BUDDHIST HISTORIOGRAPHY IN CHINA

THE SHENG YEN SERIES IN CHINESE BUDDHIST STUDIES

THE SHENG YEN SERIES IN CHINESE BUDDHIST STUDIES

Edited by Daniel B. Stevenson and Jimmy Yu

Funded jointly by the Sheng Yen Education Foundation and the Chung Hua Institute of Buddhist Studies in Taiwan, the Sheng Yen Series in Chinese Buddhist Studies is dedicated to the interdisciplinary study of Chinese language resources that bear on the history of Buddhism in premodern and modern China. Through the publication of pioneering scholarship on Chinese Buddhist thought, practice, social life, and institutional life in China—including interactions with indigenous traditions of religion in China, as well as Buddhist developments in South, East, and Inner/Central Asia—the series aspires to bring new and groundbreaking perspectives to one of the most historically enduring and influential traditions of Buddhism, past and present.

Michael J. Walsh, *Sacred Economies: Buddhist Business and Religiosity in Medieval China*

Koichi Shinohara, *Spells, Images, and Maṇḍalas: Tracing the Evolution of Esoteric Buddhist Rituals*

Beverley Foulks McGuire, *Living Karma: The Religious Practices of Ouyi Zhixu (1599–1655)*

Paul Copp, *The Body Incantatory: Spells and the Ritual Imagination in Medieval Chinese Buddhism*

N. Harry Rothschild, *Emperor Wu Zhao and Her Pantheon of Devis, Divinities, and Dynastic Mothers*

Erik J. Hammerstrom, *The Science of Chinese Buddhism: Early Twentieth-Century Engagements*

Jiang Wu and Lucille Chia, editors, *Spreading Buddha's Word in East Asia: The Formation and Transformation of the Chinese Buddhist Canon*

Jan Kiely and J. Brooks Jessup, editors, *Recovering Buddhism in Modern China*

Geoffrey C. Goble, *Chinese Esoteric Buddhism: Amoghavajra, the Ruling Elite, and the Emergence of a Tradition*

Dewei Zhang, *Thriving in Crisis: Buddhism and Political Disruption in China, 1522–1620*

Erik J. Hammerstrom, *The Huayan University Network: The Teaching and Practice of Avataṃsaka Buddhism in Twentieth-Century China*

Chün-fang Yü, *The Renewal of Buddhism in China: Zhuhong and the Late Ming Synthesis*, Fortieth Anniversary Edition

BUDDHIST HISTORIOGRAPHY IN CHINA

John Kieschnick

Columbia University Press
New York

Columbia University Press
Publishers Since 1893
New York   Chichester, West Sussex
cup.columbia.edu
Copyright © 2022 Columbia University Press
All rights reserved

Library of Congress Cataloging-in-Publication Data
Names: Kieschnick, John, 1964- author.
Title: Buddhist historiography in China / John Kieschnick.
Description: New York : Columbia University Press, 2022. | Series: The Sheng Yen series in Chinese Buddhist studies | Includes bibliographical references and index.
Identifiers: LCCN 2021053440 (print) | LCCN 2021053441 (ebook) | ISBN 9780231205627 (hardback) | ISBN 9780231205634 (trade paperback) | ISBN 9780231556095 (ebook)
Subjects: LCSH: Buddhism—Historiography. | China—Historiography.
Classification: LCC BQ280 .K54 2022 (print) | LCC BQ280 (ebook) | DDC 294.3072/2—dc23/eng/20220222
LC record available at https://lccn.loc.gov/2021053440
LC ebook record available at https://lccn.loc.gov/2021053441

Cover design: Chang Jae Lee
Cover image: *Preparing Tea*, by Liu Songnian (fl. 1174-1224). Courtesy of the National Palace Museum, Taipei.

Contents

Introduction 1

1. India 22
2. Sources 49
3. Karma 79
4. Prophecy 107
5. Genealogy 133
6. Modernity 160

   Conclusion 192

Acknowledgments 201

Appendix 1. Chronological List of Major Works 203

Appendix 2. Lineage Charts 209

Notes 215

Bibliography 263

Index 281

BUDDHIST HISTORIOGRAPHY IN CHINA

Introduction

In 1954, Yinshun 印順 (1906–2003), perhaps the most respected and certainly the most prolific Chinese monastic of the twentieth century, completed a collection of essays titled *Researching Buddhism with Buddhism.*[1] Born in the final years of the Qing dynasty and witness to political reform, modern warfare, industrialization, and revolution, Yinshun was a bridge from the traditional Buddhist background and concerns of the monks and laymen I discuss for most of this book to the scholars who research Buddhism today in the offices and libraries of modern international universities. Keenly aware that, like the politics and society that surrounded him, Buddhism too required rapid, radical reform, Yinshun rejected as antiquated many of the scholarly techniques and assumptions discussed here—recourse to prophecy, ready acceptance of the miraculous, the belief that sutras transmitted to China were all the word of the Buddha, the assertion that an unbroken genealogical chain of master and disciples transmitted Buddhist truths from ancient Indian to modern China, and so on. Nonetheless, in the preface to *Researching Buddhism with Buddhism,* rather than simply embracing the conventions of modern academic research, Yinshun instead attempted to lay out a modern but at the same time *Buddhist* approach to scholarship, and specifically to history.

This kind of deliberate, conscious effort to formulate a distinctively Buddhist historiography is rare, perhaps even unique. In Yinshun's case, it meant Buddhist analysis of causality, relentless attention to the impermanence of all things, and persistent reflection on the historian's own lack of an enduring self when reading, writing, and debating history. Few Buddhist historians have been so aware of their own methodologies (and I will return to Yinshun's ideas in more detail in the final chapter of this book).

Nevertheless, although we find few such overt statements of Buddhist scholarly principles in the study of history before the twentieth century, the premise of this book is that, in broad terms, there *is* such a thing as a Buddhist historiography, that Buddhist doctrines, literature, and institutions fostered a distinctive vision of the past. And nowhere is Buddhist historiography better represented, whether in the length of the tradition or in the sheer volume of material, than it is in China.

This book examines the historical writings of monks and Buddhist laymen. Its focus is not the modern academic study of Chinese Buddhist history, a tradition now long enough to warrant a study of its own that would examine why and how scholars working in universities in China and abroad have approached this history from the nineteenth century to the present.[2] Instead, I focus here on writings by self-professed Chinese Buddhists—mostly monks, but a few laymen as well—who wrote about the past.[3] Modern scholars of Chinese Buddhism have always been interested in its history, but relatively little attention has been given to Buddhist historical writings, not just as repositories of historical facts but as ways of thinking about the past. This is my concern here. As I outline below, there is a wealth of material for the study of the place of the past in Chinese Buddhism; dozens of large, elegant books from all periods written by well-known figures, mostly preserved in formal collections, are readily available.[4]

But the fact that the topic of Chinese Buddhist historiography has attracted relatively little scholarly attention despite the considerable body of material available for such a study is not, on reflection, all that surprising.[5] In the most general terms, Buddhist historiography in Tibet and East Asia is easily recognizable as history, though as we will see with many distinctive characteristics, while traditional Buddhist historical writings of South and Southeast Asia, rarely citing dates or engaging in source criticism, often require us to question our own assumptions about what history is.[6] But even in China, with one of the richest historiographical traditions in world civilization, Buddhist doctrine and history are not the most natural of companions.

WHY BUDDHIST HISTORY MATTERED

Strong currents of Buddhist thought and belief run against the historian's predilection for dwelling on the past. While book culture is central to Buddhist devotion in China (liturgical manuals are common, and documents are written, read, and sometimes burned as part of many, if not most Chinese rites), historical books are for the most part marginal to everyday rituals. In Buddhist devotional practice, memorizing, reciting, and copying scripture—the word of the Buddha—is above all a source of merit. This belief is testified in countless manuscripts and printed versions of scriptures in which the copyist or donor dedicates the merit for replicating and propagating a Buddhist scripture to a deceased parent or sibling. And this explains why the store of extant medieval manuscripts is dominated by hundreds of copies of a few key scriptures, reliable repositories of potential merit.[7] But the composition and distribution of historical works brings no such merit. Unlike with scripture, copying or reading a historical work does not in itself do anything; devotees do not chant biographies or historical accounts of court debates in temple halls. The most famous and important Buddhist historical work in China, the *Biographies of Eminent Monks*,[8] by all accounts has enjoyed immediate and sustained success among literate East Asians from the time of its composition in the sixth century up to the present day. Yet in contrast to the hundreds of copies of the *Lotus Sutra* and the *Diamond Sutra* discovered among the medieval manuscripts of Dunhuang, not a single copy of the *Biographies of Eminent Monks* survives there. In other words, in a devotional context, historical works lag far behind scripture in importance, if they rank at all.

Setting aside the practical matters of copying and propagating historical writing, at a higher level of abstraction, the Buddhist conception of time would also seem to suggest that history is, at best, a trivial distraction from the more pressing and fundamental matter of relief from suffering. On the grandest scale—not of a single event or a lifetime or the reign of a ruler, but of hundreds, thousands, or hundreds of thousands of years—time, for the literate Buddhist, was cyclical. Buddhist teachings, the health of the monastic order, and the collective wisdom of the people of the world looped in circles punctuated by the appearances of buddhas. On the death of a buddha, the world begins a long and inexorable period of decline—monks, increasingly corrupt, petty, and dull, eventually disappear altogether; the teachings of the Buddha are slowly forgotten; and violence reigns as the world sinks into a long, dreary era of ignorance, chaos, and suffering. Happily, when an advanced bodhisattva achieves buddhahood, the cycle resets: with the spread of Buddhist teachings, the people become more peaceful, more receptive to improvement, and the monastic institution is restored.[9]

These "buddha cycles" are themselves embedded in vast patterns of rise and fall. In the grand parabolas of time, *our time*, the age in which we live, happens to fall in a period of decline that began deep in the distant past and will only begin to improve far in the future. Descriptions of the past buddhas noted that life spans of buddhas and the people of their age have been steadily declining. To cite one example among many, the widely read eleventh-century *Transmission of the Lamp Compiled in the Jingde Era* (*Jingde chuandeng lu* 景德傳燈錄), though primarily concerned with the Chan lineage in China, begins long, long ago, before even the most ancient events in Chinese history, with the seven buddhas of the past, noting that in a deep and distant antiquity, in the time of the buddha Vipaśyin, people lived on average for eighty thousand years. By the time of the subsequent buddha, Śikhin, people lived for only seventy thousand years. Five buddhas later, in the time of our own buddha, Śākyamuni, we live more or less (mostly less) for a mere one hundred years.¹⁰ In other words, not only is the world now far removed from the last buddha and far, far away from the next, deep into a period of decline as we await the appearance of Maitreya, we are now at the tail end of an even longer period of decline encompassing the eras of several buddhas, which began in an unimaginably distant past.

Following this steady deterioration, our entire world system—including not just the continent on which human beings live but also the heavens and the hells above and below us—will eventually end in a cataclysmic *kalpa* of destruction. Nonetheless, even this lengthy and inevitable decline is part of a larger cycle; eventually all will come full circle and start from the beginning. Specifically, over the course of a period of time of such length that it can only be conceived in broad metaphors, sentient beings improve not just physically but morally, eventually emptying the hells, the animal realm, and even the human realm as all living creatures migrate one by one into the heavens, swept up on a rising tide of wholesome karma. At this point, the physical world sentient beings have left behind is destroyed as they look on from the heavens above. Eventually, these ethereal beings use up the store of good karma they so painstakingly made for themselves, and a new world is created for them, at which point they are born as humans and the whole process begins anew.¹¹

The opening section of the thirteenth-century history *Comprehensive Orthodox Transmission of the Śākya Clan* (*Shimen zhengtong* 釋門正統) nicely summarizes these interlinking patterns of time. A long succession of buddhas fall along an undulating line comprising periods of rise and decline, itself placed in an even grander cycle that moves through the four phases of appearance, existence, decay, and disappearance:

> This *sahā* world [i.e., our world] goes through periods of formation, existence, decay, and disappearance. Each of these periods includes twenty [minor] *kalpas* of decrease and increase that together are called a "great *kalpa*." This current *kalpa* of existence is called the "Good Kalpa." In all, one thousand buddhas appear in this *kalpa*. The previous eight [minor] *kalpas* [in this great *kalpa* of existence] passed without any buddhas. But in the ninth [minor] *kalpa* of decrease, the people of Jambudvīpa [our continent] lived for eighty-four thousand years. [From this time], life spans decreased by one year for each one hundred years until they only lived for sixty thousand years, at which point the Buddha Krakucchanda appeared. When people lived for forty thousand years, the buddha Kanakamuni appeared. When they lived for twenty thousand years, the buddha Kāśyapa appeared. When they lived for one hundred years, the buddha Śākyamuni appeared. In this way, life spans will continue to decrease until they reach ten years. But then, sons will begin to live to twice the age of their fathers, until their life spans increase to eighty-four thousand years. When we approach the tenth [minor] *kalpa* of decline and reach the point when people live for eighty thousand years, the buddha Maitreya will appear. In this way, by the time we reach the fifteenth [minor] *kalpa* of decline, 994 more buddhas will have appeared one after the other. Eventually, in the twentieth [minor] *kalpa* of increase, the Buddha Rudita will appear. Arriving in a [minor] *kalpa* of decline, the world will enter into the [great] *kalpa* of disappearance.[12]

This describes just one round of a cycle that will be repeated. In other words, while there have been variations in the characteristics of different segments in this grand cycle, the cycle itself is consistent, predictable, and never-ending.

Before the entry of Buddhism to China, Chinese historians also toyed with cyclical views of history. Sima Qian 司馬遷 (145–87 BCE), the most famous of all Chinese historians, for instance, commented: "In the movements of heaven, a period of thirty years constitutes a minor transformation, a period of one hundred years a mid-range transformation, and a period of five hundred years a great transformation. Three great transformations constitute an era. After three eras, there is completion, the formation of a complete cycle."[13] These cycles are marked by the rise and fall of dynasties, centered on lineages of rulers, in which, when the ruling family of a given dynasty descends into moral corruption, it loses the mandate of Heaven, paving the way for a new, more deserving family to overthrow the previous dynasty and establish a new one. Another cyclical theory held that the rise and fall of dynasties corresponded to the cycle of the five phases (*wude* 五德), each governed by a different element, the Zhou dynasty corresponding to fire, the Qin dynasty to water, the Han dynasty to earth, and so on.[14]

On a very general level, a cyclical view of time, whether Buddhist or otherwise, might suggest that history is unimportant; once the toy train of the past has gone around the tracks once, what could be more tedious than to watch it circle around the same track again and again? It would come as no surprise if Buddhist thinkers, like the twelfth-century Jewish thinker Maimonides, were to declare the writing and reading of history a waste of time.[15]

Indeed, some have invoked the prevalence of a cyclical view of time to explain why premodern South Asian writers produced so few works of history. L. S. Perera, for example, commenting on Ceylonese chronicles, writes: "This cyclic conception of history is but a reflection of their background philosophy, which places the ultimate reality and the goal of life outside the succession of births and rebirths, or what would today be called the process of history. History itself was of little significance therefore except as a means to an end."[16]

In a classic, brief study of Christian historiography, *The Phoenix and the Ladder*, C. A. Patrides evokes those felicitous metaphors to characterize the shift from the cyclical view of time of the ancients (the phoenix, referring to the mythical bird that dies in flames only to be reborn) to the finite view of time of Jews and Christians (the ascending ladder), insisting that this shift transformed history into a vital process.[17] History came to have meaning because it was going somewhere—up, like a ladder taking us rung by rung to a more elevated plane. In contrast, in the cyclical view of history a given event or moment was robbed of individuality and hence significance.[18]

All of the authors of the Buddhist histories I discuss below would have accepted a cyclical view of history. The premise of this book is that they nonetheless found history meaningful. Perhaps it is because the cycles of time that history runs through are so vast that the history of any stretch of time, in scale pales in comparison and so remains interesting: even a history encompassing centuries remains microhistory, concrete, comprehensible, relatable. At times Buddhist historians attempted to tie their own period to grand predictions of the appearance, decline, and disappearance of Buddhist teachings—and I will have more to say about this below—but for the most part, they were content to treat shorter spans of time on their own terms as meaningful and worthy of interpretation.

In short, despite doctrines laying out a cyclical model for time, not to mention doctrines emphasizing the fundamental impermanence of all things and the illusory nature of the world, Buddhists have been writing about the past as long as there have been Buddhists. Beginning with chapter 1, I focus almost entirely on Chinese works and will have little to say about Buddhist historiography in South Asia, Central Asia, Korea, Japan, or elsewhere in the Buddhist world. But before narrowing the focus, I venture a few comments here about Buddhist historiography more generally.

FOUR WAYS TO READ BUDDHIST HISTORY

Given my own linguistic limitations compounded by the vast quantity of material available, I have confined the following chapters to Chinese Buddhism, but first I propose some considerations for Buddhist history as a whole, centered on the question of what makes Buddhist historiography distinctive, a theme I circle back to repeatedly. In addressing a given historical work written from a Buddhist perspective—and in attempting to determine what, if anything is *Buddhist* about its approach—I have found useful four themes: time, doctrine, agenda, and craft.[19]

Time

As we have seen, Buddhist writers had recourse to cosmological theories of cyclical time when attempting to make sense of the past. But they also paid attention to another common means for slipping back and forth in time: prophecy, including both prophecies already fulfilled and, more rarely, speculation based on prophecies in the past about what will happen in the author's future. In writing about prophecy, authors glide right and left along a time line, recounting the prediction and the events that followed, and then often returning to the prophecy to explain the hidden points that only became clear after the events it predicted took place. I devote a chapter below to prophecy in *Chinese* Buddhist historiography, but prophecy runs throughout Buddhist historical writing from before the twentieth century.[20] Consider the *Mahāvaṃsa*, or *Great Chronicle*, one of the first sustained and self-consciously historical Buddhist works in South Asia. Composed in the fifth or sixth century, the *Mahāvaṃsa* keeps to a roughly chronological frame but often plays with time, primarily for literary effect, shifting from the historical present to the time of the authors and back to the time of the Buddha, or even the previous buddhas, and occasionally relating events from past lives to explain the event under discussion. Linking past to present throughout the book are prophecies, frequently recounted and always fulfilled. In other words, the text often employs both analepsis (flashbacks) and prolepsis (foreshadowing).[21] Prophecy is not unheard of in non-Buddhist historical writing and, at least in South Asia, combining prophecy and discussion of the previous lives of historical figures is not exclusively Buddhist. But certainly in East Asia the combination of rebirth and prophecy marked historical writing as Buddhist. In Buddhist historiography, flashbacks and foreshadowing are more than literary techniques intended to guide a reader through a story (though they did that as well); reflecting on past and future events was a way to explore and explain how people and events are connected through a Buddhist understanding of ethics, karma, and cosmology.

Aside from past lives and prophecies of future events, occasionally Buddhist historians reference liturgical time with a focus on when ceremonies should be carried out to mark remembrance of historical events such as the Buddha's birth, though this is an approach to dividing time that plays little role in formal Buddhist historiography of the sort I treat here. In East Asia, Buddhist history is most commonly structured on political time, with dynasties, emperors, and reign-era titles anchoring people and events to a recognizable time line. In this there is nothing distinctively Buddhist; in all sorts of historical writing, reference to dynasties and emperors is a convenient shorthand for locating a subject and provides context for the persistent power of the state to control the monastic community. Even for the modern historian, it is standard practice to narrate the history of Chinese Buddhism dynasty by dynasty.

From about the eleventh century, in China political time was joined with genealogy, in which "family trees" of masters and disciples were arranged such that a given monk was important often primarily as a link between his master and his disciple. At about the same time, Buddhist historians also played with the option of strict chronological history—arranging biographies and events according to a bare list of dates with little or no political or religious relevance. In China at least it was the genealogical approach that was most distinctively Buddhist—and perhaps the only historiographical trend that spread in China from Buddhist to non-Buddhist historiography. Monks could be placed in the Tang dynasty or the Song, under this emperor or that, but what mattered for the genealogical history was the identity of their teacher and of their disciples as the lineage grew across time in an ever-expanding family tree.

Doctrine

Formal doctrine appears in Buddhist historical works most commonly in moralizing commentary and in the context of causation. Before the modern absorption of Buddhist history into the newly established universities, in premodern times, while Buddhist historians make occasional reference to human agency (usually human frailty) as a driving force of history, gods and other nonhuman agents and, above all, merit are the primary causal factors behind the events and actions they recount. For instance, in his remarkable thirteenth-century history of Japan, the *Gukanshō* 愚管抄, the Tendai monk Jien 慈円 (1155–1225) explains (mostly political) events through recourse to the theory of natural patterns of rise and decline; as "fate" distinct from these patterns; as the result of the intervention of the Sun Goddess, vengeful ghosts, buddhas, demons, and other nonhuman agents; or as karmic retribution for previous acts.[22] In this panoply of causes, perhaps the most distinctively Buddhist, at least in East Asia, is karma, to which I devote a chapter below. All Buddhist historians were steeped in karmic lore about events in past lives affecting future ones as well as scholastic speculation on the subtleties of act, intent, and consequence that contribute to the karmic calculus that courses through the universe and undergirds historical development.

Agenda

Alongside attention to time and causation, which often betray distinctively Buddhist proclivities, consideration of authorial agenda is essential not only to evaluate the accuracy of a given history but also to understand why a historical work takes the shape it does. In much Buddhist historiography, the description of events is so unreliable that assessing the agenda is hardly necessary to determine that a given account is not accurate, but this does not render authorial agenda unimportant since the historians themselves are, though admittedly small in number, a fecund and influential part of the elite Buddhist tradition.

Why, then, did Buddhists write history? Buddhist historians often relate history as a series of moral lessons. Events serve to illustrate the workings of karma, the power of Buddhist deities and relics, or the virtues of eminent monks. The authors of the *Mahāvaṃsa*, for instance, explicitly introduce moralizing comments toward the end of each chapter. These may encourage readers to reflect on impermanence or to "renounce the joys of life," but most often they enjoin the reader to do good deeds and avoid evil. "In this changing existence do beings indeed (only) by works of merit come to such rebirth as they desire; pondering thus the wise man will be ever filled with zeal in the heaping up of meritorious works."[23] The moralizing tends to focus on the importance of accumulating merit ("In this way do the wise, doing many works of merit, gain with worthless riches that which is precious, but fools in their blindness, for the sake of pleasures, do much evil").[24] More specifically, the text often encourages readers to give alms ("The wise who consider how marvelously precious is the giving of alms, while the gathering together of treasures [for oneself] is worthless, give alms lavishly, with a mind freed from the fetters [of lust], mindful of the good of beings").[25] This call for charity no doubt reflects the monastic composition of the text coupled with an intended audience of rulers and merchants. We will see many examples below of historical works motivated by a desire to promote or defend the monastic community from its detractors, a tendency found wherever monks wrote history. Almost as common is the tendency to employ history to promote or defend a particular monk, monastery, or lineage against competing monks, monasteries, or lineages. Even the most methodologically sophisticated Buddhist historical works are often at root primarily fashioned as weapons in internal Buddhist sectarian disputes.

Craft

All of this is in keeping with the frequent assertion that the ideal of writing history to accurately reconstruct the past is a modern invention that would have seemed absurd to historians of previous times. If not for the sake of teaching a moral lesson, illustrating a doctrine like karma, or promoting a sectarian agenda, why would anyone want to simply arrange facts in a proper order? But somewhere between the lofty goals of moral instruction and the petty ones of victory over a sectarian rival, we do from time to time see precisely this tendency toward disinterested history in Buddhist historians' devotion to their craft. Of course, before the modern period, history was not an academic discipline with codified standards of objectivity and source analysis; authors, Buddhist or otherwise, did not even call themselves "historians." Nonetheless, historiographical rules of art and standards for practice did take shape, and most of the authors of Buddhist historical works on some level aspired to be good historians rather than simply moralists or entertainers.

Consider Tāranātha's (1575-1634) *History of Buddhism in India* (*Rgya-gar Chos-'byung*). Completed in 1608 in Tibet, Tāranātha's work covers some of the same ground as the *Mahāvaṃsa*, including, for instance, accounts of the three councils and the reign of Aśoka. And despite the centuries that separated Tāranātha from so many of the people and events he describes, his work is to this day widely cited, alongside the *Mahāvaṃsa*, for reconstructing the early stages of Buddhism in authoritative modern histories of Indian Buddhism like those of Akira Hirakawa and Étienne Lamotte, one scholar going so far as to praise Tāranātha's work as "in many ways the most important history of Indian Buddhism to be written in any language."[26]

Far from the subdued historiographical consciousness of the *Mahāvaṃsa*, often undistinguishable from epic, the *History of Buddhism in India* represents a distinct genre of writing that celebrates the marshaling and critical assessment of information. Tāranātha sorts through his sources, weeding out those "not related to the history of the True Doctrine," and ostentatiously noting, "I have myself heard many Indian legends. These also I am not recording here."[27] He relishes the opportunity to exercise his considerable analytical skills, triumphantly pointing out previous misreadings of particular words that led to misinterpretations by shoddy scholars, or miscalculations in clumsy accounts of prophecy. He reserves his most caustic criticism not for the moral failings of his subjects but for the blundering historians who attempted to recount their actions with arguments that are "irrational and groundless," "palpably wrong," "chronologically baseless," dependent on "fancy," and "empty babble."[28]

Perhaps readers more sensitive to sectarian Buddhism of seventeenth-century Tibet may detect a subtle defense of Tāranātha's Jo nang lineage (fiercely persecuted less than two decades after his death), but if he had such an agenda, it is hidden deep beneath the veneer of his devotion to solid history and contempt for sloppy scholarship. In contrast to the *Mahāvaṃsa*, links to the present (seventeenth-century Tibet) are few. Nor do we see in the *History of Buddhism in India* the sort of moralizing that ends every chapter of the *Mahāvaṃsa*. Instead, Tāranātha's driving agenda seems to be a scholarly one—a commitment to careful, reliable history, an objective ideal. Just as the *Mahāvaṃsa* opens with a salutation followed by a brief critique of its predecessors, the *History of Buddhism in India* begins:

> Even the learned (Tibetan) chroniclers and historians, when they come to discuss India, exhibit with their best efforts merely their poverty, like petty traders exhibiting their meagre stock. Some of the scholars, while trying to describe the origin of the Doctrine, are found to commit many a mistake. For the benefit of others, therefore, I am preparing this brief work with the mistakes eliminated.[29]

At times this relentless enthusiasm for rooting out the errors of previous historians verges on scholarly showmanship, as when Tāranātha notes that of seven sources for one incident, two are translated into Tibetan, but "I have seen the others in their Indian originals."[30] Passages such as these, interrupting the narrative with erudite asides, suggest that this is a scholarly work written for other scholars, or at least for those who appreciate the finer points of the historian's craft. We will see these same tendencies throughout Chinese Buddhist historiography by looking out for rare moments when the historian introduces or intervenes in a story to explain why one source is more reliable than another, or to correct a date, name, or scribal error. Even more challenging is to detect if there is anything in these technical skills that betrays Buddhist sensibilities. In China in particular, the ideals and standards for writing proper, elite history were well established before the entrance of Buddhism. Nonetheless, there are moments when a historian invokes a Buddhist doctrine to explain a source discrepancy or draws on Buddhist principles to reflect on the reason the historical record is unclear.

BUDDHIST HISTORIOGRAPHY UNDER THE SHADOW OF COURT HISTORY

Aside from any specifically Buddhist imperative to write and read history, in China history mattered in part because of the prestige of the genre; one could make a name for oneself by writing history, and educated people, including elite monks, were expected to have read the great works of Chinese historical writing.³¹ By the time Buddhism entered China in the first century, the historian's vocation was well established as an honorable and respectable pursuit with its own set of standards and models. With some qualifications, Chinese historiography can be dated all the way back to the earliest Chinese writing, the oracle bone inscriptions, from roughly 1200 BC.³² The *Spring and Autumn Annals*, a sparse annalistic history, was purportedly edited by Confucius himself, providing the genre of historical writing all the legitimacy it would need. In China the most prestigious historical works were from the beginning up to the nineteenth century essentially court history.³³

They were "court history" both in the sense that the most prominent histories dealt with war, administration, and biographies related to figures and events connected to the court, and in the sense that they were compiled by men who themselves had close ties to the court. Etienne Balazs's famous pronouncement that traditional Chinese historiography was "written by officials for officials" is, with some qualifications, largely true.³⁴ Both Sima Qian, compiler of what would become the most widely read work of Chinese history, the massive *Records of the Historian* (*Shiji* 史記, covering 2,500 years of history in over 500,000 characters), and Ban Gu 班固 (32-92 CE), compiler of the almost as famous and even more massive *History of the Han* (*Han shu* 漢書, covering 230 years in around 800,000 characters) came from families thoroughly embedded in court life, and both suffered dearly when they ran afoul of the emperor (Sima Qian was castrated for admonishing the emperor; Ban Gu died in prison). The same pattern held true for the compiler of the *Later Han History* (*Hou Han shu* 後漢書), Fan Ye 范曄 (398-445), another official, exiled for drinking too much and behaving badly at the funeral of a prince's mother, and eventually executed for conspiracy against the emperor.³⁵

As Albert E. Dien puts it, in the Han "the writing of history was a private affair, accomplished in off-duty hours and then presented to the throne."³⁶ But during the period when Buddhist historiography began to take hold in China, the fifth and sixth centuries, it became more common for historical works to receive official sponsorship. In the Tang (618-907) the writing of history became a group project within the state bureaucracy. Posts in the Historiographical Office were prestigious, and some historians working there distinguished themselves and rose to fame.³⁷ Also during the early medieval period, historical works, which in the Han were classified as "classics," now were listed in bibliographies under the separate category "history."³⁸

In these works of court-centered history, with one exception, Buddhism is largely ignored. That one exception is the "Treatise on Buddhism and Daoism" in the *Wei History* (*Weishu* 魏書). This is a brief history of Buddhism in China compiled in the sixth century by Wei Shou 魏收 (506–572), a scholar from a devoutly Buddhist family. Other standard histories have little to say about Buddhism, other than to complain about Buddhist influence on corrupt rulers or at most to devote a biography or two to monks.

Nonetheless, these court histories established the model, the standards for the craft, many of which, such as those for source criticism, precise dating, and commentary, had a major impact on the way Buddhist historians wrote about the past. More than this, before the entry of Buddhism to China, court historians had established the goal of uncovering the principles governing the past as a model for the present, and promoted the study of history as a noble occupation. This ideal is encapsulated in a famous passage attributed to Sima Qian. After recounting his fall from favor and subsequent castration, he explains how he embarked on the writing of the *Records of the Historian*:

> Lacking all humility, I have presumed in recent times to entrust my spirit to my clumsy writings. I have cast a broad net across the old accounts that have been lost or neglected. Examining these in light of past events, I have gathered together all the evidence for cosmic and dynastic cycles, having studied the underlying causes of success and failure, and of rise and decline. In altogether 130 chapters, I have tried to probe the boundaries of heaven and man and comprehend the changes of past and present, thereby perfecting a tradition for my family.[39]

In other words, history involves comprehensive collecting of accounts, examination of evidence, a search for underlying patterns, and the explanation of change, all at least in part as a way of bringing lasting honor to oneself and one's family. All of these criteria could be applied to Buddhist historical writing (if "family" is taken to include monastic lineage).

The Chinese monks and laymen who composed the works I discuss in this book were all very familiar with the court tradition. In works devoted to chronologies of Buddhist history, they pause to date the year Confucius supposedly compiled the *Spring and Autumn Annals*.[40] They refer to Sima Qian often and compare their own adjustments to the format of previous historical works to the changes Ban

Gu made to Sima Qian's format.⁴¹ They complain that in Ouyang Xiu's 歐陽修 (1007–1072) revision of the official Tang history, he removed material treating Buddhism.⁴²

In compiling their works, monks often copied accounts, inscriptions, and official documents compiled by literati. One of the most important Chan histories, the *Transmission of the Lamp Compiled in the Jingde Era*, was begun by a monk and revised by a group of court officials. At times their work was written expressly on imperial command, and most of the histories I discuss were at some point incorporated into an imperially sanctioned Buddhist canon.

Not only were the Chinese monks and laymen who wrote Buddhist history linked to the court historians intellectually, socially they moved in the same circles. Many grew up in literati families before becoming monks; most counted literati as friends; and some, like the tenth-century Zanning 贊寧 (919–1001), even held public office. Therefore they shared many of the same values as their literati counterparts. The painting on the cover of this book by Liu Songnian 劉松年 (fl. 1174–1224) is a typical scene illustrating the frequent interaction between literate monks and literati throughout much of Chinese history.

That said, monks *were* different. Most of them lived in monasteries, were celibate, and shunned meat and alcohol, in this way cutting themselves off from much of the social life of the literati. And there were comforts to living in the shadows as well. Monks for the most part were free of the dangers of writing history at court. Later we will encounter one monk fleeing arrest after a lawsuit brought against him by rivals, outraged by the revisionist history he wrote, but for the most part monk historians died old and erudite in their monasteries, avoiding the castration, exile, imprisonment, and execution that court historians risked when their work ran afoul of imperial taste or, more commonly, when they offended the powerful in some other way incidental to their work. Moreover, monastic libraries were among the best in the empire. In the thirteenth century, writing from his mountain monastery, Zhipan 志磐 (ca. 1220–1275) begins his *Comprehensive Record of the Buddhas and the Patriarchs* with a bibliography that lists 178 works, including not just Buddhist but also Confucian and Daoist texts. And we know from many sources from earlier and later periods all over China that monastic collections were similarly rich and varied. The daily needs of the erudite monks who composed history were taken care of by the monastic institution. Typically, elite monks were attended by servants and supplied with paper, brushes, and ink, their food, clothing, and baths prepared by others.

The divide between monks and court historians is mirrored in the twentieth century, when monk historians were influenced by their counterparts in the universities only imperfectly and indirectly. More significant even than this social distinction is the fact that the vast majority of Chinese Buddhist historiography concerns monks. This isn't to say that monks necessarily understood monks better than nonmonastics, but at the least they were more deeply invested in how monastics were represented.

MEMORY AND HISTORIOGRAPHY

"History" in common usage can refer either to the past itself or to the recording of the past, while "historiography" refers either just to the recording of the past or to reflections on how history is written. In the history of civilizations, formal written history is not inevitable, even in highly literate traditions. The existence of long periods without formal, sustained, chronological written history has inspired scholars of Judaism and of India to explore other ways the past can be remembered.[43] Another book on Buddhist memory in China might look at the Buddhist liturgical calendar, pilgrimage sites, painting and poetry, epigraphy preserved on steles, and oral stories as repositories of the past. Such an approach has much to recommend it. For many Buddhists, these media have provided the sort of accounting of the past most accessible to much of the population, without the time or resources to access the great written works of elite narrative history I analyze here. Chinese have for centuries been more familiar with the version of Xuanzang's 玄奘 (602–664) travels to India from the stories in the novel *Journey to the West* than from Xuanzang's more prosaic written account.[44] But a more wide-ranging and subtle study of Buddhist memory is another book for another scholar; here I focus instead on formal, mostly long, mostly single-authored Buddhist accounts of the past, readily recognizable as historiography. Even within these limitations of a relatively uniform genre, mostly composed by monks and literati of similar background, there is a rich tradition of great depth, range, and sophistication.

And even in this rarified realm of elite male scholarship, Buddhist historiography did have an impact beyond the relatively small number of scholars who read and wrote it. To give just one example, in her 2007 memoirs, the Taiwanese *bhikṣuṇī* and university professor Heng Ching 恆清 describes her experience at a meeting in 1998 in Dharamshala convened by the Dalai Lama to assess the legitimacy of the Taiwanese monastic order for nuns, in response to the suggestion that an order of nuns be established for Tibetan women. Heng Ching presented one of two reports on the legitimacy of the female order in Taiwan. Her defense was challenged by the Chinese monk Daohai 道海 (1924-2013), who questioned not just the legitimacy of ordinations of nuns in Taiwan but ordinations of Chinese nuns going back to the very beginnings of the order in the fifth century. At issue, among other things, was the interpretation of historical texts, including the fifth-century *Biographies of Bhikṣuṇīs*, the tenth-century *Brief History of the Clergy*, and the thirteenth-century *Comprehensive Account of the Buddhas and the Patriarchs*—all major works of formal Buddhist historiography that I will draw on repeatedly below.[45] More was involved in this case than questions of historiography, but the example illustrates how elite, traditional Buddhist historical works can have real-world consequences long after the time of their composition.

A BRIEF CHRONOLOGY OF BUDDHIST HISTORIOGRAPHY

The chapters that follow are thematic, at times skipping between documents separated by centuries in the interest of following a given topic. As a frame of reference, here I sketch out a brief chronology of the broad contours of Buddhist historiography in China, divided into four genres that appeared in roughly chronological order, marking four phases.

The first phase of Buddhist historiography, from approximately the fifth century to the tenth, was dominated by prosopography, biographies organized by type. The representative work in this genre is the *Biographies of Eminent Monks*, compiled circa 530 by the monk Huijiao 慧皎 (497-554), containing 257 major biographies and more than 200 shorter, subordinate biographies.[46] Various collections of biographies of monks had appeared previously, but the success of Huijiao's work largely eclipsed those that preceded his. He divided the biographies into ten categories: translation, exegesis, thaumaturgy, meditation, elucidation of the monastic regulations, self-sacrifice, recitation of scripture, good works, hymnody, and proselytism. Within each chapter the biographies are arranged in chronological order. Just as interesting, from a historiographical perspective, are the essays that Huijiao appends to each of the chapters: for the "translators" chapter, he discusses issues in the early history of translation in China; for the "self-sacrifice" chapter, he outlines the controversies provoked by monks who burned themselves to death as a form of offering, and so on.⁴⁷ Other types of historical writings appeared during this period—I make frequent reference to the *Collection of Records Concerning the Translation of the Tripiṭaka*, a work that combines textual history with biography, and another book by the same author, Sengyou 僧祐 (445–518), the *Śākya Genealogy* (*Shijia pu* 釋迦譜), that attempts a history of the Buddha's family.⁴⁸

Another massive collection of biographies of eminent monks by another erudite well-connected monk appeared in the seventh century, following on Huijiao's model with some modifications, but the next major historiographical innovation took place away from the capital under more obscure circumstances, marking the second of the four phases of Buddhist historiography in China.⁴⁹ This was the emergence of genealogical histories, texts organized not by type of monk but by teacher-disciple relationships. The earliest genealogies owe something to Tiantai works, but reach maturity in Chan lineage histories beginning in the late seventh century and finally assume a place of prestige and authority with the eleventh-century *Transmission of the Lamp Compiled in the Jingde Era*.⁵⁰ These works differ from other genres of Buddhist writings not only in their structure and unabashedly sectarian agenda but also in the style of the biographies they contain. The Chan genealogical histories are less concerned with listing the works authored, temples founded, and miracles performed by the monks they describe and instead focus on dramatic and enigmatic dialogues between masters and disciples. *The Transmission of the Lamp Compiled in the Jingde Era* inspired many epigones in subsequent centuries, a subject I cover below in the chapter on genealogy.

In the centuries following the rise of the new Chan genealogies, other, mostly Tiantai, historians introduced an alternative historical genre that modern scholars have termed "universal history."⁵¹ These are large, sprawling works, inspired by the *Records of the Historian*, that include chronological accounts, biography, and essays on the history of particular subjects. The representative work in this genre is the *Comprehensive Account of the Buddhas and the Patriarchs*, completed in 1269 by the monk Zhipan, to which I will refer often. Other genres appeared during roughly the same period, including strictly chronological works, while Buddhist authors compiled new collections of monastic biographies and, more than anything else, new Chan genealogical works.

The most recent phase in Buddhist historiography began in the twentieth century, when traditional collections of biographies, Chan genealogies, and universal histories were abandoned for modern monographs and articles of the sort written by Yinshun, and later by monks and laymen formally trained in universities in China, Taiwan, and abroad. These works mark a radical break with the tradition and increasingly have become indistinguishable from secular, academic historical writing.

In each of these categories—especially in the genre of genealogical history—there are many more works than I have listed here. And there are less common genres that I skip for the sake of clarity. I largely omit two popular genres from discussion since they are so distinctive that they merit separate treatment: autobiography and local history. Autobiography is of course limited in time frame by the author's life, but it also provides the sort of personal account from a single viewpoint lacking in the majority of Buddhist historiography.[52] Closer in nature to the works I discuss here are those that treat local history. This is a genre that goes back to the *Record of the Temples of Luoyang*, the elegant account of Buddhist temples in the capital city composed in the sixth century, and that flourished from about the twelfth century on.[53] In total, I focus on a relatively uniform body of thirty-some texts that I list in appendix 1.

SUMMARY OF CHAPTERS

All of the preceding caveats about shared tradition aside, Chinese Buddhist historiography *was* distinctive, in the context of Chinese historiography and in the context of Buddhist historiography. In chapter 1 I emphasize the importance of India's past for Buddhist historians in China. Unlike court historians, who expressed little interest in Indian history, Buddhist historians were forced to grapple with a tradition with very different historiographical practices, pushing them to develop creative techniques for dating events and mold unwieldy historical data to the needs of their Chinese audience.

Chapter 2 examines source criticism in Chinese Buddhist historiography. Like all Chinese history, most Buddhist histories are composite works that patch together previous accounts, copied wholesale, often without attribution. Nonetheless, as a part of their scholarly ethos, Buddhist historians were careful to note discrepancies in different accounts of the same person or event. And in the ways they deal with these differences, they disclose distinctively Buddhist beliefs.

Chapter 3 takes up the topic of karma, a fundamentally historical doctrine, a principle that takes effect over time. Chinese Buddhist historians, steeped in both karmic lore and scholastic writings on karma, were quick to realize its potential as a historiographical tool, a device that they believed set them apart from their counterparts at court, allowing them to see the underlying principles driving history.

Chapter 4 asks why, in works ostensibly devoted to the past, Buddhist historians spill so much ink discussing the future. At times Buddhist historians relate prophecies of what will happen after they are gone; more often, they tell stories of predictions in the past that by their own time had already been realized. One of the puzzles is that even in the stories, the prophecies are not initially understood and are only seen to have been accurate predictions of the future after the events they foretold have come to pass. Misunderstood or ignored, prophecies seldom do anyone any good, even in historical accounts that document their accuracy. Why, then, are they so pervasive?

Chapter 5 narrates the rise of genealogical history, both inspired and shaped by sectarian division. Structuring the past according to a monastic family tree raised the stakes for historical writing; it could connect the historian himself to a lineage of eminent masters extending all the way back to the Buddha, but it at the same time entailed exclusion—some branches of the tree were more central than others, and some were pruned off the tree entirely. The demands of the new genre and its consequences are the subject of this chapter.

In chapter 6 I trace the rapid turn from the tradition of Buddhist historiography that had taken shape over fifteen hundred years to new forms of scholarship, now taking place in the universities. Although monastics had always been at some remove from the more prestigious literati historians, in the twentieth century the gap grew even larger. In the first half of the twentieth century, Chinese academic historians learned foreign languages and studied abroad, keeping abreast of the latest developments in historiography in Germany, Britain, and the United States, and returned to teach in the newly founded universities in Peking, Shanghai, and Canton. Monks, while operating largely in isolation from this cosmopolitan world of the modern intellectual, nonetheless recognized the need for reform and so introduced a new style of Buddhist historiography. Examining this transformation is useful both for what it tells us about modern Buddhism in China and because it helps to clarify what came before.

My hope for the reader is that the materials I gather here will make the case for the value of incorporating Buddhist historical writings into the more developed field of Chinese historiography—every overview of Chinese historiography should take Buddhism into consideration. I also hope that this book will help to carve out a place of greater prominence for historical thought in the intellectual history of Chinese Buddhism, since working with history, aside from its own merits, is often a way of thinking through doctrine. Finally, and most ambitiously, I hope that the book will contribute more generally to a growing body of scholarship on the distinctive characteristics of religious historiography, past and present.

CHAPTER 1

India

For all of its accomplishments, Buddhist historiography in China budded and blossomed on the periphery, in the shadow of dynastic political history composed at court. In the early medieval period, monastic historians looked to Sima Qian and his *Records of the Historian* for inspiration. At the close of the middle ages, Sima Guang 司馬光 (1019-1086) and his *Comprehensive Mirror for Aid to Government* (*Zizhi tongjian* 資治通鑑)[1] set the standard for the style, scope, and format of historical writing.[2] When, from the eleventh century, the dynastic histories were collected into a set of "standard histories" (*zhengshi* 正史), Buddhist historiography was formally sealed off from the history that mattered most at the center of power, given a marginal status from which it has yet to recover.[3] Nonetheless, Buddhist historians poring over biographies of monks, sutras, and commentaries strove to demonstrate that their grasp of history equaled that of their counterparts at court, immersed in biographies of ministers, the Confucian classics, edicts, memorials, and other polished paperwork.

The two traditions—Buddhist and court history—shared most assumptions: historical narrative was to be accurate, but the historian at the same time had a duty to highlight moral lessons from his material. Both sought a balance between biography and chronology. That is, historians went to great lengths to date the events in a subject's biography so that they could be correlated to events in the lives of other figures. And chronological discrepancies—for example, sources stating that two figures met when, according to well-attested dates, they could not have done so—were rigorously exposed or otherwise explained.

One area in which the two traditions did diverge, however, was in their treatment of India. In the dynastic histories, events in India rarely encroached on the wars, court intrigue, and policy debates that absorbed the attention of most

Chinese historians. The first clear mention of India in the Chinese historical record comes in the *History of the Han* compiled in the first century by Ban Gu, in a brief essay. He describes the climate ("warm and mild"), some of the plants (alfalfa, sandalwood), the custom of employing "night soil for fertilization in their gardens and paddies," lists a few native animals, notes the use of gold and silver coins for money ("with equestrian figures on one side and human faces on the other"), and praises Indians' skill in carving, brocade, and gastronomy.[4] The *History of the Later Han* by Fan Ye contains a similar passage, now recording that the people of India "cultivate the Way of the Buddha, neither taking life nor committing aggression."[5]

Both accounts reflect the marginal status of India for the court historians who compiled them. In the first account, India was chiefly interesting for its products, some of which might make their way to China over the vast distance that separated the two regions. By the time of the second account, the increasing importance of Buddhism in China required some mention of Buddhism in any general Chinese description of India. Both essays focus on what was presumed to be the state of India at the time of the authors; neither discloses any knowledge of or interest in India's past. Even as contact between India and China became more common and information from both foreigners and Chinese who had traveled to India became more ample, dynastic historians in subsequent years relied heavily on these early accounts, repeating the same information and showing relatively little interest in even the India of their own day, much less its past. They preferred to apply their considerable historical skills to narrating the history of court struggles and military campaigns in China and on her immediate borders.

For Chinese Buddhists, however, India was always of much greater importance, its history in some ways more vital than even China's past. And despite the fact that the materials available to literate Chinese Buddhists with a historical bent were frustratingly resistant to the techniques they were accustomed to applying to Chinese history—especially the comparison of carefully dated accounts of a single figure or event from different sources—they felt compelled to employ their skills toward reconstructing the history of Buddhism in India as best they could.

Today, rather than turn to works by Chinese Buddhist historians of the premodern period, scholars in search of reliable information in Chinese about Indian history are better served by examining Chinese translations of texts from Indic languages, or, better yet, the justly famous travel accounts of medieval Chinese pilgrims. Premodern Chinese Buddhist historians devoted little attention to most of the events that most concern modern historians of Indian Buddhism, such as the early councils, the division of the monastic community into different schools, relations between monastics and the laity, the emergence of Mahayana, and patronage of Buddhism by Indian rulers (with the exception of Aśoka), much less economic history, women, or the place of Buddhism in daily life. And even when monastic historians in China discussed issues that *are* of interest to modern historians, such as the date of the birth of the Buddha or the order in which sutras appeared, they based their arguments on evidence that we now know to be utterly unreliable.

Yet for an understanding of the place of the past in Chinese Buddhism, and the manner in which Buddhist historians were forced to innovate in ways that court historians were not, Chinese histories of Indian Buddhism are invaluable. Here, rather than attempting a systematic survey of the works that treat Indian Buddhist history in China, I focus on a few themes in their treatment of India that reveal the major distinguishing characteristics of Buddhist historiography in China, specifically: the importance given to chronology, the concern with prophecy and lineage, and problems peculiar to Buddhist historians when adjudicating between conflicting sources for the history of Indian Buddhism. These themes, together with the use of karma as a historiographical tool, when appearing in *Chinese* Buddhist history, are each given separate chapters below. This chapter, in exploring chronology, prophecy, lineage, and source criticism as they related to India, sets the stage for the rest of the book. The final chapter, on Buddhist historiography in modern times, describes the abandonment of these themes and the emergence of modern, academic Buddhist history.

CHRONOLOGY

If in Renaissance Europe systematic chronology was a Christian discipline, in China it was *Buddhist* historians who were most devoted to identifying ancient dates and then tying them to a time line that led from the distant past through the present and into the future.[6] Court historians in China were certainly interested in dates, and meticulously recorded precise dates for the figures and events they documented, but they found patterns in the past that corresponded to irregular cycles—like the acquisition and loss of the "Mandate of Heaven" by a given dynasty or the gradual progression through the "five-phase cycle" (*wuxing* 五行),

neither of which was governed by preordained dates or numbers.⁷ For Buddhist historians, the stakes in determining the precise dates of a few key events were much higher. They were interested in three dates in particular: the birth of the Buddha, the Buddha's nirvana, and the date of the transmission of Buddhism to China. Of these, the first two, closely related, were by far the most important since they were needed to relate ancient Buddhist history to ancient Chinese history, and because they provided an essential reference point for tracking the greatest historical trend of all: the slow but inevitable decline of the Dharma.

Chinese Buddhist historians attempting to pinpoint the Buddha's dates faced the same problem with which modern historians of Indian Buddhism continue to struggle: the Indian sources give only the vaguest clues as to the year of the birth of the Buddha, forcing scholars to rely to a large extent on conjecture. For modern scholars, this entails employing a variety of indirect evidence such as references to political events in Buddhist scripture or dating archaeological evidence from early Buddhism.⁸ For Buddhist historians in China, the lack of chronological precision in Indian sources drove them to search the more reliable chronologies of ancient Chinese pre-Buddhist sources for clues to the elusive date.⁹

Wei Shou, in his "Treatise on Buddhism and Daoism," displays one of the most common approaches to the problem.¹⁰ Drawing on the first great work of Chinese chronology, the *Spring and Autumn Annals*, at the time widely believed to have been compiled by Confucius close to a thousand years previous, Wei writes:

> The time of Śākyamuni's birth corresponds to the ninth year of the reign of King Zhuang of the Zhou [687 BCE]. This is what the *Spring and Autumn Annals* refers to when it says, "Duke Zhuang of Lu, seventh year, summer, fourth month: *The fixed stars could not be seen, and the night was bright.*" From this date until the eighth year of Wuding of the Wei [dynasty, i.e., 550, the date when Wei Shou was writing] is one thousand two hundred and thirty-seven years.¹¹

In the original passage in the *Spring and Autumn Annals*, the reason the night was bright was a meteor shower that crossed the sky "like rain," its brightness obscuring the "permanent stars." Coincidentally, the Chinese translation of what became in China the most popular account of the life of the Buddha, the *Scripture of the Origins of the Miracles of the Prince*, translated in the third century CE, states that the Buddha was born at night, when the stars were bright in the sky.¹²

Chinese Buddhists accepted the authenticity of both the account of the meteor shower in the *Spring and Autumn Annals* and the description of the bright night sky in the Buddha's biography. Even so, there were problems with correlating the two. Wei Shou conveniently ignored a major problem with the date: according to the *Spring and Autumn Annals*, the night sky lit up in the fourth month. But according to the scriptures, the Buddha's mother *conceived* in the fourth month; it was not until ten months later, on the eighth day of the *second month of the following year*, that he was born and light filled the night sky. The months in the two accounts do not match.

The sixth-century monk Dao'an 道安 (fl. 561, not to be confused with the more famous fourth-century monk of the same name), unlike Wei Shou, recognized this problem and attempted to resolve it in two ways. First, he noted discrepancies between the calendar used at the time of the *Spring and Autumn Annals* and the calendar used in India, as well as the problem of identifying dates according to the calendar of a particular Chinese state in the *Spring and Autumn Annals*. Each of the preceding dynasties used different calendars, and there were even discrepancies between different contemporary states. All of this allowed him to conclude that in fact the Chinese date for the shower of falling stars described as taking place in the fourth month in the *Spring and Autumn Annals* corresponded to the second month of the calendar in use in India. He was even able to arrive at the proper day of the month through another series of calendrical adjustments. Second, he pointed out that, according to the Buddha's biography, the night sky was bright both on the day of the Buddha's birth and on the day he became a buddha. This then led Dao'an to conclude that the event described in the *Spring and Autumn Annals* occurred at the time of the Buddha's *enlightenment*, rather than at his birth. Once this day was determined, he could calculate the date of the Buddha's birth, the date on which he became a monk, and the date of his death, all on the basis of information about the Buddha's age at these times given in canonical sources.[13] Dao'an writes:

> According to Buddhist scripture, the Thus-Come-One entered his mother's womb on the eighth day of the fourth month. He was born on the eighth day of the second month [of the following year] and also was enlightened on the eighth day of the second month.
>
> Light was emitted both on the occasion of his birth and when he became a buddha, yet the date on which he became a buddha is [mistakenly] said [by Wei Shou] to be the date of his birth.

In the Zhou, the eleventh month [corresponds to our] first month. The fourth month in the *Spring and Autumn Annals* corresponds to the second month of the [calendar of the] Xia dynasty.[14] In India the same first month was used as during the Xia dynasty.

Du Yu[15] 杜預 calculated according to the Jin calendar, arriving at the fifth day of the second month of *xinmao* [for the date referred to in the *Spring and Autumn Annals*]. [In contrast], along with Dong Fengzhong 董奉忠 [d.u.], I employ the Lu calendar [the calendar used for the *Spring and Autumn Annals*], giving us the seventh day of the second month. If we use the former Zhou calendar, then we get the eighth day of the second month.

Moreover, the chronology of Kumārajīva and the "Stone Pillar Inscription" are in accordance with the *Spring and Autumn Annals*.[16]

[In conclusion], the Thus-Come-One was born in the *yichou* year, the fifth year of King Huan of the Zhou [714 BCE]. In the *kuiwei* year, the twenty-third year of King Huan, he became a monk. In the *jiawu* year, the tenth year of King Zhuang [686 BCE], he became a buddha. In the *jiashen* year, the fifteenth year of King Xiang [636 BCE], he entered extinction. This was one thousand two hundred and five years ago.[17]

In short, his calculations complete, Dao'an could confidently assert not just the year, month, and day of the Buddha's birth but also the date of his death and dates of other important events in his life. Yet despite such dazzling displays of energy and erudition, the puzzle continued to trouble the minds of discriminating historians, unconvinced by earlier efforts. By 597, when Fei Zhangfang 費長房 (fl. 574), a devout Buddhist and former monk, addressed the problem in his *Record of the Three Jewels Through the Ages* (*Lidai sanbao ji* 歷代三寶記), he was faced with five possible dates for the birth of the Buddha, each attested in a different source.[18] Much of Fei's book is a (famously flawed) bibliography of Buddhist works, but the first section attempts to narrate the official policy of Chinese rulers toward Buddhism in chronological order. Remarkably, Fei begins not with the introduction of Buddhism to China but with the birth of the Buddha in India, and so starts with an attempt to determine the first date in a narrative that is scrupulously tied to a continuous time line. In addition to Dao'an's solution, Fei cites a passage from the pilgrim Faxian 法顯 (d. ca. 422), who notes a legend that dates the birth of the Buddha not to the Zhou dynasty but all the way back to the Shang dynasty, specifically 1020 BCE.[19] Fei cites a monk named Fashang 法上 (495–580),

who drew on a text called the *Mu Tianzi biezhuan* 穆天子別傳 to arrive at the date of 958 BCE. Next, Fei cites a text called the *Xiangzheng ji* 像正記, like the previous, apparently no longer extant, which gives the forty-eighth year of King Ping, or 723 BCE. Finally, after recording Dao'an's date, Fei cites the *Dotted Record of the Assembled Holy Ones After the Extinction of the Buddha* (*Fo mieduhou zhongsheng dianji* 佛滅度後眾聖點記), so called because it included a dot for every year after the death of the Buddha. According to this text, Fei Zhangfang tells us, the Buddha died in 485 BCE.[20] The theories differed by up to 535 years, but which was right?

Undaunted, Fei attacks the problem through a close comparison between Chinese historical records and descriptions of the Buddha's life in Chinese translations of Buddhist scriptures. He cites one scripture to show that the night sky was bright when the Buddha was born, and another to show that falling stars were witnessed. He then addresses a reference to rain after the Buddha's birth, deftly citing and then skirting an early commentary before offering a plausible interpretation of an obscure passage in the *Zuozhuan* that states that it rained on the night of the meteor shower in 687 BCE. This last, meteorological argument reveals the extent to which Fei had entered into a world of textual scholarship in which erudition trumps reason. (He seems not to have considered that rain in India on the day of the Buddha's birth did not entail rain in China on the same day!) Fei goes on to present an argument at least as complicated as Dao'an's, in which he challenges Dao'an's conclusions.[21] Setting aside the convoluted details of Fei's argument, resting on all manner of clever moves and false assumptions, it is clear that by this time, enough variables had been introduced to the problem to make it entirely intractable. Seven hundred years later, by the latter part of the thirteenth century, when Zhipan hoped to establish a starting date for his own chronological history of Buddhism, the *Comprehensive Account of the Buddhas and the Patriarchs*, he was able to list nine different possible dates (up from five in the *Record of the Three Jewels*), according to more than a dozen different sources.[22]

Nor was the year of the Buddha's birth the only problem. Monastic historian Zanning, in the opening passage for his *Brief History of the Clergy* (*Sengshi lüe* 僧史略), dissected the problem with characteristic enthusiasm, listing seven possible dates from a number of different sources and, unlike the others, addressing not only the question of the year of the Buddha's birth but also the problem of the precise day, since, as Dao'an pointed out before him, it could be assumed that the Indians were using a different calendar from their Chinese contemporaries. Zanning cites some sources that speculate on the key issue of which month the

Indians took as the first month of the year and comes to his own uneasy conclusions. Of special interest is not so much his own solutions but that he asks the question *why* accounts varied so drastically in the first place; why didn't the scriptures provide more clarity on a point as essential as the date of the Buddha's birth? Zanning writes:

> Note: the many theories for the birth date of the Buddha differ. This is first because the manifestations of [the Buddha] are extraordinary, and he teaches according to conditions, resulting in differences in experience. Second, this is because monks who have come from the West may have been born in [different] cities or in villages, such that the information they transmit is [influenced by] different schools and sectarian considerations, resulting in different theories. Additionally, in the West the people are unassuming and simple, rarely capable of recording events in detail. They are slow and easy, and do not place emphasis on the complex and detailed. For this reason, the traditions [about the Buddha's birth] vary.[23]

This is in fact not a bad summary of the problem, with Zanning's last point being central. While few would now characterize Indian culture as "simple" or averse to "the complex and detailed," the main problem is the absence of dates in Indian Buddhist literature, which inhibits modern scholars from reaching a consensus on even the century in which the Buddha was born, much less the year, month, or day. Part of the reason for the ever-increasing number of possible dates for the Buddha's birth was the difficulty of matching calendars even when a likely astral occurrence could be identified in both Indian and Chinese sources. Another part was the regular appearance of new apocryphal accounts further muddying the waters with their spurious claims to be ancient texts providing key information about the birth of a holy man in the West. But these explanations do not address the wider question of why Chinese Buddhists were, in one tome after another, one century after another, driven to pore over hopelessly vague and contradictory ancient texts in a quixotic quest to determine a fixed date, even going so far as to fabricate new texts to provide one.

One reason was liturgical. After discussion of the problem of determining what month and day the Buddha was born on (according to some scriptures it was the eighth day of the fourth month and according to others, the eighth day of the second month), Zanning complains that in different parts of China, the ceremonies commemorating the birthday of the Buddha are held on different days, a troubling source of pious confusion and disquiet.²⁴ Zanning argues that the muddle was brought about by mistakes in translation and sloppy scholarship. He insists that the proper date of the Buddha's birth is the fourth day of the second month.²⁵ In this instance, Zanning's insistence on accuracy was in part inspired by the need for liturgical uniformity. But however important that might have been, earlier in the history of arguments over the dating of the Buddha, the stakes were even higher.

The dates of the Buddha played a prominent role in the thousand-year-long debate over the possible historical relationship between the Buddha and Laozi. The controversy had roots in an early legend that built on the biography of Laozi in the *Records of the Historian*. In the biography, after reluctantly agreeing to commit the *Daode jing* to writing, Laozi left China. "No one knows where he finally ended." According to a subsequent legend formulated in the second and third centuries, the great Chinese sage then traveled to India and the "Western Regions" where, after assuming the name and guise of the Buddha, he converted "the barbarians." Thus, Buddhism was in fact founded in India by Laozi. In this way, the legend of Laozi was used to explain the appearance of a new religion in the West and to tie it more closely to Chinese history. In approximately 300, the story was adapted to the needs of increasingly virulent anti-Buddhist polemic. A new scripture, *The Conversion of the Barbarians* (*Huahu jing* 化胡經), appeared, explaining that Laozi's intent in creating Buddhism was to control a devious and dangerous people. The promotion of celibacy among monks and nuns, for instance, was actually a clever ruse intended by Laozi (in the guise of the Buddha) to peacefully exterminate a deviant Indian race. Against the backdrop of this version of Buddhism's origins, for the Chinese to adopt Buddhism—at best a diluted form of Daoism created for foreigners—made no sense. As the legend gained currency, leading Buddhist figures fought back in court debates that are dutifully chronicled in texts preserved in the Buddhist canon.²⁶

As Erik Zürcher notes, the Buddhist response consisted on the one hand of reasoned arguments that attempted to demonstrate the absurdity of the legend, and on the other, of the creation of new scriptures explaining that in fact the conversion was the other way around: Laozi, Confucius, and other key figures in early Chinese civilization were in fact manifestations of bodhisattvas.²⁷ The arguments exchanged between Buddhists and their Daoist detractors, mostly in court debates, continued all the way up to the fourteenth century, when, after imperial intervention, the legend of Laozi's conversion of the barbarians faded, and the debate finally seems to have subsided for good.

Back when the debate was still hot, with crucial consequences for imperial support for Buddhism, Buddhist historians seized upon the opportunity to refute the "conversion of the barbarians" theory on historical grounds. One of the ways they did this was by examining the textual history of the *Scripture of the Conversion of the Barbarians* to show that it was a late fabrication. Another technique was chronological: they undermined the credibility of the legend by demonstrating that the Buddha lived long before Laozi. The biography of Laozi in the *Records of the Historian* does not give his date of birth, but it does cite traditions that he lived for either 160 years or "over 200," and, crucially, that he was a contemporary of Confucius. As the *Records of the Historian* biography of Confucius gives his dates as 551–479 BCE, it was possible to have at least a general idea of the date of Laozi's birth. All that was necessary then was to place the Buddha well before this date to demonstrate on chronological grounds that Laozi could not be the founder of Buddhism.

The argument that the Buddha predated Laozi first appears in the biography of Tanwuzui 曇無最 (fl. 520) in the *Further Biographies of Eminent Monks* (*Xu gaoseng zhuan* 續高僧傳). According to this account, during a debate in 520 at the Wei court over the tradition that Laozi founded Buddhism, the Buddhist monk Tanwuzui challenged his Daoist rival, Jiang Bin 姜斌 (fl. 520), by asking when Laozi was born. The Daoist responded to his rival with confident precision:

> He was born during the third year of King Ding of the Zhou (604 BCE) in the state of Chu, Chen Commandery, Hu District, Li County, in Quren Village on the fourteenth day of the ninth month at night. In the fourth year of King Jian (571 BCE) he was appointed archival officer. In the first year of King Jing (519 BCE), at the age of eighty-five, he saw that the virtue of the Zhou was in decline, and so he entered the Western Regions with the Keeper of the San Pass Yin Xi 尹喜 in order to convert the barbarians. All of this is clear.

Tanwuzui in turn refutes his opponent with equal precision:

> The Buddha was born on the eighth day of the fourth month of the twenty-fourth year of King Zhao of the Zhou (1029 BCE). He entered extinction on the fifteenth day of the second month of the fifty-second year of King Mu

(949 BCE). If we calculate from the time he entered nirvana, it was three hundred and forty-five years before the third year of King Ding, when Laozi was born. Laozi had lived for another eighty-five years by the first year of the reign of King Jing, making for four hundred and thirty years [from the Buddha's nirvana] before he retired to the West with Yin Xi. The chronological discrepancy is vast. What nonsense![28]

In other words, according to Tanwuzui's calculations, Laozi left for the West 430 years after the Buddha's death; it was hence mathematically impossible for the Buddha to have been Laozi in disguise.[29]

This earlier date for the Buddha's nirvana—based on two texts most likely fabricated by Buddhists in China—eventually became the dominant one in Buddhist historical sources. Indeed, 949 BCE was accepted throughout East Asia as the date of the Buddha's nirvana until quite recently.[30] It seems that the earlier date became predominant in Buddhist writing because of this polemical advantage in debates with Daoists. In the thirteenth century, Zhipan, in typically rigorous fashion, lists nine "absurdities" in the story of the conversion of the barbarians. He divides his dissection of the problem into the two categories of chronology and textual criticism. The chronological critique focuses on the gap between the nirvana of the Buddha and the birth of Laozi. Zhipan adroitly points out internal inconsistencies in the texts that relate the story of Laozi's conversion of the barbarians, including anachronistic transliterations of Buddhist technical terms. He does not, however, apply the same criteria to the *Zhoushu yiji* 周書異記 or the *Hanfa ben neizhuan* 漢法本內傳, the dubious sources used by Buddhists to argue for the 949 BCE date. The argument—however thorough and sophisticated—was ultimately in the service of polemics.

In many cases, however, more was involved in the interpretation of the Buddha's birth date than Buddho-Daoist polemics at court. Beginning in the fifth century, ancient prophecies of the decline of Buddhism, first formulated in early Indian Buddhism, gained new impetus in China. According to these prophecies, at a certain number of years after the death of the Buddha (the number varied widely), the teachings of Buddhism and the monastic community that preserves them would fall into decline and eventually disappear entirely, plunging the world into a dark age from which it would only recover long after, in a distant era that culminates with the arrival of the next buddha, Maitreya.[31] In the sixth century, leading monks like Huisi 慧思 (515-577) and Jizang pored over the scriptures at their disposal, weighed the evidence, and applied their considerable exegetical skills toward determining the precise date at which the Dharma would begin its decline, and what phases it would endure at other key dates along the way.[32]

This concern with the chronology of the inevitable decline of Buddhism may explain the final lines attached to many of the calculations of the dates of the Buddha by Chinese Buddhist historians, noting how many years have passed from the death of the Buddha to the year in which they write. Recall Wei Shou: "From then until the eighth year of Wuding of the Wei [dynasty, i.e., 550, the date when Wei Shou was writing] is one thousand two hundred and thirty-seven years." One thousand was a common number (among several schemes) for the duration of the Dharma in Indian texts.[33] It was precisely at the time that Wei Shou was writing—the latter part of the sixth century—that Chinese monks were formulating a new system for the gradual decline and disappearance of Buddhism, divided into three phases: True Dharma, Semblance Dharma, and Final Dharma. According to the timetable proposed by Huisi, Wei Shou's calculation would put the world less than two hundred years from the end of the Semblance Dharma and, in the grand scheme of things, on the cusp of the dark period of the Final Dharma.[34] In contrast, according to the timetable proposed by Jizang, the world had entered the period of the Semblance Dharma less than two hundred years previous.[35] While the early attempts by Chinese Buddhists to date the nirvana of the Buddha do not specifically link it to the decline of the Dharma, by 597, when Fei Zhangfang compiled the *Record of the Three Jewels*, the connection between these two projects—to chart the chronology of the decline of the Dharma and to uncover the dates for the Buddha—was too crucial to ignore. As we saw above, Fei settled on the date 687 BCE for the Buddha's nirvana, which placed Fei 1,284 years after the nirvana. After giving the reasons for the superiority of the argument for the 687 BCE date, Fei lists the various other theories, noting how many years had elapsed since each proposed date. At the end of this section, he addresses the significance of the dates, concluding cheerfully that, on the basis of comprehensive inquiry and rigorous historical analysis, there is cause for optimism. He writes:

> According to the teachings of the *tripiṭaka* and the *Regulations of Good Views*, the reason the Buddha did not want to ordain women was out of respect for the Dharma. The True Dharma should have lasted one thousand years, but because of the ordination of women was reduced by five hundred years. Because the Buddha instituted the "eight forms of respect" [of nuns for monks,

the period of the True Dharma] was restored to one thousand years.³⁶ After this, the Semblance Dharma also lasts for one thousand years, and the Final Dharma for ten thousand years. Up to the end of the five thousandth year, one can learn the three forms of complete knowledge and obtain the four rewards. From the year six thousand on, one cannot complete the Path through study alone. After ten thousand years, the written scriptures will naturally fall into extinction, leaving only shaved heads and kaśayas [i.e., only the superficial external signs of Buddhism]. During the period of the True Dharma, the flavor of the Great Vehicle is pure, but in the Semblance era it is diluted, and during the time of the Final Dharma there will be no Great Vehicle. Slaves will join the clergy and pollute the pure practices. Wicked kings will rule the world and impose taxes on monks and nuns. This has not yet happened. Based on this [we know that] the transition from the True [Dharma] to the Semblance [Dharma] is not yet advanced. The Three Jewels prosper and the Great Vehicle flourishes. How can we be said to be approaching the Final Dharma?³⁷

All sorts of values and assumptions are embedded in the prophecies that Fei takes as given—the ordination of women shortened the duration of the good Dharma; the fate of Buddhism depends on the quality of the clergy and the generosity of rulers. But for Fei, the immediate problem of assessing the prospects for Buddhism in the coming years came down to precise dating of a single event on the basis of historical documents.

Given the dire predictions of collapse and dark despair, founded on specific spans of time, it is understandable that Buddhist historians like Fei Zhangfang would be driven to scrutinize the historical record in search of their exact location in the phases of the Dharma. The two themes that I have focused on here—polemics and eschatology—go a long way toward explaining Chinese historians' persistent preoccupation with the dates of the Buddha. Both were of great importance at particular times, and both suggested to historians the power of chronology and the practical value of rigorous textual analysis. Other scholars who have examined the dating of the Buddha in China have also noted both themes.³⁸

But concern with the decline of the Dharma and Laozi's dates is not as prevalent in discussion of the date of the Buddha's death as we might assume. I argued above that Wei Shou, by concluding his comments on the Buddha with the number of years since his death, may have been informed by recent discussion of the decline of the Dharma. But he does not make the point specifically. Nor does

Dao'an make any reference to the decline of the Dharma; he is more concerned with establishing that the traditional date for the birth of the Buddha was in fact the date of the Buddha's enlightenment—a difference of little consequence for determining the date of the end of Buddhism. And neither mentions the problem of the "conversion of the barbarians."

After a peak of anxiety over the decline of the Dharma at the end of the sixth century, interest in these troubling predictions waned, and later historians no longer mentioned a connection between the dates of the Buddha and the eventual demise of Buddhism.[39] From the seventh century on, historians' concern with the apocalypse was overshadowed by the immediate value of weaponizing the date of the Buddha to refute the story that Buddhism was founded by Laozi. This seems to account for the shift at this time from 687 BCE to the earlier 949 BCE date, since this placed the Buddha well before the date of Laozi's birth.[40] This earlier date remained the standard in East Asia until modern times. But even after the Laozi story lost currency (by about the fourteenth century), monastic historians in China continued to rehearse the dates for the Buddha. In the seventeenth century, Jiyin 紀蔭 (fl. 1683) relates all of the sources we have seen so far and more.[41] Yet in citations, he focuses solely on the dates and eliminates references to the decline of the Dharma and the "conversion of the barbarians." Back in the tenth century, Zanning was most concerned with establishing the proper month for celebrating the birthday of the Buddha, and makes no mention of either Laozi or the decline of the Dharma.

The driving force for this concern about the dates of the Buddha—perhaps even more important than polemics, eschatology, or liturgy—was the imperative to determine precise dates in formal Chinese historiography. This is most apparent in books like the *Record of the Three Jewels* or the *Comprehensive Account of the Buddhas and the Patriarchs* that are organized at least in part chronologically; for works like these the date of the birth of the Buddha was the first of all of the dates—followed by dates for the deaths of the Buddha's most prominent disciples, for Aśoka's distribution of relics, for later masters, and for the transmission of Buddhism to China—and so naturally attracted the exegetical attention of the historian.[42] But concern with the dates of the Buddha is just as pronounced in other sorts of Buddhist historical works, and we find an attention to dates in all manner of Buddhist historical writings in China, even when the dates in question are of no particular significance. In short, in Chinese Buddhist historiography, chronology proved useful for various purposes, but it was primarily the exercise of unraveling chronological puzzles itself and the neat organization of events on a clean time line that consistently attracted Buddhist historians to dates. Dates provided the irresistible opportunity to prove their historical skills and rightful place among the best practitioners of the discipline, even at the expense of a fluid and compelling narrative, as the historians insist on interrupting their stories with chronological excurses.[43] It was in this historiographical milieu of scholars marshalling evidence and constructing intricate arguments to refute their rivals and predecessors that, provoked by the more immediate concerns of the day, their attention turned to the dates of the Buddha.

PROPHECY

Chronology was one way to bring order to a muddled past, but as we have seen, the sources Chinese Buddhists drew upon for the history of Buddhism in India, though voluminous, were frustratingly short on the calendars, reign periods, and other concrete dates that Chinese readers craved, inspiring monastic historians in China to turn to other techniques better supported by the sources. Buddhist writers used chronology in the service of prophecy in attempting to pinpoint where they fit on the time line of the Buddha's prophecies. But the opposite was also true: they used prophecy in the service of chronology. That is, prophecy was, ironically, seized upon as a means of ordering not the future, but the past. If the Buddha had predicted that something would happen at a certain date or in a certain way after his death, the Buddhist historian could assume that events had transpired as foretold, even when corroborating evidence was weak.

Writing in the early sixth century, Huijiao, for instance, at the conclusion of a chapter of biographies of monks who specialized in the monastic regulations, attempted to narrate the division of the Indian sangha into different groups, each with its own vinaya. Given the Indian sources, this is a problem of great complexity; precisely how the division took place—which groups grew out of which and in what order—continues to vex modern historians of Indian Buddhism. Huijiao attempts to organize the history of these divisions by citing a series of prophecies made long before the sangha began to split into separate factions. One such prophecy occurred when a man came to the Buddha with a dream he had had of a white carpet torn into five parts. The Buddha explained that the dream meant that "after my extinction, the regulations will be divided into five groups."[44]

Huijiao then provides more detail through reference to a passage in the *Da fangdeng da ji jing* 大方等大集經 (Skt. *Mahāvaipulyamahāsaṃnipātasūtra*) in which the Buddha prophesies that the monastic community will split into five groups: the Dharmagupta, Sarvāstivāda, Kāśyapīya, Vātsīputrīya, and Mahāsāṃghika.[45] Huijiao follows this with yet another of the Buddha's predictions, paraphrasing the *Mañjuśrīparipṛcchā*, in which the Buddha says that one hundred years after his death the sangha will divide into two groups that will further splinter into a total of seventeen schools.[46] Huijiao then attempts to place the two in some sort of order before introducing yet a third prediction. He writes:

> Other accounts refer to eighteen groups with slightly different names. Hence, the five groups are at the roots, with four schools emerging from the Sarvāstivāda, one from the Mahīśāsaka, and two from the Kāśyapīya. These together correspond to the Buddha saying at his nirvana that two hundred years later the Mahāsāṃghika would split into six groups that would continue for four hundred years.[47]

None of this, despite my best efforts, maps out into a comprehensible chronological chart. The prophecies were most likely formulated after the divisions they predict had taken place, and so vary depending on the time, place, and circumstances of those who devised them. But this was not a possibility Huijiao was willing to entertain: all were, for him, authentic prophecies of the Buddha and, as such, accurate descriptions of what must have happened between the time of the Buddha and Huijiao's own day. Later, Yijing provided another version of the story of the dream of the white carpet, in which it is divided into eighteen parts, one for each of the eighteen schools.[48] Prudently, Yijing simply ignores the other versions of the prophecy rather than attempting to show why one is more credible than another.

Prophecy can be generated by a need for legitimacy or, more innocuously, as a way to bring order to a chaotic present—proving that all that has happened was unavoidable, preordained, and understandable. For the historian who accepted a set of prophecies as true, they presented both opportunities and problems. This was particularly the case for Chinese Buddhists who, however skeptical they might have been about *Chinese* texts, accepted all Buddhist texts translated from an Indian original as the authentic words of the Buddha and so had to make sense of a diverse group of prophecies. This helps to explain the confusing picture presented by Huijiao. No Indian historian before him had clearly laid out the history of the divisions of the sangha after the Buddha's nirvana, leaving Huijiao and others to make the most of a set of contradictory prophecies that they had to accept as representing what eventually came to pass.

GENEALOGY

Genealogy is perhaps the only area in which Buddhist historiography significantly influenced other forms of Chinese historical writing.[49] And while Indian sources are largely uninterested in providing specific dates for figures and events, the use of lineage—a succession of religious masters or rulers—as a means of ordering history was not uncommon in Indian Buddhism.[50]

In his *Śākya Genealogy*, the sixth-century monk Sengyou mines the scriptures for information about the family background of the Buddha, tracing it all the way back to the beginning of human society when attachment began with the discovery of food, giving rise to divisions that led to the rise of the first ruler.[51] He then follows with a list of thirty-two Indian rulers, related either as father and son or as brothers, followed by a list of ten prominent clans that produced *cakravartin* kings, followed by another list of rulers culminating in the birth of Śākyamuni. In all of this, while Sengyou is drawing on Indian sources he is careful to cite, we can clearly see the influence of Chinese historiography, in particular the *Records of the Historian*, which presents the foundations of history as a lineage of rulers in the "Basic Annals" (*benji* 本紀) section and as a succession of prominent families in the "Hereditary Houses" (*shijia* 世家) section.[52] Sengyou even compares the difficulties of reconstructing the early lineage of rulers in India to the difficulties in tracing the biographies of the sage kings of China's past—Fuxi, Shennong, and the Yellow Emperor—the figures with which Sima Qian began his history.[53]

In a later chapter of his book, Sengyou turns to a very different sort of lineage, distinctive to Buddhism: the buddhas of the past. Drawing chiefly on the opening sutra of the *Dīrghāgama* (Ch. *Chang ahan jing* 長阿含經), he lists the buddhas of the distant past about whom we have specific information (names, classes, life spans, etc.) and notes ways these details differ or agree with the facts concerning the most recent buddha, Śākyamuni.[54] A generation later, Wei Shou began his account of Buddhism by placing Śākyamuni in the same context:

He whom we refer to as the Buddha was originally called Śākyamuni, which, translated, means "capable of benevolence." That is to say, his virtue fulfilled and his path complete, he is able to save the myriad beings. Before Śākyamuni, there were six buddhas. Śākyamuni, succeeding the six buddhas, achieved his enlightenment and dwelt in the present age, the Good Kalpa. It is written that in time to come Maitreya, directly succeeding Śākyamuni, will come down to this world.⁵⁵

Later historians followed suit, beginning their histories of Buddhism not with Śākyamuni but with the buddhas who preceded him.⁵⁶

The concept of the lineage of the buddhas in some form is a core doctrine, the common heritage of all Buddhists, but it also appealed especially to ambitious Buddhist historians who, with this tool in hand, could stretch their histories into the far distant past. As in Sengyou's lists of kings, lineages could also be used to structure time, particularly when dates were not available, like archaeologists dating evidence further and further back in time by matching overlapping tree rings.⁵⁷ For the period following the death of the Buddha, Sengyou again turned to genealogy, this time a lineage of Indian patriarchs beginning with one of the Buddha's immediate disciples, who transmitted the monastic regulations. Writing in about the year 500 in a preface to a work that no longer survives, Sengyou alludes to lists of more than fifty Indian patriarchs said to have transmitted the Sarvāstivāda vinaya across time in India.⁵⁸ In considering lineage as a historiographical tool, the key concern here is Sengyou's motivation. What was the point of introducing lineage when narrating Buddhist history in India? Sengyou himself promoted the Sarvāstivāda vinaya. But in the context of his other historical works, like his account of Śākyamuni's family, the presentation of this lineage was just as likely inspired by the historian's interest in linking past figures and events. And in keeping with the practice of formal Chinese historiography we will see in the next chapter, Sengyou lists not one lineage for the Sarvāstivāda tradition but two, preserving the discrepancies for future historians to puzzle over and hopefully reconcile.

Outside of the mainstream historiographical tradition, at about the time that Sengyou was writing, a text began to circulate that claimed to be a translation of a Sanskrit original but was in fact composed in China on the basis of extracts from Indian scriptures. This text, the *Fufazang yinyuan zhuan* 付法藏因緣傳, provided a list of twenty-three patriarchs, one following on the other, each less capable than the one who preceded him, and ending with the dramatic murder of the final, twenty-fourth patriarch in India (see appendix 2: lineage chart 1).[59] We can only speculate about the motivation for compiling such a work, as it suggests that the line of Buddhist heroes was extinguished long ago: rather than ordering the past or demonstrating the old and distinguished roots of Buddhism in general, it seems instead to have been inspired by a vision of crisis and decline, best demonstrated through charting the gradual deterioration of the Buddha Dharma over a vast span of time.[60]

Beginning in the seventh century with the Tiantai monk Guanding 灌頂 (561-632), partisan monks driven by sectarian agendas began to invent lineages linking themselves back through the history of Indian Buddhism and ultimately all the way to the Buddha himself in genealogical lines of transmission. Eventually, rival links to Indian lineages were advanced for monks identifying with the Tiantai and Chan schools, with representatives of each shoring up their own family histories while attacking the validity of the lineage accounts of their opponents. In Guanding's case, this meant forging a link, through a text, from one of the Indian patriarchs to a Chinese monk in his own lineage. Guanding was followed in the eighth, ninth, and tenth centuries by dozens of writers furiously constructing such lineages—of various levels of sophistication and authenticity—in order to legitimate their own traditions, a topic I will return to in chapter 5.[61]

Authors presenting lineages of Indian masters were cognizant of the need for convincing chronology, in the case of the Chan school providing dates for the deaths of each of twenty-eight patriarchs (see appendix 2: lineage chart 1) that account for the time between accepted dates for the Chinese Chan patriarchs and the nirvana of the Buddha in 949 BCE, with most of the Indian patriarchs living about fifty years after receiving the transmission. The challenge in constructing and then tinkering with this lineage was to space the patriarchs out evenly, so that each lived a credible life span. A significantly later date for the nirvana would have entailed extensive changes to the dates for each of the patriarchs to come out right.[62]

Yet despite its eventual prominence, including acceptance at court by the emperor himself, this shaky historiographical scaffolding continued to attract criticism from opponents of Chan, which in turn inspired attempts at revisions by more cautious Chan writers determined to reinforce their history of Indian Buddhism linking them in a genealogical chain back to the Buddha. In the middle of the eleventh century the Chan monk Qisong reassessed the Indian side of the Chan lineage.⁶³ The obvious problem was that the *Fufazang*, on which previous historians, including Tiantai monks, had based the Indian side of their lineage, clearly states that the lineage *died out* in India with the beheading of the last patriarch. But Qisong was also perplexed by the old problem of prophecy: early on in the text the Buddha commands his disciples to spread the Dharma. Taking the statement not just as a command but as a prophecy (with the Buddha saying, "you *will* respectfully follow out my wishes" 汝當於後敬順我意), Qisong considered the demise of the Dharma later in the text as inconsistent. Moreover, when the last patriarch dies, he does so without a prophecy of his own, or explanation of any sort. This is a novel twist on the historiographical use of prophecy: the lineage cannot have died with the "last" patriarch because if it had, he would have foretold these events beforehand.⁶⁴ In response, Qisong first speculates that the *Fufazang* might be a translation of an incomplete Sanskrit text, with reckless translators filling in the blanks in China. Later he dismisses the text outright as a forgery, indignantly concluding, "I pronounce this book absurd. It can be burned!"⁶⁵ Qisong's solution to the problem was not to reject the Indian lineage entirely, but rather to reaffirm the standard Indian Chan lineage prominent in his day through reference to early Chinese texts we have already discussed, and to the story laid out in the *Biographies of Baolin* (*Baolin zhuan* 寶林傳), a text at least as suspect as the *Fufazang* that Qisong so vehemently rejected.⁶⁶ In other words, while he was clearly cognizant of the problems of unearthing a lineage of masters stretching back to the Buddha, the need for such a lineage was too great to abandon the project all together.

Tiantai adherents were unconvinced. Not only was Qisong affirming a Chan lineage that excluded Tiantai monks; he was also rejecting the *Fufazang*, which presented the Indian lineage that the Tiantai tradition claimed to carry on. The Tiantai response was based largely on historiographical concerns: chronology and sources. Take, for instance, the description of the problem in the *Comprehensive Orthodox Transmission of the Śākya Clan* by the Tiantai monk Zongjian 宗鑑 (fl. 1237). The problems begin, for Zongjian, with Chan historians' dubious reconstructions of Buddhist history in India. In what had by his day become a standard description of the genealogy of buddhas, Chan works recorded distinct verses supposedly composed each time one buddha passed the Dharmic torch to the next.⁶⁷ Here the creative attempts to reconstruct Indian history overshot their mark. As the scriptures clearly indicate, the buddhas of the past were separated by vast expanses of time. How could they, as the Chan works claim, have recited verses to each other? And even if they did, Zongjian complains, what Indian text is this account of transmission based on? Who translated it and when?⁶⁸

Moreover, he points out that the Chan story of the first transmission of the Dharma from Śākyamuni to the first Indian patriarch Mahākaśyapa—in which a silent transmission took place when the Buddha held up a flower and Kaśyapa smiled—makes no sense.⁶⁹ According to the *Nirvana Sutra*, the Buddha entrusted his teachings to Kaśyapa simply because Kaśyapa's ascetic virtues ensured that he would vigorously preserve the teachings for future generations. Many were enlightened during sermons of the Buddha; Kaśyapa was hardly the only one. And besides, he was first enlightened upon hearing the Buddha preach the *Lotus Sutra*. Why would he wait until just before the Buddha's death before becoming enlightened a second time?⁷⁰ In short, Zongjian insists, Chan histories of an Indian lineage were riddled with inconsistencies apparent to any but the least discriminating reader.

This contempt for the history of Indian Buddhism in the Chan "lamp histories" was rooted not just in an objection to a particular argument but also in the way they are presented. The *Transmission of the Lamp Compiled During the Jingde Era* cites only one source for its account of the buddhas of the past, the *Dīrghāgama*, and then pads it with material, like the verses each buddha pronounces, that have no canonical source. The *Transmission of the Lamp* biography of Śākyamuni, in contrast to Sengyou's well-known biography compiled close to 500 years previous, again cites only one source, the *Puyao jing* 普耀經 (Skt. *Lalitavistara*), and states only one interpretation of controversial issues—like the year of the Buddha's birth and his age at the time he left home—all without discussion.⁷¹ This did not conform to the standards of high history, built on a solid foundation, dense with references to multiple sources and erudite asides.

In the end, narrative power trumped historiographical sophistication, at least in popular historical memory. Despite the objections of critics like Zongjian, the historically unsupported Chan story of the flower and the smile entered the Chinese vernacular as a common proverb, "holding up the flower, one smile" 拈花一笑, the *gāthas* of the seven buddhas of the past were widely quoted in poetry, and the Chan lineage of Indian patriarchs that dominated discussion of Indian Buddhist history eclipsed all others. For all of its flaws, lineage remained a powerful historiographical tool for interpreting Indian Buddhism. Aside from its importance for establishing the legitimacy of one's own tradition and its centrality for the Chan message of an esoteric essence "beyond words and letters" transmitted through time, lineage had great appeal to historians as a way of structuring the past—it was not necessary to date individual events or pore over large amounts of unfamiliar material; the important thing was to draw a neat, unbroken line of succession from the distant past to the present. Figures and circumstances external to the lineage could be ignored; all that mattered was the hard, linked structure. This was especially true for India, where dates and consistent historical accounts were hard to come by.

ADJUDICATION OF SOURCES

In the search for dates of the Buddha and lists of Indian patriarchs, Chinese Buddhist writers were forced to choose between divergent accounts that grew in number with the appearance in China of new Indian texts, mixed in with Chinese fabrications. The adjudication of conflicting sources is fundamental to most types of historical writing. Like other Chinese historians, monastic historians in China copied freely from their sources, usually without attribution. Buddhist historians, following in a long-standing Chinese historiographical tradition, at times draw attention even to contradictions in sources they are unable to resolve. In a discussion of the cousins of Śākyamuni in the *Śākya Genealogy*, for instance, Sengyou observes that the sources differ as to their order of birth, titles, and names, and explains that he must "leave the assessment of their accuracy to wise men to come."[72] Sometimes the historian notes that, given the discrepancies, he is following an Indian text that is longer than other versions and hence, presumably more complete, or he explains that he is following the majority opinion, though some sources differ.[73]

In some cases, Buddhist historians base their arguments on principles of consistency. To cite one example among many, Zhipan, in a passage brimming with erudition, observed that the scriptures differ on how old Śākyamuni was when he left home, giving either nineteen or twenty-nine. After citing some seventeen different texts, Zhipan calculates backward from the time of the Buddha's enlightenment when the scriptures agree he was thirty, subtracting the six years during which he practiced asceticism and arriving at twenty-five as the age when the Buddha must have left his family.[74] These sorts of intricate divigations separated the discriminating historian from the mere storyteller; compilers of miracle tales, for instance, do not pause to ruminate over inconsistencies in their sources.

These approaches are not particularly Buddhist; examples of similar techniques can be found in Chinese historiography more generally from at least the Han dynasty on. More characteristic of Buddhist history is reference to the miraculous to explain discrepancies between sources. Huijiao, for example, explains the troubling fact that different travelers record the presence of specific relics of the Buddha in different places, stating:

> I have searched through the travel records of śramaṇas. At times the routes they record differ. The places at which they encounter the Buddha's alms bowl and the bone of his skull are also at odds. It should be noted that there is more than one road to India, and that the skull bone and bowl [of the Buddha] miraculously move, frequently going to different places. For this reason it is difficult to bring order to the information that has been transmitted to us.[75]

Daoxuan, when confronted with different possible dates for the birth of the Buddha, draws on the doctrine of the Buddha's "three bodies," explaining: "A buddha has three bodies. The Dharma Body and Reward Body cannot be seen by [ordinary] humans, but only by those who have advanced on the bodhisattva path. The Transformation Body covers the universe. There are a hundred million Śākyamunis, manifesting themselves according to conditions, earlier or later in time with no fixed position."[76] But such explanations, or similar ones—for instance, attributing discrepancies in different accounts of a holy man to his divine powers of transformation—are common throughout Chinese Buddhist historiography whether it is addressing India or China, as we will see in chapter 2.

When Chinese Buddhists sat down to write on the history of Buddhism in India, the problem of how to assess their sources was especially acute, the stakes especially high. More often than not, Indian scriptures did not answer the questions that most interested frustrated Chinese historians—they left major gaps between key figures, made no reference to contemporary events in China, and offered no dates at all. The most telling evidence of this hunger in China for a different type of history are the apocryphal works fabricated to fill the gaps—the *Zhoushu yiji*, which gave evidence for the date of the Buddha's nirvana, or the *Fufazang*, which detailed a list of patriarchs stretching from a more recent Indian past all the way back to the Buddha.

Compounding the problem was that Buddhist historians in China seem rarely, if ever to have questioned any scripture once it could be shown to have been translated from an Indian original. All Indian works faithfully recorded the word of the Buddha, and discrepancies, which if examined too closely threatened to bring the reliability of the scriptures as a whole into question, needed to be treated with caution. Normally—as when Zhipan sorted through varying accounts of the Buddha's age when he left home—the historian applies himself toward reconstructing a credible version of events rather than speculating on why the discrepancies arose in the first place. When they do address the question of *why* sources differ, our historians tended to blame it on translation. We have already seen this in Qisong's initial reaction to what he saw as troubling inconsistencies in the *Fufazang*: the translators must have tinkered with the original text. Whereas discrepancies in Chinese texts were often explained (in many cases with good cause) as scribal errors, problems with Indian texts were blamed on problems of translation, and more specifically, with deficiencies in the translators. Take, for instance, the comments of Sengyou, himself familiar with the problems of translation discussed in the work he compiled, the *Collection of Records Concerning the Translation of the Tripiṭaka*. At one point in his biography of the Buddha, Sengyou comments:

> Note: The story of the four sons in this vinaya is for the most part the same as that of the *Āgamas*, but with some differences. In my humble opinion, these arose when the scriptures were converted to Chinese from a foreign language, and the translators made decisions. Those who translated the scriptures each were endowed with different abilities, and so there are inevitably differences. The *Records of the Historian* and *History of the Han* are recent works, yet they too contain confusion and contradictions. How much more must this be the case [when interpreting history] ten thousand *li* away and a thousand years ago?[77]

In other words, Chinese writers were acutely aware that they faced challenges greater than those faced by court historians writing almost exclusively on Chinese history because their subject, Indian Buddhism, involved a longer time span as well as daunting geographic, linguistic, and cultural differences. Buddhist historians in later periods continued to lay the blame for discrepancies in the scriptures on translation rather than question the reliability of the texts on which the translations were based. Among the reasons Zanning gives for discrepancies in the day and month of the Buddha's birth in different sources is miscommunication between translators and scribes in the translation centers.⁷⁸ In fact, discrepancies in sources had much more to do with the circumstances of their creation and transmission in India, but Chinese historians had neither the tools nor the inclination to pursue this line of inquiry, leaving them with the more proximate and convenient explanation of slips in translation.

The most famous technique in Chinese Buddhism for explaining scriptural contradictions was developed not in historiography but in doctrinal exegesis. There is a long tradition in Chinese Buddhist exegesis of classifying and ranking Buddhist scriptures according to the period in the Buddha's life in which he supposedly preached them. Such systems of doctrinal classification (*panjiao* 判教) helped to explain Buddhist doctrine, asserted the superiority of a particular sect (with the scripture most important to one's own tradition situated at the end of the Buddha's career), and also provided a graded route for study and practice.⁷⁹ Much of this sort of doctrinal classification is essentially historical; if it could be shown conclusively on the basis of scriptural evidence, for instance, that the Buddha preached the *Flower Adornment* scripture, central to the Huayan tradition, after the *Lotus* scripture, central to the Tiantai tradition, Tiantai exegesis would suffer a serious challenge.

The relative dates for the Buddha's sermons were, for this reason, enormously consequential. Moreover, doctrinal classification held great potential for historians eager to explain discrepancies in accounts of the life of the Buddha.⁸⁰ Curiously, though, despite the fact that doctrinal classification was a major theme of Chinese Buddhist exegesis from the fifth century through the ninth, it made little impression on historical writings about India or the life of the Buddha until the Tiantai historical works of the Song dynasty. Zhipan's *Comprehensive Account*, suffused with technical doctrinal terminology drawn from Tiantai exegesis, attempts to wed chronology with doctrinal classification, precisely dating each of the "five time periods" (*wushi* 五時) in which the Buddha delivered key sermons according to the Tiantai schema of doctrinal classification.⁸¹ But the "five time periods" are not employed to resolve specific historical problems; for the most part they are taken as a given, around which historical documents are to be arranged. That is, while doctrinal classification was used to explain doctrinal discrepancies in scripture, it was not used to explain chronological discrepancies. Much as Chan historians could not bring themselves to abandon some form of a lineage of Indian patriarchs, Tiantai historians were bound to the "five time periods" when narrating the life of the Buddha, despite the awkward historical problems it created.[82]

In sum, although, like all premodern Chinese historians, Buddhist historians freely copied from previous works, they were from the beginning keenly sensitive to discrepancies between their sources, employing a variety of historiographical techniques to either resolve or explain these differences. When writing about India, the most distinctive of these strategies was to ascribe a messy historical record to the problems inherent in translation and to China's geographic isolation from India, a convenient solution that masked the diverse origins of the Indian works that formed the Chinese Buddhist canon.

CONCLUSION

The fragmentary nature of Indian sources and their lack of dates, coupled with the centrality of Indian Buddhist history for Chinese Buddhists, inspired great historiographical creativity: ingenious chronologies, fanciful lineages, sedulous scrutiny of prophecy, and belief in the miraculous were all enthusiastically put to use as historical tools. None of this is unheard of in Chinese court historiography, but there these themes are more muted. Buddhist historical writings are, moreover, always informed by Buddhist doctrines and their exegesis, whether the doctrine of the eventual decline of the Dharma, the "three bodies of the Buddha," or Tiantai doctrinal classification that divided the life of the Buddha and his teachings into clearly defined stages.

In general, the approach Chinese Buddhists took to Indian history was not radically different from their approach to the history of Buddhism in China—for China as well, great attention was given to prophecy, lineage, and the evaluation of sources. Perhaps the most distinctive aspects of the historiography of *Indian* Buddhism were, first, the search for a single date—the date of the Buddha's nirvana—fueled as much by polemics and eschatology as by the historian's natural fondness for chronological precision. Second, Chinese historians, for all of their confidence when analyzing and speculating about Chinese texts, were less critical of Buddhist texts from India, at times suggesting faults in translation but never questioning the authenticity of a text accepted as originating in India. From a modern perspective, the limitations of Chinese Buddhist historiography are readily apparent, as we search in vain for exploration of issues that concern modern historians, such as the spread of and interaction among the various sects of Buddhism, popular reception of Buddhist teachings, the time and circumstances of the rise of the Mahayana, the economics of monasticism, and so on. The areas of interest to Buddhist historians were, in short, limited to a few themes.

Not surprisingly, the historical problems I discuss above were often driven by polemical or sectarian concerns—an older date for the birth of the Buddha could expose the story of Laozi's conversion of the barbarians as a fraud; amassing evidence to support a lineage extending from the Buddha to China could prove the superiority of the Chan lineage. More surprising is the extent to which much Chinese Buddhist historical writing about India approaches "disinterested history"— discussion of dates and other details when little seems to have been at stake. To the extent that even this more objective analysis was driven by personal interest, it was an interest in demonstrating the historiographical skill and awareness that the Buddhist historian hoped would earn him a place in an elite tradition of rigorous, objective historiography, dedicated to producing a reliable and convincing portrait of the past. From a modern historian's perspective, the portrait is neither reliable nor convincing—no serious historian today accepts the date of the Buddha as 958 BCE or draws on prophecy to demonstrate subsequent events— but nonetheless, we cannot help but admire the thought, creativity, and erudition that went into efforts to reconstruct the history of Indian Buddhism. More than this, Chinese Buddhist historians were keenly aware of the distinctive problems of time, language, culture, and geography that Indian history presented. And while few of their solutions are persuasive today, their assessment of the underlying obstacles to the project of reconstructing Indian Buddhist history are, more often than not, spot-on.

CHAPTER 2

Sources

Traditional Chinese historiography prized mastery of sources as much as skillful storytelling, style, and the use of the past to convey moral truths. Source mastery meant not just collecting multiple accounts of a given person or event but also comparing and evaluating them.[1] Understanding the use of sources in Buddhist historical writing is of great importance to modern scholars who want to accurately reconstruct the events these historians described. Is an account of the family background of a key monk provided in the *Biographies of Eminent Monks* copied from an earlier source we know to be unreliable? Are Song-dynasty records of early Chan history based on early sources that accurately reflect what really happened, or are they instead later projections of an ideal that never existed?

More than this, analysis of source criticism in Buddhist historiography discloses fundamental questions about how elite Buddhist writers in China conceived of the past. Did Buddhists approach their sources differently from other types of historians? Did they care whether or not the past they were reconstructing was accurate, or was their allegiance instead to transmitting instructive stories that conveyed philosophical and moral truths, regardless of their historicity? And what did they make of conflicting sources? The fact that when we have two or more accounts of the same figure or event they at times diverge, suggests just how fragile the foundations of the historical enterprise are. Do we attribute such incongruities to careless mistakes, malice, or more fundamental flaws in human perception and language? Honed in both historical methods and Buddhist doctrinal analysis, Buddhist historians in China brought great sophistication and industry to answering these questions, inspired by problems created by a large body of complex and often conflicting sources. We have caught a glimpse of these issues in the approaches to Indian sources discussed in the last chapter, but the scope of the problem of treating sources was much wider than that.

Few Chinese historical works are firsthand accounts; the most prominent are massive compilations of material gleaned from previous sources, supplemented at times with the historian's comments. Nor did Chinese historians attempt to create the illusion that they did not rely on previous works. On the contrary, demonstrating a thorough knowledge of available sources was the mark of a skilled historian; this is one of the most prominent elements of the craft mentioned briefly in the introduction.[2] Hence, from the great histories written during the Han dynasty to those of the Qing, Chinese historians often cited their sources by name and discussed their merits, at times replicating discrepancies in the historical record rather than attempting to present a "streamlined version of history."[3] Over time, the number of sources used increased, in part at least as the result of changing technology. Considering the sheer physical bulk of manuscripts written on wooden or bamboo strips, it is remarkable that Sima Qian, writing in the first century BCE, consulted the number of works he did.[4] By the eleventh century, Sima Guang could spread paper scrolls about his studio and, in the compilation of his work, literally use the "cut and paste" method to arrange and edit more than 300 sources.[5] Sima Guang even compiled a separate book to accompany his massive history, devoted to explaining his principles and method in comparing discrepancies in historical documents.[6] In subsequent centuries, the increasing availability of printed books, particularly in paginated codex form, made comparing a large number of sources even easier, allowing historians to increasingly consult written texts rather than rely on memory when compiling their works.

Buddhist historical writing followed the same trajectory. Like their counterparts at court, Buddhist historians drew heavily on written sources. Before the modern period, chroniclers of Buddhist history and biographers of monks rarely described figures they met or events they witnessed. Only in very recent times have monastic memoirs become more common.[7] One would think that stele inscriptions, written soon after a prominent monk's death to commemorate his life and broadcast his deeds, would provide direct accounts of what a close disciple saw his master do and heard him say. Similarly, steles recounting a given monastery's history and erected outside its gates would seem to provide an ideal platform for recording direct observation. But the genre of stele inscription was from early on so stylized and ornate that authors of such pieces seldom shed the bounds of convention to describe specific events they themselves saw, focusing instead on expansive praise of a monk's virtues or a monastery's glory in terms so vague and hackneyed that they could just as easily have been written by one with no specific knowledge of the subject.

It is only in the specialized genre of pilgrimage accounts that we find sustained eyewitness descriptions of Buddhist people and things, and even those drew heavily on written texts and long-standing local traditions when attempting to narrate the past.[8] Indeed, such accounts of the past, based on someone else's history, dominate the writings of Xuanzang and Faxian in their "firsthand" accounts of India, frustrating the modern scholar, who is usually more interested in the rarer descriptions of what Chinese pilgrims actually saw of the India of their day than in the legends such pilgrims collected during their travels.

This is not to say that, aside from pilgrims, monastic historians were in principle opposed to "fieldwork." When their personal experience overlapped with the events, figures, or places they describe, they note that they have personally verified certain relevant facts. For instance, seventh-century historian Daoxuan notes at the end of one of the biographies in his *Further Biographies of Eminent Monks* that the remnants of the monk in question "were buried in a valley beneath a cliff, with a stele erected behind the site. In the ninth year of the Zhenguan era (635), I personally visited the site to pay my respects. His bones are still there, and the remains of the monastery still intact."[9] Zanning, compiler of the tenth-century *Song Biographies of Eminent Monks*, similarly notes on occasion that the relics of a prominent monk survive, or explains that he himself visited a particular site mentioned in one of his biographies.[10] But such comments are rare exceptions. Nowhere does Huijiao cite himself as a historical witness in his *Biographies of Eminent Monks*. In general, monastic historians wrote from their libraries, drawing on sources provided by others.

While we cannot always determine what sources were used for a particular account, we do have a good *general* idea of the types of sources monastic historians used. Huijiao details his sources in the preface to *Biographies of Eminent Monks*, our earliest sustained statement of methodology in Chinese Buddhist historiography. He writes:

> In my leisure time I examined a large number of writings. I searched through assorted works by dozens of authors, including chronicles and histories of the Jin, Song, Qi, and Liang dynasties; the heterodox calendars of the frontier

dynasties of Qin, Zhao, Yan, and Liang; geographical miscellanies; isolated pieces; and fragmentary accounts. In addition, I went to great lengths to interview the elderly, and widely questioned those more learned than myself. I compared what one source had and another did not, and chose from among diverging accounts.[11]

The statement is remarkable for its inclusivity, reflecting the maturity of the field of historiographical method early on in the development of Chinese Buddhist historiography. Modern historians investigating the lives of monks from the period can add little to Huijiao's list of possible sources. Although Huijiao does not specifically mention epigraphy here, it is almost certain that he made use of it, as did court historians from the end of the Han onward.[12] Often, soon after the death of a prominent monk, his disciples would ask a local literatus or another prominent monk to compose an elaborate eulogy, which was then carved into a stele and erected at the monk's monastery. In addition to Huijiao, later monastic historians made ample use of stele inscriptions, as reflected in the reference by Daoxuan cited above to "a stele erected behind the site." Indeed, for later periods, steles recording the biographies of monks included in monastic histories survive, and comparison reveals that the biographies in monastic histories were often taken word for word from stele inscriptions. Hence, while modern scholars of Indian Buddhism have been criticized for relying too heavily on transmitted texts and ignoring epigraphy, the same cannot be said of medieval Chinese Buddhist historians.[13] Nor did Chinese monastic historians disparage oral accounts, or conversely consider them necessarily more authentic than written ones; information from oral sources is often blended with information taken from texts. Monastic historians prided themselves on their breadth, on their exhaustive knowledge of all relevant sources, and considered the use of a wide variety of sources a sign of erudition rather than undisciplined reading.[14]

The practice of explicitly citing source material developed only slowly and never reached the level of rigor we might hope for. Huijiao never cites his sources. Daoxuan only occasionally, and seemingly unintentionally, reveals his sources in passing. It is only in the tenth-century *Song Biographies of Eminent Monks* that the compiler, Zanning, notes his sources with some frequency. Yet even he cites them in an indirect way, at the end of a given biography, noting merely that such and such a person composed an epitaph for the monk or that a "separate account" is in circulation without explicitly stating that the biography he gives is based on the epitaph or independent biography. Aside from biographies of monks, when Buddhist historians discussed events in India or at the Chinese court, they often cited their sources. Writing just before Huijiao, Sengyou, in his biography of the Buddha's family, for instance, references dozens of canonical sources.[15] But as in court historiography, in Buddhist historiography systematic citation of sources only became prevalent in the Song dynasty.[16] As I noted above, in the thirteenth century, Zhipan began his *Comprehensive Account of the Buddhas and the Patriarchs* by listing 178 sources that he draws from in what follows. This increased volume of sources, combined with the use of history as a weapon in the sectarian battles between and among Chan and Tiantai adherents, led to increased scrutiny of the use of sources in the works of rival historians. In early criticism of Buddhist historiography, monastic historians focused on classification, scope, and style. Huijiao complained that a previous collection of biographies of monks was wrong to use mere fame as a criterion for inclusion: monastic history should propagate the stories of exemplars rather than just celebrities. Daoxuan criticized Huijiao for failing to adequately cover the biographies of monks from the north.[17] In short, the discriminating reader evaluated history not just for the stories told but also for the sources consulted when telling them.

Turning from the scale of sources historians employed to the ways they used them, the final comment in Huijiao's statement of historiographical principles is particularly noteworthy: "I compared what one had and another did not, and chose from among diverging accounts." That is, not only did he draw on a wide variety of types of sources; he also used them critically, noting their differences. Yet in general, Huijiao, like the monastic historians who followed, was not preoccupied with these differences. And while he recognized discrepancies between different accounts, he did not in general specifically mark them as such in his written work.

For modern historians, such discrepancies in sources are essential, first because they remind us that we seldom deal with absolutely accurate descriptions of historical events—or else all accounts would be the same—and second because differences often reveal the biases of the authors. The ability to recognize such prejudices in source material, in contemporary scholarship, and even in one's own interpretations of the historical record is now the mark of the critical professional historian. In contrast, the Buddhist historian, not unlike the court historian, though eager to collect all manner of materials, for the most part patched together whatever he could get his hands on, seemingly undisturbed by the shaky foundations on which his stories were built. On occasion, however, discriminating historians *did* specifically note divergent sources. And on even rarer occasions, the incongruities seemed so egregious, or so at odds with what the historian knew to be true, that he stepped out from his customary position bunkered behind his sources and passed judgment. These instances, and the reasoning behind such judgments, are my focus here.

WHEN SOURCES DISAGREE

Huijiao in his preface quotes the oft-repeated statement of Confucius: "I transmit but do not innovate."[18] This is a standard slogan of Chinese historical writers, and the temptation is to dismiss it out of hand as a sort of false humility or transparent disguise for the historian's own prejudices, advising the reader that there is no need to look too closely since what follows is no more or less than bare, indisputable facts. At one level, objective transmission is an unattainable ideal, even for historians who simply copy out accounts originally composed by others; by combining even two sources or placing one before another, one is already innovating, even if each individual source is replicated in full. And Huijiao himself was not afraid to innovate in the criteria he used for selection of subjects, focusing, he tells us, on "eminent" monks, unlike his most prominent predecessor, Baochang 寶唱 (fl. 508), who entitled his collection *Biographies of Famous Monks* (*Mingseng zhuan* 名僧傳). In the cases in which Huijiao's sources survived, we find that he often copied directly from them, word for word. Huijiao himself must have realized that even when discussing the same figure, a given biography included in a bibliography or a collection of miracle tales would be understood differently than a biography included in a collection of accounts of "eminent" monks—"eminent" implying a higher ethical standard.[19]

Well versed in Buddhist scholasticism, Buddhist historians were keenly aware of the unwieldy nature of perception and the extent to which each constructs his own reality.[20] In Buddhist exegetical writings, the assertion that the Buddha preached different doctrines depending on the capacities of his audience was a standard explanation of contradictions in the scriptures. But it was also recognized that the audience themselves interpreted what they heard differently. This insight had important implications for the historical record, explaining how two accounts of the same event could differ, even when the good intentions of the witnesses were not in doubt. The *Comprehensive Orthodox Transmission of the Śākya Clan* explains that dates given for the Buddha differ in the sources because their authors "all had different faculties and perceptions."[21] Zhipan explained apparent inconsistencies in texts ascribed to the Buddha as the result of differences in the "faculties and perception" (*jijian* 機見) of those who recorded his teachings.[22] Zanning applied the same principle to Chinese records, explaining variants in the story of a holy monk by saying, "As a story spreads, accounts of it naturally increase. It is like different people looking at the sun or moon from different positions a thousand miles apart. Even when they see the sun and moon at the same time, the shape and appearance of the clouds that surround them [in different locations] differ."[23] In short, on a theoretical level, Buddhist historians were far from naïve about the possibilities of absolutely objective history. This did not, however, lead them to abandon the pursuit of objectivity, particularly in the specific areas in which the historian's grasp of objective facts was most closely scrutinized.

For all of the preceding caveats, the injunction to "transmit without innovation" had a discernable impact on the way Buddhists wrote history. They are often careful to note differences, even when they cannot choose between them or when the differences are seemingly trivial. This attitude toward the recording of variants was well established by the time Buddhism entered China. Confucius was famously credited with carefully recording two different possible days for the death of Marquis Bao of Chen, establishing perhaps the most famous example in China of historiographical fidelity to the sources.[24] Hence, for Buddhist historians, the practice of noting contradictory sources distinguished them from vulgar writers or casual antiquarians, marking them as serious scholars committed to something more than pedantic moralizing or mere entertainment.[25] The practice of commenting on sources became more common from about the tenth century on, but examples can be found in Buddhist historical writing from earlier periods as well.

Biographers at times list variations in names without attempting to determine which is correct. Take, for example, the name of the great translator of Tantric texts Shanwuwei 善無畏 (637–735). Zanning's biography of the monk begins, "His Indian name was Śubhakarasiṃha (Ch. Xupojieluosenghe 戍婆揭羅僧訶), which in Chinese literally means 'lion of purity.' This is translated as 'good and fearless' [*shanwuwei*]. But according to another tradition, his name was Śubhakara (Ch. Lunpojialuo 輪波迦羅), which means 'fearless.'" Zanning's hesitation is understandable, as even today scholars puzzle over the transliteration of the monk's name, and Zanning knew little or no Sanskrit.[26] This is hardly a gripping opening to a biography of a thoroughly fascinating figure. But while other works concerned with the monk's thaumaturgical feats would simply state the most common Chinese form of his name and pass quickly to the more entertaining episodes in his life, the serious monastic historian pauses over the name and lists its possible derivations.

One subtle way of including material that the historians themselves considered somewhat dubious—but were not prepared to criticize outright—was to preface it with the phrase "some say" (*huoyun* 或云). Huijiao writes in the case of Dharmaruci (Ch. Tanmoliuzhi 曇摩流支, fl. 405) that he "wandered to various parts, and the circumstances of his death are unknown. *Some say* he died in the Liang region, but we have no details."[27] Huijiao shows similar restraint in the question of dating the death of the great translator Kumārajīva (Ch. Jiumoloshi 鳩摩羅什, 350-409). He writes,

> Yet the records regarding the year and month of Kumārajīva's death differ. Some say he died in the seventh year of the Hongshi era, some in the eighth, and others in the eleventh. Looking into the matter, we see that the characters for "seven" 七 and "eleven" 十一 may be mistaken for each other. Moreover, a catalogue of scripture translations gives the "first year." I fear that in attempting to adjudicate among the three different dates we have no means of arriving at the correct one.[28]

Here, Huijiao suggests that the problem may have arisen through a scribal error. Elsewhere, though, with no apparent knowledge of Sanskrit, he takes a reasonable stab at explaining discrepancies in the transcription of the name of a prominent Indian translator-monk when he writes, "His name was Tanwuchen 曇無讖. Some give it as Tanmochan 曇摩懺, others as Tanwuchan 曇無懺. This must come from differences in Sanskrit pronunciation."[29]

Again, where a writer concerned more exclusively with narrative would have picked a given tradition and ignored the rest, Huijiao is at pains to include all possibilities. Subsequent Buddhist writers continued to demonstrate pride in historiographical integrity, inherited from the Chinese historiographical tradition. They would present the facts at their disposal even when they themselves could make little sense of them.

In addition to names, Buddhist historians filled their accounts with numbers. The vast majority of biographies of monks give a precise date for the death of the monk, along with his age at time of death and often the number of years he had been a monk. This scrupulous attention to dating in the earlier works inspired and allowed for later chronological works that centered on a precise timeline.

In keeping with this tradition, when examining the sorts of differences in sources that Huijiao alluded to in his preface, monastic historians were particularly alert to discrepancies in names and dates, often going beyond merely recording such differences and attempting instead to determine which source got the name or date right and which wrong.

Zanning at various points trains a sharp eye on dates and names to question the material he cites, noting that meetings between certain figures could not have taken place. In his biography of a Chan monk named Rumin 如敏 who lived after the fall of the Tang dynasty under the reign of the Later Tang (923–936), Zanning records that early in his monastic career Rumin was said to have met the prominent monk Daan 大安 who, according to Zanning's biography of him, lived from 793 to 883. Commenting on the passage, Zanning does not let the discrepancy pass, noting, "For Rumin to have met Daan, Daan would have had to have lived a very long time, much longer than is normal. I suspect that there is an irregularity in the transmission of the account."[30]

By the thirteenth century, the meticulous attention to source discrepancies was even more pronounced. Zhipan, in his *Comprehensive Account of the Buddhas and Patriarchs,* in an account of the Tiantai patriarch Huisi, lists the sources he used and then notes that the Song Chan work the *Transmission of the Lamp Compiled in the Jingde Era* records an exchange between Huisi and the famous thaumaturge Baozhi 寶誌 (418–514) on the Southern Peak. "According to the *Transmission of the Lamp,* Sire Baozhi had someone say to Master Huisi, 'Why don't you come down from your mountain to teach the myriad beings?' The master replied, "I've swallowed all of the buddhas of the three times in a single gulp. What myriad beings are there to teach?'" For modern specialists, the style of the exchange, typical of Chan "encounter dialogue," clearly marks it as an invention of the late Tang dynasty. But Zhipan instead objects to the passage on chronological grounds, writing:

> Now if we examine the preface to the *Nanyue yuanwen* 南岳願文 we see that the date of birth [of Huisi] should be the fourteenth year of the Tianjian era

under Emperor Wu of the Liang (515). He only arrived at the Southern Peak in the second year of Guangda (568) of the Chen. At that time, he was fifty-four years old.[31] Baozhi had long since died under the reign of Emperor Wu of the Liang. This exchange could not have taken place. Now I fear that there was another master, and that it has simply been mistakenly passed down that he was Baozhi.[32]

We can speculate that the story was invented out of a desire to imagine the meetings of famous figures—the eccentric thaumaturge Baozhi and the brilliant exegete Huisi. We will see the same dynamic below in the imagined meeting between the exotic Tantric foreigner Shanwuwei and the staid Chinese disciplinarian Daoxuan. But later, elite historians quickly noted the chronological impossibility of such stories and dismissed them as unreliable.

The practice of dwelling on what are at times only minor discrepancies in names and dates of sources has significance for the larger historiographical question of the attitude of Buddhist historians in China toward their vocation. One could conceivably interpret Confucius's injunction to "transmit without innovation" not as a call to objectively reconstruct the past—what really happened—but instead simply as a call to transmit conventional wisdom, to tell the story as it had been told in the past, imbued by previous masters with a moral lesson, whether or not it accurately represented events in the lives of the people it described. To continue this hypothetical argument, perhaps the concern with reconstructing the past as it happened is a modern concern, alien to the medieval historian: only we care about a notion of historical truth; historians of the past were preoccupied instead with moral truths embodied in ancient lore.[33] The material we have seen thus far, however, suggests that a more conventional interpretation of what medieval Chinese historians were doing is in fact accurate. In most of these cases there are no apparent moral or ideological issues at stake, driving the historian to question the proper interpretation of Shanwuwei's name or the dates of Kumārajīva's death. The primary concern seems instead to have been with determining accurate historical facts. Indeed, Buddhist historians were prone to overlook the doctrinal or moral significance of passages in their zeal to verify their historicity. The meeting between Baozhi and Huisi ("'Why don't you come down from your mountain to teach the myriad beings?' The master replied, 'I've swallowed all of the buddhas of the three times in a single gulp. What myriad beings are there to teach?'") calls out for interpretation. Is the point that Huisi, as a representative of the virtues of meditation and insight, is superior to thaumaturgy, as represented by the wonder worker Baozhi? Or is the point that every person must discover buddha nature for themselves, independent of a teacher? Our historian does not comment, only noting coldly that the event in question could not have taken place since the dates of the two figures do not match. We will see below and in subsequent chapters that at times Buddhist historians did derive moral and doctrinal lessons from their materials, but their first instincts were almost always to identify and root out chronological discrepancies.

CARELESS MISTAKES

While monastic historians felt obliged to supply conflicting accounts even when they could not adjudicate between them, when possible, they did attempt to determine which version was right. To this end, they employed various strategies. Below I focus on three: blaming discrepancies on careless mistakes by sloppy scribes and poor historians, citing bias and slander as the cause of unreliable accounts, and finally, referring to the marvelous or supernatural nature of the figures about whom the stories were told. I begin with the charge of careless mistakes in the historical record.

Owing to the relatively narrow range of possibilities, the names of Chinese monks and nuns have long been a source of confusion. Modern scholarship has shown that because of a misunderstanding of names in biographical accounts, a given monk may be split in two and presented as two different figures, each with a separate biography, while elsewhere the opposite is the case and two separate figures are conflated into one biography.[34] The influential fourth-century monk Dao'an 道安 (312–385) was in part responsible for the name problem since he instituted the practice of all monks adopting the same surname, Shi 釋 (part of a Chinese transliteration of Śākya), indicating that all monks belong to the family of Śākyamuni. It is hence fitting that Dao'an's own legacy suffered from the problems created by this practice. As Huijiao notes when commenting on a famous letter Dao'an received from the writer Xi Zuochi 習鑿齒 (d. 384):

> According to a separate record, "In Hebei there is another monk called Zhu Dao'an 竺道安, who shares his name with Shi Dao'an." This account claims that it was to Zhu Dao'an that Xi Zuochi wrote his letter. Originally, Dao'an

followed his teacher,³⁵ choosing the surname Zhu. Later, he changed his surname from Zhu to Shi. When people saw the two surnames, they took them as representing two different people. This is an error.³⁶

That is, because Dao'an changed his surname, a subsequent writer mistakenly split his biography in two.³⁷ Here, Huijiao thought it his duty not only to give information from the "separate account" but also to point out its compiler's mistake.

In contrast to Indian sources, in which authors were largely uninterested in chronology, the best Chinese Buddhist historians, in addition to larding their writings with dates, took sorting out problems of dating in the sources as one of their major duties and often exercised great skill in doing so. In his biography of An Shigao 安世高 (fl. cerca 150 CE), the first prominent translator of Buddhist scriptures, Huijiao quotes from a source ("another account," *biezhuan* 別傳) that relates a story that at the end of the Taikang era (ca. 289), An Shigao sealed a letter, which he left in a monastery with the instruction that it not be opened until four years had passed. When the letter was opened, four years later, it read, "The one to revere my teachings is the layman Chen Hui 陳慧; the one to transmit the *dhyāna* scriptures is the *bhikṣu* Senghui 僧會." After recording the story, Huijiao raises doubts about its accuracy, writing:

> The content of An Shigao's sealed letter states: "The one to revere my teachings is the layman Chen Hui; the one to transmit the *dhyāna* scriptures *is* the *bhikṣu* Senghui." Now, in [An Shigao's work] *Ānapāna*, *dhyāna* is spoken of at great length. From this we can believe that the record in the letter is true. But as it says that his teachings will only be spread with the two men he mentions, how can they be his contemporaries?
>
> Moreover, the account states [that in An Shigao's letter he wrote], "The one to transmit the *dhyāna* scriptures is the *bhikṣu* Senghui." Yet Senghui died already at the beginning of the Taikang era [280]. How could the Master of the Way, the Marquis of An [i.e., An Shigao], appear [and compose his letter foretelling that Senghui would transmit his teachings] at the end of the Taikang era [289]? The beginning and end of the text contradict each other.
>
> There must be another document mistakenly dating this to the beginning of the Jin [ca. 265]. Later writers then dated it either to the Taikang or to the end of the Wu [ca. 280]. Attempts at adjudication compete with each other, and there is insufficient data to resolve the issue. Even the claim that this

happened at the beginning of the Jin is troubling. Yet Tanzong's record (*Tanzong ji* 曇宗記) states that only during the time of Emperor Ai of the Jin [r. 362-365] did An Shigao return to administer his monastery. This is in error to the point of absurdity.³⁸

The story that An Shigao wrote in a sealed letter that the layman Chen Hui (d.u.) and the monk Kang Senghui 康僧會 (d. 280) would propagate his teachings is in one way an accurate description of what happened. Kang Senghui and Chen Hui wrote a commentary to what is perhaps the most influential of An Shigao's works, his translation *Da anban shouyi jing* 大安般守意經.³⁹ Perhaps even more widely read than the commentary or the text itself was Kang Senghui's elegant preface to the work.⁴⁰ And Chen Hui is credited with yet another commentary on one of An Shigao's translations on meditation.⁴¹ But rather than observing that these two figures were important in the propagation of An Shigao's translations, the text Huijiao drew on couches their role in a dramatic story of An Shigao mysteriously predicting the future. The point was apparently more to underline An Shigao's supernormal abilities than to describe the influence of his teachings.

Disturbing to Huijiao, however, was the fact that the dates the story supplies don't add up. First of all, An Shigao is said to have made his "prediction" in 289, close to ten years after Kang Senghui's death. What is more, even allowing for a scribal error, if Kang Senghui, Chen Hui, and An Shigao were contemporaries, it would have made no sense for An Shigao to make predictions about how they would act in the future; he would have seen the actions he predicts with his own eyes. Equally troubling was the claim that An Shigao was still alive in the fourth century, which would have made him several hundred years old. At this point, Huijiao cannot help but express his disdain for those who neglect the principles of accurate dating of events to such an extent.⁴² At the same time, rather than dismiss the entire story of An Shigao's prophecy as a pious myth, Huijiao ascribes the discrepancy to a mistake in the dating of the letter.

Similarly, commenting on a famous story of an encounter between Kang Senghui and the ruler Sun Quan 孫權 (182-252) in which the doubting Sun foolishly attempts to destroy holy relics that Senghui has miraculously produced on demand, Huijiao notes:

One record states that it was [the later ruler] Sun Hao 孫皓 who smashed the relics and that this did not happen during the [earlier] time of Sun Quan. To this I note that when Sun Hao was about to destroy a monastery, his ministers responded by saying, "This monastery was created by the Great Emperor [i.e., Sun Quan] in response to the auspicious miracle performed by Senghui." From this we can know that the first śarīra miracle must have taken place during the time of Sun Quan. Hence various accounts all say that Sun Quan experienced the śarīra miracle in his palace. Later, if there were other tests of the divine power [of the relics], these may perhaps have been carried out by Sun Hao.[43]

In other words, while the relics continued to respond miraculously to tests of their power during the reign of the later Sun Hao (r. 264–280), the first test was in fact carried out by the previous Sun Quan.

Comments such as these are remarkable not only for their critical rigor but also because the authors include the passages they dismiss as implausible, recording for later readers the historiographical puzzle along with its solution. At the same time, they also highlight the historians' limitations. Although they recognized problems in a given source, Buddhist historians seldom took the next step of challenging the source's authenticity altogether. From the perspective of the modern historian, suspicious of the whole notion of prophecy, the inconsistency in dating in the story of An Shigao's prophecy suggests that the story was rooted in legend and does not reflect an actual event in the monk's life. But monastic historians were extremely reluctant to pass such extreme judgments and so, even in these cases, turned to favorite explanations of faulty dating and confusion over names to resolve historiographical conundrums.

BIAS

In the preceding examples, the monastic historians did not question the motivations of the authors of implausible accounts. Instead they attributed mistakes to the sloppy editing or uncritical reading of credulous amateurs who relied on only one source, paid no attention to dates, and were unfamiliar with the peculiarities of monks' names. For the most part, Buddhist historians were better equipped to detect shoddy history than they were to uncover outright deception. Only rarely did they sense more pernicious forces at work.

For the early phase of Buddhist historiography, the most sophisticated critical analyses of sources are in bibliographies, in particular Zhisheng's 智昇 (fl. 730) remarkable *Buddhist Bibliography of the Kaiyuan Era* (*Kaiyuan Shijiao lu* 開元釋教錄). For instance, in his determination that a text called the *Yaoxing sheshen jing* 要行捨身經 is a forgery, Zhisheng points first to its suspicious lexicon. The byline of the text says that it was translated by Xuanzang, but the text itself translates Gṛdhrakūṭa-parvata as "Sacred Vulture Peak" (Lingjiu shan 靈鷲山), the common translation *before* Xuanzang, who always translated it simply as "Vulture Peak" (Jiushan 鷲山). Second, Zhisheng complains, the text claims that there is a cemetery beside Vulture Peak, but "according to various accounts, Vulture Peak is within a mountain city [i.e., Rājagṛha] in the kingdom of Magadha, fourteen to fifteen *li* northwest of the royal city. How could there be a site for disposing of corpses inside a city?" After listing two more dubious claims in the scripture, Zhisheng concludes: "I do not know who fabricated this scripture. There are devious sorts everywhere."[44]

Accusations of attempts to deceive, very rare in early Chinese Buddhist historiography, burst onto the historiographical scene in the Song dynasty, when history, as much as doctrine, became a battlefield of sectarian rivalry, particularly in disputes between proponents of the Tiantai and Chan lineages. Tiantai histories like the *Comprehensive Account of the Buddhas and the Patriarchs* and the *Comprehensive Orthodox Transmission of the Śākya Clan* on which it was partly based compared the new Chan histories to the ecumenical collections of biographies of monks of the past and bluntly accused Chan monks of fabricating stories to advance their sectarian agenda. Chan monks, most famously Qisong, for their part dissected the sources on which the Tiantai lineage was based, most notably the *Fufazang yinyuan zhuan*, which, as we saw above, Qisong insisted was a Chinese fabrication rather than an Indian original, concluding that it "should be burned."[45] No longer scribal slips or translation blunders, these mistakes were intentional and malicious.

In Buddhist historical writings, the suspicion of the motivations of other historians spilled over to accusations of bias by court historians who, Buddhist historians complained, intentionally ignored the role of Buddhism in Chinese history, and when they did mention it, attempted to cast it in a bad light. Chief among these culprits was Ouyang Xiu, one of the most important court historians of his day, responsible for two major historical works, the *New Tang History* and the *New History of the Five Dynasties*.[46] Buddhist historians read his work with great irritation, carefully noting the many instances in which, in his rewriting of what was henceforth known as the *Old Tang History* and the *Old History of the*

Five Dynasties, Ouyang blithely passed over the contributions of major Buddhist figures and ideas.⁴⁷ When he did mention Buddhist monks, it was, Buddhist historians lamented, only to criticize them unfairly. In an informal collection of anecdotes, *Records of Returning to the Fields* (*Guitian lu* 歸田錄), Ouyang Xiu in a typical passage highlights the sycophancy and hypocrisy of a monk, this time Zanning, compiler of the *Song Biographies of Eminent Monks*, with a story of Zanning's obsequious behavior before the emperor. In Ouyang's telling, when the emperor asked Zanning if even an emperor should bow before an image of a buddha, Zanning replied no, since one buddha need not bow before another. Thirteenth-century monastic historian Zhipan immediately seized on this passage to criticize Ouyang Xiu's anti-Buddhist bias.

> According to the *Record of Returning to the Fields*, when [Song emperor] Taizu entered a monastery, he asked Zanning Tonghui 贊寧通慧, "Should I bow to the Buddha or not?" Zanning replied, "A buddha of the present does not bow to a buddha of the past."
>
> [However, (and now it is Zhipan speaking)], Zanning gave his allegiance to the capital along with the king of Wuyue under Taizong [Taizu's younger brother]. He never even met Taizu. Ouyang Xiu's record is false. Now if we examine [the later Song Emperor] Zhenzong, he bowed to buddha [images] more than a hundred times, without delegating responsibility for it to his closest officials. This must have been the family custom handed down from his ancestors [including Taizu]. Subsequently there were emperors like Huizong who bowed to a tooth of the Buddha. After the passage to the south [that is, the Southern Song dynasty], each court bowed to the bodhisattvas. Hence we can know that from the beginning of the dynasty, there has been no reason for an emperor to refrain from bowing before buddhas. Ouyang looked on Buddhism with derision. It is because he did not want the ruler of men to show such respect for the Buddha that he invented this story. It is meaningless to speak here of present and past buddhas. In this way he slandered both the ruler above and Master Zanning below. This is egregious.⁴⁸

Here, not only does the Buddhist historian note the mistake in chronology that demonstrates the story could not have taken place as described—and what pleasure he must have taken in exposing Ouyang Xiu's blunder—he then takes the additional step of speculating on the bias behind the faulty account, in this instance an ingrained loathing for all things Buddhist.

In these cases, careful reading of sources for prejudice was a powerful polemical tool, allowing historians to dismiss specific arguments of their opponents while impugning their credibility more generally, a technique with which readers of any modern scholarly journal are familiar. But once the possibility of bias in the sources gained currency, even anonymous sources came in for scrutiny when historians attempted to verify a questionable account.

In the biography of Xuanzang's greatest disciple, Kuiji 窺基 (632–682), one of the most admired Buddhist exegetes of his day, Zanning depicts Kuiji as brilliant, but not entirely suited to the restrained life of a monk. When Xuanzang, impressed by the boy's precocious intellect, asked Kuiji's father to allow his son to become a monk, the father, a military man, insisted that the boy was too wild for the monastic life. On finally receiving the father's consent, Xuanzang broached the subject with Kuiji, who replied, "Only if you agree to three conditions will I vow to become a monk: that I do not have to cut off emotional desires, that I can eat meat, and that I can eat after noon." Subsequently, we are told, whenever Kuiji traveled, "he carried these objects of his previous desires (i.e., for women and meat) with him, so the people of the Guanfu region referred to him as the 'Reverend of the Three Carts.'"[49] Yet after relating this account—irresistible as a story of the peculiar first meeting of two of the greatest Buddhist thinkers of their day—Zanning discredits this characterization of Kuiji's dissolute youth through reference to Kuiji's own writings, commenting: "This is said to have taken place in the twenty-second year of the Zhenguan era [648]. Kuiji himself once wrote, 'When I was nine years old [that is, in 640], my mother died and I gradually distanced myself from the secular world.'[50] This being so, the three-cart story is a vicious slander." That is to say, according to Kuiji's own firsthand account, he lost interest in worldly pleasures already as a child.

The point is clarified at the end of the biography, when the story is repeated, but with a more pious twist:

According to one tradition, when Kuiji went to Taiyuan to spread the Dharma, he traveled with three carts. The first cart carried crates and bundles of scriptures and treatises. The second cart carried Kuiji himself, and the last cart carried courtesans, female servants, and provisions. On the road, he met with an old man who asked who the people in the cart were. "Members of my family," replied Kuiji. The old man said, "Your understanding of the Dharma is refined, but traveling with members of your family is not, I fear, worthy of the [Buddha's] teachings." Hearing this, Kuiji immediately regretted his former faults and then walked on, transcendent and alone. The old man was none other than the bodhisattva Mañjuśrī.[51]

One modern scholar has suggested that the story was invented to explain a nickname, "Three-Vehicle Ji," which stemmed from Kuiji's interpretation of the three vehicles famously described in the *Lotus Sutra*.[52] Although Zanning did not, apparently, consider this possibility, in addition to his assessment of Kuiji's spiritual maturity from an early age, he casts doubt on the three-cart story for practical reasons, writing, "This tradition is certainly mere hearsay. During the period when Kuiji followed Xuanzang to participate in translation activities at the Yuhua Palace, where would he have kept the carts?"[53] In other words, when Kuiji was hard at work in a translation center at the heart of a major monastery, he would not have been permitted to keep women, wine, and meat. Again, despite the fact that he considered the story absurd, Zanning relates it twice in the space of a relatively short biography: first following the encounter between Xuanzang and Kuiji, and second at the end of the biography, in each case refuting the story on the basis of compelling textual evidence. Unlike most such accounts that he criticizes, however, Zanning here questions the original author's motivations, rather than his competence. The story, he is at pains to tell us, smells of slander. And, in fact, given Kuiji's reputation for contentious rivalry with other exegetical monks, this is not an unlikely explanation.

Perhaps not accidentally, the morals of one of Kuiji's rivals, the Sillan monk Sun-kyŏng 順璟 (fl. 666), were questioned in an even more pointed manner. "According to one tradition," the biography notes—hinting, as we have seen, that what follows is of doubtful veracity—"when Sun-kyŏng was bed-stricken and ordered his disciples to lift him to the ground, the ground split open and he fell immediately into the earth. He had fallen into hell in the body of his present life [i.e., without being reborn]. To this day there is a ditch about a *zhang* wide. In fact it is just a crevice, but they call it 'Sun-kyŏng's Hell.'"[54] After citing this damning detail, Zanning refutes it, claiming that the story is surely a mean-spirited fabrication and reminding the reader of how common such slander is, comparing the monk on the one hand to the Chinese figure Zhao Dun[55] 趙盾 (d. 601 BCE), described in the *Records of the Historian* as the innocent target of slander, and on the other to the Buddha, himself the victim of the calumnies of his evil cousin Devadatta.

Even here, uncovering bias contributes ultimately to the glorification of eminent monks. These are Buddhist historians defending their heroes from false claims. We must search very hard indeed to find instances in which Buddhist historians defend evidence that runs counter to their interests. This is perhaps the highest standard of historical objectivity: citing sources that contradict one's own argument. In at least one case, a Buddhist historian's attention to detail led him to reject previous accounts that served his purpose and to question the impartiality of even historians he admired.

In his remarkable twelfth-century work *Comprehensive Discussion and Chronology of Buddhism Compiled in the Longxing Era*, Zuxiu relates a well-known story of a magical contest between Buddhists and Daoists at the court of Emperor Wenxuan in 555 of the Northern Qi. The Daoists, led by Lu Xiujing 陸修靜 (406–477), levitate a monk's robe, a feat the Buddhist monks in attendance are unable to match. But in the second round of the competition, with imperial favor on the line, the Buddhist team brings in a mysterious monk named Tanxian. Tanxian challenges the Daoists to levitate the robe of the great Buddhist meditator Sengchou 僧稠 (480–560). The emperor orders his attendants to try to lift the robe manually, but even they cannot. Tanxian then picks up the robe himself with ease.[56] He follows this with another similar feat, and then even defeats Lu Xiujing in a brief debate on the merits of Buddhism. Some six hundred years after these events supposedly took place, Zuxiu highlights a discrepancy that the reader may have noticed from the dates of Lu Xiujing I gave above: he had died close to a hundred years before the date of the debate. Before noting the chronological discrepancy, Zuxiu begins with praise for the Daoist:

> Lu Xiujing visited Sire Huiyuan of Mount Kuang at the end of the Jin. Master Huiyuan 慧遠 (334–416) escorted him beyond Tiger Stream. And Ziliang, Prince Jingling of the Southern Qi 南齊竟陵王子良, gave Lu Xiujing a white-feather fan. For these two gentlemen to have honored him in this way, Lu Xiujing must have been an extraordinary man.
>
> [But] from the Jin to the Northern Qi was more than one hundred seventy years. And the skills employed in the competition are extremely primitive. I suspect that [the magical feats] were not in fact carried out by Lu Xiujing.
>
> Yet Sire Daoxuan of the Southern Mount in his disquisition on biographies of monks, and Shenqing 神清 [d. ca. 814] in his *North Mountain Record* (*Beishanlu* 北山錄), both record this story.[57] Neither of these two distinguished men was a slanderer. Yet if Lu Xiujing was approaching the age of two hundred and was in fact present, then he must have had extraordinary magical

talents. I posit that the Daoist in the competition was a follower of Lu Xiujing. Because the Daoist lost, these two gentlemen [Daoxuan and Shenqing] exploited Lu Xiujing's name and then condemned him. This is a story in need of clarification.[58]

What is particularly notable here is that Zuxiu is suggesting that two prominent Buddhist historians have, for the sake of a cause Zuxiu himself supported (the primacy of Buddhism over Daoism), presented false evidence. He stops short of accusing them of slander or outright fabrication, but hints that they allowed their prejudices to cloud their judgment. They should have noted the problem with dates, but in their eagerness to demonstrate the superiority of a Buddhist monk to one of the most prominent figures in Daoist history, allowed an obvious error to slip into their works. Nor does Zuxiu suggest that such slips are acceptable in the service of a good cause. Even here, events should be related as they happened.

However, only in a few such cases do monastic historians probe the biases of their sources, questioning not only the author's competence but also his intention, and never do they do so in a sustained manner. Again, while the ability to recognize authorial bias is a basic skill of the modern historian, monastic historians, like their court counterparts in premodern times, focused chiefly on errors of technique, such as faulty copying, rather than the possibility of intentional distortion. Hence, although monastic historians did to an extent subject their sources to criticism, it was in general limited in scope and nature.

HISTORIANS OF THE MARVELOUS

Much of the preceding discussion could just as easily apply to dynastic court historians as to Buddhist writers. One area in which the two types of history part is in the realm of the marvelous. "Marvelous" here is imprecise, encompassing a wide variety of phenomena, some of which traditional historians would accept as extraordinary and others they would relegate to common sense. Even the most sober dynastic histories include accounts of miraculous omens that reflect the will of Heaven, and some of the dynastic histories contain more fabulous material than others. In general, however, it is safe to say that Buddhist historians were more at ease admitting accounts of supernormal, extraordinary events. To cite one example among many, Huijiao's biography of the thaumaturge Fotucheng explains that the monk

> had a hole in his left breast, four to five inches (*cun* 寸) in circumference, that opened straight through to his insides. Sometimes he would remove his intestines. He at times stopped up the hole with floss. At night when he wished to read, he would remove the floss, at which point the entire room would fill with light. Also, on days of fasting, he would go to the river, take out his intestines, wash them, and then place them back in his body.[59]

For all of his attention to source criticism and chronological impossibilities, Huijiao apparently had no problem accepting that a holy monk could regularly remove and wash his intestines; for saints like Fotucheng, all sorts of extraordinary feats were possible. Beyond simply recording such things, Buddhist historians contemplated and categorized them. We can assume that the supernatural, broadly conceived to include the existence of deities and demons, was a part of the worldview of the compilers of court histories, but, with the exception of omens, they did not in general consider the analysis of the marvelous to be a part of their craft. Buddhist historians, on the other hand, embraced the marvelous, applying the same sort of rigor in their analysis of supernatural events that we have already seen in the case of names, dates, and dubious sources. In this respect, Buddhist historians distinguished themselves from compilers of fabulous stories (*zhiguai* 志怪), who collected and transmitted stories, usually without comment.[60] Take, for example, Huijiao's attempt to evaluate the spiritual attainments of the monk Zhiyan 智嚴 (350–427). Huijiao writes:

> He then walked all the way back to Jibin 罽賓 (Kashmir) where he passed away, though without outward signs of illness. At that time he was seventy-eight. According to the laws of that country, the ordinary and the holy are cremated in separate areas. Although Zhiyan was lofty in his command of the precepts, his actual practice was not well understood. When they first attempted to move his corpse to the cemetery for ordinary monks, the corpse became so heavy that it could not be moved. When they attempted to move it in the direction of the cemetery for holy monks, it became as light as could be. Zhiyan's disciples Zhiyu 智羽 and Zhiyuan 智遠 returned from the West to

report this auspicious omen. They both then returned to their country abroad. From this we can conclude that Zhiyan had achieved the Way; it is just that we cannot determine the depths of his attainments among the "realizations and accesses."[61]

The "realizations and accesses" 四果向 (Skt. catvāraḥ pratipannāḥ) refers to the four basic levels of spiritual attainment: the level of one who has "entered the stream" and is hence irrevocably on the way to enlightenment; a "once returner," that is, one who will only be reborn one more time before achieving enlightenment; a "nonreturner," that is, one who will achieve enlightenment in this life; and finally, an arhat, or enlightened being. Passages like this demonstrate that for Huijiao and other Buddhist historians, it was not enough to praise a monk's spiritual attainments; a part of the historian's job was to apply technical Buddhist literature to provide an accurate assessment of a monk's abilities, something mere storytellers would not and could not do.

Daoxuan, one of the most prolific Chinese Buddhist historians, was particularly interested in the marvelous and filled his collection of biographies with accounts of miracles. In his later years, he even composed several works based on conversations he held with divine beings or other sorts of visions.[62] While such revelations are common enough in the writings of Daoists, they are rare among works by Buddhist monks in China. In the writing of history, however, a monk did not need personal experience to verify a miraculous account. The Buddhist historians I discuss in this book in general professed no skills or experience in mysticism, revelation, or thaumaturgy. They could instead turn to Buddhist doctrinal writings to verify that the account was in the realm of the possible and to interpret it more fully. For instance, the *Song Biographies of Eminent Monks* recounts a story in the life of the famous seventh-century thaumaturge Wanhui 萬迴 (632–711) in which the monk travels ten thousand miles in an instant to visit his brother. According to the story, when Wanhui was a child of ten, his brother was stationed in the north. After some time had passed without news of him, Wanhui's mother became distraught, convinced that her child had died. At this point, the young Wanhui remarked,

"It's actually quite a simple matter to find out if big brother is well. Why are you so worried?" He then wrapped up some of the leftovers from the meal and headed straight out the door. That night he returned, holding in his hand a note from his brother saying, "All is well." They asked him where he had found the note, but he said nothing in response. [In fact] he had traveled ten thousand *li*. Later, when the brother returned he reported, "On that day I talked with Wanhui. He'd come from home with some steamed buns. We ate them together and then he left for home again." The entire family was astonished and delighted.⁶³

As in the case of Fotucheng opening up his innards for reading light, few modern readers would accept this as historically accurate. While granting the importance of such stories for understanding medieval mentalities and religious beliefs, we also recognize that the story contradicts common sense: even on horseback an eleven-year-old boy could not travel ten thousand *li* (over three hundred miles) in less than a day; this of course is the point, the reason the story warrants telling. We can surmise that the story may well have been invented to explain the monk's name (literally, "ten thousand and back"). It is usually very difficult to determine just how readers would have reacted to it during medieval times. However, we can gauge the reaction of at least one tenth-century reader: Zanning, compiler of the *Song Biographies of Eminent Monks*. Like most of the material in Zanning's work, the story of the ten-year-old Wanhui's journey to the north was taken virtually word for word from an earlier source, in this case either the *Tan bin lu* 談賓錄 or the *Liang jing ji* 兩京記, both Tang-dynasty collections of tales preserved in part in the later collection *Taiping guangji*.⁶⁴ Not only did Zanning include the story in his collection, implying that he accepted it as reliable, but he also commented on it.

He begins by remarking that Wanhui was "certainly no human," and asking himself whether he was a demon, a god, or a practitioner of the "arts of the sylphs," that is, a student of Daoist magical techniques. The question itself reflects that while the medieval reader found the story of Wanhui's journey extraordinary, because of commonly accepted beliefs in various sorts of spirits, it was deemed quite possible. But by drawing on his knowledge of Buddhist scripture, Zanning felt that he could go a step further and explain the precise source of Wanhui's powers. Zanning explains that they came neither from the dark demonic arts nor from Daoist practices, but from his cultivation of Buddhism, which, as any number of canonical Buddhist texts attest, can result in supernormal powers. Specifically, Zanning continues, "The *Treatise of the Virtue of Great Wisdom* lists four categories of one possessing this type of power: 'One, he can fly as freely as a bird;

two, he can travel great distances effortlessly; three, he can disappear in one place and appear in another; and four, he can arrive anywhere in an instant.'"[65]

"This type of power" refers to the power of "divine feet," the first of the six supernormal powers possessed by a buddha.[66] Zanning concludes his explanation by noting that the *Yoga Treatise* equates this power with the "realm of the divine."[67] Zanning's references to Buddhist texts, translated by his day from Sanskrit to Chinese, are accurate and fully support his assertions. Given the almost universal belief in flying spirits in Chinese society at large, and detailed analysis in Buddhist scholastic writings of the supernormal ability to move great distances quickly, we can easily understand his belief in the Wanhui story. He did not indiscriminately accept it as true; he applied his own set of criteria to what on the surface appears to be a remarkable feat and determined that, while extraordinary, Wanhui's abilities were within the realm of the possible. Comparison to Buddhist doctrinal literature convinced him that his source was credible.

With the notion that one of the historian's duties is to assess supernatural events according to lists of the "four realizations" or the "six supernormal powers" discussed at length in the abhidharmic literature, we begin to see the rift, not just between the Buddhist historian and contemporary historians—whether official court historians or compilers of more racy unofficial histories—but also between monastic and modern historians. That is, Chinese Buddhist historians seem quite like modern historians in their attitudes toward dates and names, their broad ecumenical interest in a wide variety of sources, and their critical attitude toward sources that betray bias. But their ready incorporation of miracles, tested against Buddhist technical literature, sets them apart.

Most jarring for the modern reader are the moments when the Buddhist historian, with characteristic rigor, notices a discrepancy in sources but then proceeds to invoke the miraculous to explain it. Huijiao, for instance, puzzles over the differences in accounts of the life of An Shigao, saying, "I have gone through all of the writings, but there are discrepancies between the records of An Shigao. It is perhaps that his provisional manifestations disappeared and appeared again, responding [to conditions] in many ways."[68]

In his biography of the translator Shanwuwei, Zanning recounts an amusing encounter with Daoxuan. In the story, Daoxuan—who, in addition to being known for his collection of monastic biographies, was perhaps even more famous for his works on the monastic regulations—shares a room with Shanwuwei, who "behaves crudely" (in another version, he staggers in drunk one evening and vomits on the floor).⁶⁹ Later, Daoxuan discovers to his surprise that Shanwuwei maintains the spirit of the monastic regulations with even greater vigilance than he, when Shanwuwei criticizes him for killing a single flea. After narrating the story, Zanning duly notes that the two monks could not have met, as Daoxuan died shortly before Shanwuwei arrived in the capital.⁷⁰ The most likely explanation for this discrepancy is that the story is a fiction. I have proposed elsewhere that the two figures were brought together for literary and psychological purposes. That is, Daoxuan, as a renowned master of the monastic regulations, was paired with Shanwuwei, a Tantric master, representing for the general reader a more flexible approach to the regulations. Such pairings are common, not just in hagiography but in literature in general. One character is a foil for the other, each bringing out, through contrast, a particular characteristic.⁷¹ Needless to say, Zanning does not resort to this sort of explanation. He recognizes the problem with dating a meeting between the two figures, noting, "Examining this story closely, Daoxuan's death [in 667] was fifty years before the middle of the Kaiyuan era" (713-741), when Shanwuwei arrived in China. Nonetheless, he is reluctant to dismiss the story out of hand, so he offers the unlikely explanation that there might have been another, otherwise unknown figure, also known as Shanwuwei, living in the capital fifty years previous. But in his biography of Shanwuwei, Zanning suggests an alternative, commenting that "Shanwuwei's unusual appearances and disappearances cannot be fathomed by mere men."⁷² Here, Zanning reaches the limits of skepticism. Because he accepts the possibility of supernormal phenomena, and the existence of not only deities but also figures of great spiritual attainment who blur the distinction between man and deity, he was reluctant to pass judgment even when attention to dates, one of the foundations of Chinese historiography, told him that the stories were likely spurious.⁷³

A similar case appears in Zanning's biography of an eccentric holy monk named Daojian 道鑑 (fl. 516?) said to have lived in the sixth century. The biography contains a number of stories related to the monk. In one, based on a Tang collection of anecdotes, a young student surnamed Feng befriends a venerable monk in the capital who tells him the name and location of his monastery and invites him to visit one day. Some time later, when the student, now an official, visits the monastery, he is told that there is no monk there by that name, but when he wanders about the grounds he comes across a wall painting depicting Daojian and explaining that the monk died many years previous. Only then does the student realize that the monk he met in the capital was a divine being. A second story relates how Daojian appears at the gates of an official named Lu and cures his ailing son, whom doctors had pronounced beyond cure. Daojian tells the official the location of his monastery and departs. Again, when the official later visits this monastery, he is told that no monk by that name lives there, but discovers a holy image of the monk who saved his son. After relating these and a few other anecdotes, Zanning addresses their contradictions: in versions of the story, the locations given for Daojian's monastery differ, and while the two accounts are similar in many respects, they feature protagonists with different surnames. Zanning writes:

> Historical sources often supply us with varying accounts. If we look closely at the accounts given here, both describe monasteries named Lingyan 靈巖, and both describe paintings of monks. But in one, the prefecture is given as Lixia 歷下, while in the other it is Gusu 姑蘇. In one case the one who encountered the holy man is called Lu 陸, and in the other, Feng 馮. This probably stems from irregularities in what people saw or heard, resulting in different recorded accounts.
>
> The "response body" of a holy man may appear in the south or in the north; he may be Chinese, or foreign; he may take the shape of an ordinary person, or of a strange being. Thus the accounts inevitably vary, and as the story spreads, accounts of it naturally increase. It is like different people looking at the sun or moon from different positions a thousand miles apart. Even when they see the sun and moon at the same time, the shape and appearance of the clouds that surround them [in different locations] differ. As an unfathomable manifestation, Daojian appeared according to the conditions of the moment, so that it is unlikely that accounts of him would be the same. We can characterize the case with the phrase: "Different words used to transmit the tale."[74]

The source for the first story of Daojian was apparently the Tang collection of fantastic tales *Xuan shi zhi* 宣室志.[75] The second story presumably came from another such collection, and it is likely that originally both stories came from an oral source or a story copied in informal writings, in which divergent details appeared as different narrative branches as the story's transmission extended. Zanning comes close to offering precisely this explanation when he says that "as the story spreads, the accounts naturally increase," but at the same time he attributes the variations to the miraculous and mysterious powers of the monk the stories are about. The lesson he draws from comparing sources and discovering discrepancies is not that at least one of the sources must be inaccurate, but that Daojian must have been a divine being capable of appearing at different times to different people in different places: an "unfathomable manifestation."

Immersed in a surfeit of dramatic accounts of holy monks, bodhisattavas, ghosts, ghouls, incantations, and omens, Buddhist historians chose carefully, applying the same standards of source criticism to stories of the marvelous as they did to records of court debates. Some of course were more careful than others, but the criteria they employ to test stories of the supernatural are consistent. Take for instance Zuxiu's criticism of an extraordinary event recorded by Zanning close to two centuries previous. Zanning had written of a monk who, while visiting a mysterious community of monks in a remote monastery, saw a wandering, disembodied spirit that the monks identified as belonging to the soul that would soon be born as An Lushan 安禄山 (d. 757). An Lushan was the Sogdian trader who led a rebellion that brought the mighty Tang empire to the verge of collapse. The account fits a type of prophetic story, as we will see in another chapter, common throughout Chinese Buddhist historiography. But Zuxiu, reading his sources with a thorough knowledge of Tang history and a keen eye for chronological discrepancies, quickly seized on a fatal flaw: at the time the spirit was seen, An Lushan had already been born. Zuxiu writes:

> Zanning in his *Biographies of Eminent Monks* states, "Faxiu 法秀 once entered the Huixiang Monastery. While he was speaking with one of the elders, a spirit suddenly appeared before the main hall. Startled, Faxiu asked, 'What spirit is this?' The elder said, 'He is the one who will on another day bring chaos to the Tang empire.' Later, An Lushan did indeed wreak havoc throughout the world."[76]
>
> Alas! The author of this account is in grave error. Why? It was in this year that Faxiu obtained the jade flute and submitted it to the emperor.[77] Sixteen years later An Lushan rebelled. Yet at the time that Faxiu saw the spirit, An Lushan was already approximately thirty or forty years old. Truly, the story would be possible if before An Lushan was born Faxiu saw his spirit, but how could he see his spirit when he had already been born and was alive on the earth?
>
> It is true that from ancient times, the bizarre doings of ghosts and spirits have always been peculiar and strange and difficult to fathom. Yet some matters are credible and others not. If An Lushan were in any way different from

other men, we could grant the veracity of the account since the goings and comings of ghosts and sprits are difficult to fathom. But An Lushan was of the lowest sort of ignorant and depraved men. His son played a role in the murder of his own father, and he died at the hands of Li Zhuer 李猪兒, a slave in his own house, who sliced open his master's belly.[78] How could this be an appearance of a sylph in the world? For Zanning to write this brings a blemish to the inhabitants of the Huixiang Monastery. Therefore I have eliminated [the story from my history] in order to cover over Zanning's great error. It is with reluctance that I have refuted the story.[79]

A key point here comes right in the middle: "It is true that from ancient times, the bizarre doings of ghosts and spirits have always been peculiar and strange in any number of ways. Yet some matters are credible and others not." Given the world in which he lived, and particularly the world of the Buddhist monk, in which no doctrine was more fundamental than that of rebirth, it would have been a sign of ignorance to reject outright the possibility of the story being true. If An Lushan had died, the figure could be his ghost; if he was not yet born, it could be a ghost or demon that had not yet been reborn as An Lushan. If An Lushan were a powerful deity or holy man, he might be capable of appearing in different places or guises at the same time. But because of the chronology of events and what we know of the sordid details of An Lushan's character, none of these possibilities pans out; the story, Zuxiu assures us, must be a fabrication.

Just as Sima Qian, who held the title of Grand Astrologer, could apply his professional expertise to the verification of claims of portents and omens, so too Zuxiu could apply his historical acumen to rooting out false claims of prophecies, and censure a previous Buddhist historian who should have seen a suspect story for what it was.[80]

CONCLUSION

Much of the preceding seems far removed from the genre "religious literature," if we understand the term in this context to refer to vivid narrative on religious themes. It is not simply that monastic historians considered their writings history as opposed to fiction, but that their principal allegiance was to explanation and criticism rather than effective storytelling. Most of the tendencies I have described disrupt the narrative, breaking up often entertaining stories with meticulous dates, dry excurses on alternative names, digressions on alternative readings, and rambling doctrinal ruminations.

At the same time, however, the problems Buddhist historians set themselves to solve were often driven by literary tendencies in the materials they drew upon. The meeting of Shanwuwei and Daoxuan is a story that seems to have been generated by a desire to achieve the delicious literary effect of bringing two figures with opposing characteristics together, a tendency that may also explain the entertaining but dubious story of a sober Xuanzang bargaining with a profligate young Kuiji over whether or not he could indulge in wine and women once he became a monk. We can detect another type of literary tendency in the story of An Shigao prophesying the names of the figures who would best propagate his teachings in a sealed letter, not to be opened until four years had passed. Here is the narrative device of prophecy (the wild cousin of foreshadowing). The original story was conceived to demonstrate the miraculous powers of the foreign monk, able to see into the future. That in both cases the authors of the legends bungled their facts underlines the power of the narrative forces urging them on. The original storytellers would bring Daoxuan and Shanwuwei together even if one died in the capital years before the other reached it. And despite their blemishes, such stories persisted, leaving it to cautious monastic historians to sort out the discrepancies and propose solutions.

Despite their sophistication and erudition, our historians seem to have been blind to the influence of structural literary concerns on the sources they drew upon, just as they were reluctant to explore bias. After carefully pointing out why the events could not have taken place as recounted in their sources, they struggled to understand how scribal errors and sloppy editing might account for such anomalies, or else threw up their hands and ascribed the discrepancies to the mysteries of the supernatural. I have found only one example of a monk more attuned to the way such stories take shape. Zuxiu, writing in the twelfth century, returns to the now familiar story of the encounter between Shanwuwei and Daoxuan. Like Zanning before him, Zuxiu explains that, given their respective dates, the two monks could not have met. But then he goes on to cite a passage in the official *Tang History* that narrates the appearance in the capital in 750 of an enormous viper that emitted a poisonous vapor, killing all who came into contact with it. According to the *Tang History*, Shanwuwei intoned an incantation that killed the viper after three days.[81] Once again, Zuxiu notes, this event could not have taken place since Shanwuwei had died some fifteen years previous. Rather than follow Zanning and suggest that Shanwuwei transcended the limits of time or speculate that there was yet another monk with the same name, Zuxiu hypothesizes that Shanwuwei must be a mistake for the famous Tantric master Amoghavajra (Ch. 不空, 705-774).[82] But resisting the temptation to congratulate himself on resolving another historiographical puzzle, Zuxiu pauses to reflect on *why* previous authors would have confused Shanwuwei with Amoghavajra: "It is because Shanwuwei was famous in history for his divine deeds that his name was appropriated in case after case."[83]

In the analysis of sources, it is only very recently that historians of Chinese Buddhism have achieved a significant technological advantage over our premodern counterparts. The hard-won erudition of the medieval monastic historian, poring over a library of manuscripts painstakingly collected and studied over a lifetime, is now acquired cheaply with an internet connection and a laptop.[84] Some new sources have appeared—the cache of medieval manuscripts discovered at Dunhuang, large collections of epigraphy, new archaeological finds—but then, earlier monastic historians had access to many sources that have since been lost to us. Nor is there a clear divide in the way we analyze sources. We can find examples of Buddhist historians in the past who recognized the problems of textual transmission, intentionally and unintentionally biased sources, translation problems, split biographies, amalgamated biographies, clustering motifs under a single figure and, more fundamentally, the impossibility of complete objectivity in any historical account. And while Buddhist historians of the past were more reluctant than scholars today to detect bias in the sources or to see how literary values shaped the historical record, differences in approach owe less to a realization of the tools of analysis and more to differences in the historian's worldview and the beliefs that underpin it. The difference then is not so much in the range of techniques available or the skill in their application, as in the themes of interest and the limits of credulity.

CHAPTER 3

Karma

In one of the most celebrated passages of the first-century BCE *Records of the Historian*, compiled well before the arrival of Buddhism to China, Sima Qian recounts the story of the virtuous brothers Shu Qi 叔齊 and Bo Yi 伯夷 (fl. ca. 1046 BCE). Because of their loyalty to a fallen state, they were forced to retreat to the mountain wilderness where, rather than compromise their principles, they chose instead to starve to death. By Sima Qian's time, the two brothers had already become emblems for unbending virtue, and subsequent writers continued to draw on their story for inspiration. But their fate presents a moral quandary as well in that it illustrates that the good are not necessarily rewarded for their virtue, leaving the ultimate purpose of virtuous action open to question and suggesting that if there is a greater power overseeing human affairs, it is not just.

For Sima Qian, as for most Chinese historians, the writing of history was an essentially moral endeavor. That is, while he was no doubt inspired in part by curiosity about the past and drawn to the challenge of reconstructing it, the highest calling was to draw moral lessons from history. But what, precisely, was the lesson of the tragic story of Shu Qi and Bo Yi? Sima Qian wants to praise their virtue, but at the same time recognizes the disturbing truth of their dismal demise: "Some say, 'It is the Way of Heaven to show no favoritism. It is forever on the side of the good man.'[1] Should men such as Shu Qi and Bo Yi be called good, or bad? They accumulated such virtue, in conduct were so pure, and yet died of starvation!"[2] Sima Qian's question should, given the following line, be read rhetorically: the brothers were unquestionably virtuous. In short, then, Sima underlines the contradiction that while Heaven favors the good and Shu Qi and Bo Yi were paragons of virtue, Heaven allowed them to starve alone in the wilderness.

He follows with the example of Yan Hui 顏回 (521-490 BCE), the favorite disciple of Confucius. Like Shu Qi and Bo Yi, Yan Hui was virtuous, but he too suffered in life, grinding out his final years in abject poverty and dying young. In contrast, the infamous Bandit Zhi 盜跖 (d.u.) "killed innocent men daily, feasted on their flesh, was cruel and ruthless, willful and arrogant, gathered a band of thousands of men and wreaked havoc throughout the world, yet finally died of old age. How does any of this illustrate how Heaven repays the good?"[3] Faced with the immense body of biographical evidence that he had mastered to compile his great work, showing how the good sometimes meet hard, pitiful ends and the wicked so often prosper, Sima Qian could only throw up his hands and lament the caprices of fate, the cruel and inscrutable workings of destiny.

Surprisingly for an era in which history was laden with exemplars, while stories of men who got the fate they deserved are common enough in the *Records of the Historian*, stories of good men suffering bitter injustice are at least as famous. Prominent examples include Wu Zixu 伍子胥 (d. 484 BCE), a brave general forced to commit suicide for offering honest advice to an ungrateful ruler; Confucius, who during his lifetime did not win the respect he deserved; and even Sima Qian himself, who endured the humiliation and physical pain of castration for displeasing a fickle emperor.[4] From a reader's perspective, accounts of failed heroes are even more compelling than the successful ones, inspiring empathy for those who have suffered unfairly.[5] The slights and petty injustices we poor readers have endured in our daily lives are mirrored on a grander, more noble stage by giants of the past. Sima's approach set the standard for historiography in the centuries that followed, the period in which history became an independent genre in Chinese letters; throughout the medieval era, the emphasis in historiography was on the moral choices of individuals and the consequences of their actions, even when these difficult moral choices were not rewarded.[6]

As it was for Sima Qian and his epigones, the focus of Buddhist historiography in the medieval period was on exemplars who fit into a larger scheme. For the court historians, the unit of analysis was the individual—emperor, soldier, official—who contributed to the rise and fall of a dynasty. For Buddhist historians, the challenge was to document how individual monks contributed to the dissemination of the Dharma from the land of the Buddha to China, and how they nourished and protected Buddhism once it sank its roots into Chinese soil. Unlike Sima in the *Records of the Historian*, which included lengthy accounts of despots and even established a special section for biographies of cruel officials, monastic historians decided early on to limit their works to only virtuous, "eminent" monks. This means that the problem of moral justice is less pronounced in Buddhist historiography than in court historiography, with little ink spared for failed monks, heretics, imposters, and other petty men. But over the centuries, as historical data piled up and Buddhist historians became more adventurous in the scope of their work, the issue of fate, morality, and justice elbowed its way to the fore.

Some seven centuries after Sima Qian, Buddhist historian Daoxuan returned to the problem of moral justice, equipped with the powerful new conceptual tool of karma. Daoxuan writes that when previous historians like Sima Qian or his successor Ban Gu attempted to understand what they termed "destiny," they were like one who sees woven silk without knowing how it was made on a loom, or one who sees grain in a storehouse without knowing that it was originally harvested from a field. That is, non-Buddhist historians, for all of their erudition, see the events of history race by but don't understand the rational mechanism driving these events. "That which the Confucians term 'destiny,'" Daoxuan explains, "Buddhists call 'karma.' Destiny is tied to karma and karma is tied to the mind. As the products of the mind are uneven, the results of karma vary."[7] In other words, there is an intelligible moral order governing the course of history, but it is more complex than men like Sima Qian, ignorant of Buddhism, understood, since reward and punishment are distributed in different degrees and spread out over many lives, depending not just on action but on the intentions, the mental states, of those involved in a given action.[8]

> There are a thousand ways to create karma, and ten thousand ways to experience retribution. One may be good at the start but finish badly, and so begin with a flourish and wither in the end. Or good fortune and bad may appear together, and so calamity and blessings occur at the same time. Form is one thing, covering divergent aspects in different guises. The mind is another, spread over a hundred transformations with no fixed pattern. Thus an arhat may create no further karma in this life, and still only completely eliminate previously accumulated karma at the time of his death. [The arhat] experiences affliction because of retribution from previously created karma. [Karma] is not limited to this present life.[9]

The price for moral deviance and the reward for virtue can only be understood when the ebb and flow of karmic retribution, spanning many lives, is factored in. Shu Qi and Bo Yi suffered starvation as compensation for bad karma left over from previous lives and would be rewarded for their virtue in subsequent ones. Even arhats, spiritually advanced, enlightened beings who no longer create karma, still may suffer for karma left over from previous lives. Robber Zhi and other villains squandered the fruits of good karma accumulated in past lives by generating bad karma in cruel acts for which they would one day, in a future life, suffer. If the details of these past and future lives escaped Daoxuan's grasp, he was at least confident of the principle. Moreover, as we will see below, at times the historical record *did* disclose the unfolding of karma over many lives. Karma, explained and supported in Daoxuan's time by reams of technical Buddhist literature (not to mention Buddhist lore and even art), opened up a new approach to history that Sima Qian could not have imagined. Equipped with an understanding of karma, Daoxuan and other Buddhist historians saw the patterns of the past with unprecedented clarity.

That karma should play a prominent role in Buddhist historiography in China should not surprise us, first, because karma is an essentially historical doctrine—a principle that plays out most clearly over vast stretches of time and provides a general theory of causation for human behavior (and indeed for that of all living creatures). Moreover, if, perversely, we had to pick one Buddhist doctrine that had the most profound effect on not just China but all of East Asian civilization, it would be karma and the related doctrine of rebirth. The subject of sophisticated analysis by the greatest Chinese exegetical monks, karma became equally prevalent in literature, material culture, ritual, and popular religion.[10] Even Daoists drew inspiration from the notion, developing their own variants of karma theory.[11] In fact, from the medieval period on, belief in karma and rebirth was so common in China that few would have insisted on labeling it Buddhist at all, much less "Indian"; it became more common sense than an article of faith for any one tradition.

Before the entrance of Buddhism, the nearest equivalent to karma in China was the notion of the collective moral responsibility shared by ancestors and descendants. Here the link connecting the ethics of actions to their just consequences in future lives was the family. This belief held that a man could suffer for the misdeeds of, for instance, a long deceased grandfather. This is an idea with roots stretching back to the Shang dynasty, when kings suspected ancestors of regulating the fortunes of their descendants. One oracle bone inscription famously records the humble query of one of the Shang kings to his ancestors in the beyond, asking if one of them is responsible for his toothache.[12] The idea was further articulated much later in the Daoist notion of "received burden" (*chengfu* 承負), developed—perhaps independently—at about the time Buddhism entered China. According to this doctrine, misfortunes are often brought on as compensation for the immoral conduct of our ancestors. The belief led some to attempt to locate the source for their illnesses, inability to produce heirs, or other forms of bad luck in the family's past in what one scholar has termed a "witch-hunt into the past," in which the sick called on mediums to communicate with the netherworld in order to pinpoint the source of their suffering in the dark past of a flawed ancestor.[13]

Like karma, this is a historical doctrine, linking events in the present to those of the past. There is no indication, however, that those who adhered to these views applied them to history. Daoists were not driven to search the historical record for examples of, for instance, how the reprehensible acts of one man who died long-lived and prosperous in the end resulted in the impoverishment and early death of his sons or grandsons. On the contrary, the seventh-century Buddhist layman Li Shizheng 李師政 (fl. ca. 620) does precisely this, arguing in a treatise on karma that the doctrine of inherited burden does not hold up to the historian's scrutiny.[14] Li writes:

> Some say that good and ill fortune come from one's ancestors and that suffering and happiness extend to one's children and grandchildren. But when we examine the historical record we see that this is not necessarily so. The lineages of Bo Zong 伯宗 and Yang Xi 羊舌 were extinguished in the Jin dynasty. The descendants of Qing Fu 慶父 and Shu Ya 叔牙 prospered in the Kingdom of Lu. How could either fate have been caused by their ancestors?[15]

Needless to say, Bo Zong and Yang Xi were virtuous men; Qing Fu and Shu Ya were not.[16] Nonetheless, their virtue or villainy had little effect on the fortunes of their descendants. The reason Li felt it necessary to refute the notion of collective responsibility for the family was the central place of karma in Buddhist thought, which, at least in the scholastic literature, places the responsibility for one's fate on the individual rather than any collective.[17] As Li put it: "Destiny is tied to karma, and karma arises in the individual. It is the destiny a man receives that determines whether he is successful or not. And the quality of one's destiny depends on karma. The quality of one's destiny comes from oneself alone. It is absurd to blame Heaven and complain about what lies above!"[18] The last line—"It is absurd to blame Heaven"—reiterates the superiority of the precise Buddhist understanding of karma over not just the Daoist notion that tied fate to family history but also Sima Qian's recourse to the inscrutable workings of Heaven.

Although proponents of "collective burden" did not try to argue on the basis of documented family histories, for karma, Buddhist historians did think they could prove their case on the basis of the historical record. The search for karmic explanations of causation in history is one of the areas in which Buddhist historiography in China was shaped by Indian precedent. There is no direct Indian equivalent to the major Chinese collections of biographies of monks, which follow patterns established for biographies in the dynastic histories. Nor, as we have seen, were there carefully dated chronological surveys of the history of Buddhism in India on which Chinese historians could draw. While famous Indian exegetes and logicians were admired and emulated in China, there were no Indian historians to inspire Chinese Buddhist writers. Nonetheless, despite the gulf between the Chinese concern for tying people and events to a calendar and the Indian disregard for dates, it is clear that history, more broadly understood as the events of the past, was very important to Indian Buddhism. And the main principle used to interpret the past in Indian Buddhist texts was karma and rebirth. Buddhist writings are suffused with analysis of how events were shaped by the previous lives of those involved, from jataka tales recounting the progress of the Bodhisattva through countless lives to the biographies of Aśoka and the immediate disciples of the Buddha, or the precedents for individual regulations in the vinaya. From the sixth century, when Buddhist historiography in China begins to develop in earnest, historians were without exception deeply familiar with all manner of Indian Buddhist writings in Chinese translation.

Karma encompassed at least three interrelated phenomena: causality, ethicization, and rebirth.[19] In each of these areas, Chinese Buddhists had to prove the theory to an often skeptical audience through reasoned argument and, in the case of historians, on the basis of the historical record.

PROVING KARMA WITH HISTORY

The past held subtle clues to the workings of karma, though they were not always apparent to the untrained eye. One of the tasks Buddhist historians set themselves was to uncover, buried in monastic libraries, proof of the veracity of basic Buddhist doctrines, or simply to illustrate these principles for readers who already accepted them as true. Drawing on the tradition in Buddhist scripture of recounting the previous lives of the Buddha and his disciples, they compiled seemingly irrefutable evidence of rebirth in Chinese history.

Evidence for rebirth is hard to come by since in theory only those of great accomplishments, especially in meditation, obtain the supernormal power of being able to see into their own past lives or the lives of others. But there are ruptures in the natural order that allow glimpses into past lives. For instance, in a passage often cited in Buddhist historical writings, the *History of the Jin* (*Jin shu* 晉書) tells a story from the childhood of the prominent third-century official Yang Hu 羊祜 (221-278). When Yang was five he asked his wet nurse to fetch his gold ring. When she explained that he owned no such thing, he dug beneath a tree on the property of the neighbors and retrieved it himself. The startled neighbors, surnamed Li, explained that the ring had belonged to their deceased son. "The people of the day were astonished," concludes the story, "and said that the Li child was the previous incarnation of Yang."[20] Buddhist historians retold the account of the official Bao Jing 鮑靚 (fl. 318), also in the *History of the Jin*, who, also at the age of five, explained to his parents that in a previous life he came from the Li family in Quyang and that he had died at the age of nine when he fell into a well—a story his previous parents later confirmed.[21] In both cases, the suggestion is that children are close enough to their previous existences that they can still at times remember their past life, or at least elements of it.[22] There are many claims for rebirth in Buddhist historiography, not all of them involving children.

Daoxuan was said to be a reincarnation of the equally eminent Buddhist historian Sengyou. This was revealed to Daoxuan's mother in a dream when she was pregnant with him. In the dream, a foreign monk appeared, announcing: "The child with whom you are pregnant is [the reincarnation of] Master of the Regulations Sengyou of the Liang dynasty. Sengyou was in turn the reincarnation of Senghu 僧護[23] of the Yinyue Monastery of Shanxi in the Southern Qi dynasty. You should permit him to become a monk and work to implement the teachings of Śākyamuni."[24] Daoxuan himself claimed that an ancient spirit appeared to him late in life and informed him that he was the reincarnation of Sengyou.[25]

Absent the revelations of children or visions revealed to adults, at times historians took it as a part of their job to look for connections between people of different times, report claims of rebirth, and speculate that one might be the reincarnation of another. The tenth-century monk Deshao 德韶 (891–972) was said to have instantly recognized the former abode of the eminent sixth-century monk Zhiyi 智顗 (538–597). What is more, before becoming monks, the two shared the same secular surname, all of which suggested that Deshao was a reincarnation of the great Tiantai patriarch.[26] Zanning, while arguing for the identity of a Tang-era monk as a reincarnation of an earlier one, stated matter-of-factly that the official Cai Yong 蔡邕 (133–192) was the reincarnation of the scholar Zhang Heng 張衡 (78–139),[27] the Tang general Wei Gao 韋皋 (746–806) was the reincarnation of the general Zhuge Liang 諸葛亮 (181–234),[28] and the monk Zhiwei 智威 (d. 680) was originally the official Xu Ling 徐陵 (507–583).[29] "The evidence for these things is secure," he tells us, "the principle behind them assured."[30]

But while stories such as these confirmed the existence of rebirth, they do not illustrate the ethical principle of karmic retribution, without which rebirth would be random and ethically neutral. That is, this type of reference notes that one person was a reincarnation of another, but does not explain why the actions of one led to his rebirth as another. Here too, even cursory knowledge of the history of Buddhism in China provided clear proof of near instant karmic retribution. In a well-known account of the efforts of the early Buddhist missionary Kang Senghui to spread the Dharma in eastern China, the sixth-century *Biographies of Eminent Monks* recounts the importance of the doctrine of karma in early Buddhist proselytizing while illustrating the frightening consequences of ignoring it. According to the story, when Kang Senghui first arrived in the region, the local ruler Sun Hao invited the monk to his court, where he asked him to explain the Buddhist doctrine of "retribution for good and bad acts." Kang explained that karma was similar to the traditional Chinese idea of auspicious omens appearing when a sage ruled, a concept that he noted was well supported by the Chinese classics. "In that case," Sun Hao asked, " then [the Duke of] Zhou and Confucius have already explained the matter. What need is there for Buddhism?" Kang Senghui replied, "The words of the Duke of Zhou and Confucius in general address the proximate circumstances, but the teachings of Buddhism explain these matters completely and with great subtlety. Thus we know that bad actions lead to long periods of suffering in a hell, while cultivating goodness leads to perpetual bliss in a heavenly palace. As a means to encourage and restrain, this is great indeed!" Here, as in the case of Daoxuan's critique of Sima Qian, we see a key area in which Buddhist thinkers thought themselves superior to the sages of

Chinese antiquity. The story continues with a concrete incident that illustrates just how karma works. Unconvinced by the monk's brief sermon, Sun Hao brazenly urinated on a Buddhist image on palace grounds, boasting to his smirking attendants that he was "bathing the Buddha." But to his horror, he was immediately afflicted with "swelling throughout his body, and especially acute pain in his genitals."[31]

This is the first of the three types of karma, famously catalogued by Huiyuan in a fifth-century essay: immediate retribution, retribution in the subsequent life, and retribution in a later life.[32] Stories of immediate retribution, "instant karma," are common in Chinese Buddhist literature, and Buddhist exegetical writings certainly allowed for the possibility of karmic retribution within one's lifetime. But this does not solve Sima Qian's problem of the virtuous who suffer and the bad who prosper. To demonstrate the workings of karma adequately, to see a full turning of the karmic wheel, it is necessary to trace a person's experience beyond his death, to link karma and rebirth over more than one existence. To decipher the ethical reasons for a given event or personality in past lives required more than a child's passing reference to a toy owned in a previous life.

This presented historians with a version of the problem we saw above: in theory, only one who has attained exceptional supernormal powers can recognize the past lives of himself or of others. Knowledge of one's previous existences is coupled with knowledge of the previous existence of others as two of the six supernormal powers of a buddha.[33] Short of buddhahood, both of these powers could, in theory, be obtained through meditation, though few in Chinese history ever claimed such powers for themselves. Exceptions are rare. In the biography of An Shigao, the biographer states matter-of-factly that the monk "had mastered principles and comprehended their nature. *He knew his karmic conditions*, exhibiting many divine feats, beyond the estimation of ordinary people." He goes on to relate that An Shigao, according to his own account, was the reincarnation of a Parthian prince who, after becoming a monk, was killed by bandits in Canton.[34]

Daoxuan, unique among Chinese historians, claimed to have received visits from very ancient spirits who helped him fill in gaps in the historical record, but even he did not claim to possess the power to see into his past lives; he only learned of one of them with the assistance of one of his helpful spirits, old enough to have witnessed it. Buddhist historians were known more for their erudition than their prowess in meditation, and I know of none who claimed to possess these useful skills. Nor did historians easily grant credence to claims of having such powers.

As Li Shizheng put it in his treatise on karma: "Unless he is a greatly awakened one with all-pervasive knowledge, who can fully understand the principles involved and eliminate delusion?"³⁵

Nonetheless, wide and careful reading of textual sources revealed to the discriminating historian intriguing ruptures that disclosed the intricate web of causes and conditions, stretched over many lives, that lay just beneath history's surface. We have already seen some of the ways these karmic detectives uncovered evidence pointing to rebirth: Deshao's déjà vu at the remains of a former monk's residence, the dream of Daoxuan's pregnant mother, and children who, closer to the moment of rebirth, in rare cases retained some memory of their former existence. And while the prominent historians I have focused on prided themselves on their critical approach to sources—which distinguished them from mere tellers of tall tales—they made ample use of popular stories that focused on just these breaks in the everyday, and in these disjunctions revealed the workings of karma and rebirth. These stories were not read as parables, but as history that could be verified through careful examination of dates and sources.

Chinese miracle tales reveal the underworld in the return-from-death narrative, in which a protagonist dies, descends to the netherworld, and then returns to tell their tale.³⁶ Such stories, not limited to people who agreed with Buddhist doctrines, at times describe an underworld governed by non-Buddhist deities, a fact that Buddhist historians disguised by choosing their evidence carefully, selecting only those details that conformed to a Buddhist cosmology. Buddhist historians were particularly drawn to stories in which the (temporarily) dead protagonist witnesses the fate of some well-known person or people. More than remarkable stories, such accounts provided historically valuable material, completing the biography of an important figure while at the same time illustrating the principles of karma and rebirth.

An early example comes at the end of the biography of the monk Fazu 法祖 (d.u.) in the early sixth-century *Collection of Records Concerning the Translation of the Tripiṭaka*, according to which, soon after Fazu's death, a certain Li Tong 李通 is said to have died, but to have revived soon after. After his death, Li "saw Dharma Master Zu in the presence of King Yama [lord of the underworld], for whom he lectured on the *Śūraṅgama Sūtra* (Ch. *Shoulengyan jing* 首楞嚴經). When he finished lecturing, he was to proceed to Tuṣita heaven. Li also saw the libationer Wang Fu 王浮 (according to one source, the Daoist Priest Master Ji 道士基公). He was in shackles and begged Fazu to repent on his behalf."³⁷ The biography goes on to explain that the Daoist Wang Fu ("libationer" is a Daoist title) had previously debated with Fazu at court and repeatedly lost. Furious and hungry for revenge, Wang Fu (fl. ca. 300) composed the famous *Scripture of the Conversion of the Barbarians*, which, as we saw above in the chapter on India, explained that the Buddha was in fact a magical impersonation carried out by Laozi. For this despicable act, Wang was consigned by Yama to a hell, while Fazu was rewarded for his diligent recitation of scripture with assignment to a heaven.

Such stories were produced no doubt in part for their entertainment value, though this is not to suggest that those who related them did not believe them. But beyond expressing a timeless fascination with life after death, Buddhist accounts of the netherworld transparently propagated instructions for the world of the living. The *Biographies of Eminent Monks* explains how an ordinary man, fond of hunting, at the age of thirty-one died and, after one day, returned to life. While dead, he saw those who suffered for their actions in various hells, and saw as well a monk who explained to him that he had been his teacher in a previous life. This former teacher then encouraged him to repent for his faults and pay reverence to a specific stupa. On reviving, the man becomes a monk and devotes himself to "cultivating merit," at the same time "giving precedence above all to repentance."[38] In addition to generic calls to "cultivate merit," stories such as the following must have been appealing to monastic historians, themselves often leaders of monasteries concerned with protecting monastic revenue from corrupt officials or, as in this tenth-century account from the *Song Biographies of Eminent Monks*, charged with raising funds for a new bell.

> In the second year of the Jinglong era [708] Censor-in-Chief Feng Si 馮思 suddenly died. [In the netherworld] he entered a place where there were two young boys carrying documents who led him to a judicial court for questioning. While [the records of] his faults were being inspected, he was ordered to look out over an area of giant trees with branches spread out over several hectares.[39] Beside the judge was an old acquaintance of Feng Si's named Zhang Siyi 張思義. Zhang called Feng Si over and said, "I am your uncle. I was once a storage officer in Luoyang and was murdered by a senior official. At that time I had borrowed cash, oil, and grain from the Taiping Monastery, and so [owing to this debt] I have yet to be released [from hell]. Your punishment is not fitting. You survived the chaos that occurred in the palace of the Celestial Consort [Wu Zetian], only to die suddenly.[40] You should vow to copy the *Nirvāna*

Scripture and to forge a bell." When Feng Si went up to appeal his case, the judge permitted him to return to the world of the living. As he was about to leave, Zhang said to Feng Si, "If you do good deeds for one day in Jambudvīpa,[41] the merit acquired is immeasurable. How can people go for their entire lives without doing any good deeds?"[42]

Although the origins of the story remain obscure, its appeal to the monks who compiled the *Song Biographies of Eminent Monks* is readily apparent. It at once conveys the truth of Buddhist doctrines, warns of the dangers of stealing from monasteries and the benefits of donating to them, and is couched in comforting historical detail: both of the men mentioned in the story, Feng Si and Zhang Siyi, were historical figures.

In addition to the harrowing accounts of men who died just long enough to witness the horrors of the hells, another source Buddhist historians eagerly exploited for information about the connections between lives was holy men with special powers. The *Song Biographies of Eminent Monks* tells of an obscure monk named Jiankong 鑑空 said to have lived in the early part of the ninth century. As a young man, before he became a monk, Jiankong was a sincere but unaccomplished scholar. Born to poverty, he was a diligent student but was cursed with a poor memory. Moreover, though he was fond of poetry, his verse was never better than mediocre. Unlucky in life, whenever he managed to save a bit of cash he would take ill and only recover when he had exhausted his savings. At this point in his dull and frustrating life, Jiankong was approached one day by a strange Indian monk who claimed to recognize him and to know something of his past lives. The monk then offered him a date, saying "This is grown in my country. If one of higher wisdom eats it he will know events past and future, while if one of lower wisdom eats it, he will only know of events from past lives." When Jiankong ate the fruit, he immediately fell asleep and, on awakening, remembered that he had been a monk in a previous life. He asked the Indian what had become of several of his colleagues, whereupon the monk explained that one had in his current life again become a monk while another friend was soon to become a monk. Yet another who once jokingly made a vow in front of a Buddha image that if he did not realize supreme enlightenment he would return in his next life as a soldier, had in fact, the Indian monk explains, become a soldier, eventually rising to the rank of general. The monk continued by explaining that only he himself had achieved liberation and only Jiankong had become destitute. The reason for

Jiankong's misfortune is that he misinterpreted the Buddha's teachings in his lectures in that previous life, misleading his audience and generating bad karma. After this encounter, Jiankong determined to become a monk and devote himself to improving his karma.[43]

Elsewhere, we read of the mysterious Indian monk Qiyu 耆域 (Skt. Jīvaka, fl. ca. 290), who could perceive the former lives of those around him, explaining that one was in his previous incarnation a man, another was an ox.[44] The story of this great holy man, that of the obscure monk who discovered his previous lives, that of the former official in the underworld, and even the story of a ruler punished for his mistreatment of a Buddha image all fit neatly into a genre of religious literature. Robert Ford Campany has argued convincingly that, in addition to the function of such stories as entertainment, they were also serious attempts to order the world, to map out its boundaries, and to explore its mysteries.[45] When incorporated into formal Buddhist historical works, stories like these also served to verify Buddhist doctrines of karma and rebirth and to promote specific interests, like state policy toward Buddhism or the protection of monastic assets. But in addition to using historical accounts to disseminate belief in karma, historians turned to karma to interpret history. This is one of the areas that distinguished formal Buddhist historiography, on the one hand from the less formal collections of strange tales and on the other from historiography centered on the court.

EXPLAINING HISTORY WITH KARMA

For Buddhist authors, the past was more than factual fodder for propagating Buddhist doctrine. We have already seen how Daoxuan was convinced that, through recourse to karma, he understood historical justice better than Sima Qian. To wring one's hands at the caprices of fate was a sign of ignorance, a failure to appreciate that justice is often only realized after many lives. Stories like those discussed above were plentiful enough that all but the most skeptical of readers were convinced of rebirth and ethical compensation. But of karma's main three components—rebirth, ethics, and causation—historians in particular found the third, causation, a powerful tool for understanding both the motivations behind individual acts and the forces dictating larger historical trends. That is, history was not just a way of explaining karma and rebirth; it was often the other way around. Equipped with a thorough grounding in the doctrine of karma—unavailable to court historians at best reluctant to draw on Buddhist concepts in their work—Chinese Buddhist historians approached their two central concerns—the lives of eminent monks and imperial policy toward Buddhism—with an eye for the reasons behind apparently random events. The doctrine of karma, for all of the speculation it inspires, insists that no event is entirely random, and that with skill, attention, and a bit of luck, the historian can determine precisely why the past played out the way it did.

Every biography is in some sense a puzzle in which author and reader alike scrutinize the family background, birth, and early childhood of the subject in search of clues that will explain why she or he became the woman or man who would one day be worthy of a biography. This mystery at the heart of every life story accounts in large measure for the continued success of biography as a genre. In the case of monks, family background is not as useful as it is for other types of figures since, assuming early vows of celibacy are strictly maintained, one cannot come from a long line of Buddhist monks. And even when, for instance, a great exegetical monk can be shown to come from a family famous for producing scholars, this still leaves open the question that shapes the opening of every monastic biography: Why did the boy become a monk in the first place? To answer this question, Buddhist historians could draw on a rich hagiological repertoire. Before the birth of a great monk, his mother has an auspicious dream, and during her pregnancy she loses all taste for meat. Fortune-tellers prophesy that the child will do great things, and on his birth a bright light and pleasing fragrance fill the room. Such motifs became commonplace early on in Chinese Buddhist hagiography and continued into modern times. The modern monk Xuyun 虛雲 (d. 1959) went so far as to recount his own miraculous birth in his autobiography.[46]

But the surest evidence that a boy is destined to become an eminent monk is in his own actions, and here the alert historian typically underlines the presence of karma, as the subject of the biography finds himself drawn to the life of the monk. "A few years after he was born," an account early on in the *Song Biographies of Eminent Monks* tells us, "Vajrabodhi [Ch. Jin'gangzhi 金剛智, 669–741], began to daily chant ten thousand words. Whatever he read passed directly into his mind, so that he would never forget it. When he was sixteen, he awakened to the principles of Buddhism. He found no pleasure in studying the various treatises of the *nirgranthas*, and so he took the tonsure and became a monk; *this must be owing to the force of his karma.*"[47] How else can one explain his interest in Buddhism from such an early age, or his innate talent for studying Buddhist doctrine? Karma explains the exceptional erudition of an eighth-century monk named Langran 朗然 (724–777): "When he encountered a principle or teaching, he would master its doctrines as he read; all said that *this was through the force of his accumulated karma*."[48] The modern scholar of Buddhism can easily sympathize with the medieval historian's wonder at the ability of the foreign monk, Sun-kyŏng, to quickly master the study of Buddhist logic under the tutelage of the great Xuanzang. "Very few of the Chinese monks were able to comprehend it. Were it not for the force of his *karma*, how could Sun-kyŏng have done so?"[49] And even when the role of karma is not specifically mentioned, it was no doubt assumed by authors and readers alike when they read accounts of monks who as boys refused to join in the frivolous play of other children,[50] or spontaneously composed poems on the ephemerality of all phenomena,[51] or, silent from birth, uttered "Buddha" as their first word.[52] While hagiographical motifs may have been *inspired* by more general notions of divinity, historians *interpreted* them through a karmic lens. If Christians saw in the early life of Jesus signs of his divinity—in particular in his ability to debate with learned men already as a child—Buddhist historians would have seen evidence of qualities carried over from a previous life.

To this day, Chinese Buddhists often speculate about the possible karmic reasons for their present personality and circumstances, a therapeutic technique that, regardless of its accuracy, may be at least as useful as searching for clues to one's psychological makeup in one's childhood or dreams.[53] In Buddhist historiography, in addition to explaining why boys decided to become monks and why certain monks had a natural affinity for Buddhist doctrines and practices from an early age, karma explained otherwise puzzling parallels between eminent monks of different generations, as in the case of Daoxuan and his previous incarnation Sengyou.

Seen through the lens of karma, new aspects of the past came into focus. A natural affinity for doctrine or devotion at an early age signaled not only that a boy *would become* a monk, but that he *had been* a monk in a previous life. Unlike other types of historians, Buddhist historians were attuned to these karmic clues. They could decipher other puzzles in the historical record on the basis of karma as well, including, for instance, accounts of how a young girl with no formal training could recite Buddhist scriptures that no one in China had previously heard of. At the end of the fifth century, word spread of this remarkable young girl who at the age of eight would fall into a trance and recite entire scriptures. These episodes continued until she was sixteen. "At times she would close her eyes and sit in meditation, then recite these scriptures. Some said that she ascended to heaven; others that she received them from a spirit. She spoke fluently, as if she had learned them in another life.[54] She had others write them out. All at once, she would stop again."[55] After recording these events, Sengyou in his great catalogue of scriptures classified the text revealed to the girl as "dubious." A century later, Daoxuan returned to the case. Like Sengyou, he was particularly troubled by the assumption that the scriptures had been transmitted by spirits.[56] As we saw above in the chapter on sources, Buddhist historians in China judged the authenticity of scriptures claiming to be the word of the Buddha by examining the dates and circumstances of their translation. Any texts that were not translated by well-known figures, preferably as part of a large team sponsored by the court, were suspect. Instances of spirit writing threatened to erase the divide between Buddhism and Daoism and, perhaps even more important, between Buddhism and popular religion. For elite monks like Daoxuan, who had himself participated in one of Xuanzang's famous translation teams, Buddhist scriptures were brought to China by sophisticated, well-traveled monks, as learned as they were intrepid, and then translated by state-sponsored committees staffed by eminent monks and court literati; they were not produced in an afternoon by an eight-year-old girl in a trance. For an explanation of what *must* have happened, Daoxuan turned to karma:

> If we examine this according to Buddhist scriptures, we see that it is just a matter of remnant karma; there is nothing more to say about it. I have read in non-Buddhist writings, "Those who are born with knowledge are the highest. Next come those who attain knowledge through study."[57] This is limited to discussing this life and ignores past [lives]. If not, how did she distinguish the differing qualities between Buddhist and non-Buddhist and between the levels of the sages? This is just as in a previous biography when Tandi remembered the paperweight,[58] or the recent layman Cuizi remembered the golden bracelet.[59] Such things happen in every period. She certainly did not receive [the scriptures] from an external [spirit].[60]

The point then is that the girl must in a previous existence have memorized these scriptures. This is an example of one of the rare instances of overlap in which a young child happens to maintain an especially close connection to their previous life.

In this new way of reading history, the historian was not just assessing the qualities of the individuals he described and highlighting the moral lessons we as readers should derive from their stories; nor was he simply using the stories to drum home the truth of Buddhist doctrine. In addition to all this, based on his knowledge of Buddhist doctrine and his training as a karmic sleuth, he was explaining what happened and why.

This powerful combination of familiarity with Buddhist learning and historical erudition allowed the historian (and through him the readers of his works) to understand the past more clearly than even those present at the time of the events he described. Take, for example, the case of the ninth-century monk Zhixuan 知玄 (811–883). Zhixuan compiled a number of exegetical and liturgical works, most of which are not extant, and maintained close relationships with prominent literati. He enjoyed great success at court and was even attacked by one Xiao Fang 蕭倣 (793–867) for the extravagance of the favors he accepted from the emperor. Yet, far from a sycophant, Zhixuan later heroically defended Buddhism at court during the reign of Emperor Wuzong (r. 840–46), one of the most virulently anti-Buddhist emperors in Chinese history. His biography also relates that, as a native of what is now Sichuan province, on moving to the capital Zhixuan was ashamed of his provincial accent until one day he had a vision in which a "divine monk" removed his tongue and replaced it with a new one. From that time on he could speak like an urbane native of the capital. But the incident in his life that attracted the most attention among historians was the claim that he was a reincarnation of the second-century BCE figure Yuan Ang 袁盎 (d. 150 BCE). This was revealed to Zhixuan himself when a protuberance appeared on his left foot. When it burst, a small sphere emerged with the two characters *chao* and *cuo* inscribed on it. Now Chao Cuo 晁錯 (d. 154 BCE), as every student of Han history knew, was the mortal enemy of the high court official Yuan Ang, the man eventually responsible for engineering Chao's execution.[61] The story of the signed cyst first appeared in the tenth-century biography of Zhixuan in the *Song Biographies of Eminent Monks*.[62] Close to two centuries later, in his chronological survey of Chinese Buddhist history, Zuxiu fleshed out the story with more historical detail and karmic analysis, explaining that in the back-and-forth between Zhixuan and his court rival Xiao Fang, Zhixuan argued on the basis of principle, while Xiao Fang resorted to personal attacks. This contrasts with Zhixuan's previous incarnation, Yuan Ang, who, like Xiao Fang, eventually succumbed to a thirst for revenge, creating a karmic footprint that continued to influence events even centuries later. Reflecting on these events, Zuxiu writes:

> It is said that Zhixuan was probably a reincarnation of Yuan Ang of the Han. Zhixuan's remonstrance was the result of this remnant karma. When Wuzong, seduced by a heterodox path, was on the verge of banning the great teaching of Buddhism, Zhixuan remonstrated. This was in order to proclaim his own position and so was acceptable. But [for Xiao Fang] to cast aspersions on Zhixuan's clothing and food and memorialize the throne on the subject of the rites and administration was to attack him personally, to compete with him [as an individual]. This is different from the instance in which Yuan Ang remonstrated the throne over removing the king of Huainan, insulting Zhao Tan for riding in his carriage, or removing the seat of Lady Shen.[63]
>
> However, from [Emperor] Wen of the Han to [Emperor] Xizong was more than seven hundred years. This should have been enough time for Yuan Ang to repay the debt he owed for the events concerning Chao Cuo. Yet [Zhixuan] still died as a consequence of the burden of bad karma. How can this be? It must be because of his personal enmity with Chao Cuo. When Chao recommended reducing the seven states that then revolted, Yuan Ang asked that he be executed.[64] When Chao was executed, the armies of the seven states did not retreat. Hence, Ang had used the authority of the state to avenge a personal grievance. For this reason, the karma was still not spent after some tens of generations. Is this not cause for caution?[65]

Here secular political history and religious monastic history meet, requiring the historian to demonstrate knowledge of both ancient history—the personal rancor driving policy decisions at the Han court—and Buddhist doctrine—the possibility of the karma from a single event lingering, dormant, for a dozen lives before awakening to exact its inevitable effect.

Buddhist historians, wending their way through a series of karmic labyrinths, saw the relentless force of karma at work in the lives of all their subjects, monks and laymen alike. Emperor Gao of the Northern Qi was in a previous life a *rakṣa*, which explains his violent disposition early on in his reign.[66] Emperor Shizong carried out a persecution of Buddhism in 955 because of his "old karmic aspirations."⁶⁷ Nor did karma stop with the effects brought on by previous deeds, for the new acts of the living only created more karma that would bear fruit one day sooner or later. In the case of Emperor Wu of the Zhou, notorious in Buddhist history for his persecution of the sangha, later historians related sightings of the former emperor undergoing punishment in hell.⁶⁸ Zhipan, relying on a variety of sources, including historical events in the lives of rulers and accounts of their miserable rebirths in the netherworld, confidently demonstrated that the emperors responsible for all of the major persecutions of Buddhism in Chinese history to his day had all suffered retribution for their actions.⁶⁹

In fact, whether it be the karma of the emperor at the time or of others involved, Buddhist historians saw karma as the key to understanding the vagaries of official policy toward Buddhism at the Chinese court. As Zhipan put it,

> The Buddhist Path is at root constant. If at times it encounters misfortune, this is in response to the karma of people of the world. For this reason, in the case of the greater and lesser of the "three types of catastrophe," the karmic response is great.⁷⁰ In the case of the destruction of the clergy under the "three Wu" [i.e., three great persecutions of Buddhism in China by three different emperors coincidentally all with the title Wu "martial"], the karmic response was small.⁷¹

If karma lay just beneath the surface of imperial campaigns to destroy Buddhism, it was just as central to the success of Buddhism in happier times. Zanning wrote that the victories and failures of Buddhism in China depended on "karmic conditions," citing the (legendary) rejection of Buddhist missionaries at the Qin court of the First Emperor, and the later (equally legendary) welcoming of the Buddhist missionaries at the Han court of Emperor Ming as examples of, respectively, bad and good karmic conditions.⁷²

THINKING ABOUT KARMA WITH HISTORY

For all of its utility, karma also presented historians with unique difficulties. On a technical level, claims of reincarnation needed to be verified, or at least shown to be free of obvious internal contradictions; Buddhist historians, like all historians, were sensitive to the charge of credulity. We have already seen how one historian, Zanning, slipped up, claiming that Cai Yong was a reincarnation of Zhang Heng, when in fact the two overlapped by a few years. In this case the mistake seems to have gone by unnoticed, but in another case (discussed in the previous chapter) Zanning's story of the appearance of a spirit soon to be reborn as An Lushan was shown by a later historian to be impossible, since the date of the spirit's appearance was after the date of An Lushan's birth. Though sloppy in these two instances, Zanning notes that claims that the monk Zhixuan was both the reincarnation of Yuan Ang and the reincarnation of another monk are *not* in contradiction because the time span separating the three figures was enough to account for three generations of men.[73] In short, historical evidence for karma was subject to the same sorts of scholarly scrutiny as other historical claims. This was part of what made the doctrine compelling: it could be neatly incorporated into the historian's toolkit for textual analysis.

Ultimately more troubling than such technical problems, easily addressed (if not necessarily resolved) by traditional historiographical techniques of comparing sources and dates, doctrinal conundrums discussed by Buddhist exegetes also crop up in historical works. Perhaps chief among these is the inherent tension between the doctrine of rebirth and the Buddhist rejection of the self. As the great ninth-century thinker Zongmi 宗密 (780–841), in an influential discussion of karma, put it: "Granted that we receive a bodily existence in [one of] the five destinies as a result of our having generated karma, it is still not clear who generates karma and who experiences its retribution."[74] Zongmi goes on to further critique the doctrine of karma as a foundation of ethical behavior and then moves on to what he considers the higher doctrine of dependent origination. Unlike doctrinal exegetes, Buddhist historians rarely discuss this knotty problem, perhaps in part because it threatened the utility of karma as an ethical incentive (why should I care what happens to the one who suffers for my bad actions or profits from my good actions, if in the end, my next life is not in any substantial sense experienced by me?), but also perhaps because the problem did not detract from the utility of karma as a historical theory. That is, regardless of how we understand the overlap between the person in this life and a previous life or a future life, each is profoundly affected by the actions of the past; the historian can hence still appreciate the role of karma in the way history unfolds—it often explains *why* people did what they did and why their circumstances were what they were.

Zanning at least skirts the problem of self in one passage in his *Brief History of the Clergy*, in a discussion of the karmic consequences of the first great persecution of Buddhism by Emperor Wu of the Zhou dynasty. Zanning writes:

> Emperor Wu of the Northern Zhou dismissed Buddhism as if it were a trifle. He once attended [a debate] in the main palace hall to evaluate the three teachings. He placed Confucianism before Buddhism, with Daoism above them all since it "emerged before the nameless" [...] In all of this, he insulted holy men. According to one source, this planted the seeds that led him to Avīci hell. Hence, when Toba Hu 拓跋虎 entered the netherworld, he saw Emperor Wu of the Northern Zhou receiving judgment. Wu then sent word to Emperor [Wen] of Sui, saying, "Deliver me from this suffering." Emperor Wen subsequently solicited funds from throughout the empire to generate merit in order to save him.[75]

So far this is a standard story of karmic retribution: the emperor committed an evil deed and was punished for it in a subsequent life in hell. But Zanning then concludes the passage by questioning who, precisely, was harmed by the emperor's persecution. "Yet a buddha does not possess the concept of self, and even when harmed, does not seek retribution. Hence, it must be that when one prepares to inflict damage on another, [the will to do so] burns first in the mind. As the mind is the source of suffering, the body is afflicted with retribution. The one who acts is the one who receives. Is this not frightening?" This too is a standard interpretation of karma. In contrast to notions propagated in popular stories—like the one we saw above of the continuation of a rivalry between two Han officials in the cyst suffered by a monk in a later life—monks versed in Buddhist doctrine understood that it is not that the one who is harmed in one life personally seeks revenge in a subsequent life; it is that by intentionally harming another—or even intending to harm another but not carrying through on the act—one plants karmic seeds *in one's own mind* that later manifest themselves in retribution in a subsequent life.[76] Only people *seek* revenge; karma coolly, remorselessly exacts just compensation without recourse to intention or indignation.

In fact, on closer inspection, despite his reference to "no-self" (*wuwo* 無我), even here Zanning does not address the problem of the self directly, since he asks only who was harmed in the initial act—he might just as easily have highlighted the suffering of monks at the time—and then points out that this is not important since it was the mind of the emperor that generated the karma and his body (in a subsequent incarnation) that suffered the consequences. Zongmi and Huiyuan dealt with the more profound problem of whether or not the mind and body of the one who generates the karma exist in an enduring sense.[77]

This same problem—just who it is that is the creator and recipient of karma—lurks behind attempts to assess the karma of historical figures. While many circumstances can be ascribed to karma, and these circumstances can influence one's decisions, it would be nonsensical to attribute all actions to the effects of past karma, since it is through actions—whether physical or mental—that one creates karma, good or bad. Hence when evaluating the life of a famous person of the past, the discriminating historian had to balance karma and will, circumstance and action, taking the impact of karma accumulated in former lives into consideration but not relying on it as an excuse for the decisions the person made. The problem becomes particularly complex when evaluating emperors who, though they promoted the Buddhist cause in some of their policies, were also known for acts of great violence and cruelty. Zhipan avoided the challenge in the case of the Northern Qi emperor Wenxuan 文宣 (526–559), ascribing to good karma created in a previous life—Zhipan says the emperor was a novice monk in a former life—his promotion of the translation of scriptures, practice of meditation, reception of the lay precepts, and prohibition against killing either people or animals on certain days, while ascribing his "fondness for killing" and cruel punishments to "the activity of his remnant [bad] karma."[78] Similarly, when attempting to assess the life of Emperor Yang of the Sui, who on the one hand murdered his own father to usurp the throne and on the other was a great patron of Buddhism, Zhipan offers two possible explanations: either the murder of his father was the result of a "former condition" (specifically, there was a grievance between two men in a previous life that led to them coming back in this life as father and son) or the act was an apparent sin committed in service of a greater good (that is, only by killing his father could he become emperor and only by becoming emperor could he most effectively promote Buddhism).[79]

Buddhist historians also worked around the equally perplexing problem of collective karma. At the level of the individual, karma provides an elegant solution to the problem of justice with great explanatory power. But in practice, karma was always a collective concern in that, from early on, the vast majority of devotees believed that one could transfer good (though never bad) karma to another.

This is the foundation of Buddhist death ritual, in which children pay for rituals to generate karma to be passed to their deceased parents. The tension between these two theories of karma (that it is solely the provenance of the individual, and that it can be transferred) troubled Buddhist exegetes and, at times, historians. Moreover, beyond the problem of transference of merit, in the Chinese conception of the afterlife, how one was to be rewarded or punished for behavior in the preceding life was decided not by the impersonal, impartial, and precise mechanism of karma alone but also by a subterranean bureaucracy subject to the same failings—namely, incompetence and corruption—as the bureaucracy among the living.

These two problems cropped up simultaneously for Zanning after he described the near-death experience of an obscure holy monk called Hongzheng 洪正 (d.u), originally surnamed Chang (this surname will be important in the story). On the night when Hongzheng was about to die, a neighbor (either in meditation or in a dream) caught a glimpse of two messengers from the netherworld with an official rescript in their hands. The neighbor even overheard their conversation in which they described their own bureaucratic nightmare: they had been dispatched by the king of the underworld to take Hongzheng away from the world of the living, for his time to die had arrived. Unfortunately for the two underworld officers, Hongzheng was chanting the *Diamond Sutra* and, owing to the apotropaic power of the sutra, which protects one who chants it from all manner of ghosts, demons, and other figures in the other world, they could not even approach him, much less complete their mission and take him to the world of the dead. At the same time, they feared the reaction of their supervisor if they returned empty-handed. At this point, one of the emissaries devises a plan: "I see that there is someone else with the surname Chang at the Office of the Eastern Gate. He even has the same given name as the monk, and was once a monk himself. Let's take the other man to fill the hall [in the netherworld]." The next day, the neighbor investigates the matter and discovers that a man who lived nearby named Chang Hongzheng had died suddenly during the night.[80]

The story fits a pattern of miracle tales told to promote the efficacy of a particular scripture. The *Diamond Sutra* inspired many such stories, some of which were included in miracle-tale collections.[81] The protagonist is not so much Hongzheng—a monk of little historical significance, if he did in fact exist at all—as it is the sutra itself, so powerful that it can protect one against even death. But, as we have seen in other cases above, when historians like Zanning took such stories into their works, they found troubling inconsistencies. In this case it is an inconsistency not in dating but in doctrine. Why should an innocent layman take over the burden of the monk's karma? Was karma in this case really subject to the whims of a pair of bungling bureaucrats?

[QUESTION:]

Can two different men of the same name take each other's place in death? As karma cannot be transferred, how can this be? It is like a common sorcerer who makes an image in one's likeness, saying that it will take on their misfortune.

RESPONSE:

King Yama may well be a bodhisattva. If there are two men of the same name, he lets the good one go and takes the one who is not good. This may be a case of official leniency[82] leading to an increase in the allotted life span. It is for this reason that the man was allowed to continue to live. Moreover, when a man's "vessel of evil" reaches its full, his days must come to an end. It was for this reason that the other man was taken.[83]

If the two were not exchanged in order to spread the Teaching, then these events cannot be understood according to common principles.[84]

Again, Zanning fudges the answer, at first speculating that the karma of the two men was originally such that in fact the monk should have lived and the layman died; it was not their karma that changed, but merely the assessment of their karma by the agents of the underworld. But then in the end, seemingly dissatisfied with his own answer, he raises the possibility that the king of the underworld can manipulate karmic recompense—speeding it up or delaying it—in order to better "spread the Teaching."

Zhipan similarly grapples with the question of the relationship between the victim and the agent of karmic retribution in a historical account of assassination. The problem arises when he recounts the story of how Juqu Mengxun 沮渠蒙遜 (368–433), ruler of the Northern Liang, became angry with the translator Dharmakṣema (Ch. Tanwuchen 曇無讖, 385–433). When the monk insisted on returning to his homeland, the furious king dispatched an assassin to kill him.

Earlier, just before Dharmakṣema left for the West, the monk said to a friend sending him off, "The time for my karmic [retribution] has arrived." After Dharmakṣema's murder, Juqu Mengxun, filled with regret, had a terrifying vision of a divine being wielding a sword and promptly fell dead. The question for Zhipan was, if Dharmakṣema himself saw that he was to die for his own karmic reasons, why should Juqu Mengsun suffer for being the agent of this inevitable death? Zhipan writes:

> When [the king of] Kashmir attacked Siṃha, the king's arm fell off and he too died.[85] When Juqu Mengxun dispatched an assassin to kill Dharmakṣema, a divine being felled the king with a sword. Some say that since these holy masters [Siṃha and Dharmakṣema] fully understood their karma and so allowed their own karmic debt to come to completion, why should their killers receive retribution in this way?
>
> It must be that deities who protect the Dharma were angered over these assaults on the worthy. Moreover, the malevolent minds of the kings were sufficient in themselves to bring their fate upon them. This cannot be compared to the exchange of blame and retribution between ordinary people.[86]

In other words, the agent of Dharmakṣema's murder, whether the king or a spirit, was responsible for their own actions, regardless of the state of Dharmakṣema's karma, and so would in turn carry the burden of the karmic consequences of the act. We see in examples like these historians using cases from the historical record to think through knotty ethical problems that the doctrine of karma presents. Abhidharma and formal doctrinal essays aren't the only genres in which Buddhist thinkers contemplate the ramifications of doctrinal problems; history too provoked this kind of speculation and debate, often by authors steeped in Buddhist doctrine and often at a sophisticated level.

CONCLUSION

The preceding may give an impression of a stiff and mechanical interpretation of history, as if karma were such a powerful tool of explanation that it crowded out all others. True, when karma was applied to interpret events, it often led to hermeneutical overkill: we can speculate that every action was the direct result of karma from actions in a previous life, in the end leaving historical actors as little more than automatons—wind-up dolls propelled by forces set in motion long ago, blindly following a course long since determined. Taken to its extreme, this is an approach that undermines karma, which depends on an assumption of free ethical choice. In fact, Buddhist historians availed themselves of a number of models for understanding causation in history, particularly for interpreting long-term trends. The modern scholar Cao Ganghua has argued that in the Song dynasty, traditional Buddhist historiography with its emphasis on karma and the decline of the Dharma gave way to less Buddhist historiographical concepts like destiny (*yunshu* 運數 or *tianming* 天命) and "temporal shifts in power" (*shishi* 時勢).[87] Destiny (though not amoral) is less moral than karma, and allows greater leeway for tragic themes, taking us back to cases like that examined by Sima Qian at the beginning of this chapter: great men who, *through no fault of their own*, could not realize their full potential. I disagree with Cao that such concepts ever eclipsed karma in Buddhist historiography; the examples above draw heavily on Song sources, and Cao himself gives many instances of Buddhist historians employing karma to explain history. But it is true that Buddhist historians, particularly from the Song period on, were comfortable using both Buddhist notions of karma and non-Buddhist notions of destiny to interpret the past.

Aside from destiny, the issues of human nature, personality, and political dynamics received attention. Under the shadow of the prestigious tradition of court history, Buddhist historians were well aware of the political factors that shaped virtually all of Chinese history, Buddhism included. Zuxiu, for instance, interpreted the course of Chinese Buddhism as a parallel story to that of the rise and fall of dynasties. He writes:

> The flourishing and withering of the Buddha Dharma is often related to the Way of emperors. The empire was never greater than in the Tang, and Buddhism relied upon it to flourish throughout China. Buddhism and the Tang drew from each other to reach completion.... After the Huichang persecution, Buddhism declined in the world, and the Tang also ended in weakness. Alas! This is the constant principle of rise and fall. Yet it is also in this way tied to men.[88]

There is no inherent contradiction between discussion of the role of dynastic politics and karma, nor was it necessary for a Buddhist historian to invoke karma to explain every event; they did not consider it naïve or superficial to point out that Buddhism's fortunes, like so many other aspects of Chinese civilization, were linked in no small measure to the proclivities and abilities of individual emperors.

Nor did belief in karma inhibit historians from assessing the relative merits of men. That is, one might be tempted to attribute the adverse circumstances in which a given monk found himself to his past karma—it was, in effect, his own fault. But Zuxiu, when comparing three of the greatest monks of early medieval Chinese Buddhism—Fotucheng, Dao'an, and Huiyuan—notes that, unlike Huiyuan, Fotucheng and Dao'an suffered under despotic rulers; it is hence unfair to say that Huiyuan was more unbending in his virtue than the other two monks, since his principles were not put to the test to the degree that theirs were.[89] The emphasis is on their response to circumstances, not on the karmic conditions that brought these circumstances about. Similarly, in assessing the moral character of Emperor Taizong of the Tang dynasty, one of the most revered emperors in Chinese history, Zhipan raises the disturbing fact that Taizong killed countless men when assisting his father to establish the dynasty. Rather than ascribe this early burst of violence to some karmic debt or to lament the debt Taizong incurred by doing so, Zhipan explains that the violence was natural to one raised in the military and that Taizong's early military campaigns were necessary to pacify the empire. Moreover, once the empire was secure, Taizong held Buddhist rituals for the well-being of the war dead. Overall, Zhipan concludes, Tang Taizong was a "humane and generous ruler."[90] In keeping with the characterization of Tang Taizong in non-Buddhist historiography, Zhipan portrays him as a man very much in control of his own destiny. His early violent years were the product of justifiable ambition rather than karma. And after the empire was his, he controlled his karma—performing rituals for those who died in his cause—rather than the other way around.

Daoxuan insisted that Chinese Buddhist historians, equipped with the doctrine of karma, understood better than their predecessors like Sima Qian why sometimes great men suffered and petty men prospered. But the search for the heroes who propelled history along its path or fought valiantly to bend history's course to their will is just as prominent in Buddhist historiography in China as it is among other types of historiography. Among Sima Qian's many accomplishments is raising the individual life—as opposed to principles, events, or wise pronouncements—to the status of key building block of history in a process one historian of historiography describes as "the discovery of the individual" 人之發現.⁹¹ Despite occasional experiments with the history of Buddhist official posts and practices, as in Zanning's *Brief History of the Clergy*, and the eventual emergence of the history of particular places as a respectable genre of historical writing, the predominant form of Buddhist history was biographies of monks. And while karma could help to explain the development of history, monks, like all men and women, made their own karma, often at great personal risk. It was these incidents, when monks bravely faced up to bandits, wild animals, demons, and, perhaps most important of all, hostile emperors, that most attracted the attention and admiration of Buddhist historians in China.

Yet in the end the two—conditions created by karma generated by past actions and new free decisions by individuals—are inextricably bound. In the words of Sengyou in the preface to one of the first Buddhist histories in China, "The Way is spread by men, and the Dharma is revealed only when the conditions are right. Though the Way exists, if there is no one to propagate it, even if the words are present no one will understand them; and if the Dharma exists but the conditions are not right, even if it is in the world, no one will hear it."⁹²

CHAPTER 4

Prophecy

THE HISTORIOGRAPHY OF THE FUTURE

There is something decidedly odd about predictions of the future in historical writing; after all, history is supposed to be about the past, or at best a dialogue between the past and the present.[1] In the modern era, historians often express their reluctance to predict the future on the basis of past events, characterizing the work of those who do as "utterly untestable and inconclusive."[2] History suggests possibilities and even general trends, but the level of complexity and opportunity for change dooms specific predictions to embarrassing failure.[3] Premodern historians, while similarly reluctant to conjecture about the future, had no such compunction when they could base predictions on well-attested prophecies. Indeed, in most premodern history, and certainly in Buddhist histories, predictions of the future are standard fare.

One theme in predictions of the future that virtually all Buddhists writing about the past has accepted is that wherever and whenever historians find themselves, things are about to get worse: in coming years, monks will only become more corrupt, rulers less sympathetic to Buddhism, our capacity to understand Buddhist teachings even more diminished. Chinese Buddhist historians, like most Buddhists before modern times, accepted a notion of cyclical time and the premise that within this cycle, they lived in a period of decline. As we have seen, these historians actively engaged in the discourse of "decline theory." Historians in China primarily applied their talents to correctly dating the Buddha's nirvana; only when that date was correlated to a Chinese calendar was it possible for them to follow the prophecies and plot out the precise date when the final age of the Dharma would begin or, in other cases, just how deep into decline they were.

Beyond discussing prophecies of the future decline of Buddhism, at least one Buddhist historian in China analyzed a prediction of specific events that extended into the future beyond his day. Zhipan, in his thirteenth-century *Comprehensive Account of the Buddhas and the Patriarchs*, predicts the total number of emperors and total number of years of his own dynasty, the Song (960–1279). Of course the incentive, given the power and temperament of the imperial family, was to foretell a *very* long reign. To predict the length of the dynasty he lived in, Zhipan combed through the historical record and examined ancient predictions of the number of emperors and number of years for various dynasties—the Zhou, the Han, the Jin, and the Tang—that previous historians had made. In some cases Buddhist figures played a role, but others had nothing to do with Buddhism; since so many Chinese historical writings treat dynastic history, at times historians of all stripes reported prophecies of the duration of their own dynasty. After detailing how the previous predictions panned out (in general, according to Zhipan, successfully, though in one case the dynasty, on the strengths of its own merits, outlived the prophecy of its demise by a few years), he focused on the sort of intricate puzzle that fascinated Chinese historians.

During Zhipan's own dynasty, the Song, a mysterious stone inscription was discovered and submitted to the throne. It prophesied that the dynasty would last for a total of twenty-one emperors, all in the Zhao family line. Another prediction, some time later, foretold that the dynasty would last for 788 years.[4] The problem came when Zhipan put the two prophecies together. By Zhipan's time (ca. 1269) there had already been fourteen emperors, and just over 300 years had passed, which seemed to suggest that there were not enough emperors left to fill up the remaining 480-some years. Happily, a quick calculation allowed Zhipan to optimistically conclude that, with proper spacing, each of the remaining seven emperors would reign for an average of seventy years—unusually long for an emperor, but not unheard of.

This is a rare case of a historian venturing to predict future political events. It is one thing to note that the world in general has long been in decline and to predict that it will soon get worse; it is another to predict the precise length of the next emperor's reign. Of course, as modern historians, skeptical of prediction, might have predicted, such prophecies rarely go to plan. Zhipan's forecast was far from accurate. Instead of his prediction of seven, in fact only three more emperors governed during the Song, and instead of 480 years, the dynasty lasted only nine years more, each emperor ruling for an average of three, not seventy, years.

Historians making new predictions about the future are actually quite rare in Chinese Buddhist historiography. My focus here is not on predictions set to be fulfilled after the day the historian put ink to paper but on *ex eventu* accounts—the prophecies historians claimed had already been fulfilled in the past.[5] And here, the evidence is rich. If we read through the thirty or so standard major historical works composed in China by Buddhist writers from the sixth century to the twentieth century, we find many examples of *this* kind of prediction, which according to the historians, had already been proven true.

For all their reluctance to dwell on the future, the search for clues in the distant past to subsequent events—that is, causation—was the bread and butter (rice and turnip?) of the Chinese Buddhist historian. To do this, the historian must move back and forth in time. More often than not, historical events, whatever their time frame, were understood in moral terms; dynasties rose and fell on the moral quality of the families that ruled them. Emperors granted favor to or inflicted persecution on Buddhist figures and institutions as a consequence of the integrity of the ruler and those who surrounded him. On a grander scale, historians, as we have seen, attempted to explain history according to the workings of karma. But given that Buddhist historians seldom discussed economic trends, climate, crop failure, or psychology, this moral framework left all manner of historical events unexplained. One way to clean up a historical record littered with seemingly random events was to look for a different type of clue to development, not in moral behavior, much less economics or class struggle, but in ruptures in time that suggest a given event was somehow *meant* to happen, providing not an explanation per se, but at least some sense of order. In search of these clues, Buddhist historians in China were fascinated by ancient prophecies, fortune-tellers, prophetic dreams, and omens.

Accounts of prophecies were almost always taken as literal records of what really happened, as opposed to legends composed after the fact, which the vast majority of these accounts almost certainly were. Moreover, in Buddhist history, past predictions of the future always come true. I know of no case in which a Buddhist historian records a prediction of the future that had since been proved wrong; as soon as the reader encounters an omen or a prophetic dream, its fulfillment is inevitably just a few lines away. When a prophecy did prove wrong, as in Zhipan's prediction of the length of the Song dynasty, subsequent historians quietly ignored it, however confident the prediction or prominent the prophet.

THE CULTURE OF PROPHECY

The fascination with historical records of successful attempts to predict the future—mantic historiography—grew out of a rich culture of prophecy. Our earliest Chinese writings, the oracle bone inscriptions, are records of divination. And divination by scapulimancy, cracking bones, may go back even into the Neolithic. From that time on, techniques for predicting the future never ceased to multiply—by divination stalks (the foundation of the *Book of Changes*), days of the calendar, physiognomy, the stars, dice, time and date of birth, geomancy, the sounds of birds and bells, flipping "moon blocks," and nowadays even reading palms. Forms of divination, especially calculations based on the date and time of birth (*bazi* 八字), remain an integral part of many people's lives today up and down the social scale, in shops across from the local temple or from tables in the park.[6] Beyond daily life, palace coups, persecutions, and uprisings all drew inspiration from prophecies that highlighted their urgency. It is not surprising, then, that Buddhist historical writings reflect this widespread belief so deeply ingrained in the culture. At the same time, Buddhist historians wrote not only as part of a rich, dynamic culture of prophecy but also within a historiographical tradition in which documenting and analyzing predictions of the future was part of the historian's job. As we will see, this historiographical tradition placed greatest emphasis on political predictions, usually in the form of omens, dreams, and prophecies.[7]

The same holds true for Indian culture. That is, divination techniques were widespread. And if we understand "history" broadly, Indian historical writings, whether set in the past or purporting to record events of the past, are just as suffused with accounts of predictions, omens, and prophetic dreams as pre-Buddhist Chinese writings are.

In many cases in Buddhist literature, pronouncements about the future are made by men, or, more famously still, by buddhas. Buddhist scriptures are rife with such prophecies, most characteristically predictions of future *spiritual* progress. The Buddha announces that a devotee will in his next life be born in a heaven and achieve extinction there, never to be born again in this world. Others will achieve the status of "once returners," meaning they will be reborn in this world or in a heaven one more time before achieving release, while others still will at least achieve stream entry in their next life, signaling their start on an ever-upward path toward enlightenment.[8] The Buddha predicts the opposite of spiritual progress as well, prophesying that, upon his death, the incorrigible scoundrel Devadatta will suffer for an entire *kalpa* without hope of relief.⁹ Deeper in the past, the Buddha himself had received such a prediction many lives before from a previous buddha.¹⁰ The genealogy of buddhas (a topic I will visit again in the next chapter) was linked not by blood but by prophecy, with each future buddha receiving a prophecy of buddhahood from the previous buddha in a previous life. In his record of his travels in India, Xuanzang notes the spot in Vārāṇasī where the buddha of our era, Śākyamuni, was said to have prophesied that Maitreya would one day become the next buddha.¹¹

Such predictions are so prevalent in Buddhist literature that passages concerning "prophecy" (Skt. *vyākaraṇa*) were traditionally considered one of the twelve divisions, or genres, of the Buddhist canon (Ch. *Shierbu jing* 十二部經; Skt. *dvādaśa-aṅga*).¹² The ability to make such predictions is one of the powers of a buddha, well attested in Buddhist scholastic writings. The *Dazhidu lun*, for instance, lists as the second of ten powers the Buddha's ability to "know the past, present, *and future* karma of all beings, to know where they receive karmic consequences, and where they create karma. He can know the causes and the karmic retribution for each and every act."¹³ Such prophecies would have been well known to any literate Buddhist. A legend popular in the Song dynasty included, among other places, in the *Comprehensive Account of the Buddhas and the Patriarchs*, held that the Song emperor Taizong long ago in a previous life not only was present at the Buddha's nirvana but also received a prophecy from him.¹⁴

The ability to predict the future is not limited to buddhas; though few could ever attain a buddha's complete mastery of knowledge of the future, others, including even non-Buddhists, could foretell the future through various techniques. The most famous soothsayer in Buddhist history is probably the sage Asita (Ch. Ayi 阿夷 or Asituo 阿私陀), who predicted soon after Śākyamuni's birth, based on the child's physical appearance, that he would one day become either a great king or, if he left the household, a buddha.¹⁵ The Chinese pilgrim to India Faxian is said to have visited the site where this prophecy took place, and Asita is depicted on stelae in China recounting the Buddha's life.¹⁶ The episode resonates in stories of Chinese monks, whose eminent careers as monastics are predicted by wandering soothsayers and sagely monks.¹⁷ While monks were forbidden by the monastic regulations from accepting payment for predicting the future, the holiest of monks often offer up predictions free of charge, though usually in terms that mystify their less spiritually advanced listeners.¹⁸ The biography of the fourth-century monk Fotucheng claims that he could foretell events on the basis of the "sounds of bells."[19] Fotucheng makes frequent predictions, including a double murder and kidnapping, the capture of hostile commanders, the invasions of armies, and an uprising. There are scattered examples in Buddhist histories of a monk's ability in the more technical corners of the mantic arts—reading the stars, making numerical calculations, and so on.[20] But perhaps in order to distinguish monks from professional fortune-tellers, in Buddhist historiography monks rarely draw on particular techniques; their knowledge of the future is a testament to their spiritual cultivation and innate powers rather than tricks learned especially for the purpose.

Writing in the twelfth century, Zhipan attempted to put Buddhist prognostication in the context of traditional Chinese techniques for predicting the future, noting that the common employ "diagrams and books, divination stalks and tortoise shells, astrology and dream divination" to predict the future, while the Buddha demonstrates his ability to foresee the future through his prophecy of who will one day achieve buddhahood, and in his predictions of the names of kingdoms and *kalpas* of the future and "the fortunes and destinies of ordinary people."[21] Buddhist predictions are not, in fact, always so grand. It is common in biographies, for instance, for monks to predict the time of their own death. Typically, just before dying, the monk announces that his time has come, assumes the lotus posture, and dies with quiet, *punctual* dignity.[22] Rarely do they die at night or unexpectedly or in pain. Omens precede their death and follow after, most often indicating birth in a pure land.

In Zhipan's discussion of prophecy, the chief target of his critique is the skeptics in his day and earlier who dismiss the efficacy of fortune-telling. "Men who know nothing of this branch of learning yet condemn prophetic writings as false are intolerable. And the ability of the Buddha and other holy men to foresee the future is not something common people of the world can understand."[23] He notes that there are many instances of demonstrably accurate prophecies recorded in the histories and the classics, and concludes his argument by citing the commentary to the *Book of Changes*, in which the Dao "by virtue of its numinous power, [...] lets one know what is going to come."[24] Accepting the traditional attribution of the commentary to Confucius, Zhipan questions how any could doubt the viability of prophecy.[25] This attempt to persuade (or at least discredit) skeptics reminds us of a less credulous strand of thought—vocal from early on, but certainly in the minority—that challenged omens, a tradition that goes all the way back to Wang Chong's 王充 (27-ca.100) attack on omens in the first century.[26]

THE CULTURE OF OMENS

Even more than prophecy, omens were a staple of Chinese historiography long before the entrance of Buddhism to China. Drawing on even older traditions, court historians during the Han dynasty filled their books with accounts of all manner of signs in the past that prefigured subsequent events, almost always in a political context. These signs are not generated by gods or holy men but are instead cracks in the natural order, hinting at the future for those with the patience and intelligence to unravel their hidden secrets. In the Han, when unusual phenomena were witnessed, including dramatic natural events like solar eclipses, comets, and earthquakes as well as a wide variety of strange occurrences—the appearance of sweet dew, divine mushrooms "with nine stalks," two birds joined at the wing, red rabbits, unicorns, and one-legged beasts—they were dutifully reported to the throne. Fan Ye, compiler of the *Later Han History*, gives a sense of just how widespread the fascination with recording omens was when commenting on one short reign particularly rich in omens: "In those thirteen years of government, of all the auspicious omens presented to the court from the various prefectures and states, those which have been recorded in books number in the hundreds of thousands."[27] The *History of the Three Kingdoms* records that when Liu Bei 劉備 (161-223) rose to power "over 800 officials submitted memorials which recorded in detail the auspicious omens."[28] Implied in these exasperated comments on the extravagant numbers of omens is the suggestion that many were fabricated to curry favor with a powerful ruler. Historians looking back on the political history of a previous dynasty duly sifted through this surfeit of material, recounting events, signs, and pronouncements rich in portentous meaning, choosing the most extraordinary or significant, and on rare occasion questioning the authenticity of some reports.[29]

Some of these portents were consistently interpreted as auspicious and others as inauspicious. Many were read as responses to the policies or moral character of the ruler. Because of the political implications of such reports, it is usually difficult to pinpoint the motivations of those who generated them—whether they were a form of indirect censure of the emperor or of particular policies, or fawning attempts to curry favor. Some records of omens, like records of eclipses, were probably honest reports of verifiable phenomena. Others, like records of green dragons and unicorns, might generously be read as misperception or reports of hearsay or even creative interpretation of real flora and fauna. Specialists in Han thought agree that, for the most part, it was contemporary officials who were active in the complex gamesmanship of manipulating and interpreting omens for political ends; historians merely collected and, on occasion, commented on reports of omens from earlier times.[30]

Removed from the immediate political context of the reporting and interpretation of an omen, the historian was faced with a large body of documents related to portents and omens—if we are to believe Fan Ye, cited above, "hundreds of thousands" of them. Of course, the report of an omen and the imperial response to it are themselves historical events with significant consequences worth commenting on. The historian was also tasked with interpreting the mechanism behind omens, explaining what they presaged and, ideally, commenting on their moral meaning, often only apparent after the passage of time. All of this presented a unique set of problems. Accepting the Chinese traditions of omens, historians were tasked with absorbing a similar tradition in India—well documented in Buddhist writings—into their histories. More fundamentally, Buddhist historians looked for ways of incorporating distinctively Buddhist figures, doctrines, and motifs into their explanations of these ruptures in time.

Take, for example, portentous signs preceding the birth and early childhood of eminent monastics. In sixth-century collections of biographies, omens related to the birth of monks and nuns are rare. We are told that when the nun Sengguo 僧果 (fl. 429) was a breastfeeding infant, she only ate before noon—a clear sign that she would one day be ordained and follow the monastic practice of eating only in the morning.[31] The biography of Kumārajīva notes that when his mother was pregnant with him, her intelligence increased markedly.[32] For reasons that I do not understand, it is only with a seventh-century collection, the *Further Biographies of Eminent Monks,* that birth omens become commonplace. Here we see frequent reference to unusual lights accompanying the birth of an eminent monk. On the night of Zhiyi's birth, the "room was illuminated with a light that did not dissipate for two days, delighting one and all."[33] On the night of Huichao's 慧超 (d. 526) birth, "a divine light shone in the room."[34] Again from Daoxuan's seventh-century *Further Biographies* on, the birth of a boy destined to become a monk is at times marked by a pleasing fragrance.[35] From the seventh century up to the present, such omens during the mother's pregnancy and at the child's birth are standard fare in biographies of eminent monks.

Divine light and extraordinary fragrance are signs that the child will one day do great things, and these motifs, with many variations and permutations, are legion in Chinese Buddhist hagiography. But of particular interest are signs, like that of the nun Sengguo above, that suggest the emergence of a distinctively Buddhist repertoire of omens—only an infant destined for the monastic life would refuse to eat after noon. Following the rise of vegetarianism as the standard monastic diet in China in the sixth century, a pregnant mother's sudden aversion to meat and other "unclean" foods (presumably garlic, Chinese chives, onions, leeks, and so on) up until the birth of her child becomes a common trope in Buddhist hagiography. The author of the biography of Huijin 慧璡 (d. 634) felt the need to explain this omen: "When his mother was pregnant, she rid herself of desire, and did not so much as look at spicy foods, meat, or other vulgar fare. Those who understood such things said that this was brought on by the child, since they shared the same body."[36] And just as new omens followed the rise of vegetarianism in birth stories, in the same way references to eminent monks born with purple placentas reflected the growing practice of the emperor conferring purple robes on prominent monks as a sign of respect and reward for service to the state.[37] Before leaving home, as children, monks gave other signs of their future careers, for instance, spontaneously forming stupas while playing in the sand.[38]

Similarly, Buddhist historians were in a unique position to reflect on both Indian and Chinese omens. Commenting on the story that lotus blossoms sprouted from the mouth of the ninth-century monk Suiduan 遂端 (d. 861), Zanning notes that this is the mark of a *cakravartin*, a universal ruler, and asks how such a thing could occur in this decadent age, so far removed from the Buddha. He then answers his own question by framing the Indian omen of the lotus in the Chinese contexts of "stimulous and response" and enlightened rulership: "Such resonances to holy men are not restrained by time. It is like the unicorn (*qilin* 麒麟), which, though not a Chinese animal, can be stimulated to come to China by the appearance of a worthy ruler."[39]

THE CULTURE OF DREAMS

Similar to their role as vehicles for omens presaging promising monastic careers for their children, perhaps the main role monks' mothers play in the biographies of their sons is to dream.[40] Mothers pregnant with remarkable Buddhist babies dream of swallowing a pearl or the moon.[41] They dream of a flowering tree that produces only one fruit or of climbing to the top of a stupa—all premonitions that the children in their wombs will one day become eminent Buddhist monks.[42] In many cases, the dreams are even more direct, with monks entering to announce to the expectant mother that the child will one day join their ranks. I haven't found any reference in Buddhist historical writings to the sorts of handbooks recovered at Dunhuang explaining how to interpret dreams. There is, however, at least one reference to a specifically Buddhist interpretation of dreams, in the biography of the great sixth-century exegete Zhiyi. Zhiyi's mother had two dreams while pregnant. In one, she dreamed that she swallowed a white rat. Understandably puzzled, she consulted a specialist, who reassured her that the dream foretold the birth of a "white dragon" (i.e., a great man). More interesting from a strictly Buddhist perspective was her first dream, of five-colored fragrant smoke that swirled around her bosom. She attempted to wave the smoke away, when she heard a voice telling her, "The causes and conditions of previous lives signal the path of kings; when blessings and merit arrive, why should you chase them away?"[43] The point here is that the child's karma, accumulated over previous lives, had prepared him for a life of greatness, reflected in the auspicious smoke she had unthinkingly waved away in her dream.

We find a distinctively Buddhist discussion of dreams outside of historiography in the *Mahāvibhāṣāśāstra*, a scholastic treatise translated into Chinese by Xuanzang in the seventh century, which includes discussion, for instance, of whether or not beings in hell can dream (it concludes that, theoretically, they can) and whether a buddha dreams (he does not). Here, dreams are divided into five categories: dreams induced by external factors such as gods, spells, or medicines; dreams arising from one's experiences; predictive dreams showing glimpses into the future; dreams reflecting one's concerns, hopes, or fears; and dreams caused by illness.[44] The category that matters is the one confirming that dreams can predict the future, but the passage also makes it clear that dreams rise from different causes, some requiring more attention than others. In the same spirit, Zhipan distinguishes between imperial dreams that are favorable to Buddhism and those that are not. After listing a number of accounts of imperial dreams that supposedly encouraged the emperor to promote Buddhism, Zhipan explains that these are owing to "the power of the Buddha" and to "the power of the kind and wholesome faculties of eminent monks." Another instance of a famous imperial dream, in which Song emperor Huizong was visited by Daoist masters, however, represented the work of sorcerers.[45]

Elsewhere, Zanning finds further justification for accepting the predictive power of dreams, first citing the *Summary of the Great Vehicle* to the effect that the waking world and the dream world are equally products of consciousness, and then citing a story from the *Liezi* that describes a kingdom in which the people spend most of their time in sleep, waking up only once every fifty days.[46] For them, the dream world is more real than the waking one, and they take events that occur when they are awake as omens for their dreams. "The dream world and the waking world," he tells us, "are two halves to a whole."[47]

In these cases, whether dreams, prophecies, or omens, there is little work for the historian other than to record them; the actors in the stories themselves understand their significance or discover their significance after consulting specialists. But at times the historian does intervene with an explanation. For example, when describing the birth of the ninth-century monk Tansheng 曇晟 (d. 829), Zanning notes, "his 'fetal robe' [*taiyi* 胎衣, that is, the placenta] naturally left the right shoulder exposed, as if he were wearing a monk's robe." Zanning goes on to comment in an addendum to the biography that this is different from the case of the great Indian master Śāṇavāsin, one of Ānanda's disciples, who was born with a miraculous "fetal robe" that changed as he grew, such that he wore it his entire life, the "robe" disappearing only when he was cremated. For the Chinese monk Tansheng, Zanning tells us, the so-called "robe" was "simply the covering with which all infants are born." Zanning then cites other examples of more miraculous placenta robes and explains that Tansheng's apparently less impressive "fetal robe" should be appreciated in its historical context. Since he was more distant in time from the Buddha than the other cases Zanning cites, Tansheng's omen is in its own way equally remarkable.[48] But even here, the story suggests that at the time of the monk's birth, the implication that a child born with a placenta baring his right shoulder would one day become a monk was clear to all.

Given the prevalence of divination techniques in the society and all serious historians' practice of recording prophetic pronouncements, omens, and dreams, it was natural for Buddhist historians to do the same. On top of this tradition in the dynastic histories that Buddhist historians admired and emulated, monk-historians in China were steeped in an Indian Buddhist literature that is suffused with stories of the Buddha's predictions of the spiritual progress of his disciples and others—who will be reborn in a heaven, who is a stream enterer, who will be born in hell, etc. And the Buddha himself received predictions of his eventual buddhahood in previous lives. In short, for the compiler of a Buddhist history, divination and prophecy were everywhere. To challenge the theoretical possibility of seeing into the future would have been for a literate Buddhist either a bizarre eccentricity or a sign of colossal ignorance.

PROPHECY AND POLITICS

The fact that many everyday types of divination are largely ignored in historical writings alerts us that there is more going on than straightforward documentation of social practice. In historical writing at court, attention to prophecy, omens, and dreams was often driven by a political agenda. This makes sense since most omens in the dynastic histories emerge from and have direct implications for court politics. As we have seen, reporting auspicious omens to the throne (the appearance of nine-stem mushrooms, phoenixes, green dragons, and so on) was a means of winning the favor of the ruler, and reporting inauspicious omens was an indirect form of criticism. An elaborate imperial bureaucracy traded in omens on multiple levels and left behind detailed records for subsequent historians.

The principle behind omens of the imminent decline of a ruler or dynasty was laid out clearly in the second century BCE in a memorial to the throne by the prominent thinker Dong Zhongshu 董仲舒 (179–104 BCE), later recorded in the *History of the Han*: "When a country is about to lose its Way, Heaven first sends down calamities in order to warn [the ruler]. If the ruler does not rectify himself, Heaven sends down omens to frighten him. And if the ruler still does not understand these signs, then catastrophes and losses inevitably occur. From this it is clear that, loving the ruler, Heaven is willing to prevent disorder."[49] In other words, inauspicious omens signify not only that a ruler has lost the approval of Heaven but ultimately that even greater catastrophe is just around the corner unless he takes immediate action to correct his ways. Nonetheless, the historian's task was different from that of the court official or ruler: the historian was not charged with reporting on how a given emperor should respond to events in his reign; it was instead his job to sift through *previous* omens related to the reigns of *previous* rulers. Granted, at times the historian might use a previous case of a failed ruler, signaled beforehand by omens from Heaven, as a warning to a current ruler, but often one senses that historians are simply trying to make sense of the material at their disposal to tidy up a jumbled past.

In this context, when the sixth-century monk Sengyou duly recorded the omens that accompanied the Buddha's birth (the spontaneous appearance of enormous lotus blossoms, withered trees bearing fruit, etc.), in his sixth-century history of the Buddha and his family, he assured his readers that the Buddha was at least as worthy of historical attention as a dynasty-founding emperor. Sengyou draws on the *Buddhāvataṃsakasūtra* to list ten remarkable phenomena that occurred when the Bodhisattva entered his mother's womb. These ten, though distinct from traditional Chinese omens such as sightings of nine-stemmed mushrooms or phoenixes, nonetheless are similar in that they consist of unusual activity in nature: the forest suddenly expands, lotus blossoms spontaneously appear in ponds, trees line up in rows, etc., all in response to the appearance of a great man.[50] Sengyou then turns to the thirty-three omens that immediately preceded the Buddha's birth: desiccated trees suddenly produced leaves and fruit, lotus blossoms bloomed as big as carriage wheels in nearby pools, and so on. But, comparing his sources and with an eye to concision, he lists only ten of the thirty-three, noting, "I do not list the majority of the omens, on which the accounts of the [two scriptures], the *Ruiying* and the *Xiuxing,* are identical."[51] All of this would have been familiar to Sengyou's readers, no doubt themselves raised on similar accounts of miraculous conceptions of dynastic founders in Sima Qian's *Records of the Historian.*[52] The same can be said for the thirty-two marks on the Bodhisattva's body, listed in full by Sengyou in his biography of the Buddha.[53] Again, even Sima Qian, generally considered less interested in miraculous phenomena and strange occurrences than other historians, suggested that the physiognomy of important figures, like the founder of the Han, Liu Bang 劉邦 (256–195 BCE), indicated a glorious destiny.[54] Whether the miraculous appearance of flowers on withered trees or signs on the body of the Bodhisattva, these were at once responses to what had just happened and signs of what was to come. That they had implications for the future is clearest in the case of the marks on the body of the Bodhisattva since in most accounts, including that of Sengyou, the Buddha's father was at first puzzled and asked for guidance as to what these signs meant for the future of his child. Nor was there any conflict in the theory behind the appearance of such omens. In Indian texts, these are spontaneous responses in nature to remarkable figures or events. Although the theory behind such occurrences is not articulated, Chinese notions of "resonance," in which nature resonates with an exceptional figure or event just as one musical note resonates with another, explain the Indian examples perfectly.[55]

Sengyou's *Śākya Genealogy* is representative of the approach of other Chinese Buddhist histories to the place of omens in the life of the Buddha. Daoxuan's history of the Śākya family also recites the ten omens that took place when the Buddha was conceived.[56] The *Comprehensive Account of the Buddhas and the Patriarchs*, though primarily concerned with chronological matters (what year the Buddha was conceived, when he was born, at what age he left his family, etc.), still finds space to cite the *Ruiying jing* and the *Yinguo jing* to note the omens that ornamented the life of the Buddha.[57] The *Transmission of the Lamp Compiled in the Jingde Era*, though primarily interested in Chan genealogy, in its brief account of Śākyamuni's life duly notes the omens attending his birth.[58] This is all very much in keeping with court histories, which typically begin with the life of a dynasty-founding emperor, his birth marked by omens that presage his glorious reign. Historians are at once sifting through and ordering the historical documents before them, littered with omens, and also employing the omens to validate the importance of the figures they write about, whether rulers, buddhas, or eminent monks.

The court historian's practice of glorifying a ruler through omens and the Buddhist historian's commitment to glorifying monastics through omens come together in Daoxuan's work. While recounting how the early seventh-century monk Daomi 道密 (d. ca. 605) was selected by the emperor to escort relics of the Buddha to a prominent monastery, Daoxuan explains that the monastery had previously been a convent and that the emperor had been born there. On the day the child who would one day become Emperor Wen of the Sui was born, "a vermilion light shone in the room, reaching outside the door. Purple vapors filled the courtyard taking the shape of buildings and towers. Its color stained the people's clothing so that all, within and without, were astounded."[59] This is followed by the story of a nun at the convent who, recognizing something special in the child, protects him from harm. Returning to the story of Daomi's delivery of relics to the monastery, Daoxuan recounts that when the relics were placed inside a stupa there, "the entire cloister was filled with light. Between the yellow and the white, speckles of vermilion vapor weaved throughout, remaining for some time before dissipating. Monastics and laypeople from within and without the monastery all saw it."

Both accounts, though linked to Buddhist elements—a monastery, a nun, relics—are primarily testaments to the power and majesty of the ruler. Daoxuan himself notes the origins of these accounts in the writings of the official court historian Wang Shao 王劭 (fl. 601). He tells us that Emperor Wen 文帝 (541–604) commissioned Wang Shao to write a biography of the nun who had raised him, long before his rise to rule. And later Daoxuan notes that his version of the miraculous events surrounding the installment of relics also followed Wang Shao's work. While later historians would criticize Wang Shao for his penchant for "the strange," his accounts of omens appearing as a response to imperial actions would have fit easily into standard court historiography.[60]

Prophetic dreams—essentially internal omens revealed in the mind rather than in nature—tell a similar story, providing clues to what is about to happen in stories the historian relates. The most famous dream in Buddhist history is that of the Buddha's mother who, at the moment of conception, dreamed of a white elephant with six tusks that entered into her through her right side, filling her with joy.[61] When she tells her husband of the dream, he summons a team of prognosticators who agree that she is with child and that the child will one day become a buddha.[62]

As in the case of omens, the story of the Buddha's mother's dream would have resonated with Chinese historians, steeped in a culture of dream interpretation and familiar, for instance, with an account in the *Han shu* of the Empress Xiaojing 孝景皇后 (173–126 BCE) who, pregnant with the future Emperor Wu of the Han 漢武帝, in 156 BCE claimed that she had dreamed of "the sun entering her bosom." When she reported this to her husband, he is said to have remarked, "This is a precious omen."[63] Against the backdrop of fierce and dangerous competition at court—the emperor and his sons had many wives, and the throne did not necessarily pass to the eldest son—this account may well be an accurate depiction of an actual report of a dream. And given the attention to dreams for signs of the future, it is not unreasonable to speculate that the empress may in fact have had the dream she claimed to have had.[64] In court historiography, the birth of the first emperor of the Han dynasty, Liu Bang, was preceded by an (erotic) dream.[65] Not surprisingly, the rise of subsequent emperors, including the first emperor of the Latter Han, were also said to have been predicted in dreams.[66] With precedents like these on both the Indian and Chinese sides, Chinese Buddhist historians were keen to highlight accounts of dreams foretelling the birth of great men among the clergy. Absent such signs, even the most prominent monk was likely to fade into the background of more exotic biographies of monks enveloped in light, fragrance, auspicious dreams, and wondrous omens.

PROPHECY AS PUZZLE

Historians recorded many omens, prophecies, and dreams, and only on rare occasions felt the need to defend their reliability. Nonetheless, they were particularly attracted to cryptic prophecies marked by word play and symbolism. One senses that historians were drawn as much to the challenge and satisfaction of solving the historical puzzles embedded in enigmatic prophecies as they were to advancing any agenda. Happily for them, the two usually overlapped.

Take, for example, the case of the Tang-era nun Zhenru 真如 (d.u.), said to have received "thirteen treasures" (that is, thirteen pieces of extraordinary jade) in 762 from a deity (the Celestial Thearch 天帝). The treasures came with the instruction that, since China was in a state of calamity (in the midst of civil war provoked by the An Lushan Rebellion), the second of these treasures should be employed immediately. The treasures were submitted to a prefect who in turn presented them to the emperor. The standard dynastic histories record that this occurred when the previous emperor, Xuanzong 玄宗 (r. 713-756), had just died. His son, Emperor Suzong 肅宗 (r. 756-762), took the sudden appearance of these marvelous treasures as an auspicious omen. Noting that the pieces of jade were revealed in Chu 楚 and that his eldest son was first enfeoffed with the kingdom of Chu, Suzong turned over power to his son, the future Daizong, the "second treasure" of the prophecy, and declared a new era name: Baoying 寶應, "Response of the Treasures."[67] Three days later, Suzong died.

This in many ways reads like a typical omen recorded in the dynastic histories. A local official presents to the court an auspicious omen that mixes aspects of Buddhism (the vision of a Buddhist nun) and Daoism (the jade objects include talismans and the "white bracelet of the Queen Mother of the West"). These are accepted as signs of Heaven's approval at a time of great political strife and complex court intrigue—the dynasty had not yet recovered from the greatest revolt in its history, and two emperors died within thirteen days of each other as leading figures at court jockeyed for power. Ever alert to reports of omens, court scribes duly recorded the submission of the treasures. But once recorded, long after the events took place and memory of the political circumstances that inspired them had faded, cases like these proved irresistible to subsequent historians, eager to disentangle the puzzles previous historians had left unsolved.

On reviewing the relevant documents, the monastic historian Zuxiu, writing in the twelfth century, zeroes in on the total number of treasures: thirteen. He complains that, while recognizing the significance of the prophecy of the "second treasure" and that it came from Chu, previous historians had missed the point. In particular, he singles out the compiler of the *New History of the Tang*, Ouyang Xiu, famously hostile to Buddhism and a frequent target of Zuxiu's criticism: "From Suzong to Zhaozong, there were thirteen emperors, after which the Tang collapsed. The Supreme Thearch had predicted the fate of the dynasty with great accuracy. The *New Tang History* recorded the thirteen treasures in its 'Annals,' and lists them again in the 'Treatise on the Five Phases,' but never did understand what they predicted. How lamentable!"[68] That is, whether in the moment or later, historians had missed the meaning of the prophecy: the thirteen treasures symbolized the thirteen remaining rulers of the Tang, after which the dynasty would fall.

Here again the Buddhist historian, in the shadow of the more prestigious court historians, demonstrates that he is at least as capable as they (we will see a similar dynamic between monks and academic historians in the twentieth century). In Zuxiu's case, it is hard to see how his argument would have been driven by a desire to assert legitimacy for an emperor or for any Buddhist cause. The rulers belonged to a previous dynasty, long since defunct. A Buddhist nun did play a role in the prophecy, so perhaps demonstrating her accuracy does lend some support to a Buddhist agenda. But the argument seems to have been motivated at least as much by a desire to demonstrate Zuxiu's own historiographical abilities; in moments like these, the historians' hard-won erudition and keen eye for detail allows them to see patterns previous readers missed, to unravel intricate puzzles from the past and clean up the historical record.

A hundred years later, yet another monk, Zhipan, returns to the story, now bringing legitimation more clearly back into the mix by explaining that not only had court historians missed the significance of the thirteen treasures, which in fact predicted the number of emperors before the collapse of the Tang; they had also misidentified the source of the nun's prediction. What they recorded as the "Celestial Thearch" (Tiandi 天帝) must in fact have been Indra (Dishi 帝釋).[69] In other words, this was a *Buddhist* prophecy, not only revealed by a Buddhist nun but also derived from what (in China at least) was a Buddhist deity.[70] Certainly politics, local legitimation, and other polemical agendas lay behind the recording, interpretation, and propagation of prophecies, omens, and prophetic dreams

124 *Prophecy*

in Buddhist historical writing, but the allure of the historian's craft was also a powerful force pulling attention toward hints to the future in the past. We can see this tendency even more clearly in examples of Buddhist historians who employed prophecy as a way of establishing chronology.

PROPHECY AS A HISTORIOGRAPHICAL TOOL FOR ESTABLISHING CHRONOLOGY

We catch a glimpse of prophecy in the service of chronology only rarely in Chinese Buddhist writings, and almost exclusively in relation to India, where dates were scarce, vague, and contradictory. In these instances, unable to line up undated sources and events chronologically, the historian, perhaps with some measure of frustration and reluctance, turns to prophecy to plot out a reliable time line. That is, if the Buddha predicted something would happen at a certain point in time, we can safely assume that it did happen precisely at that point. And since, as we saw in a previous chapter, historians in China presumed to know the Buddha's dates, this allowed them to date the events he foretold as well.

One such event, referred to by a number of Chinese monastic historians, was the date for the splintering of the monastic community in India. According to a version of events commonly accepted in China, interpretation of the monastic regulations early on divided into five distinct schools. Part of the evidence for this division was the prophetic dream of a torn carpet mentioned in passing above in the "India" chapter. Following his predecessors, Zanning in the tenth century related the argument as follows:

> When the Buddha entered nirvana, the Repository of Regulations was compiled. At first, [the monastic community was as harmonious as] the blending of water and cream, or a family trade. Later, [monks drifted apart] like the *shen* 參 and *chen* 辰 constellations,[71] each to different regions, as the community divided into five separate schools.[72] The prophecy of the carpet in the dream was realized,[73] and sectarian discourses were composed.[74]

In the reference to the dream of the carpet, we see the historian hard at work, marshalling his facts in order to provide an accurate account. Zanning is following on a treatise from some four hundred years earlier, referenced above, when

Huijiao similarly referred to a "dream of a carpet" when the Thus-Come-One was still in the world that predicted the division of the monastic regulations into five schools.[75] The slightly earlier *Collection of Records Concerning the Translation of the Tripiṭaka* gives a fuller account, noting, "When the Buddha was in the world, there was a householder who dreamed of a white carpet that was suddenly torn into five pieces. Startled, he went before the Buddha to ask what this meant. The Buddha replied, 'This means that after my extinction, the repository of the regulations will be divided into five schools.'"[76] Here, our chroniclers draw on prophecy simply to determine the precise number of divisions of the monastic community since different sources described the divisions of the monastic regulations differently.

Zhipan takes a similar tack when he draws on a story that recounts that just before leaving the palace, the Buddha predicted that his pregnant wife would remain pregnant for a full six years before giving birth to his child. The story itself is interesting, but for our purposes it is Zhipan's use of the story to establish chronology in the Buddha's life that is most intriguing. Having established that the Buddha was born in 1003 BCE, Zhipan wants to chart the Buddha's life year by year. But different sources did this in different ways. In particular, Zhipan is determined to ascertain how old the Buddha was when he left the palace, how long he practiced austerities, and how old he was at the time of his enlightenment. Zhipan argues that the Buddha left the palace at twenty-five and practiced austerities until he was thirty, at which point he achieved enlightenment. He then preached for fifty years, dying at the age of eighty. But the sources were far from uniform, with some claiming the Buddha left his home at the age of nineteen and others at the age of twenty-nine. Below I translate the whole convoluted passage. In the midst of sophisticated analysis and erudite recitation of sources, note how prophecy slips into the argument.

> The *Auspicious Response*, the *Causes and Conditions*, the *Central Origin*, and the *Great Treatise* all say that the Bodhisattva left his home at nineteen.[77] The *Life of Śākyamuni to His Twelfth Year*, the four *Āgamas* (that is, the *Incremental*, the *Middle Length*, the *Various*, and the *Longer*), the *Scripture of the Appearance of Light*, and Vasumitra's commentary all say that he left home at twenty-nine.[78] Which should we follow?
>
> Now, the Thus-Come-One lived to the age of eighty. If we take away the fifty years during which he preached the Dharma, then we can accept the

Brahma's Net, the *Markless Samādhi,* and the *Storehouse of Valuables* scriptures, which claim that he achieved enlightenment at thirty.[79] If we take away from thirty the six years during which he practiced austerities, then we can accept the position of Jingxi 荊溪 [a.k.a. Zhanran] that the Buddha left home at the age of twenty-five,[80] which accords with the theory proposed in the *Storehouse of Valuables.*

To determine the chronology, there are two points that can be used to verify this position [i.e., that the Buddha left home at twenty-five]. First, [if we posit that he was twenty-five at the time] he left home, once he had practiced six years of austerities, his age then accords exactly with that at which he is said to have achieved enlightenment.

Second, when he was about to leave home, he pointed at the belly of his consort and said: "Six years from now, you will give birth to a child." Later, in the year in which he achieved enlightenment, she did in fact give birth to Rāhula. According to the *Scripture of the Wise and the Foolish,* "After leaving home to cultivate the path, he practiced austerities for six years and obtained complete insight."[81] The *Scripture of What Had Never Been Before* says, "The Prince fled to the mountains and marshes where he diligently practiced austerities for six years and achieved buddhahood before returning to his kingdom."[82] The *Extensive Display Scripture* says, "Six years after his father, the king, had heard that the prince had achieved buddhahood, he ordered Udaya to invite him back, saying, 'It has been twelve years since you parted.'"[83] It also says, "The Buddha returned to the kingdom, entered the palace, and sat down. Rāhula came to ask after him, at which point the ministers became suspicious, saying, 'The prince abandoned the kingdom twelve years ago. How is it that he has a child?'"

Scriptural passages like these all insist that he became a buddha six years after leaving home and returned to his kingdom six years after that. Working backward, it is clear that he must have been twenty-five years old when he left home. Gushan 孤山 [a.k.a. Zhiyuan 智圓] claimed that the Buddha wandered for five years, but there is no basis for this.[84] Shenzhi 神智 [a.k.a. Congyi 從義] in his *Supplemental Notes* discusses the different theories in detail.[85] Please consult Jingxi for the correct interpretation.[86]

In this impressive display of textual mastery and close analysis, prophecy drifts in almost as an afterthought—one piece of evidence among many ("when he was about to leave home, he pointed at the belly of his consort and said: 'Six years from now, you will give birth to a child'"). More jarring to modern sensibilities is that in the midst of the arithmetic, Zhipan matter-of-factly accepts as a given a pregnancy said to have taken six full years to come to term. In either case, there is no clear agenda here.

Nowhere does Zhipan explain why we should care about the Buddha's age at the time he left home. One can imagine reasons this might matter, but for Zhipan this seems not to have been important. In this instance, prophecy was so much a part of the historian's repertoire that there was no need to justify its use or question its reliability; the point instead was to recognize its value and apply it to reconstructing chronology.

PLAYING WITH TIME

For all of their confidence in the cyclical nature of history, even in cases where their ultimate goal was to use the past to understand or affect the present, Buddhist historians in China were primarily concerned with the past. When unearthing and ordering the past, their vision was relentlessly chronological: ideally, history is related as a series of events beginning with an origin and proceeding in a linear direction through time. Zanning's *Brief History of the Clergy*, compiled in the tenth century, was intended, at least in part, as a manual for court bureaucrats to quickly bone up on the history of key Buddhist terms and institutions, so it is a series of disjointed entries rather than a continuous narrative. But even in this book, closely wedded to the present, entries begin with a search for origins in an attempt to start each story at the beginning before proceeding chronologically up to the present. He begins his entry on monasteries with the foundation story of the first Buddhist monastery in China; the entry on the history of the translation of the monastic regulations begins with the first translation; his essay on Chinese monks traveling to the West begins with a review of different theories of who was the first, and so on. The same concern with origins inspired Zuxiu in his twelfth-century *Comprehensive Discussion and Chronology of Buddhism Compiled in the Longxing Era*, a chronological history of Buddhism in China, to begin with Emperor Ming's famous dream that prompted him to dispatch an emissary abroad to introduce Buddhism to China. Though a collection of biographies rather than a strict chronology, Huijiao's *Biographies of Eminent Monks* begins with a biography of Shemoteng 攝摩騰 (d.u.), according to tradition, the first monk to be welcomed to China after having been summoned in response to Emperor Ming's dream. Zanning goes a step further in his brief entry on the coming of Buddhism to China by suggesting that, while Buddhism arrived in China already during the Zhou dynasty, the relevant records were destroyed by the First Emperor in the Qin.[87] In other words, virtually every historian tracing the history of Buddhism in China wanted to start at the beginning, to pinpoint a particular moment and mark it as significant.

Histories that attempt to stretch back to India, in turn, begin with the Buddha; we saw above the concern in the *Brief History of the Clergy* and other texts with the dates of the Buddha. "Lamp histories" like the *Transmission of the Lamp Compiled in the Jingde Era* go back even further, beginning with the six buddhas that preceded Śākyamuni.

Once the historian establishes origins, he proceeds chronologically. And unlike, say, the *Mahāvaṃsa*, in a Chinese historical work, the reader always knows where they are in time. In China, the primary reference point is almost always political time. In the *Biographies of Eminent Monks*, each entry is preceded by the name of the dynasty in which the monk was active. And within each biography, the historian frequently interrupts to provide dates for particular events, almost always according to the year within a reign period of a dynasty; at times other systems were employed, such as the Chinese sexagesimal cycle or, less commonly, the date in relation to the nirvana of the Buddha. The same holds true for works like the *Comprehensive Discussion and Chronology of Buddhism Compiled in the Longxing Era* and the *Chronology of Lineages and Transmission* (Zongtong bianlun 宗統編論) that are strictly chronological.

Rarely do Chinese historians interrupt the narrative to refer to events from before those under discussion, that is, the past of the past, or what one scholar inspired by the pluperfect tense (e.g., By the time I arrived at home, *he had eaten*) has termed the "plupast" (e.g., Monk A arrived at the city of such and such. Ten years previously, Monk B had arrived at the same city).[88] At times a biographer refers to the plupast to put a figure in context. When recounting Dao'an's life and coming to his compilation of the first detailed catalogue of Buddhist scriptures, Huijiao explains that throughout the previous Han and Wei dynasties, the names of translators and dates of translation were not recorded. Similarly, when noting that Dao'an took "Shi" (Śākyamuni) as his surname, Huijiao states that in the Han, Wei, and early Jin, this *had not been* the practice.[89] Huijiao's biography of Faxian explains that he traveled farther than the Han-dynasty emissary Zhang Qian 張騫 (d. 114 BCE) because between the times of Zhang and Faxian, paths had been cut in the rock and bridges constructed over dangerous passages.[90]

Straightforward temporal shifts like this provide context, but they are far removed from a historical work like the *Mahāvaṃsa*, which *plays* with the past, often primarily for literary effect, shifting from the historical present to the time of the authors and back to the time of the Buddha, or even the previous buddhas, and occasionally relating events from past lives to explain the event under discussion. While Chinese Buddhist historians at times speculate on the past lives of important figures, such references are rare, and seldom integral to the account. Nor were Chinese historians in general fond of analepsis (flashbacks); that is, in China, only very rarely is any event experienced by a single figure presented out of chronological order.[91] This is true of all of Chinese history, perhaps in part owing to the self-conscious attempts of Chinese writers to distinguish the work of serious history from that of mere storytellers; not unlike the ways historians cite sources and dwell on the verification of names and dates at the expense of narrative, Chinese historians had little taste for flashbacks or revelations of past events late in a story. And despite the potential for using karma and rebirth to explain historical events, in China even Buddhist historians preferred a strict chronology.

Turning to the focus of this chapter, the exception to this tendency to tell time step by step, from past to present, is in reference in the past to sudden leaps into the future. And if analepsis is rare in Chinese historical writing, prolepsis (foreshadowing) is common, particularly in Buddhist historiography. This is not to say that Buddhist historians were unconcerned with predicting the future beyond the present—all of them believed in the inexorable decline of the Dharma—but as historians, for the most part they discussed the decline of the Dharma only as it was useful in explaining the past.

Playing with time brought order to the past, and hence order to the present in its own uncomfortable relation to the future. Aside from the quotidian references to dreams, omens, and fetal peculiarities signaling the birth of an eminent monk, Buddhist historians were drawn to signs of more momentous changes, presaging key events in the political history of Chinese Buddhism. Historical predictions, that is, events discovered to have been foreshadowed by omens or prophecies, helped to mitigate the shock of radical historical change. Perhaps no event in these histories attracted as much attention as the most devastating persecution of Buddhism in premodern China, by Emperor Wu of the Tang, known as the "Persecution of the Dharma During the Huichang era" 會昌法難 from 841-46, reaching its peak in 845.[92] Zanning, for instance, recounts the history of a monastery that was destroyed during the Huichang period, noting that just before the campaign of persecution, seven glowing relics emerged from the monastery's stupa and flew off to the West. Moreover, in the year in which the persecution was to begin, a date tree suddenly dried up.[93] Only when Buddhism returned to favor just a few years later with the following emperor did the tree again flourish. Zanning then raises the question of whether or not such periods of favor and persecution are pre-established. Specifically, he argues that even the Buddha Dharma is not exempt from the general pattern of the "four marks of existence" (*sixiang* 四相): arising, abiding, changing, and ceasing.

> The times are indeed established; the points on the sundial cannot be altered. For example, before the Huichang persecution, *śarīra* scattered, and the date tree withered. We know that when the fortune of decline grows in strength, the fortune of ascent must be weak; it cannot hold off the declining fortune. When Buddhism ascended again during the Dazhong era [in 847], the fortune of decline could not withstand the fortune of ascent. If [the Buddhist teachings] were not affected by the changes of the "four marks" then there would be no pre-established times for its ascent and decline. But the teachings are themselves conditioned elements, and as such cannot escape change. Alas![94]

In moments like these the historian employs his grasp of the vagaries of Buddhist institutions over time—not just in the vast cycles of decline and rise but also in the shorter episodes of imperial favor and persecution—and his attention to the signs that these events were to happen, overlooked by contemporaries. For all of its ups and downs, such prophecies tell us, history is not an aimless flux. Here the historian no longer simply documents events but penetrates beneath them to the forces that propel history, revealed in the cracks in time that produce omens. In fact, modern historians now recognize the Huichang persecution as marking profound changes in Chinese Buddhism; it *was* a radical break with the past. Yet it is in precisely these moments of rupture that the premodern historian is at pains to uncover evidence that the change was not as rapid and unpredictable as it first seemed, that all was foreshadowed well in advance.[95]

CONCLUSION

Modern historians of Buddhism look at the period leading up to major rebellions or persecutions of Buddhism for clues to shifts in court politics or underlying economic trends that sent history down the path to discord, dissolution, and violence. We look at the opening passages in biographies of prominent monks for signs that their class background, early education, or region of birth may have paved the way for a career of influence and innovation. Premodern historians interpreted history differently. While they too were sensitive to politics, class, geography, and, to a lesser extent, economics, they put confidence in another interpretive tool that was only abandoned in Buddhist historiography in the twentieth century: clues to what was to come embedded in omens, dreams, and prophecies.

The preceding examples, a small sampling of a wealth of material, should be sufficient to illustrate the extent to which Buddhist historiography in China is riddled with predictions of the future revealed in the past. On the one hand, this is not surprising, given the ubiquity of the mantic arts throughout Chinese history in general and in Chinese historiography in particular—Buddhist or otherwise. But while it is easy to point out the prevalence of prophecy in Chinese Buddhist historical writings, the reasons Buddhist historians returned to such stories again and again are less apparent.

Prophecy is seldom used to illustrate Buddhist doctrine. At most, in a few rare examples Buddhist historians explain prophecy through Buddhist scholastics—a division of dreams into categories in which only the Buddhist ones matter, or the assertion that at heart the world of dreams and the waking world are the same. But in these cases, the doctrine is invoked to explain the prophecy and not the other way around. With the notable exception of the spiritual predictions of a buddha explaining future rebirths of those he encounters, most of the predictions covered here could have been arrived at by non-Buddhist means—divination stalks or tortoise shells, astrology or calendrical calculations.

More fundamentally, only rarely are these prophecies of what will happen beyond the time of the historian; they are instead usually *ex eventus* predictions that had already proved true by the time the historian put ink to paper. Buddhist history in China remains, perhaps not surprisingly, firmly anchored in the past, not the future. Why then is there such interest in prophecy on the part of historians intent on reconstructing the past?

At times in Buddhist histories, predictions of the future were used for more strictly historiographical ends—for instance, reconstructing the history of the monastic regulations on the basis of supposedly earlier predictions of what was supposed to happen. Once it was accepted that a prophecy was legitimate, it made sense to use the framework of the prophecy to establish a timeline, especially when, as in the case of Indian materials, dates were scarce. And at times prophecy served raw polemical purposes, demonstrating the attainments of an eminent monk or suggesting imperial support for the Buddhist cause. We saw this clearly in the case of Zhipan, who argued against skeptics of Buddhist prophecy by insisting that ordinary people were not qualified to question the power of Buddhist foresight and claiming that the second emperor of his own dynasty had himself received a Buddhist prophecy in a previous existence. For the current emperor, he seems to suggest, to trifle with the Buddhist institutions that protect and interpret such prophecies would be folly.

Often, however, the predictions serve little purpose even within the stories themselves. Cryptic augurs pass by with little consequence since no one understands them until they are fulfilled. At times, those credited with predictions of the future are obscure figures of no historical importance. Ultimately, the forces driving the attention to prophecy were probably more literary than political or chronological. Predictions of the future in the past are inherently suspenseful, hints hanging in the reader's mind that drive the narrative to a conclusion in which at last all of it makes sense. Finally, omens, dreams, and prophecy served the overriding historiographical concern with linking together moments embedded in the flow of time. In historical writings, prophecy tied time together, but rather than projecting the present into the future as in a visit to a fortune-teller, prophecy linked together any two points in the past. In this stew of motivations and possibilities, there was no need to choose one intention over another: politics, belief, craft, and comfort all pointed to the value of documenting and interpreting predictions of the future in the past.

CHAPTER 5

Genealogy

In a strange but, on reflection, logical development, men and women who were said to have "left the family" to become monks or nuns, who abandoned their secular surnames and vowed to forgo producing offspring even if it meant cutting off the family line, eventually came to organize their connections to the past and future with terms and metaphors borrowed from the traditional family. Nowhere is this more evident than in Chinese Buddhist historiography.

Up until about the year 1000, the primary genre for Buddhist historiography in China was biography, specifically large collections of biographies grouped according to topic, exemplified by the genre "biographies of eminent monks," which divided accounts of monastics into categories such as translators, exegetes, ascetics, and so on. In addition to collecting the biographies, these works included essays on each of the categories, discussing the history and issues specific to translation, exegesis, asceticism, meditation, wonder working, etc. But the three centuries following the year 1000 (more or less) was a period of great experimentation in which Buddhist historians tried other formats, often modeling their works on court histories. Some attempted, for instance, to create a Buddhist history in the image of the most famous of all Chinese historical works, the *Records of the Historian*, which combines annals of a succession of rulers; chronological tables of major events; historical treatises on topics such as music, ritual, and geography; "hereditary houses" (*shijia*) for semi-independent states; and finally biographies, some of which are grouped into categories like "cruel officials," "assassins," and "jesters."[1] The representative Buddhist work to follow this model is Zhipan's *Comprehensive Account of the Buddhas and the Patriarchs*, which in place of imperial annals gives an account of the life of the Buddha, and in place of treatises on music and ritual provides treatises on pure land practices and cosmology.

Inspired by the monumental eleventh-century *Comprehensive Mirror to Aid in Government* by Sima Guang—chronology on a grand scale (at over two million characters, over four times as long as the already lengthy *Records of the Historian*)[2] covering most of Chinese history up to that time, from 403 BCE to the year before the founding of the Song dynasty in 959 CE—in the twelfth century the monk Zuxiu produced the *Comprehensive Discussion and Chronology of Buddhism Compiled in the Longxing Era*, a chronological history of Chinese Buddhism, beginning with the entry of Buddhism to China in the Han up to the beginning of the Song dynasty.

In sum, large ambitious models for innovative historiography were readily available in works by court historians, and enterprising monks were eager to try out these formats on Buddhist material. Nonetheless, what came to be the dominant genre of Buddhist historiography in China from about the year 1000 was instead genealogical history, organized according to lines of descent in which, in place of fathers and sons, historians arranged monastic masters and their disciples. Genealogical records were hardly new when Buddhists adapted the format to their own needs—records of royal descent lines were among the earliest records of any kind in China.[3] And genealogical records or "family histories" (*pudie* 譜牒 or later *zupu* 族譜 or *jiapu* 家譜) were early on established as a genre of historical writing.[4] But such works were necessarily limited by the reach of a given family; in the Buddhist case, historians eventually recognized that virtually every monk could in some way be tied to one lineage or another in a vast genealogical tree with innumerable branches in which all monastics shared the same surname: Shi, short for Śākyamuni. Every monk and nun could in this way trace their monastic transmission line back to the Adam-like figure of the Buddha.

As the tradition of Buddhist genealogical history reached its maturity (I will cover the formative period of the genre below), a series of massive tomes appeared one after the other, beginning with the *Transmission of the Lamp Compiled in the Jingde Era*, completed in 1004, which focused on Chan monks, organized according to master-disciple relations in one resplendent genealogical tree, including over 1,700 biographies stretching from the age of the six buddhas who preceded Śākyamuni all the way up to the early Song dynasty. This work was followed by four more Chan genealogical collections together compiled into an immense collection, the *Compendium of the Five Lamps*, completed in

1252. The "lamp" in the titles of these works was their central metaphor: every monk they describe passes on the Dharma, like a flame transmitted from one lamp to another.⁵ These two works in particular continued to be widely read in subsequent centuries, inciting comment and controversy up into at least the seventeenth century, though many more works in the same mold emerged to update or revise them.⁶

The rise of Buddhist genealogical history entailed a shift not just in format but in content as well. Though still essentially biographical, the content of the biographies of monks in these works is markedly different from traditional monastic biography. Previous biographies in the eminent monks series drew on prefaces, epigraphical biographies composed by disciples or local literati soon after a monk's death, and miracle tales. Some composed in ornate prose, others more prosaic, traditional monastic biographies focused on events in the subject's life and on the works he composed. In contrast, compilers of the "transmission of the lamp" genre relied almost exclusively on the "recorded sayings" of monks, focusing on dialogues that supposedly took place between master and disciple.⁷ The new style of biography often reads more like theater than history. And unlike the language of traditional biography—sometimes flowery and full of allusions, sometimes direct and concise, but always elegant—the dialogues in the genealogical histories are full of colloquialisms and all manner of crude jokes and vulgar references, making them a treasure trove for linguists intent on reconstructing the history of spoken Chinese.⁸

To cite one among hundreds of possible examples, consider the biography of the Tang monk Linji 臨濟 (d. 866). The tenth-century *Song Biographies of Eminent Monks* includes a conventional biography of the Chan master, providing the basic information about Linji's secular surname, place of origin, the master he studied under, and where he established his own monastery—in the city of Linji. It briefly characterizes his teachings ("Those who had cast aside the preaching of scriptures and treatises were drawn to his hall. There the master showed them the essentials of the mind"), and concludes by noting the precise date of his death (in 866) and the imperial bequeathal of a posthumous name and stupa for him. The whole biography takes up a mere 113 characters.⁹ This is traditional biography in the "eminent monk" mold—concise, elegant, and informative.

In contrast, the thirteenth-century *Compendium of the Five Lamps* biography of Linji is close to five thousand words long. It provides only cursory details about Linji's background before launching into an account of his first encounter with his master, Huangbo 黃檗 (d. ca. 850). When Linji approaches Huangbo to ask for the "meaning of the Buddha's teachings," even before he has finished asking the question, Huangbo strikes him. This happens three times until, frustrated at his inability to understand the intent behind the master's blows, Linji takes his leave and seeks the counsel of another master, Dayu 大愚 (d.u.). When the puzzled Linji relates the beatings he has received at the hands of Huangbo, Dayu responds, "What a kind old lady Huangbo is to tire himself in this way on your behalf. And still you come here to ask if you have done something wrong." At this moment, the biography tells us, Linji, at last enlightened, exclaims, "In the end there isn't much to Huangbo's Buddhist teachings after all." At this point, Linji has once again let himself in for physical and verbal abuse, but this time, freshly enlightened, he is ready with a response. "Dayu grabbed hold of him and said, "You little bedwetter! Just now you came here asking, 'Have I done something wrong?' Now you say, 'There isn't much to Huangbo's Buddhist teachings.' What truth have you seen? Speak quickly, speak quickly!" Master Linji then punched Dayu three times in the ribs. Freeing himself, Dayu said, "Your master is Huangbo. This has nothing to do with me."[10] Linji returns to Huangbo for another series of dramatic encounters, punctuated by shouting, beating, and cryptic comments. Stories in the transmission of the lamp genre are filled with thousands of similar accounts of what modern scholars term "encounter dialogue." These encounters, which eventually formed the basis of *kōan* ("public cases"; Ch. *gongan* 公案) in which subsequent writers comment on the exchanges with their own abstruse commentary, have long attracted both popular and scholarly attention, and Chan specialists have taken a variety of approaches to explain how these slippery texts function and how they should be read.[11]

But if here we set aside the shift in the content of the individual biographies and consider instead the structure into which they were placed—that is, genealogical trees—the implications for historiography are just as important. The *Transmission of the Lamp Compiled in the Jingde Era* is a good example of Chan genealogy in its mature form. It begins with biographies devoted to the "seven buddhas of the past" (that is, the most recent seven buddhas whose biographical details are described in the scriptures) beginning with an account of the ancient buddha Vipaśyin and ending with the most recent buddha, Śākyamuni. These biographies of buddhas from an unimaginably distant past are disappointingly short, quoting from the *Dīrghāgama* a few details for each (the age in which they appeared; their class, surname, parents' names; the name of the tree under which each achieved enlightenment, and so on) and providing a brief *gāthā* each was said to have spoken.

The connection between the ancient buddhas is not explicit (just how did one "transmit the lamp" to the other when they were divided by vast stretches of time?), but the assumption is that they are in some way the ancestors of the figures to follow. The genealogical pattern for the text begins in earnest with the biography of Śākyamuni. More detailed than the preceding biographies, the account of Śākyamuni provides dates for his birth (the fourth day of the eighth month of the twenty-fourth year of King Zhao of the Zhou 周昭王—1029 BCE), the day he left his family, his enlightenment, and his death. But what marks the biography as genealogical is the reference to the special link between Śākyamuni and one of his disciples, Mahākāśyapa. Here the cosmological time linking the lives of previous buddhas shrinks down to the more manageable time of human life spans.

The text explains that the Buddha, in a key moment for Chan history, "told his disciple Mahākāśyapa, 'I confer upon you the subtle, correct Dharma that is true, devoid of marks, the marvelous mind of nirvana, the pure Dharma eye. You should keep and uphold it.'" The Buddha goes on to intone a *gāthā* and to confer his robe on Mahākāśyapa, who vows to follow the Buddha's instructions. The transmission complete, the Buddha passes into nirvana.[12] Like a list of a succession of rulers, each legitimated by their connection to the lineage, for the ancient period the Chan lineage establishes a single line of legitimate caretakers of the Dharma, with only one person charged with this duty at a time.

The biography of Śākyamuni, including his conferral of the flame on Mahākāśyapa, is followed by a separate biography of Mahākāśyapa, now listed as the "first patriarch," which gives a slightly more detailed account of Śākyamuni's instructions before recounting how Mahākāśyapa conferred the Dharma on Ānanda. And so the story proceeds over time and through patriarchs, each linked to the previous by a physical meeting and a formal acknowledgment of conferral (see appendix 2: lineage chart 1). At the twenty-fourth patriarch, Siṃha, the trunk branches off to include multiple disciples, but in each generation only one continues the line of transmission. With the twenty-eighth patriarch, Bodhidharma, this true Dharma comes to China and is conferred upon Chinese monks. Once the lineage tree is transplanted in China, subsequent developments in India can be safely ignored.

For the early patriarchs, "superfluous" disciples are noted from time to time, but these are branches off a central trunk. It is only when the lineage reaches the

Sixth Chinese Patriarch, Huineng, that the trunk itself divides, eventually, in the decades following the appearance of the *Transmission of the Lamp Compiled in the Jingde Era*, splitting into five main branches, the "Five Houses" of Chan (see appendix 2: lineage chart 2).[13] In subsequent centuries, the genealogical tree continued to grow from the foundation of this basic structure.

The new format brought a new sense of urgency and relevance to Buddhist historiography. Much more than in other genres of Buddhist historical writing—chronology, collections of biographies, or some combination of the two—genealogical history selects clear winners and losers; a given monk from the past is on a main branch or a minor one or, even worse, not on the tree at all. Just as importantly, the genealogical tree either links *the author and his contemporaries* to a specific lineage or leaves them out. Both of these factors shaped how books in this new historical genre were written and how they were received.[14]

WHAT IS AT STAKE IN GENEALOGICAL HISTORY?

The decisions historians made in arranging their subjects in lines of transmission carried heavy consequences since their contemporaries and later monks scrutinized their texts to verify or challenge how their own teachers' teachers fit into the lineage. For a sense of the emotional charge and practical consequences of these genealogical decisions, consider the case of the seventeenth-century monk Feiyin Tongrong 費隱通容 (1593–1661), who was forced to flee arrest and go into hiding in response to a successful legal suit brought against him by irate monks, furious over his genealogical history of Chan, the *Strict Transmission of the Five Lamps* (*Wudeng yantong* 五燈嚴統).

Officially, the charge brought against him was sedition for challenging imperial authority because in his work Feiyin questioned the traditional explanation of the branches that eventually fed into the "five houses" laid out in the *Transmission of the Lamp Compiled in the Jingde Era*, which by his day was a part of the imperially sponsored official version of the Buddhist canon. But monks had for centuries questioned this or that point in all manner of texts contained in the canon without legal consequences. The real source of outrage was more immediate: monks in a rival Chan lineage felt that they had been slighted in this new version of the history of the lineage; Feiyin's rearrangement had placed their ancestors in the category of "affiliation unknown," leaving their followers off the tree.[15]

This is an extreme example of the sort of sectarian infighting over controversial historical works that became commonplace from about the year 1000, with Tiantai monks criticizing lineages proposed by Chan monks, Chan monks attacking Tiantai lineages, Chan monks picking apart earlier nonsectarian works for not being sectarian enough, and Chan monks of one lineage lambasting proposed transmission lines for other Chan lineages.[16] These disputes were rooted in even earlier tensions during the formative period of lineage histories.

While we have already seen examples of Buddhist historians critical of other Buddhist historians before the rise of genealogical history (after all, historians who don't disagree with other historians hardly deserve the name), sectarian tension and dispute are inherent in the genealogical genre in a way that they are not in other types of historical writing.[17] It is not just the prevalence of dispute swirling around genealogical histories but the level of intensity that is striking. In Buddhist historical works in other genres, the primary danger for the historian was in somehow offending the state. Zanning's *Song Dynasty Biographies of Eminent Monks* primarily covers monks who lived during the preceding Tang dynasty. It is called the "Song" biographies because it was compiled by order of the Song emperor Taizong. Not surprisingly, in the preface to the text and at various points in the text itself, Zanning praises the Song imperial family in effusive language typical of materials submitted to emperors. None of the preceding dynasties compares to the imperial support for Buddhism under the "august" and "mighty" Song.[18] And throughout, the compilers of the *Song Biographies of Eminent Monks* are careful to avoid "taboo characters"—that is, characters that appear in the names of members of the imperial family. All of this is very much in keeping with the dynamics in the compilation of the dynastic or "standard" histories (*zhengshi* 正史) at court to recount the history of the preceding dynasty. Here too, the most immediate danger to the compilers was in somehow offending the hypersensitive sensibilities of the ruling family. Needless to say, treatment of the fall of the previous dynasty and rise of the new one were particularly fraught. Staying with the example of the *Song Biographies of Eminent Monks*, the chief compiler of the text, Zanning, before rising in the administrative ranks of the Song dynasty, was himself a prominent figure in one of the states (the Wu-Yue kingdom) that surrendered to the Song. In other words, like many of the monk historians I discuss in this book, he was thoroughly familiar with the precarious world of court politics. That said, *within Buddhist circles*, before the advent of genealogical history the composition of a historical text was not especially dangerous. Doctrinal positions, rather than historical ones, sparked controversy. In contrast, Buddhist genealogical history was contentious from the outset.

THE RISE OF BUDDHIST GENEALOGICAL HISTORY

Scholars in recent decades have had great success in excavating and clarifying the complex formative period in the creation of the Chan and Tiantai lineages that appear in mature form only centuries later in the large, polished, well-sponsored historical works in the early Song. In a few cases, the authors of early lineage histories are well-known figures. In the Tiantai lineage, for example, the prominent monk Guanding, disciple of one of the most prolific and eminent exegetes in Chinese Buddhist history, Zhiyi, was largely responsible for drawing on a combination of Indian and Chinese sources to construct a lineage history stretching from Zhiyi back through two Chinese masters to India, and eventually all the way back to the Buddha.[19] Guanding does this very briefly, in a few comments as part of a preface to his teacher's magnum opus, the *Mohe zhiguan*.[20] In these comments, Guanding draws on the *Fufa zang yinyuan zhuan*, an earlier work discussed above in the "India" chapter that presents a lineage starting with the Buddha and ending with the twenty-third patriarch, Siṃha, who, tragically, is killed by an evil ruler, thus ending the transmission of the true Dharma (see appendix 2: lineage chart 1).

This dramatic history of the death of an Indian lineage would seem to offer little hope to a Chinese one. But happily, Guanding tells us, a previous Indian patriarch, number thirteen in the list, preserved the correct Dharma in a book, the *Dazhidu lun*. Long after, Guanding's master's master's master, the Chinese monk Huiwen, recovered the Dharma by correctly understanding the *Dazhidu lun*. He then transmitted the Dharma to the monk Huisi, who transmitted it to Zhiyi, Guanding's master. Far from a fully formed history, these are a few lines at the start of a preface to a doctrinal work. Guanding gives only minimal biographical details for each of the patriarchs, provides no dates, cites no sources, and gives little justification for the leap in the lineage from the person-to-person transmission in India to the transmission to China via a text. It wasn't until much later that this minimalist lineage history was expanded upon as the foundation of a grand, full history of the Tiantai lineage in the great Tiantai historical works of the Song: the *Comprehensive Orthodox Transmission of the Śākya Clan* and the *Comprehensive Account of the Buddhas and the Patriarchs*.[21]

The motivation for Guanding to forge these ties from Zhiyi back through a succession of masters in China, and through a book to tap into an Indian lineage all the way back to the Buddha, was in part presumably to legitimize the large and original doctrinal text attached to Guanding's preface. The work you are about to read, he implies, was written by the legitimate and singular heir to the Buddha's true Dharma. He may also have been eager to establish the pedigree of his master at a time when Guanding and his monastic brothers were attempting to establish a major monastery with imperial support.[22] At roughly the same time, Guanding asserted in another text that Zhiyi, together with his teacher, Huisi, had long ago in previous incarnations been present when the Buddha pronounced the *Lotus Scripture* on Vulture Peak.[23] In short, the spare Tiantai lineage Guanding sketched out in his preface was part of wider efforts to promote a text, a teacher, and a monastery in order to garner respect, readership, and patronage.

Chan monks made similar efforts on a broader scale in order to establish a lineage for their own teachings, teachers, and monasteries. As in the case of the Tiantai lineage, the Chan lineage began with relatively simple lines of descent. One of the great contributions of modern Chan scholarship has been to piece together the formation of the lineage through meticulous work on a wide range of texts that had effectively disappeared from the historical record until they were rediscovered in the twentieth century.

Sometime in the late seventh and early eighth century, Chan genealogical histories begin to appear in works by obscure figures far from the erudite, court-centered world of most of the Buddhist historians I discuss. Among the earliest, the *Record of the Teachers and Disciples of the Laṅkāvatāra Scripture* (*Lengqie shizi ji* 楞伽師資記), compiled by a monk named Jingjue 淨覺 (683–ca.750), provides a list of patriarchs in eight generations, beginning with the Indian master Guṇabhadra (Ch. Qiunabatuoluo 求那跋陀羅, 394–468)—who it claims was the teacher of Bodhidharma—and ending with the disciples of Shenxiu 神秀 (606?–706), known subsequently as the representative of the "Northern School" of Chan.[24] Another lineage history from roughly the same period, the *Record of the Transmission of the Dharma Treasure* (*Chuan fabao ji* 傳法寶記), presents nearly the same lineage with some variations—supplying the names of a few Indian patriarchs and placing a monk named Faru 法如 (638–689) immediately after Hongren—but still arrives at the end at the patriarch Shenxiu[25] (see appendix 2: lineage chart 3).

These Northern School histories are primarily collections of teachings on the mind, emptiness, and meditation, draped over a bare skeleton of genealogical history; they devote little time to the deeds of the patriarchs, focusing instead on their words. For understanding what was at stake in the genealogical structure of these works, the final line of the *Record of the Teachers and Disciples of the Laṅkāvatāra Scripture* is revealing. "Since the [Liu] Song dynasty [420–479], generation after generation of Chan masters of great virtue have followed one on the other, beginning with Tripiṭaka Master Guṇabhadra of the Song. Over generations, the lamp was transmitted up to the Tang dynasty. In total, there were eight generations. Of those who obtained the Way and reaped its fruits, there were twenty-four men."[26] Scholars have puzzled over this last number—twenty-four men. Why twenty-four?[27] In his notes on the text, the modern scholar Yanagida Seizan explains the number as consisting of, first of all, the first six patriarchs beginning with Guṇabhadra up to Hongren. If we add to them the eleven monks the text mentions who were disciples of Hongren, we get to seventeen. Add to these the four disciples of Hongren's disciple Shenxiu and we reach twenty-one. The text also mentions in passing two additional disciples of Bodhidharma. This brings us to twenty-three. For the final, twenty-fourth disciple, Yanagida posits the author of our text, Jingjue[28] (appendix 2: lineage chart 4).

Even if this ingenious, convoluted explanation is wrong, it can still serve to illustrate what is at stake in genealogical history. The author is almost always an inheritor of the family legacy; the story he tells is his own. This is true to a certain degree for virtually all of the Buddhist historians I discuss in this book to the extent that they considered themselves Buddhists. In many cases, such as the biographies of eminent monks genre, the historian was a Buddhist monk recounting the history of Buddhist monks and championing their cause. But the genealogical genre is much more limited in scope, and much more personal. Moreover, its power lies in the delicate lines that connect each patriarch to another and every branch back to the trunk. In the loose Tiantai lineage Guanding constructed, the line could jump from India to China merely by one monk reading and intuitively understanding a text composed by another monk he never met (appendix 2: lineage chart 1), but this one exception aside, for the rest of genealogical history, a physical meeting—a historical event—was, with rare exceptions, required for each iteration of what eventually became long and tenuous lines of transmission.

The two similar lineages proposed in the *Record of the Teachers and Disciples of the Laṅkāvatāra Scripture* and the *Record of the Transmission of the Dharma Treasure* did not ultimately come to dominate Chan historiography in subsequent centuries. Both of these histories were lost for centuries, and are only known (primarily by scholars of Chan Buddhism) thanks to their unlikely preservation among the medieval manuscripts at Dunhuang, discovered in the twentieth century. They are relatively simple lineages, with a small number of patriarchs, relying on only a few transition nodes, evidently compiled by men who were affiliated through their own teachers with Shenxiu, the key figure in what came to be known as the Northern School.

The early history of the more successful Southern School lineage, which eventually formed the skeleton for the massive compilations of the Song dynasty, has also been meticulously pieced together by Chan scholars, again mostly on the basis of Dunhuang manuscripts. One of these newly discovered texts from Dunhuang, the "Treatise on Establishing What Is True and What False in the Southern School of Bodhidharma" (*Putidamo nanzong ding shifei lun* 菩提達摩南宗定是非論), compiled in 732, lays out what was to become the standard list of the first six Chinese Chan patriarchs, ending with the "Sixth Patriarch" made famous in the *Platform Sutra* (i.e., Bodhidharma → Huike 慧可 (487-593) → Sengcan 僧璨 (d. 606)→ Daoxin 道信 (580-651) → Hongren → Huineng). It also tells us that as a mark of the transmission from one master to another, a robe was passed down, at least from the time of Bodhidharma. This robe was left behind by Huineng and "was not again transmitted to another. [When it is said that] other objects have been transmitted, these are all lies."[29]

With this last sentence, even if we did not have extant evidence for written histories of competing lineages, we could still get a sense of the environment of sectarian competition that must have inspired works like these. Moreover, for the first time, this text tells us that in "the six generations [of the transmission of the Dharma in China], only one person is allowed [to represent the lineage] for each generation; there cannot be two. Even if a patriarch were to have a million disciples, only one would be entrusted to carry on the lineage."[30] This insistence on a single line of transmission (all others are lies) raises the stakes for lineage histories: it is not enough to belong to a lineage; one must belong to the lineage that carries the true Dharma—all others are at best weak imitations of the true lineage, brazen imposters at worse.

One example of just the sort of lineage history this text is complaining about is the entertaining version of transmission given in the *Record of the Dharma Jewel Through the Generations* (*Lidai fabao ji* 歷代法寶記), compiled toward the end of the eighth century in Sichuan.[31] According to this text, which provides a more extensive lineage of Indian patriarchs, the Dharma was transmitted from Hongren in the north to Huineng who traveled south—the traditional transmission story of the Southern School—but from there took a turn westward, arriving at the Baotang Monastery 保唐寺 in Sichuan through a succession of relatively obscure monks (Zhishen 智侁 [609–702], Chuji 處寂 [669–736], Wuxiang, and Wuzhu 無住 [714–774]) (appendix 2: lineage chart 3). Moreover, while the "Treatise on Establishing What Is True and What False" insists that the ancient robe that served as a mark of transmission was not transmitted beyond Huineng, the *Record of the Dharma Jewel* claims that before his death, Huineng gave the ancient robe, passed down to him from Bodhidharma, to Empress Wu, who later conferred it on Zhishen to take to Sichuan, where the true lineage of the Dharma continued.[32] Criticized by Zongmi in his overview of Chan schools in his day, this lineage and the historical details that went with it were effectively forgotten in the subsequent decades and only rediscovered with the Dunhuang finds in the twentieth century.[33] In other words, like the various Northern School lineage accounts, it was a genealogical history that eventually lost its argument as the legitimate family line.

That alternative family line, the "Southern School," which proceeded through Huineng to his disciples, first appears in all its splendor in yet another genealogical history, the *Collection of the Hall of the Patriarchs* (*Zutang ji* 祖堂集), initially compiled circa 952 by two otherwise obscure monks. A large work containing biographies of over 250 monks arranged according to lineage affiliation, the *Hall of the Patriarchs* is much more expansive than the previous works not just because it includes more biographies but also because it documents many lineages; rather than legitimating a single line of succession ending in the compilers themselves, it celebrates a large and powerful family with many branches spread over all of China.[34] Like virtually all of the Chan genealogical histories discussed above, the *Hall of the Patriarchs* faded quickly from view, only to be discovered, again in the twentieth century, this time in Korea. Nonetheless, the lineage it presents was absorbed and expanded on in what came to be the dominant vision of Chan history for subsequent centuries.

Not everyone was happy with the new genre of Buddhist genealogical history, both for its exclusivist sectarian bias and for its content: the often cryptic sayings and peculiar encounters between masters and disciples. Zanning, when composing his *Song Biographies of Eminent Monks*, notes at various points the circulation of "recorded sayings" of Chan masters but declines to incorporate them into his collection.[35] We have already seen above an example of the contrast in styles in the biography of Linji—straightforward and concise in Zanning's telling, but full of lengthy encounter dialogue in subsequent Chan versions.

Dialogue aside, in Zanning's work, based on the traditional format of collecting monastic biographies according to category (translators, exegetes, ascetics, etc.), he laments the lineage disputes that marked much of Chan writing for the period. Both Zanning and the ninth-century monk Shenqing reference a story about two jealous disciples, each charged with massaging one of their master's sore feet. Whenever the monk in charge of the right foot is away, the disciple assigned to massage the left foot bashes the master's right foot with a rock. When the monk in charge of the right foot steps away, the other monk does the same to the other foot, until in no time both of the master's feet are bruised and battered.[36] It is perhaps too simplistic to say that the writing of lineage history is responsible for the rise in tension within the monastic community—wrapped up in matters of pride and livelihood, lineage-based rancor could manifest in all manner of ways—but lineage histories certainly contributed to sectarian identity and sectarian strife. If the lineage metaphor brought the promise of identity and the shared cause of a united family, it carried its perils as well; nothing tests family bonds like a disputed inheritance.

More fundamental, and seldom challenged, is the underlying assumption behind lineage histories: that one can only achieve enlightenment by receiving transmission from an enlightened master. "There are those who even after a long period of practice do not succeed," Shenqing explains, "and those who achieve realization right after taking a vow to do so. There are men of mediocre abilities who achieve enlightenment and brilliant talents who don't. What matters is their understanding, not whether they have received transmission or not."[37] In other words, not only is lineage divisive, it is founded on a false premise that prioritizes master-disciple relations above all else. Take away this assumption, and the whole massive corpus of lineage history loses its reason for being—a point I will return to below.

MATURE, OFFICIAL BUDDHIST GENEALOGICAL HISTORY

Whatever reservations Buddhist thinkers and historians like Shenqing may have had about the new lineage history, it eventually eclipsed all other genres. The *Transmission of the Lamp Compiled in the Jingde Era*, containing over 1,700 biographies spread over fifty-two generations, was an expanded version of the already extensive *Hall of the Patriarchs*.³⁸ And unlike previous lineage histories, the Jingde *Transmission of the Lamp* received imperial support, including the assignment of a prominent court literatus and experienced editor of other historical works at court, Yang Yi 楊億 (968–1020), to lead a group of scholars to revise the work, first compiled by the monk Daoyuan 道元 (fl. 1004).³⁹ This work inspired a series of other large lamp histories aimed at expanding on an already substantial collection of biographies of Chan monks arranged according to lineage. *The Expanded Lamp Record Compiled in the Tiansheng Era* (*Tiansheng guangdeng lu* 天聖廣燈錄), completed in 1029, was produced with official support by a member of the imperial family.⁴⁰ Subsequent expanded versions of this official Chan genealogical history appeared in 1101, 1183, and circa 1204. These previous five lamp histories were consulted and combined into what became, after the Jingde history, the most widely read Chan lineage history, the *Compendium of the Five Lamps* (*Wudeng huiyuan* 五燈會元), completed by a group of monks in 1253.⁴¹ With the genre well established by the end of the thirteenth century in this string of prominent works sponsored by prominent men, Chan genealogical histories continued to proliferate in subsequent centuries; one scholar estimates the compilation of no fewer than eighty such works in the Ming and Qing period.⁴²

Inspired by these sweeping, popular, and prestigious Chan histories, in the thirteenth century, Tiantai monks returned to the rough, simple lineage Guanding proposed in a preface to his master's work centuries before. As in the later Chan histories, the two representative works of Tiantai historiography—the *Orthodox Lineage* and the *Comprehensive Account*—built a much more complex edifice over what began as a simple straight line of a few dozen "patriarchs" linked one by one back to the Buddha.⁴³ In these works, the pedigree of generations of subsequent Tiantai monks ran through Guanding to his teacher Zhiyi and ultimately through the Indian patriarchs, like train stations on a single track leading back to the Buddha. In the face of the intricate Chan genealogical tree with branches in every part of the empire, those outside of this structure ran the risk of becoming a marginal, regional group of loosely related monks and monasteries, orphans in the wilderness. The expansive Tiantai lineage of the *Comprehensive History* exhibited instead a flourishing monastic family with multiple branches distributed over all of China. But as in the Chan case, creating this lineage meant choosing not just between two central lineage stories (Chan and Tiantai) but also between different branches within the lineage.⁴⁴ The virtual erasure of many unsuccessful lineage histories (some of which were preserved only by chance in a Dunhuang cave) points to the stakes for authors invested in the legacies of their work; but more poignantly still, the case of Feiyin Tongrong—the monk forced to flee his monastery to avoid arrest following on a lawsuit from monks outraged over their place in his published genealogy—illustrates that compiling a genealogical history was a serious business, the stakes high for preserving not just a particular picture of history but the historian himself.

HISTORIOGRAPHICAL STANDARDS

In the context of Buddhist historiography, a key point of concern in this flurry of genealogical creativity over the course of centuries is the place of historiographical standards in the rush to promote one lineage over another. The earlier, Tang-era lineage histories in particular play very loose with facts, dates, and events, which opens up their narratives to attacks on historical grounds. But this line of analysis assumes that the authors and readers of lineage history cared about historical accuracy. One possible reading of genealogical history is that it was intended primarily to convey a general notion of the sacred origins of the thing transmitted. In this understanding, who transmitted the Dharma to whom at what time and in what way is of only marginal interest; the important point is that the transmission took place. In other words, the brief, hazy sketch of the transmission of the lamp in the earliest accounts is not the result of sloppy history but rather of concise narrative focused on the point of it all.

The extent to which an ideal of historical accuracy matters in Buddhist genealogical history has been discussed most prominently by Chan scholars. John C. Maraldo's 1985 article, "Is There Historical Consciousness in Ch'an?," marks a moment of reflection on the implications of decades of scholarship—most notably by Yanagida Seizan—employing newly discovered manuscripts to demonstrate that the lineage presented in the authoritative Song transmission of the lamp compilations was just one among many possible stories, and that each Chan genealogy reflects the biases and sectarian affiliations of its compilers.⁴⁵ Maraldo begins by recapping an exchange at the beginning of the twentieth century between two giants of early Chan scholarship: Hu Shih 胡適 (1891-1962) and D. T. Suzuki 鈴木大拙 (1870-1966).⁴⁶

After an early career as a reformer, philosopher, playwright, diplomat, and critic of "superstition," Hu Shih turned to the study of Chan, discovering in the Dunhuang manuscripts housed in Paris many of the texts mentioned above that called the received tradition into question. Hu insisted that the duty of modern scholarship is to dismantle the romantic façade created by the transmission of the lamp compilations and reconstruct the sectarian squabbles over social, political, and economic advantage that inspired them.[47] Suzuki, then as now the most famous proponent of Zen teachings and practice in the West, took exception to Hu Shih's sneering delight in exposing Chan hypocrisy. Suzuki insisted that the stories contained in these collections were attempts to convey higher truths, and that reading them in search of historical inaccuracies was fundamentally misguided—to borrow a Chan metaphor, remaining focused on the finger that points to the moon rather than turning one's attention to the moon itself.

Maraldo posits a middle ground in which the modern scholar, after demonstrating that a given claim in a Chan transmission story is historically inaccurate, rather than discard the story asks what it does as a form of literature expressed according to the rules of a particular literary genre. Subsequent scholars have given attention to the creation of new genres of writing in Chan (most importantly, lineage history, recorded sayings, Chan monastic regulations, and koan).[48] More relevant in the context of a study of Buddhist historiography, Maraldo argues that in general, while Chan writers treat their lineage as a historical entity, they are with rare exceptions either wed to a sectarian agenda or primarily concerned with conveying a particular message, and so do not possess historical consciousness in an empiricist, Rankean sense in which the goal is to objectively reconstruct what really happened in the past.

"The historical awareness of the Chan chronicles seems to be limited to a sectarian concern to establish a lineage leading back to the historical Buddha and thus to justify a particular school. A commitment to investigate the stories in an objective manner, as modern historiography would have it, is conspicuously absent." Moreover, in establishing the lineage, the focus of lineage history is not on the circumstances of the transmission of the Dharma such as details of time, place, and date, but on the quality of the transmission, the understanding between disciple and master. "Of significance for the distinction between factual and literary historical approaches is the stance of the recorded saying toward historical transmission. While this question remains a theme that needs closer investigation, it appears that they are concerned more with demonstrating an understanding of the dharma than with demonstrating its historical transmission."[49]

Dale S. Wright returned to these themes in 1992 in an essay titled "Historical Understanding: The Ch'an Buddhist Transmission Narratives and Modern Historiography."[50] Like Maraldo, Wright makes the case for the value of lineage history even when it can be shown to be based on inaccurate descriptions of events, with faulty dates and place names and improbable quotations. The writing, reading, and repetition of transmission stories, he argues, created meaning by forging an identity for members of the lineage. But this is a distinctively Chan sense of history, grounded in the family metaphor and recorded sayings rather than traditional historiographical concerns.

> Furthermore, while drawing heavily on forbearing texts, the editors have made no effort at attribution. Innumerable bits and pieces of other texts are woven together into a new one without citation, quotation, or other devices that might credit the appropriate sources. In addition, editors seem very little concerned over the accuracy or legitimacy of their sources. Epistemological concerns—how do we know that this story about Mazu really did occur—seem to be subordinate interests at best. From our modern perspective, what we notice is that objective authentication of sources is not the reigning criterion of inclusion. What seems to matter is not where the story came from but how good it is and how well it might serve the purposes of transmission. This realization pushes us toward the question: Were these editors really historians, and if so, what kind?[51]

The point of departure in these discussions is the difference between compilers of Chan lineage histories and the modern historians who study them, which is, of course, substantial. A modern historian like Hu Shih, who dismissed these Chan narratives as self-serving fabrications, had little or no commitment to the tradition; there is a big difference between writing about the history of one's own family and writing about someone else's. This is true for virtually all of the writings I discuss in this book. But in examining genealogy as a historical genre, the more interesting aspect is the exploration of the understanding of history reflected in the lineage accounts. In short, whether today or in the past, does writing a genealogical history, as opposed to other historical genres, demand a different approach?

Maraldo and Wright suggest that the construction of Chan transmission accounts entails overlooking the historiographical niceties of source criticism and chronology in favor of dramatic narratives that convey Chan principles about the nature of mediation and truth.[52] There is some validity to the observation. If we look not just at how Chan history was written but also at how it was read, we see that when the transmission of the lamp compilations became popular reading material for the literati, these readers were primarily interested in the dialogue and poetry contained in the accounts and showed relatively little interest in their historical context or accuracy.[53] For instance, when the official Wang Sui 王隨 (ca. 975-1039) compiled his *Collection of Gems from the Transmission of the Lamp* (*Chuandeng yuying ji* 傳燈玉英集), he extracted from the Jingde *Transmission of the Lamp* only the dialogue, poetry, and other exchanges that revealed doctrine, leaving out details of the lives and deeds of the masters.[54] He didn't bother himself with comparing sources or explaining discrepancies in dates or names. And critics of the transmission histories often focused on what they considered crude, clumsy language rather than inaccuracy.[55] In other words, when literati read these Chan histories in their studios or discussed them over tea with their literati friends, they often took them more as either books of wisdom or entertainment than as formal history, as they would do when reading, say, the *Records of the Historian*.

Nonetheless, many readers of the Chan genealogical histories, including both monks and laymen, *were* troubled by discrepancies that seemed to undermine their claims for historical accuracy, and the authors of the texts themselves at times *did* follow historiographical conventions even when it meant interrupting the narrative flow. For instance, even the schematic and crude *Transmission of the Dharma Jewel* (*Chuan fabao ji*) includes a comparison of source discrepancy of the sort we see in more formal historiography. When recounting the story of Bodhidharma's disciple Huike cutting off his own arm as a sign of commitment and devotion, the text notes that this is not the only version of the story: "The master casually remarked: 'Would you give up your life for the Dharma?' Huike then cut off his arm to prove his sincerity. Note: another text says that Huike's arm was cut off by bandits. This is a false version that was circulated at one time."[56] The "false version" refers presumably to the biography of Huike in the more famous *Further Biographies of Eminent Monks* by Daoxuan. Huike intentionally severing his own arm to prove his sincerity certainly makes for a more meaningful story than losing it to bandits. As I noted above, Maraldo posed two questions to assess historical consciousness in Chan accounts like these: 1) Does the historian commit to an attempt to objectively reconstruct history?, and 2) Is the historian at pains to convince the reader of the historicity of the account? In some cases discussed in chapter 2, Buddhist historians do approach an objective ideal, introducing alternative readings and sources that do not seem to advance any agenda (other than to demonstrate the historian's skill). In contrast, with this reference to the "false" account of Huike's arm loss, this text is clearly in the realm of history in service to sectarian polemic. That is, by noting an alternative source, the author of the *Transmission of the Dharma Jewel* is following historiographical convention, but the choice of the more meaningful version (he cut off his own arm as a mark of commitment to Bodhidharma) over the less meaningful one (he lost his arm in a bandit attack) is asserted rather than argued.

Such discussions of alternative sources are rare in early Chan genealogical history; these are mostly collections of teachings stretched over a bare historical frame. Nonetheless, however crude the early Chan genealogical histories may be in the context of formal, elite Chinese historiography, they do present themselves as historical works and give every indication that they were meant to be read as literal reconstructions of the past. The *Record of the Teachers and Disciples of the Laṅkāvatāra Scripture* is sprinkled with dates (telling us the reign period when the patriarch Guṇabhadra reached Canton), place names (noting the place of origin of Bodhidharma's disciple Huike), and referencing one other historical text, the *Further Biographies of Eminent Monks,* while condemning another purported collection of a Chan master's sayings as "lies."[57]

Despite its outlandish claims for the Dharma transmission extending from central China to Sichuan via Empress Wu, *The Record of the Dharma Jewel Through the Generations* is closer to traditional historiography, beginning with a list of the books the compilers claim to have consulted before launching into the famous story of the entrance of Buddhism to China with the dream of Emperor Ming of the Han, including a precise date for the dream (the third year of the Yongping era, 60 CE). This account, it notes, is based on the *Inner Commentary on the Dharma in the Han* (*Hanfa ben neizhuan*), which we now know to be a late forgery rather than a Han text, but in the Tang was a respectable historical source.[58] In fact, this early Chan genealogical history is full of references to sources and dates, though it does not discuss discrepancies.

The *Biographies of Baolin,* recounting the transmission of the lamp in India, supplies dates for the patriarchs, details that are not essential to the stories themselves, at times digressing into chronological calculations to situate events in India with those in China. For instance, when recounting the death of the Buddha, it notes awkwardly (the text was later maligned for its lack of linguistic elegance): "The extinction of the World-Honored-One corresponds in China to the fifty-second year of King Mu of the Zhou [i.e., 950 BCE], the *renshen* year, on the fifteenth day of the second month. One thousand seventeen years after the extinction of the World-Honored-One, Buddhism arrived here in China, that is, in the tenth year of the Yongping era [67 CE] in the *wuchen* year."[59] Later, it advances the timeline, writing, "One thousand seventy years [sic] after the Buddha entered nirvana, [Buddhism] reached China. One hundred sixty-five years after Buddhism arrived, it reached the Wu region."[60] These chronological calculations are interesting because they are not essential for the genealogy and break up the narrative; they are inspired by the impulse to conform to Chinese historiographical practice, even in works that the elite tradition would later criticize as crass and historiographically flawed.

The same tendencies crop up on rare occasion in the *Collection of the Hall of the Patriarchs*—a lamp history in its mature form. Granted, much of this work is taken up with encounter dialogue: "The master asked Dongshan 洞山 (807–869), 'What was the intention of the Patriarch?' Dongshan replied, 'When the Dong River flows backward, then I will tell you.'"[61] Or, "The master asked the First Seat, 'Are the patriarchs in the ancestral hall?' He replied, 'Yes.' The master said, 'Then call them here to wash my weary old feet.'"[62] Often the compilers don't even bother to note the circumstances of a monk's death, ending an account with dialogue instead of a date. And they rarely cite sources. The main detail, and the cement that holds the structure of the text together, is the lineage affiliation that identifies each monk before his famous bon mots are given. But even in this text, the compilers supply dates from time to time, the early chapters do cite sources, and even the later chapters (taken up almost exclusively with encounter dialogue) mention stele inscriptions for monks (though they don't cite them precisely) or other extraneous historical detail. The account of Shunzhi 順之 (fl. 858) of the Ruiyun Monastery 瑞雲寺 notes that his monastery was originally called Longyan 龍巖 and only later changed to Ruiyun.[63] Another account ends by stating, "Later it was said the old woman [mentioned earlier] had once met National Master Zhong when she was young."[64] These details have no bearing on Chan teachings.

In sum, there are enough concessions to historiographical convention to conclude that the authors and readers of these texts took them to be historically grounded in events of the past rather than allegories for which historical detail was irrelevant. But at the same time they are often vague about places and dates. Even worse, when they did supply dates and places, they created problems for subsequent readers with greater historiographical acumen. From about the year 1000, with the emergence of the officially sponsored lamp history genre, the scholars working with this material were no longer preachers and visionaries championing a new approach to the quest for enlightenment; they were instead sophisticated, deeply literate monks at court, accomplished literati, and even members of the imperial family. For these men, the fascinating but clumsy history of the transmission stories created problems they could not ignore. In short, the problem wasn't that the early genealogical histories refused to participate in the Chinese historiographical tradition, it's that they did so badly.

Take, for instance, the biography of Bodhidharma. In Chinese Buddhism, no figure attracted more hagiographical attention. His legend grew from the briefest of comments in the sixth century to a full-blown biography in the sixteenth, as his story accumulated new dialogue, episodes, and motifs in both texts and art, rendering him not only a key figure in the history of Chan but also the most recognizable monk in East Asian art. The gradual expansion of his biography has also made Bodhidharma particularly susceptible to source-critical analysis. Modern scholarship has suggested that early sources on Bodhidharma are so loosely connected to his later legend that it is virtually impossible and not, in any event, very useful to search for a historical core to his legend.[65] By examining the dates of the earliest sources for each of the motifs that entered the ever-expanding legend, it is possible to chart the gradual growth of the legend.[66] Most of the interesting developments took place outside of formal historiography. Daoxuan's biography of Bodhidharma in his *Further Biographies of Eminent Monks* focuses on a summary of abstruse discussion of doctrine and practice; Daoxuan avoids dates, saying only that Bodhidharma himself said at one point that he was a hundred and fifty years old, and noting that the circumstances of his death are unknown. But with the publication in 1004 of the *Transmission of the Lamp Compiled in the Jingde Era*, the biography of Bodhidharma included all manner of details carelessly thrown together, leaving a series of puzzles for more discriminating historians. As Bodhidharma was now a key figure in all Chan lineages, they were reluctant to strip his legend down to the bare frame of a story provided in the earliest sources. At the same time, as historians who saw themselves as a part of a tradition of exacting scholarship, they had to address discrepancies in dates and sources.

Tiantai monk Zhipan complains in his *Comprehensive History* that the *Biographies of Baolin* contain "all manner of absurd stories, for instance that Bodhidharma returned to the West carrying one sandal or that [Huike] stood in the snow and cut off one arm."[67] Both of these came to be famous episodes in the Bodhidharma legend (it was after his supposed death that he was seen carrying a single sandal as he returned to the West—the other sandal was found in his otherwise empty grave). However, Zhipan points out, "the events are very different from those found in Daoxuan's *Further Biographies of Eminent Monks*." Recall that the earlier *Record of the Transmission of the Dharma* at least mentions that the account it gives of Huike cutting off his arm differs from the account in the *Further Biographies of Eminent Monks* that his arm was severed by bandits. Because the *Biographies of Baolin* did not even mention the alternative account, much less make the case for why its version was superior, it left itself open to criticism.

Even Chan monks were bothered by discrepancies in Bodhidharma's biography. Among other problems, the details of Bodhidharma's arrival in China at Canton, when the local prefect, one Xiao Ang 蕭昂 (483–535), supposedly reported his arrival to the throne, didn't make sense. The Chan monk-scholar Qisong, in a work completed in 1061, notes the problem:

> The compilers of the various "transmission of the lamp" texts of the past all say that Bodhidharma came to the Liang dynasty (i.e., China) in the eighth year of the Putong era. Now, according to historical writings, there were only seven years in the Putong era. Only by using the dates of the long calendar of Wang You 王佑 might we arrive at eight years, but this is suspect.[68]
>
> Moreover, they all say that [Prefect] Xiao Ang 蕭昂 reported Bodhidharma's arrival to the emperor. But when we examine Xiao Ang's biography [in the official histories], it does not say that he was ever governor of Guangzhou. It was Xiao Ang's nephew, Xiao Li 蕭勵, who had once been governor of this prefecture. I fear that the one who recorded this event mistakenly took Xiao Li for Xiao Ang. As the previous records [on Bodhidharma in the *Transmission of the Lamp*] are official records of state,[69] even if the truth of the matter is beyond doubt, I do not dare to remove this detail, but leave it here while marking it as suspect.[70]

Here we see again the tendency to view discrepancies in Buddhist histories as careless, but ultimately harmless, mistakes. Just as interesting are the seemingly minor points that Qisong chooses to focus on. Rather than challenge the claim in earlier biographies that Bodhidharma lived for more than 150 years (a claim he accepted), he discusses a possible discrepancy of a single year. Nor does he address the absence of references to Bodhidharma in the dynastic histories despite the fact that, according to Bodhidharma's biography, he had an interview with Emperor Wu of the Liang and was summoned to the court by a later emperor, and yet another emperor supposedly ordered his tomb to be opened. Instead, Qisong notes that a very minor figure in Bodhidharma's biography is probably a mistake for another.[71] In instances like these, we see that more is involved in the historian's comparison of sources than a quest for historical accuracy. If Qisong went to the trouble to check the biography of the official said to have received Bodhidharma in Canton, surely he must have combed the dynastic histories for references to Bodhidharma's meeting with the emperor. Yet rather than draw attention to the gap between the official histories and Bodhidharma's biography, he comments instead on a trivial problem. In this way, he lends a veneer of credibility to an otherwise implausible account of a key Chan figure, no doubt demonstrating for at least some of his readers that the story of Bodhidharma had been properly vetted and shown, on the whole, to be reliable.

A century after Qisong, another Chan monk, Zuxiu, in his annalistic history of Buddhism came up against the persistently problematic biography of Bodhidharma. Among other issues, the dating of Bodhidharma's arrival in China was fraught with problems. The traditional account did not allow enough time between his arrival and his supposed invitation to the capital from the emperor, since it would have taken more than a few days for couriers to inform the emperor of events on the southern border. There was also a need to link the dates given for Bodhidharma's teacher in India and his disciple in China while allowing for his teacher's instruction that Bodhidharma was not to leave for China until sixty-seven years had passed after his death. All of this inspired Zuxiu to engage in complicated calendrical calculations in an attempt to make sense of it all.[72]

Writing at roughly the same time, the late twelfth century, the great Confucian Zhu Xi 朱熹 (1130–1200) seized on what he saw as slips in Chan lineage history as part of his relentless criticism of Buddhism. The Jingde *Transmission of the Lamp* account includes "transmission verses," part of the poetry of the transmission histories that many literati singled out for praise and discussion. But for Zhu, the poetry betrayed a clear forgery, for "how could these Buddhist patriarchs of ancient times, barbarians from the Western regions, know how to write rhymed Chinese poetry?"[73] The criticism reflects, perhaps, Zhu Xi's rigid view of translation practice, but it shows at the least that he took these works as *attempts* to create a credible history.[74] In this context, efforts by Buddhist scholars—monastic and lay—to clean up the historical record are easy to understand. A 1316 edition of the eleventh-century *Transmission of the Lamp Compiled in the Jingde Era* contains interlineal notes that endeavor to tidy up some of the sloppy chronology of the text inherited from the *Biographies of Baolin*. While the *Transmission of the Lamp* gives the year Mahākāśyapa entered Cockfoot mountain to await Maitreya as "the fifth year of King Xiao of the Zhou, the *bingchen* year," the note explains, "'Fifth year' should be 'fourth year.' From here up to the thirteenth patriarch Kapimala the dates are wrong. We have corrected them, following the chronology of Chart 6A in the *Records of the Historian*."[75] Elsewhere, these meticulous fourteenth-century editors drew on epigraphy to add biographical data that the original lineage history, as was its tendency, left out, or to clarify points of historical geography.[76]

This fastidious, erudite tinkering—a date fixed here, a rare piece of inscription referenced there—demonstrates that despite their rough beginnings, lineage histories were gradually incorporated into the elite historiographical tradition. But as we have seen, the inherently sensitive nature of lineage history, in which real-world consequences rested on fragile historical connections, meant that even the most seemingly innocuous historiographical moves carried the potential to provoke rancor and controversy.

In one of the most famous of these controversies, the problem began when Huihong came across what he believed was a mistake in the *Transmission of the Lamp Compiled in the Jingde Era*.[77] The cantankerous monk Huihong earlier had criticized the representation of Chan in Zanning's *Song Biographies of Eminent Monks*. This time his sharp eye fell on the biography of Tianhuang Daowu 天皇道悟 (748-807), which describes his determination to become a monk as a child. When his parents object, he fasts, eating only once a day until his parents give in and allow him to take the tonsure. He is credited with taking part in a few typically cryptic encounter dialogues (e.g., he asks his master, "Setting aside concentration and insight, what Dharma is there to teach?" His master, Shitou, replies, "I have no slaves here. What is there to set aside?").[78] But he is mostly known as a link between his master, the famous Shitou Xiqian 石頭希遷 (700-790), and disciples that came later in his lineage: Fayan Wenyi 法眼文益 (885-958) and Yunmen Wenyan 雲門文偃 (864-949), the eponymous head figures in two of the five "houses of Chan."

That is, the *Transmission of the Lamp Compiled in the Jingde Era* places Tianhuang Daowu in the lineage of Shitou Xiqian, and lists Longtan Chongxin 龍潭崇信 (d.u.) as one of his disciples⁷⁹ (appendix 2: lineage chart 2). About a hundred years later, Huihong, in keeping with the practice of elite historians, read the *Transmission of the Lamp* account of Tian*huang* Daowu alongside several alternate accounts of a monk named Tian*wang* Daowu 天王道悟 (738-819) in epigraphical sources and concluded that there were in fact two monks named Daowu.⁸⁰ As we have seen, both modern and premodern scholars have noted a number of instances in monastic biography in which a work joins two different monks or, conversely, splits one monk in two—reflections of the unfortunate limitations of Chinese monastic names. But in this case, there are important implications not just for reconstructing the biography of one or two monks but for subsequent branches of the lineage. Huihong argues that once we sort out which Daowu did what, three of the "five houses of Chan" are closer relations than previously thought—more like cousins than first cousins twice removed. And hence, Huihong tells us, the "absurd bickering between the Yunmen and Linji lineages is laughable." The "two Daowu theory" might well have gone unnoticed had it not been picked up in the *Compendium of the Five Lamps* a little over a hundred years later. The *Five Lamps*, perhaps out of sectarian concerns but more likely as one of many efforts to fix mistakes in the previous *Transmission of the Lamp Compiled in the Jingde Era*, includes a long note laying out the "two Daowu theory" in great detail and arguing that two of the five main houses of Chan should be grouped on the side of the family with two other houses, rather than off on their own⁸¹ (appendix: lineage chart 5). A later edition of the Jingde *Transmission of the Lamp* included a note fixing the perceived error as well.⁸² All of this was very much in keeping with standard historiographical practice and more specifically, efforts by Chan monks and laymen to clean up the at times sloppy Chan genealogical histories. But when Feiyin Tongrong compiled yet another lamp history, the *Strict Transmission of the Five Lamps* (*Wudeng yantong* 五燈嚴統), the two Daowu problem erupted into controversy. Monks from the Caodong 曹洞 lineage attacked Feiyin both in writings (challenging the evidence for the two Daowu theory, which is not at all clear-cut either way) and in legal proceedings (claiming maliciously that by challenging material that was in the imperially sanctioned canon, Feiyin was guilty of sedition). The debate continued unabated through much of the seventeenth century.⁸³ What began as a bookish, technical historiographical discussion inspired by a slipshod historical work that did not give due attention to sources gradually descended into strident sectarian bickering with serious legal consequences for the hapless historian Feiyin Tongrong.

THE SEARCH FOR ORDER

The rise of lineage history and Chan and Tiantai sectarianism are inseparable. In fact, to a large extent sectarianism in Chinese Buddhism was a product of a historical vision rather than, say, doctrinal differences. One can detect general differences in style in the five houses of Chan, but these seem more the product of lineage history than the other way around.

As Shenqing implied in his critique of genealogical history back in the ninth century, if we take away the premise that transmission is necessary for enlightenment, genealogical history loses its reason for being. And to be truly meaningful, transmission must also imply exclusion. In this respect, genealogical history is primarily a tool of legitimation, a means of demonstrating that monks who belong to a particular lineage are superior to those who don't—most pronounced in the early transmission histories in which winners and losers are clear. But we have seen enough at this stage to know that more was going on in the historian's construction of lineage histories than the legitimation of a small group of monks. Unlike some of the earliest rough, brief lineage histories in which authority was transmitted in a single line, the mature lamp history genre detailed many lines of transmission in a grand family tree that was close to all encompassing, particularly as the rival Tiantai lineage faded in importance in late Imperial China.

More telling still are instances in which the compiler of a history didn't privilege his own lineage.[84] When compiling his nonsectarian work the *Song Biographies of Eminent Monks*, Zanning, in addition to noting the early Chan lineage, also referenced a lineage of masters and disciples in the new "Esoteric School," with Vajrabodhi as the first Chinese patriarch, Amoghavajra as the second, and Huilang 慧朗 (fl. 774) as the third.[85] Zanning had no particular investment in either of these lineages. In his summary of the history of the monastic regulations in China, thirteenth-century Chan monk Zuxiu in his *Comprehensive Chronology of the Longxing Era* runs through a list of monks who transmitted the *Dharmaguptakavinaya* in China.[86] This too was a lineage that did nothing to legitimate Zuxiu. In both cases, listing a succession of masters and disciples has inherent historiographical value: it allows the reader to trace influence and, above all, brings order to a long and complex history of Buddhism in China, filled with hundreds of monks connected in various ways. In other words, lineage history didn't only fill a need of the historian to demonstrate his proud family history; it also produced a grand but tidy narrative of interconnected stories, combining the two great passions of all Chinese historians, biography and chronology, linking the two in a satisfying, logical order. Doctrinal concerns and sectarian agendas aside, the structure of genealogy held great appeal for Buddhist historians as a tool for ordering and presenting the past.

CHAPTER 6

Modernity

In 1914, Taixu 太虛 (1890–1947), who would one day be recognized as the most controversial and influential monk of the twentieth century, retreated into confinement on Putuoshan. Sealed into his rooms in a formal ceremony, he remained in isolation—food delivered to him through a trap door—for three years.[1] In his autobiography, Taixu describes his daily routine as meditating and making reverence to an image of the Buddha in the morning, reading Buddhist scriptures starting around noontime, followed by venerating an image of the Buddha and more meditation at night. Wedged between study of scripture at noon and evening devotions, he reserved the long afternoons for general reading from the substantial collection of books he brought with him and installed on bookshelves in his rooms before beginning the retreat. These included works of classical prose and poetry, but also recent translations of Western works on psychology, philosophy, ethics, and biology. He read from a collection of works of the polymath reformer Liang Qichao 梁啟超 (1873–1929) and from "educational journals." And every day, he scoured the Shanghai newspaper, *Shenbao* 申報, looking especially for disparaging remarks about Buddhism that he responded to immediately with combative letters to the editor and ardent articles of his own.[2] In short, even as a monk in confinement, devoting much of his time to meditation and self-cultivation, Taixu was caught up in the new ideas and attracted to the controversial figures that dominated one of the most intellectually exciting periods of Chinese history. While Taixu is hardly representative of the monks of his day—he was far more enthusiastic about all manner of reform and even revolution than most of his contemporaries—his period of confinement is an apt illustration of the position of monastic intellectuals in China during the twentieth century. However separate they may have been socially and even physically from the major figures in Chinese academic and political life, away from the centers of power they too swam in the intellectual currents of the day.

For the first half of the twentieth century, these trends included a new openness to Western writings, a call for sweeping political and economic reforms, a move away from literary to vernacular Chinese writing, and radically new approaches to various forms of scholarship, including literary criticism, philosophy, and history.[3] The examination system that had dominated scholarship for centuries had by 1914 entirely collapsed, marking a break with the past that even the most trenchant conservative could not deny. The world was changing at an unprecedented pace in unpredictable ways, and those swept up in these changes knew it. No field of scholarship went untouched in the early decades of the twentieth century, and many new disciplines—as reflected in Taixu's reading list—emerged. Historiography was at the forefront of these changes. Liang Qichao had just returned from political exile in Japan and was deeply involved in the politics of the new republic. In his writings on history, Liang called for an examination of the ancient Chinese classics not just as repositories of wisdom but as historical sources.[4] In subsequent decades, Gu Jiegang 顧頡剛 (1893-1980), the most widely discussed historian of the period, would expand the possibilities of history, promoting "doubting antiquity," in which he subjected the authenticity of long-revered ancient works to intense critical scrutiny. Gu further championed folklore, searching for the roots of the elite tradition in popular culture, and insisted as well on the importance of identifying evolution and progress in history instead of the traditional penchant for cycles or decline.[5]

Yet as Taixu's seclusion illustrates, while leading monks were aware of these developments, they were at the same time cut off from them both socially and intellectually. Some of the monks I will discuss below responded directly to writings of academic historians, but for the most part monks moved in different circles from their academic counterparts. In contrast, the key figures in the historiography of the early twentieth century—all academics at some point employed by China's newly founded elite universities and research institutes—interacted socially as well as intellectually. Gu Jiegang and the prominent historian Fu Sinian 傅斯年 (1896-1950) were college roommates; Gu Jiegang was first a student and then a colleague and friend of Hu Shih; and Hu Shih was president of Academia Sinica when Fu Sinian took up his position as head of its Institute of History and Philology. These men studied and taught at the same universities and published in the same journals. They came from the same social background—proud representatives of respected, well-educated families, sons of serious, learned fathers—and shared the same experiences, many of the most prominent of them having studied abroad—Hu Shih at Columbia, Tang Yongtong 湯用彤 (1893-1964) at Harvard, Fu Sinian at Berlin University. And even those who didn't study abroad avidly kept up with the latest trends in historiography from Germany, England, and America, meeting in China with eminent visiting scholars like John Dewey and Bertrand Russell. This was a lively, cosmopolitan society that was beyond the reach of monks, even had they aspired to belong to it.

The clearest impact of the new history on *Buddhist* scholarship was not in the writings of monks like Taixu, but in the works of these academic intellectuals.[6] Liang Qichao himself wrote a series of essays on Buddhist history, followed in the first half of the twentieth century by other academics like Tang Yongtong, Chen Yuan, and Hu Shih. Although Liang's pioneering writings are now dated and seldom cited, those of Tang, Chen, and Hu, consistently erudite, original, and clear, have held up well and continue to be read and discussed by historians of Chinese Buddhism today.[7] While these scholars had occasional contacts with Buddhist figures of their day—Hu Shih once met Taixu, Tang Yongtong once sat in on some of the lectures of the Buddhist layman Ouyang Jingwu 歐陽竟無 (1871-1943)—their primary influences were from foreign historians and from each other.[8]

Despite the political and economic instability of the times, in the twenties and thirties, academic scholars made rapid progress in the field of Buddhist history. Liang Qichao's attempts to sort through legends of the arrival of Buddhism to China and analyze the history of Buddhist translation are filled with inaccuracies and faulty assumptions, but he at least established examination of Buddhism as a legitimate branch of the new historiography.[9] Hu Shih pioneered the use of the documents discovered at the turn of the century at Dunhuang for reevaluating Chinese Buddhist history. Chen Yuan opened up the field of Qing Buddhist history and was the first to critically examine a wide swath of Buddhist historical writings, while Tang Yongtong identified the key themes in early medieval Buddhism and published a standard study of the earliest phase of Chinese Buddhism that remains a model of elegance, insight, and concision.

Nonetheless, these scholars were not Buddhists. The academic historians might pride themselves on their knowledge of Buddhism, but their commitment to the truth claims of the religion was ambivalent at best. Liang Qichao once commented that ideally China should have no religion, but if it needed one, Buddhism was probably the best of the available options.¹⁰ Hu Shih, especially in his English essays, expressed open contempt for Buddhism and lamented the Indian influence on Chinese culture, instilling in China traditions of extremism and superstition that impeded reform and modernization.¹¹ Chen Yuan insisted that he was a scholar of religion and not an adherent to any faith.¹² Even Tang Yongtong, born in Huangmei 黄梅, the county where Chan Buddhism was born, never expressed particular sympathy for Buddhism in his masterful studies of Buddhist history. Their interest in Buddhism stemmed from their voracious appetite for new sources, overlooked by previous scholars, and by a new open-minded fascination with the role of non-Han people in the formation of Chinese culture.¹³

Of course for monks like Taixu and those who followed in his footsteps, Buddhist history was not a subdiscipline of Chinese history; it was the other way around. In contrast to their counterparts in the universities who had to demonstrate to themselves and their followers their objectivity and distance from the Buddhist cause in order to be taken seriously, monks had to demonstrate that their academic work was ultimately in the service of the Dharma. The gap between the historiographical trends among the new generation of academic historians teaching and writing in universities and monks writing Buddhist history in their monasteries was not just the product of their social estrangement or even differences in their access to resources, though both, as we will see below, were significant. The constraints of faith did not allow monastic historians the freedom to pursue the same paths of scholarship as their academic contemporaries. Gu Jiegang is perhaps most famous for dismantling the "golden age" of Chinese history, said from ancient times to have existed at the earliest phase of Chinese civilization in the time of sage kings. Gu demonstrated that the sage kings were myths and that this golden age of wise rulers was a later creation. Now Buddhism too had its golden age in the time of the Buddha, and biographical materials on the Buddha are notoriously scant and difficult to date. But for Buddhist monks, the stakes were far too high to challenge the existence of the Buddha as Gu had done with the Yellow Emperor, or even to probe the sources for the oldest strata of Buddhist history with the sort of critical rigor Gu Jiegang so eagerly applied to ancient Chinese culture heroes.¹⁴

Similarly, Gu insisted that even when early texts could be shown to be forgeries, they could still prove valuable sources for reconstructing the age in which they were forged. Academic historians of Buddhism have since taken the same approach to Buddhist apocrypha, but with one exception discussed below, monks never showed much interest in such a project, wed as they were to either highlighting Buddhist truths or defending Buddhism from its detractors. Nor was Gu's interest in folklore as a source for elite culture appealing for Buddhist historians. Academic historians might explore the vital role of popular culture in shaping the history of Buddhism in China and elsewhere, but these were precisely the elements—in particular folk customs incorporated into death ritual—that the Buddhists I will discuss objected to most strenuously.

For historians writing *as Buddhists*, old problems like refuting the story that Laozi created Buddhism or dating the periods of the decline of the Dharma paled in the face of an array of new challenges created by academic scholars at home and abroad as well as by the encounter with thriving Buddhist traditions in other parts of Asia. With academic historians like Gu Jiegang effectively demonstrating that even some revered Chinese classics were late forgeries, Buddhist historians were forced to abandon traditional dates for the Buddha based on what were obviously apocryphal texts. But was it possible to establish new dates based on more reliable evidence? And could such dates bring together disparate Buddhist traditions from different parts of the world, each with its own understanding of Buddhist history? Hu Shih and others, using the newly discovered Dunhuang documents, pointed out troubling inconsistencies for key texts and figures in the Chan lineages. Did this mean it was necessary to abandon the sacred history of the transmission of the Dharma in the Chan lineage, or was there enough historical evidence to refute such challenges to the legitimacy of modern Chan? More troubling still, scholars outside of China suggested that the entire Mahāyāna tradition emerged long after the time of the Buddha. Did this mean that all Mahāyāna scriptures—the foundation of Chinese Buddhism—needed to be abandoned as worthless fabrications? These were not simply articles of faith; they were (and are) essentially historical problems that can be addressed through recourse to modern historical methods informed by the lengthy tradition of Buddhist historiography we have examined thus far.

TAIXU'S HISTORIOGRAPHY

Taixu was the quintessential "revolutionary monk" of the modern era. The orphaned son of a small-town construction worker, raised on the edge of poverty, he received an erratic education as a child, primarily from his affable but unreliable opium addict uncle, before deciding to become a monk, in part in hopes of achieving mystical powers, a motivation he ridicules in his own charming and chatty description of his youth. To this point he followed a pattern of countless monks of similar background, destined to a life of monastic administration and ritual service to the lay community. But when he was eighteen, Taixu met a monk who introduced him to the works of the new modernizing intellectuals at the turn of the century: Kang Youwei 康有為 (1858–1927), Yan Fu 嚴復 (1854–1921), and, most important, Liang Qichao. From this time on he devoted himself to reforming Chinese Buddhism, both to preserve Buddhism from the new threats it faced in the twentieth century and out of a belief that Buddhism could provide a cure for the modern illnesses of inequality, materialism, and anomie.[15] With boundless energy, Taixu proposed any number of reforms, from innovative ideas for a new monastic economy to a new design for monks' robes. The most important were his efforts to change the way monks were educated and to introduce a systematic curriculum based in format on that of a secular school. In addition to his tireless travel across China and to Taiwan, Japan, Europe, and America, Taixu wrote voluminously. His works bristle with new ideas that mark him off from reform-minded monks of a previous generation. He cites Marx and Bakunin, Darwin and Tolstoy alongside Nāgārjuna, Tsongkhapa, and Dōgen. He dashed off book reviews, poetry, philosophical lectures and treatises, and, above all, polemics intended to defend Buddhism from its contemporary detractors and establish its relevance for the modern world.

During his life and after his death, Taixu was seldom known or read for his historical writings. Nonetheless, as he leaped enthusiastically from one topic to another, he often returned to history. Taixu's works are scattered with references to important historians of his day, including some of those who were pioneering new historical techniques. He claims that Gu Jiegang (along with Lu Xun 魯迅, 1881–1936) attended one of his lectures and drops the names of Tang Yongtong and Chen Yinke, but he does not describe conversations with them or discuss their writings at any length. He never even mentions his near contemporary Fu Sinian who, on his return from Germany, was in the twenties and thirties actively promoting Leopold von Ranke's historiography with its emphasis on critical analysis of primary sources and suspicion of interpretation.[16] Perhaps more important for Taixu than any of the works of the leading Chinese historians was H. G. Wells's *A Short History of the World*, which Taixu read in translation. Rather than the meticulous source analysis of scholars like Chen Yinke and Tang Yongtong, not to mention Ranke, this was the sort of writing—popular, grand, sweeping, and brief—that captured Taixu's interest. In a review of Wells's book, full of references to evolution, geology, progress, and science, Taixu criticizes Wells for his treatment of both Chinese and Buddhist history.[17]

Perhaps it was with Wells in mind that Taixu composed *A Brief History of Buddhism*, beginning by noting that though there are millions of Buddhists in the world, "there is as yet no complete history that records events marking the rise and decline of Buddhism, its highs and lows, that conveys the spirit of its import. Is this not a great pity!"[18] We have already followed a number of attempts in Chinese historiography to compile universal histories of Buddhism—the *Comprehensive Discussion and Chronology of Buddhism Compiled in the Longxing Era*, the *Comprehensive Account of the Buddhas and the Patriarchs*, and the *Chronology of Lineages and Transmission*. But before the twentieth century, these were essentially histories of *Chinese* Buddhism, with Indian Buddhism included as background. Taixu proposed a history of a larger Buddhist world that would include Tibet, Ceylon, and the rest of East Asia. He divides Buddhist history into periods defined by their characteristics as well as their time frames: the "era of creation," followed by the "era of dissemination," further divided into the "Indian era," the "Asian era," and the "global era." Unlike Wells's *Short History of the World*, however, Taixu's work was never more than a sketch, taking up only a dozen or so pages in all.[19]

And despite the radical new frame for his history, its brief contents are strikingly conventional. He begins by dating the Buddha's birth to three thousand years ago. As we will see below, this was a date that a source-critical approach would soon expose as untenable. In his account of the Buddha, Taixu states that the first scripture the Buddha preached was the *Buddhāvataṃsakasūtra*. This is another notion that is firmly rooted in medieval attempts to classify Buddhist scriptures (*panjiao*) and would soon be rejected by more exacting scholarship. Much of his discussion of India is taken up with relating a conventional Chinese lineage of Indian masters that can easily be shown to be spurious. When he turns to the arrival of Buddhism in China, he begins with the legend of Emperor Ming of the Han first encountering Buddhism in a dream. Taixu's political hero, Liang Qichao, was among the first to dismiss the story as a pious legend, and was soon followed by Tang Yongtong, who scrupulously examined the sources for the early transmission of Buddhism to China with even greater rigor.[20]

In short, Taixu's work is entirely in keeping with themes we have already seen in premodern times: attempts to reconstruct Indian Buddhist history on the basis of dubious sources in service to Chinese polemics, a critical use of sources that stops short of questioning Indian texts, an obsession with genealogy as a way of ordering history, and a reliance on accounts of dreams and prophecy to explain the past. Unlike the new historiography emerging in the universities, Taixu did not cite the works of other scholars, relied entirely on Chinese texts, and showed no interest in the critical evaluation of his sources. If scholars like Gu Jiegang and Fu Sinian were becoming more suspicious of traditional texts and attempted to challenge traditional narratives through the use of unconventional sources, the lesson Taixu learned from modernity was to do the opposite: to synthesize, simplify, and generalize.

Taixu's brief attempt at a global history of Buddhism reflects a nascent response to a rising challenge: as international communication and travel became increasingly common for leading monks, they were confronted by the great disparities among different Buddhist traditions and the possibility of forming a united front against the challenges they faced. One way of uniting Buddhists from different regions was to appeal to their shared history. But when outlining his optimistic, confident history of Buddhism, Taixu had not yet realized just how difficult adjudicating regional differences would prove. For instance, the gap between the standard date for the birth of the Buddha given in Buddhist histories of South and Southeast Asia and the date Taixu gave was some three hundred years.[21] More fundamentally, Taixu's claims for the chronology of Buddhist scriptures placed Mahāyāna scriptures—which the Theravada tradition does not recognize—before and above scriptures (the *Āgamas* and *Nikāyas*) at the heart of the canon employed by Buddhists in South and Southeast Asia. Attempts to reconcile these different historical interpretations continued long after Taixu's death.

Although Taixu did not immediately recognize the historical challenge of incorporating Chinese Buddhism into the world history of Buddhism, he did perceive the threat to Chinese Buddhist tradition from the new, critical historiography emerging from the universities. When scholars like Liang Qichao, Tang Yongtong, and especially Hu Shih examined the history of Chinese Buddhism, they were drawn to traditions built on shaky foundations, ripe for demolition. While scholars of ancient Chinese history challenged the historicity of ancient Chinese texts like the *Book of Documents* or ancient culture heroes like Yao and the Yellow Emperor, Tang and Hu questioned the authenticity of early Chinese Buddhist scriptures or pointed out glaring lacunae in Chan lineages. In the past, Chinese monastic historians had responded to attacks from Daoists that argued that Laozi was the true founder of Buddhism, or from opposing Buddhist sects that asserted the superiority of one lineage over another. They complained that court historians like Ouyang Xiu excised Buddhism entirely from their histories. Most anti-Buddhist polemic from court figures focused on the moral character of the sangha; the low, foreign origins of Buddhism; its economic costs to the state; or the supposed fallacies of its doctrines. But the threat from academic historians was new. It was disinterested, cold analysis in place of the hot polemics of the past, and called for a more cautious, more nuanced response.

In the twentieth century, much of the most exciting research on the history of Chinese Buddhism focused on a radical reassessment of the history of Chan in light of documents discovered at Dunhuang at the turn of the century that brought into question the traditional account of how Chan teachings were brought to China by Bodhidharma and transmitted in a lineage of succession down to the present day. As we saw in the last chapter, Buddhist historians had long since argued over lineage, but this modern challenge to the tradition, coming from scholars intent on rewriting all of Chinese Buddhist history with no investment in a rival lineage, felt more decisive, more final. Once again, these discoveries were made almost exclusively by academic historians. Among Chinese scholars, the key figure in exploiting Dunhuang documents for reconstructing Chan history was Hu Shih. But the problems with Chan history were not limited to those exposed by the Dunhuang documents. In the modern period, as scholars began to look more critically at the traditional story of Chan, they saw discrepancies everywhere and began to piece together how the history of Chan had been invented centuries after the events it purports to describe.

Take, for instance, the biography of Bodhidharma. According to tradition, Bodhidharma is the pivotal figure who brought to China the essential, unspoken teachings of the Buddha, passed down in a secret transmission through a series of Indian patriarchs. But early accounts of Bodhidharma are contradictory and fragmentary, and some of the most important stories about him—that he met the Chinese emperor, that he faced a wall in meditation for nine years, that he floated across a river on a reed—only appear for the first time in very late texts. Modern scholarship suggests that the standard biography of Bodhidharma was created long after the death of the historical figure, if indeed Bodhidharma ever existed at all.[22]

Initially, Taixu's writings on Chan history show little awareness of the challenge to traditional accounts from academic historians. He had heard of the Dunhuang documents but didn't have access to them.[23] And rather than trace the growth of the legend of Bodhidharma through the arrangement and dating of texts that refer to him, Taixu accepts the traditional account, generally held by Buddhists from the thirteenth century on. That is, Bodhidharma came from southern India to China during the Liang dynasty, met the emperor, traveled north to Shaolin Monastery where he faced a wall in meditation, refusing an imperial summons, and, most important, passed on to his disciple Huike an ineffable essence that had been transmitted to him through twenty-eight patriarchs stretching back to India and ultimately the Buddha himself.[24]

Taixu suggests that discrepancies in accounts of Bodhidharma may result from his extremely long life (he was said in one early account to have lived more than 150 years).[25] Here we are very much in the realm of traditional Buddhist historiography, with a technique for explaining anomalies described earlier in the chapter on sources: in accounts of holy, extraordinary men, it is natural that there should be discrepancies, since their abilities transcend normal historical patterns. Alternatively, Taixu employs the equally traditional explanation of ascribing incongruities to the problems of oral history. The account of Bodhidharma given in the seventh-century *Continued Biographies of Eminent Monks* differs from that of the eleventh-century *Transmission of the Lamp* not because the events described in the later text were invented long after Bodhidharma's death, but because before the eleventh century these details of his life were only transmitted orally among Bodhidharma's lineage of disciples and were not recorded—an explanation that resonates with the Chan characterization of itself as a "separate tradition outside the (written) teaching" 教外別傳.[26] Taixu gives the same explanation for why it is only in very late texts that we first read the seminal story of how the Buddha began the great silent transmission of the Dharma when he held up a flower and Kāśyapa smiled: this event was not at first recorded in written texts; it was instead passed on orally for centuries before finally finding its way into a text.[27] The same, he assures us, is true for problems with the lineage of Chan patriarchs that, as we have seen, Chan historians like Qisong had discussed more scrupulously centuries previous: textual problems were the product of faulty recording of more robust oral traditions.[28]

In contrast, in 1927 Hu Shih published an article on Bodhidharma that begins provocatively:

> The legend of Bodhidharma is an extremely important koan in the history of the Chan school. The Chan school, revering Bodhidharma as its first patriarch, manufactured many absurd myths, raising doubts in the minds of later

scholars to the extent that there are those who suspect that Bodhidharma was a "Monsieur Never-existed," a "Mr. Nobody." If we examine the historical evidence, we must admit that he was a historical personage, but his actions were far less important than those recounted in his legend.[29]

Hu goes on to systematically examine relevant texts in the order of their appearance, not only pointing out inaccuracies—the claim that Bodhidharma arrived in China in 527 "is incorrect," the claim that he met Emperor Wu is "entirely fabricated by later writers," the legend that when his tomb was unearthed only a shoe remained is "a later myth"—but also attempting to trace, through Dunhuang documents, how the legend of Bodhidharma gradually changed and grew over time. In style the article is concise, but it leaves enough room to lard analysis with sarcastic asides on the absurdity of the legend. For later texts to supply dates for the meeting of Bodhidharma with the emperor when texts hundreds of years earlier didn't even mention it is Bodhidharma's "greatest miracle of all." Hu concludes by noting that the legend of Bodhidharma grew like a rolling snowball, but like a snowball melts away under the "light of the historical method."[30]

Taixu read Hu Shih's sardonic article and responded with a different line of defense from the traditional approaches he had taken to the material previously. The figure first described in the sixth-century *Luoyang qielan ji* 洛陽伽藍記, he explained, did in fact exist, but he was another Bodhidharma of no relation to the Bodhidharma of the Chan tradition. The historical figure who was the first Chan patriarch was in fact a monk known as Buddhaśānta, whose name was corrupted to Bodhidharma in later texts.[31] Again, we have seen a similar historiographical move in the writings of the tenth-century monk Zanning, explaining that one story places Shanwuwei at a time after his death because there must have been two monks of the same name. As in the case of Shanwuwei, it is not impossible that Bodhidharma's biography is an amalgamation of different figures and confused names (we know of a number of such cases in Chinese Buddhist biography).[32] But the more likely explanation, as scholars like Hu Shih recognized, is that the biographical material we have for such figures today is a network of legends with little basis in historical fact. Academic historians eventually came to recognize the value of such legends, even when of little use for reconstructing historical figures, since they reflect more general mentalities of the era they emerged from and often had a great impact on later generations of readers. And, as we will see below, at least one monastic historian recognized that even when accounts of a Buddhist figure could be shown to be historically inaccurate, they were still valuable both for understanding the history of Buddhism and more important, for illustrating Buddhist doctrines. But Taixu was not yet ready to leave the familiar harbor of traditional notions of historical accuracy for such murky waters. Instead he turned to the explanations we have seen in previous chapters: errors of transmission, secret transmission, and the miraculous.

Here, as elsewhere, Taixu's response to the troubling questions raised by academic historians is strained and unconvincing. Taixu was a reformer, a polemicist, and an activist more than he was a textual scholar. But he did at least engage, if only fleetingly, with academics, reading some of their works and corresponding with some of them as well at a level that the monastic historians who followed him did not. Taixu's brief response to Hu Shih signals the beginnings of a Buddhist historiography in which monks recognized the need to adopt or at least respond to the lessons of the new history.

Perhaps more important still, in addition to his attempts to analyze specific historical problems raised by academic historians, Taixu was among the first to discuss how a Buddhist monk's approach to Buddhist history should differ from that of a university professor. In one of his general works on Buddhist scholarship, Taixu writes:

> Scholars who do not [exclusively] research Buddhist texts take the study of Buddhist texts as a type of academic research. There is no shortage of such scholars at home or abroad. Indeed, it is no simple matter for a scholar to engage in analysis of Buddhist texts and to research their doctrines in order to become a specialist. Yet they often suffer from a tendency to draw attention to a single discovery to extol their own originality and praise their own accomplishments.
>
> When the average person reads from my works they think that I am an academic scholar of Buddhism who parses every word and phrase, tracing the roots of each subject and verifying every detail. In fact, when I read Buddhist texts I focus on the big picture. I don't commit it all to memory and I don't attempt to achieve in-depth understanding. My goal is to use texts as a tool of self-cultivation and instruction of others. Hence among my ambitions, I have never hoped to become a scholar, but have instead striven only, through these means, to revive Buddhism, awaken others, and save the world.[33]

In other words, not only are the goals of Buddhist historians of Buddhism different, but even the way they conduct themselves as reflected in their research should be different—one senses here the sting of Hu Shih's acerbic style, and perhaps the exclusion born both from Taixu's status as a monastic and from his humble social background. On a less personal level, Taixu hints that all authors press historical study into service for purposes other than a disinterested love for the past. For monks, these purposes ideally should include the promotion of Buddhism and, more interesting still, self-cultivation.

In a compelling portrait of Taixu's character written in the 1960s, Holmes Welch portrays him as a flawed and at times ridiculous man, constantly promoting his grand schemes—a complete reorganization of the Buddhist clergy, a revamped system for educating monks, and the founding of large Buddhist universities—without the patience to implement them properly; his seminaries collapsed, one by one, a year or two after they were founded; his support of an attempt to modernize a leading monastery ended in failure; his lectures abroad were poorly received; and many of his plans for great scholarly works never completed.[34] But by the end of the twentieth century, fifty years after Taixu's death, it was clear that Welch's assessment was premature, since many of Taixu's ideas about education and monastic reform did come to fruition among a later generation of monks in Taiwan who established seminaries and even universities on Taixu's model.[35] Even the new monastic robe he designed is now commonplace. The same is true of Buddhist historiography; Taixu's ideas for reforming Buddhist approaches to history had their greatest impact among those he inspired only after his death, chiefly in the person of the monk Yinshun.

YINSHUN'S HISTORIOGRAPHY

Outside the tight circle of cosmopolitan, innovative academic historians, reshaping forever the principles of Chinese historiography, a number of figures active in the first half of the twentieth century helped to bridge the gulf between the monk-historian, writing history from a Buddhist perspective in his monastery, and the academic who, with no particular allegiance to Buddhism, presented the history of Buddhism for his students and other scholars. Jiang Weiqiao 蔣維喬 (1873-1958) in 1928 published *A History of Chinese Buddhism*, a translation with revisions of *Shina bukkyōshi kō* 支那佛學史綱 by Sakaino Satoru 境野哲 (1871-1933).[36]

Unlike other nonmonastics mentioned above, Jiang was well known as a *Buddhist* layman and is probably best known for his popular works in which he describes his religious experiences and promotes meditation.[37] Similarly, Zhou Shujia 周叔迦 (1899-1970) wrote a series of monographs on Buddhist history in the thirties, including two histories of Chinese Buddhism and another history of Indian Buddhism. A member of one of the most remarkable academic families in modern Chinese history, Zhou was originally trained as an engineer but devoted most of his adult life to his interest in Buddhism, including giving classes on Buddhism in a number of prestigious universities in Beijing and publishing extensively on the topic.[38] Like Jiang Weiqiao, Zhou was a self-proclaimed Buddhist, with close ties to several Buddhist groups, and was a founding member of the Chinese Buddhist Association 中國佛教協會. But his historical writings, while broadly sympathetic to Buddhism, leave few clues of the distinctive challenges the study of Buddhist history presents to Buddhists. His first history of Chinese Buddhism (*Zhongguo foxue shi* 中國佛學史) is a bare collection of documents.[39] His second history (*Zhongguo fojiao shi* 中國佛教史) is a useful survey, innovative in its attention to social history and particularly the history of Buddhist art, but without a hint of the author's own affiliation with Buddhism.[40] We will never know how these incipient historical efforts might have developed in Buddhist circles; on the mainland in the decades that followed, studying Buddhist history from any but a stilted Marxist-Maoist perspective became increasingly difficult and ultimately impossible.

Yet one figure provides a bridge from the first attempts at a modern history of Buddhism from a distinctively Buddhist perspective to contemporary times. Yinshun, easily the most prolific scholar of Chinese Buddhism of the twentieth century, devoted much of his prodigious effort and deep familiarity with the Chinese Buddhist canon to tracing the development of Indian Buddhist thought. Like Taixu but unlike all of the academic historians discussed so far, Yinshun came from humble beginnings. The son of a provincial shop clerk, he studied through elementary school, but as his family could not afford further education, he was sent to learn a trade in Chinese medicine until he was sixteen. He soon thereafter abandoned the study of medicine, took a job as a primary school teacher, married, had a daughter, and settled down to small-town life. But restless for intellectual stimulation, he applied by mail in 1929 for entry into a new Buddhist seminary and, leaving his young family behind, set off to become a monk.[41] For the rest of his long life, Yinshun dedicated himself to Buddhist scholarship, first in the mainland, then, briefly, in Hong Kong, and finally in Taiwan. The source for his material and his inspiration was almost exclusively the Chinese Buddhist canon; and he published his extensive writings in Buddhist journals (primarily *Haichao yin* 海潮音) and through Buddhist publishers. Unlike Taixu, he demonstrated little interest in recent trends in Western thought and for most of his life had little interaction with academics. It was only on the insistence of his teacher Taixu that Yinshun published a critique of the characterization of Buddhism in the writings of the prominent Christian intellectual Lin Yutang 林語堂 (1895–1976), and even this was published only in a Buddhist journal directed at a Buddhist readership.[42] Yinshun's reclusive isolation was no doubt in large measure the product of his natural proclivities—he was an exceptionally introverted, bookish man—but his reluctance to explore new areas of thought or develop contact with intellectuals outside of Buddhist circles is also easily understandable given the times in which he lived. In 1949 Yinshun left China for Hong Kong, and some years later moved to Taiwan, where he lived for the rest of his life. There, in 1954, his book *An Overview of Buddhism* (*Fofa gailun* 佛法概論) came under suspicion for its supposedly pro-Communist ideas. At issue was a passage in the book, written by Yinshun when he was still in the mainland, in which he identified references in Buddhist scripture to the "Northern Continent" (Skt. Uttarākuru), a mythical land of freedom and equality, with an actual geographic region somewhere on the Tibetan plateau, his argument being that the mythical geography of ancient Indian works was rooted in conceptions of actual places. But since the book was written at a time when the center of Communist power was at Yan'an, in the Chinese northwest, and published around the time Tibet was occupied by the People's Liberation Army, the passage (identifying a land of freedom and equality) was taken by Nationalist Party hacks, charged with rooting out any hint of dissent, as veiled support for the Communist Party.[43] The charge was absurd, but the potential consequences for Yinshun were no less terrifying. Yinshun escaped the incident without imprisonment, but the book was banned for a time, and rumors that he was in hiding swirled in Buddhist circles. The affair made a lasting impression on Yinshun, a quiet scholar with no taste for political conflict; even had he had an interest in new ideas of foreign writers or academics, the effect of the political atmosphere in Taiwan at the time was utterly stifling, and he resigned himself to independent research largely confined to the Chinese Buddhist canon.[44]

Nonetheless, just as his decision to become a monk was inspired by the very modern possibility of mailing in an application to a Buddhist seminary, his scholarly interests were inspired by translations of Tāranātha's history of Buddhism and a Western book on the history of India, works that a previous generation of Chinese monks never would have considered.[45] More important, his approach to Buddhist works was in many ways a sharp break with traditional Buddhist historiography, from his critical stance to sources to his sophisticated use of legend and myth. Twentieth-century culture was so permeated with new ideas that even a reserved scholar like Yinshun, who spent most of his life reading the Chinese Buddhist canon without commentary or secondary scholarship, was still imbued with modern sensibilities.[46]

Working alone in monastic libraries, Yinshun never had the obligation or opportunity to present his findings to students in a systematic way. His books were not critically reviewed, and he did not have occasion to defend his positions at conferences or public lectures. Perhaps because of this relative isolation, Yinshun never explained his criteria for evaluating the sources of Buddhist history. He was not a rationalist, empiricist, or positivist in a strong sense, in that he did not explicitly argue against *all* claims of the supernatural or insist that all historical interpretation needed to be tied directly to verification through contemporary documents. In practice, however, he brought an unprecedented level of skepticism to the study of Buddhist history.

Consider for instance a passage that echoes Hu Shih's sarcastic characterization of Bodhidharma's biography, in which Yinshun writes that

> the greater Bodhidharma's fame in China, the more texts were attributed to him. In the Daoist canon there is the *Secret of the Marvelous Use of the Inner Mind of the Great Master Bodhidharma Who Lives in the World but Left His Form Behind* in one fascicle, in which Bodhidharma is said to be a sylph who lives forever. In the *Scripture of the Tendon Change of Bodhidharma* (*Damo yijin jing* 達磨易筋經), and *Bodhidharma, Fists of Gold* (*Damo yizhang jin* 達磨一掌金), Bodhidharma has become through legend some sort of martial artist or fortune teller! This truly is the burden of fame![47]

In this telling, not only were many of the texts attributed to Bodhidharma not his; even the iconic story of Bodhidharma facing a wall in meditation for nine years is a late legend.[48] More striking still, he concedes that the Chan lineage as a whole "may be at some remove from the facts."[49] We have seen in previous chapters that Buddhist historians in China were not averse to questioning the authorship of texts or to challenging the Chan lineage. What distinguishes Yinshun is, first, the fact that his critiques did not stem from a sectarian agenda, and, just as important, that the scope of his criticism extended to Indian Buddhism as well.

Yinshun wrote a book on the early history of Chan that earned him an honorary PhD from Taishō University in 1973, and he even published a book on ancient Chinese myths—his only work unrelated to Buddhism.⁵⁰ But the primary focus of his research was on the history of Indian thought. He read neither Sanskrit nor Pali, but his deep familiarity with Chinese translations of Indian Buddhist works in the Chinese Buddhist canon provided enough material for a series of thick, densely documented tomes with titles like the *History of Buddhist Thought in India* (*Yindu fojiao sixiang shi* 印度佛教思想史), the *Formation of the Canon of Scriptures of Primitive Buddhism* (*Yuanshi fojiao shengdian zhi jicheng* 原始佛教聖典之集成), *Texts and Teachers of the Sarvāstivāda* (*Shuoyiqieyoubu wei zhu de lunshu yu lunshi zhi yanjiu* 說一切有部為主的論書與論師之研究), and the *Origins and Development of Early Mahāyāna Buddhism* (*Chuqi dasheng fojiao zhi qiyuan yu zhankai* 初期大乘佛教之起源與開展), to name just a few. His access to and familiarity with scholarship on India was limited. In 1990, when Yinshun was eighty-four years old, he published an article on the authorship of the important Mahāyāna work *Dazhidu lun* that responds to theories proposed by prominent scholars like Hirakawa Akira, Étienne Lamotte, and others.⁵¹ Yinshun makes the case for the traditional attribution of the text to Nāgārjuna, an argument as plausible as those of Hirakawa and Lamotte. More generally, the article hints at an approach Yinshun might have taken—fully engaged with international scholarship—had his circumstances been different. And, as Marcus Bingenheimer argues, perhaps the most influential aspect of Yinshun's scholarship is his adoption in his later writings of the academic monograph—probably under the influence of European scholarship via Japan—which signaled a turn in Buddhist historiography to academia.⁵² But instead of incorporating his work into the wider academic world, Yinshun rarely cites scholarship of any kind, cutting trails on his own through a thicket of canonical sources.

In part because of this isolation, Yinshun's approach to Indian Buddhism is a curious blend of the traditional and the modern.⁵³ Although the sources he drew upon were essentially the same as those that had been available to Chinese monks for centuries—works translated from Indic languages into Chinese between the third and tenth centuries—his approach to them was radically different.

Consider, for instance, his take on what, as we have seen, had been for centuries a central issue in Chinese Buddhist historiography: the dates of the Buddha's nirvana. In response to a request from Taixu, Yinshun returned to the question that had vexed generations of Chinese Buddhist historians, eventually publishing in 1950 *A Discussion of the Determination of the Date of the Buddha's Extinction* (*Fomie jinian jueze tan* 佛滅紀年抉擇譚). This meticulous examination of sources signaled a new approach to an old problem, shaped by modernizing strands in Chinese Buddhism. In this short monograph, Yinshun notably does *not* discuss Chinese legends of the birth of the Buddha, focusing exclusively on medieval Chinese translations of Indian texts. The majority of the book is an argument for dating the death of the Buddha to approximately 100 years before the reign of Aśoka—what scholars now term the "short chronology"—specifically, 390 BCE.[54] Of especial interest here are Yinshun's motivations for the project. Nowhere does he mention the decline of the Dharma or the birth of Laozi (or any other event in China). He argues instead, in keeping with the Chinese historian's commitment to chronological precision, that "practical needs demand the dates of Buddhist history."[55] Released from the constraints of the Laozi debate, which no one any longer took seriously, Yinshun was free to follow the most reliable sources to whichever date they led. He ends his book with a call to Buddhists throughout the world to agree upon a date for the Buddha's nirvana and proposes 390 BCE. This, the unification of Buddhist traditions worldwide based on a single event located at a precise moment, is, one suspects, the main motivation for the book, and as such marks a turning point in Chinese Buddhist historiography that nonetheless shares with previous Buddhist historians some of the protocols for reading the history of Indian Buddhism we have already seen.

In the context of Chinese Buddhist historiography, Yinshun's dating of the Buddha's nirvana is radical not so much for the date itself—though this is novel—as it is for rejecting the premise that *Chinese* texts from the time of the Buddha—that is, before the entry of Buddhism to China—are of any use at all for uncovering signs that the Buddha had been born. Yinshun implicitly dismisses the notion that events in the life of the Buddha were accompanied by astronomical phenomena that would have been recorded in China, avoids all discussion of prophecy, and does not shirk from questioning the authenticity of texts composed in India—all clear breaks from Buddhist historiography as practiced in China before the twentieth century.

In addition to establishing new dates for the Buddha, throughout his scholarly corpus Yinshun persistently attempted to establish a new chronological framework for the development of Buddhist doctrine in India. His efforts built in part on similar attempts by Taixu. In one of his works, Taixu describes a shift in his thinking from relying on a conventional "doctrinal classification" (*panjiao* 判教) approach that, as we have seen, was standard in Chinese Buddhism since medieval times to a new approach that he introduced in 1934. Unlike the doctrinal classification schemes, which attempted to place all essential Buddhist texts and teachings at various moments in the life of the Buddha, Taixu tried to cover all of Indian Buddhist history, which he divided into three five-hundred-year periods: in the first five hundred years after the Buddha's death, "the Lesser Vehicle circulated while the Greater Vehicle was concealed" 小行大隱; in the following five hundred years, the "Greater Vehicle was predominant while the Lesser Vehicle followed" ;and from the period beginning one thousand years after the Buddha's death, the "Greater Vehicle circulated, the Lesser Vehicle was concealed, esoteric Buddhism predominated, and exoteric Buddhism followed" 大行小隱，密主顯從.[56] Although different from traditional periodization, Taixu's tripartite division avoided controversy on two fronts: first, by noting that the Mahāyāna (the "Greater Vehicle") remained "concealed" in the first five hundred years after the Buddha's death, he leaves open the possibility that the Mahāyāna scriptures were spoken by the Buddha rather than created centuries after his death, a position Western scholars had already held for some time; second, although there is a hint of criticism of Tantric (or "esoteric") Buddhism—Taixu writes that esoteric Buddhism absorbed "vulgar" Indian practices—he does not rank the periods he set out, as was standard and indeed the point of previous systems of doctrinal classification. Only with Yinshun and his discussion of the periods of Indian Buddhism are these sensitive problems broached.

In Yinshun's writings, from early works like *Indian Buddhism* (*Yindu zhi fojiao* 印度之佛教), published in 1942, through to later works like *A History of Indian Buddhist Thought* (*Yindu fojiao sixiang shi* 印度佛教思想史), completed in 1987, he developed his own terminology for characterizing periods of Indian Buddhist thought. He divided Indian Buddhist thought into three periods: an early period that emphasized the doctrine of impermanence (*wuchang lun* 無常論); a middle period corresponding to early Mahāyāna that emphasized emptiness, or the absence of self nature (*xingkong lun* 性空論); and a late period characterized by an assertion of "true permanence" (*zhenchang lun* 真常論), roughly corresponding to *tathāgathagarba* texts, the foundation of much of Chinese Buddhist thought.[57] This is a fairly standard presentation of Indian Buddhist thought, prevalent especially in Tibet, and usually termed the three "turnings of the wheel."[58] What made Yinshun's use of this scheme distinctive is his open disdain for the third category as a late accretion and product of non-Buddhist influence that, he argued, reestablished the notion of an enduring self in contradiction to what he considered the core Buddhist doctrine of non-self.[59] His greatest contempt was reserved for Tantric Buddhism, which he ascribes to an even later period. With the rise of Tantra, he laments, "conservative, mystical, formulaic, opportunistic religion raised its head. In other words, this was a decline in the spirit of religion."[60] Here, this explanation for the disappearance of Buddhism in India replaces prophecy and the belief in an inevitable "period of decline" (*mofa* 末法). The decline of Buddhism in India was not destiny; it was instead a human failure to maintain the principles of early Buddhism, willfully abandoned in exchange for crass worldly advantage. And unlike classical decline theory, in Yinshun's view the problem could be rectified through scholarship and persuasion. While this is still a traditional rhetoric of corruption, unlike the long-standing practice of "doctrinal classification" in Chinese writings on India, Yinshun is rejecting outright that a large portion of the Chinese Buddhist canon represents the teachings of the Buddha at all. And although Yinshun's periodization (minus the value judgment) may appear standard to modern scholars of Buddhism, within the tradition of Chinese monks writing on Indian Buddhist history it was a radical departure from convention.

More than providing a new chronological framework of Indian Buddhism, Yinshun approached Indian Buddhist scriptures with a critical acumen that previous generations of Buddhist historians had reserved for texts composed in China. While traditional Buddhist historians drew on the Buddha's prophecies to reconstruct Indian history, Yinshun was more circumspect, at one point explaining, "The legends and prophecies of the scriptures are often parables, hints, intimations, combining fact and imagination. One cannot take every character and every line as reliable historical material. When treating this material and researching it, one must be especially careful and without prejudice or bias if one is to extract the truth from legends and prophecies."[61]

This willingness to question the authenticity of Indian Buddhist scriptures opened up a new array of explosive problems that previous generations of monastic scholars had been unwilling even to entertain. If some canonical scriptures claiming to be the word of the Buddha that came to China from Indian originals are not in fact from the Buddha's day, can we show that *any* of them are? At the same time, this new attitude allowed Yinshun to critique the tradition, not just as a scholar, but as a Buddhist monk attempting to define just what is of value in Buddhism. In Yinshun's telling, the Buddha's opposition to class distinctions, ritual, and superstition, his reflections on impermanence and the false nature of the self, led not just to the flourishing of Buddhism but also to the flourishing of India;[62] when it lost these ideals to formalism, mysticism, and empty ritual, Buddhism perished and Indian culture as a whole fell into decline.

Yinshun was equally eager to apply this new modern skepticism to elements in the Buddha's biography, even those that he acknowledged were of great antiquity. Modern rationalists have long been frustrated by the biography of the Buddha, not just because it is embedded with accounts of miracles but also because it is tightly bound with accounts of previous buddhas of the far distant past, and also with stories of the Buddha's previous lives.[63] In China, one of the most influential account of the Buddha's life, the *Scripture of the Origins of the Miracles of the Prince*, translated into Chinese already in the first half of the third century, opens with the Buddha describing his meeting with the previous buddha, Dīpaṃkara, in a previous life.[64] One standard source for the life of the Buddha, the *Scripture of the Great Origin*, the first text in the *Dīrghāgama* and the first text in the modern Chinese Buddhist canon, is not really a biography of *the* Buddha at all, but rather a collective biography of the past seven buddhas, including buddhas who are purported to have lived in extreme antiquity, long before recorded history.[65]

Both texts are typical of a general approach. Before the modern period, Chinese Buddhist historians always took canonical accounts of the Buddha's previous lives and of the lives of previous buddhas as factual. Chan histories of the "transmission of the lamp," for instance, typically begin not with Śākyamuni but with Vipaśyin 毗婆尸佛, the most ancient of the seven previous buddhas. In a clear break with the past, Yinshun rejects both stories of the Buddha's previous lives and accounts of events in the lives of previous buddhas as pious fiction. Characteristically, he diffuses potential objection to such a radical stance not through reference to modern scholarship or appeals to rationalism but through reference to the canon. Even among Indian Buddhist masters of the past, he tells us, there were some who rejected such stories. In his massive (1,300-page) study of early Mahāyāna, he cites the *Sapoduo pinipiposha* 薩婆多毗尼毗婆沙 (Skt. *Sarvāstivādavinayavibhāṣa*): "The accounts of the Buddha's previous lives or related stories are not reliable. The information they contain is in neither the sutras nor the vinaya and cannot be employed to draw definitive conclusions."[66]

While accepting that legends of the seven buddhas of the past were shared by virtually all Buddhists in the early period,[67] Yinshun assures us that at least one group of Buddhists in medieval India, the Sarvāstivāda, were skeptical of such accounts. The Sarvāstivāda position "is deeply rational, and not given to lightly relying on legends."[68] As one example, Yinshun addresses the story of how in a previous incarnation the Buddha Śākyamuni had encountered Dīpaṃkara, the previous buddha, and received a prediction that he too would one day become a buddha. According to Yinshun, the story was accepted by all of the schools of Indian Buddhism except the Sarvāstivāda, since in the end it is merely a legend, "and legends may contain, in their transmission, errors." More specifically, he cites the *Apidamo dapiposhalun* 阿毗達磨大毗婆沙論 (Skt.*Abhidharma mahāvibhāṣāśāstra*), which discusses the legend in the form of a dialogue.

> How are we to explain the accounts concerning Burning-Lamp Buddha (Dīpaṃkara Buddha)?
> Answer: There is no need to explain them. Why? Because they are not spoken of in the sutras, vinaya, or abhidharma.
> They are just legends, and all legends may or may not be true.[69]

But what distinguishes Yinshun's approach to such material from that of a pure rationalist like Hu Shih, gleefully ripping apart the legends of Bodhidharma, is that after praising the skepticism of the Sarvāstivādins ("certainly superior to those of other schools"), he goes on to praise the legends he has just discredited as "synthesizing the virtues, the very heart of the spirit of the Indian people."[70] Legends are historically useful reflections of the mentalities of those who created and propagated them and useful for the virtues they embody, the examples they set. Already in his first major work, *An Introduction to Buddhism* (*Fofa gailun* 佛法概論), Yinshun argued that Buddhist cosmology as it was later transmitted was an idealized projection of an ancient understanding of real geographic regions.[71] Yinshun did not flinch at the potentially disruptive consequences of this attempt to reread the tradition as myth—myth filled with meaning, but myth nonetheless. He argued that the buddha Amitābha, central to popular devotion in Chinese Buddhism, was the product of the evolution of myths about the sun.[72] The bodhisattvas Mañjuśrī and Samantabhadra were in fact idealizations of the historical disciples of the Buddha, Śāriputra and Maudgalyāyana.[73] Guanyin (Skt. Avalokiteśvara), he suggested, may have originated in the Iranian goddess Anāhita, combined with Apollo and Īśrava, but "from a Buddhist perspective, is nothing more than a vulgarization of Śākyamuni's compassion."[74] Even the pure lands of the buddhas Akṣobhya and Amitābha are essentially projections of an ideal world without physical suffering and perfectly suited for self-cultivation, inspired by disappointment with the real world.[75] Many of these iconoclastic positions are raised in a lengthy, densely documented and hence little-read study on the rise and early development of Mahāyāna. They share some features with attempts by Western scholars to link buddhas and bodhisattvas with earlier deities and myths. But for Yinshun, as a Buddhist monk, historical explanation is not enough; he finds Buddhist ideals—the "salvific compassion" of the Buddha, or ideals of a more perfect world—better suited to Buddhist practice than the flawed world in which we live. Such comments suggest that, unlike a secular historian of Buddhism, who can content her or himself with reconstructing the past, the Buddhist historian must go a step further and employ the lessons of Buddhist history, however faulty and corrupted it may be, to illustrate and promote Buddhist doctrines and values.

Yinshun's monograph, *Researching Buddhism with Buddhism*, first published in 1954, is a collection of essays, primarily on Indian Buddhism, that covers many of the themes touched on above, including the social context for the rise of Buddhism in India, the failings of Tantric Buddhism and *tathāgathagarbha*, and the authorship of Mahāyāna scriptures.[76] But perhaps the most remarkable part of the book is the preface, in which, like Taixu before him, Yinshun lays out a Buddhist approach to the study of Buddhist history, built on the principles of impermanence and non-self. As all phenomena are essentially impermanent, Yinshun argues, it is foolish for the scholar to cling to notions of continuity in Buddhist doctrine and history. History, in the final analysis, is composed of a series of individual, ephemeral moments. The same holds true for Buddhist doctrine. The Buddha's teachings, "Once formulated in the intricate splendor of language become scriptures comprising words and phrases, forming theories made up of distinct ideas. These are then propagated as mundane truths, subject to the principle that all actions are impermanent, changing continuously." What is true of language is equally true of institutions, like the monastic order, and of material expressions of Buddhism. More precisely, "Impermanence is arising and extinction. Arising occurs according to conditions. It is not that something arises because the consequence is present in the cause, or that it arises without consequence. We must use arising without self nature as a principle of impermanence to research and understand the occurrence of a given Buddhist sect, type of thought, practice, institution, or event."[77] To employ this skepticism toward the illusion of continuity and simplistic models of causation—a skepticism that derives from strong currents of Buddhist thought—makes for better history, a history less concerned with a search for ultimate origins and singular causes and more sensitive to complex processes. He gives as an example the perplexing problem of the origins of Yogācāra. According to tradition Yogācāra begins with the two half-brothers Asaṅga and Vasubandhu, with Asaṅga receiving the teachings from the future buddha Maitreya.[78] This legend has troubled modern scholars of Yogācāra, leading to theories that "Maitreya" may in fact have been a historical figure who lived at the time of Asaṅga, sharing by chance a name with the future buddha, thus later sparking misunderstanding and the subsequent legend. At stake here for many is the legitimacy of Yogācāra teachings. Even if the involvement of the buddha Maitreya is a later legend, it reflects a perceived need to link Yogācāra thought to a buddha since Asaṅga lived long after the last buddha's nirvana. That is, is Yogācāra inherent in the teachings of the Buddha or a novel creation of a later time?

Rather than relying exclusively on precise empirical research and textual analysis, Yinshun tackles the problem by employing the classical Mādhyamika explanation of the relationship between cause and effect. It is illogical, he explains, to claim that something causes itself without external intervention. At the same time, something cannot be caused by another intrinsically distinct entity, since if it is intrinsically distinct there can be no causation. Nor can something originate from no cause at all.[79] But where does all of this leave the historian? Returning to the case of the origins of Yogācāra, Yinshun runs through the various options. One approach, he tells us, is to claim that the Yogācāra championed by Asaṅga was in fact fully present at the time of the Buddha, and that all Asaṅga did was to correctly transmit what he had heard from the bodhisattva Maitreya. But "this is equivalent to saying that something that was already completed appeared anew, and this, 'self-production,' is not in accord with the principle of all actions arising in impermanence according to causes and conditions." Similarly, to say that the doctrines of Yogācāra did not exist in the time of the Buddha and were invented by Asaṅga without the assistance of Maitreya or were the direct result of another school of thought is an example of the fallacy of seeing "external production" (*tasheng* 它生), production of an event or idea in which the agent of production plays no role in bringing it about.

After running through other faulty, fragmentary approaches, Yinshun explains the correct approach: "First, you must understand, Asaṅga's Yogācāra is the formative stage of Yogācāra's development. At this time, the distinguishing characteristics and refined doctrines of Yogācāra were fully and concretely established. But there is no self nature that does not change, and in the process of formation through constant transformation, the formation itself is constantly transforming." At the time of the Buddha, he continues, there were already nascent Yogācāra tendencies. And by the time of Asaṅga, doctrinal problems and approaches developed in a process of "unlimited transformations." He goes on to insist that there are of course primary and secondary causes, geographical factors, and personal factors. Nor did this process of constant change come to a conclusion with Asaṅga; it continued with his disciples and later Buddhist thinkers in a process without end, for "certainly that which has ended is passed; history does not repeat itself. But the truth of history is that, in the transformations of causes and conditions, [the past] always exerts an integral influence on the future."[80]

In addition to this sensitivity to the contingency of any historical moment, the Buddhist approach to history, Yinshun asserts, is equally committed to resisting the illusion of the self. "According to the position of Buddhist doctrine, cognition is a faculty formed through the conditioned interaction of the knowable and the act of knowing. There is no act of cognition that is purely objective and divorced from the subjective." We are, moreover, heavily conditioned by our past experience. Yet the only way to at least approach the original meaning of the scriptures, and historical truth, is to recognize and account for our subjective biases. Proponents of a given school of Buddhist thought, Yinshun explains, tend to be so wedded to their own interpretation that they cannot be objective. Yinshun goes on to describe the effort required to recognize and root out one's biases as a scholar and to strive for objectivity as a form of religious self-cultivation and implementation of the Buddhist rejection of self. For Yinshun, who was never known as a meditator or chanter, scholarship was his principal form of cultivation and could be valued as much for the process of self-discipline as for the results derived from it.

Linked to this notion of scholarship as a form of self-cultivation, the third area in which Yinshun argues that the Buddhist historian should be different is in a commitment to the quest for the realization of ultimate truth in nirvana.[81] Here he defends scholarship from a strong tradition, especially in Chan Buddhist thought, of skepticism toward the ultimate value of formal study. He points out that Buddhist literature is full of examples of sages, from Śāriputra to Huineng, who achieved enlightenment through reading or hearing the recitation of scripture.

Nirvana signifies truth, it signifies release. Until one who studies Buddhism has directly encountered nirvana, he should take it as an ultimate goal and fervently strive to attain it. Hence, one who studies Buddhism must be equipped with a desire to search for truth, with a genuine resolve to achieve release. One does not study Buddhism just to acquire material for conversation. Nor it is just a tool to enhance one's reputation or gain material benefits. The purpose is instead, through study, to grasp truth.[82]

Much of what I have presented in previous chapters, while important for understanding the development of Buddhist historiography and interesting in its own right, has been abandoned in the face of challenges to tradition in the twentieth century. No serious Buddhist historian, monastic or otherwise, any longer cites karma as an explanation for imperial policy in medieval China, suggests a supernatural cause for discrepancies in sources, or uses ancient prophecies as evidence for subsequent events. Yinshun suggests an approach to Buddhist history distinct from yet compatible with modern sensibilities. Whether he carried out this ideal in his own work—the essays that follow the introduction to *Researching Buddhism with Buddhism* are relatively conventional and do not consistently apply a historical methodology informed by Buddhist doctrine—is less important.

Yinshun's contemporaries and successors did not adopt his methodology or propose other distinctively Buddhist approaches to Buddhist history. Owing to the suffocating political atmosphere in the People's Republic of China, monastics there made little, if any contribution to Buddhist scholarship before the final decade of the twentieth century. In Taiwan, however, the tradition of the monk-scholar continued (albeit at first also in a socially and politically stifling environment), producing some historical works that continued to probe the boundaries of how Buddhism's most committed followers, monastics, interpreted Buddhism's past.

DONGCHU, SHENGYAN, AND THE TURN TO ACADEMIA

In June 1949, with China at the height of revolution and the fate of Chinese Buddhism more precarious than ever, Dongchu 東初 (1907-1977), who had only just fled to Taiwan from the mainland a few months earlier, published an essay on, of all things, the dates of the Buddha's birth.[83] In it, he rejects at the outset the traditional Chinese date of 956 BCE for the Buddha's nirvana and sets himself the task of deciding between the date of 623 BCE for the Buddha's birth, the view he attributed to Taixu, and that of 565 BCE, held by the eminent Japanese Buddhist scholar Takakusu Junjirō 高楠順次郎 (1866–1945). After a long, complex analysis of sources, including consideration of Chinese and Pali texts and references to, among other works, H. G. Wells's *A Short History of the World* and Vincent A. Smith's *Early History of India*, Dongchu settles on a new date: 563 BCE. As we have seen, Yinshun at roughly the same time, though in his case having fled to Hong Kong, was writing a whole book on the subject in which he would come to the more radical conclusion that the Buddha entered nirvana as late as 390 BCE. Setting aside historiographical technique and the merits of the date Dongchu proposes, given the historical context, what is most remarkable is the choice of topic. In such desperate times—even after managing to find passage on a commercial liner to Taiwan in the midst of a chaotic mass exodus from war-torn Shanghai in January 1949, Dongchu was detained by port officials in Taiwan for lacking proper papers—monk-scholars like Dongchu and Yinshun took solace and found meaning in historical scholarship.[84]

Dongchu's biography shares many characteristics with those of other monk-scholars of his generation. Like Taixu and Yinshun, he came from a village near Shanghai, born to a family of modest social standing. He became a monk as a child of thirteen but later followed the new trend of attending a Buddhist seminary, where he met on several occasions both Taixu and Yinshun. As in the case of Taixu and especially Yinshun, Dongchu lived in relative intellectual isolation, publishing exclusively in Buddhist journals for Buddhist readers. He responded to the writings of Hu Shih and once met the intellectual historian Xu Fuguan 徐復觀 (1904–1982), but otherwise seems to have had little contact with academics. He late in life attempted to improve his English but was never able to master any foreign language. In addition to his brief study of the dates of the Buddha, he wrote a number of articles on Indian and Chinese Buddhist history, but his representative works are three books he published after his sixtieth birthday: *A History of Buddhist Relations Between China and India*, *A History of Buddhist Relations Between China and Japan*, and finally, *A History of Modern Chinese Buddhism*.[85] All three are sprawling, ambitious books, remarkable more for the choice of topic—before the twentieth century, Chinese Buddhists expressed little interest in, for instance, Japanese Buddhism—than for the originality of the analysis.

Of these, Dongchu's most important book is his *History of Modern Chinese Buddhism*, a large work in two volumes, with the second devoted primarily to biographies of Buddhist figures in the first half of the twentieth century. The first volume—staunchly patriotic and fiercely anti-Christian—chronicles the government's relentless dismantling of Buddhist resources during the Republican period and the swift erosion of Buddhist economic and political influence in China. Written in the early 1970s before Taiwan's economic boom, the book reflects the spartan conditions under which Dongchu worked. He cites few sources, relying almost entirely on materials published in Buddhist journals. He does not make use of government archives, newspaper reports, or oral history. Nor does he cite scholarship on modern Chinese history.[86] Here history is employed as a tool of reform in a book punctuated with passionate pleas for improvements in the education of monks, calls for cooperation between members of the sangha, and condemnation of the external forces that Dongchu held responsible for impeding the progress of Chinese Buddhism: imperialism, Christianity, and Communism.[87] In this project, there was no place for either traditional historiographical concerns with dating, sources, and lineage or Yinshun's new Buddhist historiographical agenda focused on finding truth in history and meaning in myth.

Despite the sheer volume of his work, Dongchu is best known as the ordination master of Shengyan 聖嚴 (1931–2009), the final monastic historian I will examine in this book. Shengyan's greatest significance for Chinese Buddhist historiography is his status as the first Chinese monk to receive a PhD.[88] More than formal recognition of his work, the PhD reflects Shengyan's attention and access to the wider scholarly world, representing a trend that has continued in the generation of monks and now nuns writing history today.[89]

At the time of his death in 2009, Shengyan was best known as an organizer and public figure, and as author of dozens of widely read popular books on Buddhism. But before he became involved in the founding of Dharma Drum Mountain, a large monastic organization with a seminary, university, and publishing house, Shengyan was a scholar whose work focused on Buddhist history. The early part of Shengyan's life is very much in keeping with the pattern of other monk-scholars of the twentieth century discussed above, all of whose historical writings, even when they dealt with the minutiae of Buddhist history in India in the distant past, were informed by their personal experience. Born to a poor family in the same general area of China, near Shanghai, that Taixu, Yinshun, and Dongchu came from, Shengyan (a.k.a. Sheng Yen) became a monk at thirteen in part because his parents could not afford to arrange a desirable marriage for him. As a consequence of the family's poverty, he received only a minimal education as a child. Indeed, it is remarkable that he received any education at all. Again, this is in marked contrast to the academic historians of his generation who received intensive training in the Chinese classics as children; most of Shengyan's knowledge of Chinese history and philosophy was self-taught.

Like the other leading monks of his day, Shengyan attended one of the new Buddhist seminaries, and his career was repeatedly disrupted by social and political unrest. As in the case of Taixu and Yinshun, he was put off by the dependence of monks for survival on what he saw as the empty, rote recitation of liturgy in Buddhist death rituals. His description in his autobiography of the dreary ceremonialism of monastic life in the forties in Shanghai is especially poignant, including claims that many Shanghai monks turned to heroin to cope with the frantic ritual schedule in the belief that it would boost their energy level, and no doubt for relief from the boredom of a relentless ritual routine.[90] Rather than ritual, the monastic ideal Shengyan aspired to was a life devoted to study, meditation, and social work. This vision of a more perfect life for Buddhist monks was reflected in a history of Indian Buddhism he wrote years later in which he expressed this longing through his reconstruction of Buddhism at its beginnings: "Buddhism originally emphasized only the internal construction of character and spirit; it did not emphasize formalistic worship. For this reason, primitive Buddhism had no sacrificial rites of any kind and had no use for the worship of idols."[91]

With the economy in shambles and the entry of Mao's troops into Shanghai, monastic life of any kind became increasingly precarious. In exchange for safe passage to Taiwan, Shengyan disrobed and joined the Nationalist army for some years where, as he describes it in his autobiography, he lived a semimonastic existence, remaining celibate and largely vegetarian and never engaging in combat. His autobiography describes the years he spent in the army in almost comical terms, a wan, intellectually minded ex-monk marching about the countryside "training," at times with a bamboo stick on his shoulder since the army could afford neither uniforms nor guns for its most recent conscripts. After eventually receiving permission to leave the army under the pretext of poor health, Shengyan immediately requested and received reordination under Dongchu. Soon thereafter he left Dongchu's monastery for a period of self-imposed exile and self-study, followed in the late 1960s by a period of active teaching and research that included publication of three historical works: a history of Japanese and Korean

Buddhism, a history of Tibetan Buddhism, and a history of Indian Buddhism.[92] These works share with the historiography of Taixu and Dongchu a commitment to the world history of Buddhism presented for a general audience. The rationalist historiography of Taixu and Yinshun is very much in evidence, particularly in his history of Indian Buddhism. The section of the book devoted to the biography of the Buddha, for instance, does not discuss the previous lives of the Buddha, the lives of previous buddhas, or the extraordinary physical characteristics of the Buddha—all standard in traditional accounts. Shengyan gives us instead a very human thinker. He dismisses the legend that the Buddha's child was the result of a miraculous conception, for instance, and sides with scriptures that argue that before the Buddha set out on the life of an ascetic, as a prince he was required to have sex with his wife and consorts in order to maintain his reputation as a nobleman.[93]

But tensions between the tradition represented by the Buddhist canon and modern sensibilities frequently bubble to the surface, though Shengyan is less radical in his willingness to sacrifice traditional Buddhist history for a more credible one than Yinshun (whose long life encompassed most of Shengyan's). Shengyan notes, for instance, that immediately after his birth, the Buddha took seven steps and announced, "I am the most honored among men and gods," but concludes by explaining: "After saying this phrase, he became like an ordinary infant, and did not walk or speak."[94] Similarly, he recognizes the chronological problem with Mahāyāna scriptures—though claiming to be the word of the Buddha, they do not appear in the historical record until centuries after his death—but dances around the problem by noting that many Mahāyāna ideas are present already in early Buddhist scriptures, that the Buddha Dharma is not limited to the sayings of the Buddha, and that many of the apparent exaggerations of the Mahāyāna scriptures were intended to be read metaphorically.[95]

This "metaphorical" or "religious" reading as an alternative to a "historical" reading of material is a common trope in Shengyan's historiography. Take, for instance, the familiar topic of prophecy. In keeping with his rationalist tendencies, Shengyan is skeptical of scriptural claims of accurate prophecies, but is reluctant to dismiss them entirely, writing, "From the perspective of a religious attitude, prophecies in the scriptures are all the word of the Buddha; from a historical perspective, the dates and figures provided by prophecies are sufficient for establishing the date and place of appearance of the scriptures in which they appear."[96] In other words, from a historical perspective, prophecies of the future reveal not the word of the Buddha but the time and circumstances of those who claimed the prophecy for the Buddha long after his death.

He takes a similar approach to the problem of the story that key Yogācāra texts were dictated to Asaṅga by the bodhisattva Maitreya in Tuṣita heaven, discussed by Yinshun. Shengyan provides a summary of Chinese texts that mention the legend and of various explanations, including the argument of Ui Hakuju 宇井伯壽 (1882–1963) and Yinshun that Maitreya, in addition to referring to the bodhisattva, was also the name of a separate historical figure, and the reservations of Kimura Seitan 木村泰賢 (1881–1930), who was content with the assertion that the contents of the texts were in accord with Asaṅga's teachings. But at the same time, Shengyan admits the possibility that Asaṅga, in a meditative state, might in fact have communicated with Maitreya. Here, as in the case of prophecy, Shengyan proposes a "two-truth model":

> If we adopt the perspective of religious experience or religious belief, then indeed we have reason to firmly believe that this Maitreya is the bodhisattva of compassion of Tuṣita heaven, because what the Yogācāra masters saw in their meditative states would certainly not be a fabrication. It is entirely possible that the Yogācāra masters through supernormal powers attained during meditation ascended to heaven to ask for instruction or asked Maitreya to descend to preach the Dharma.[97]

But he balances this acceptance of Buddhist tradition with a "historical" approach according to which the legend of Maitreya the bodhisattva was an outgrowth of a historical figure who taught Asaṅga and who also happened to be named Maitreya. Here and elsewhere in his historical works, Shengyan is reluctant to take the harder line of proposing that such claims are fabrications intended to win legitimacy for new and controversial teachings. Tangled in the conflict between the force of tradition and the demands of the new critical history, in his early works he attempts to accommodate both, producing arguments that more often than not satisfy neither.

Like the other monk-historians of the twentieth century, Shengyan was content to rely on printed sources. Hu Shih read Dunhuang manuscripts in Paris and London and analyzed their significance for Chan history while working in Taiwan at Academia Sinica in the fifties, and other academics of Hu's generation like Chen Yuan recognized the importance of archaeology, epigraphy, and local history for the study of Buddhist history; Shengyan, like Yinshun before him, drew almost exclusively on the printed canon. And compared to Yinshun's, Shengyan's analysis of the canonical materials is unexceptional. Shengyan's *History of Indian Buddhism*, like his histories of Japanese Buddhism and Tibetan Buddhism, was intended as a textbook, summarizing the work of others, rather than a radical, original interpretation of the Buddhist path. In fact, the most original aspect of the work—striking in the context of writings by Chinese monk-scholars in the twentieth century—is his repeated reference to scholarship, especially Japanese scholarship. This pronounced turn to academia and recognition of professional historians is new. Soon after completing this book, Shengyan moved to Japan where, after six years, he received a PhD in Buddhist literature from Rissho University with a dissertation on the seventeenth-century Chinese monk Ouyi Zhixu. He later expanded on this work to complete a study of late Ming Buddhism in Chinese.[98] These works follow standard scholarly conventions, citing original sources with precise references in the footnotes and making extensive use of Chinese, Japanese, and English-language scholarship. Shengyan's later works focused on scriptural studies and were generally popular, less scholarly in nature.

But by the 1980s, for all of the tensions that remained between the rationalist tendencies of modern historiography and the commitment of monks to the Buddhist tradition, the gap between monk-historians and academic historians began to narrow. And in the decades that followed, increasing numbers of monks and nuns earned PhDs, in Taiwan, abroad, and most recently in mainland China, almost all in Buddhist studies and some in Buddhist history. But in the years to come, the question remains whether or not *Buddhist* historiography—Taixu puzzling over how to maintain Bodhidharma as a historical figure, Yinshun coming to terms with the value of Mahāyāna scriptures once they could be shown not to be direct records of the word of the Buddha, Shengyan struggling to separate "religious" from "historical" readings of scripture—has, for better or worse, come to an end, absorbed by the standards and sensibilities of modern academic historiography.

Who knows? Perhaps one day a distinctive form of Buddhist historiography will rise in the shadow of academic history just as it did in the shadow of court history. But for now, this seems unlikely.[99]

Conclusion

In the introduction, I tried to place Chinese Buddhist historiography in the broader context of Buddhist historical writings throughout Asia by examining the four themes of time, doctrine, agenda, and craft. Given the large geographic region Buddhism has covered, the multiple languages and cultures in which it is practiced, and the long stretch of time over which it has existed, it is not surprising that Buddhist historical writing differs widely across the Buddhist world. Now, after pursuing a series of particular problems Buddhist historians in China faced, it is worth returning to those four themes to explore what they reveal about Buddhist historical writing in China in particular.

TIME

With the cyclical view of history that all of the Buddhist historians I draw on would have accepted (perhaps with the exception of some of the modern ones), in South Asian works, historians turned to either karma or prophecy to move back and forth along a vast timeline, linking disparate events and, in effect, playing with time and narrative. Past lives provided an opportunity for historians to leave a given event and slip back to its precedents and causes; prophecy allowed them to jump ahead to future events. But while Buddhist historians in China make frequent reference to karma and to prophecy, and give an occasional nod to cyclical time, their sense of time is, in the end, overwhelmingly conventional. They order their books chronologically from the most distant date up to the present. Even in the *Biographies of Eminent Monks*, within each of the ten categories compilers created for their subjects, the monks are arranged chronologically, according to dynasty and reign title. The search for karmic sources for events or attempts to interpret prophecy rarely take us out of a standard narrative, progressing methodically from the past forward toward the present. But this is a summary of the function of time within these works. Equally interesting is the way the works and their authors were themselves affected by the flow of time.

In the last chapter, the transition from the early historical works of Taixu, emerging from a traditional monastic education at the dawn of the twentieth century, to the late works at the beginning of the twenty-first century by Shengyan, whose academic career culminated in a PhD in Japan, signals the rough passage of Buddhist historiography from the standard concerns and techniques of centuries of Buddhist historical writing—basically everything covered in the first five chapters—to modern academic ones. But for all of the drama of this sudden transformation in the twentieth century, this was just the latest shift in the constantly changing history of Buddhist historiography in China. I hope that my thematic approach in most of the previous chapters hasn't overshadowed what should by now be obvious: that Buddhist historiography itself has a history.

The contours of this history, outlined very briefly in the introduction, should be clearer now. The first phase of Buddhist historiography, from roughly 500 CE to 1000, was dominated by prosopography, in particular, collections of biographies of eminent monks grouped according to shared qualities. This grand project to document the lives of the most admirable and important monks of the first millennium of Buddhism in China is represented most famously in the first three collections of the *Biographies of Eminent Monks*, covering close to two thousand biographies of monks. Themes discussed in the first chapters of this book, from the attention to dates to the adjudication of conflicting sources and fascination with prophecy, pervade this brand of history. These same themes saturate other genres of Buddhist historical writing from the same period.

In the second phase, from roughly 1000 to 1900, the traditional format gave way to the dictates of genealogical history in which monks were arranged in lineages of orthodox transmission from masters to their disciples, though Buddhist historians experimented with a range of formats, especially in the early centuries of the period. Certainly, dates, source analysis, and prophecy can be found in the grand Buddhist genealogical works, but the new format and its overriding concern with picking winners and losers in the forging of orthodoxy often overshadowed the old concerns, leaving a messy historical record of gaps and contradictions for more sober historians to clean up, as they aligned dates and moved monks from one branch to another in their efforts to construct a more plausible family tree for the monastic community. While a number of innovative formats were introduced with great success—most notably the return to Sima Qian's format that combined annals, biography, and essays, and a strictly chronological format inspired no doubt by Sima Guang's *Comprehensive Mirror for Aid to Government*—it was in the arena of genealogical history that the greatest historiographical battles took place; this, for roughly a thousand years, was the history that mattered.

Finally, the third phase, from 1900 to 2000, was perhaps the most rapid and tumultuous of them all. In this briefest of periods, most of the old historiographical rules and techniques—decline theory, the unquestioned reliability of Indian sources, the value of prophecy, miracles and supernormal power, the role of karma as a historical force—were quietly and quickly abandoned in favor of the new call for rational, secular analysis of the past, in substance no different from political, military, or intellectual history, as Buddhist historiography was gradually absorbed into academic discourse.

The reasons for these shifts in style and emphases—in Buddhist parlance, their "causes and conditions"—are for all of their complexity generally comprehensible and obvious for the first and the third phases of Chinese Buddhist historiography. In the first phase, in the early centuries of Buddhism in China, Buddhist scholars drew on an already well-established tradition of writing the life stories of important people, beginning with the time and place of birth, family background, and childhood, and proceeding to narrate their major accomplishments and events in their lives, and ending with the time, place, and circumstances of their death, noting along the way any progeny. These were all conventions ready to hand, as was the practice of grouping biographies by category. The genre of historical biography was already prestigious, with well-known models both for genre and for the calling of the historian. All that was needed was to apply conventions of genre developed at court among literati to a new subject: the Buddhist monastic. The new subject required of course a series of adjustments. In place of progeny, Buddhist historians listed disciples; in addition to family background, they gave special attention to their subject's monastic teachers. The rich Buddhist lore that grew up around eminent holy men, whether imported from India or developed independently in China, was woven into the biographies, including accounts of miraculous births, interaction with deities, the power of Buddhist scripture, ascetic acts, and prophecy. In addition to drawing on Chinese historiographical practices of comparing different accounts, pointing out discrepancies, and if possible resolving them, Buddhist historians drew as well on Buddhist doctrines to explain the stories they narrated, referencing karma and technical classifications of supernormal powers, and stages on the bodhisattva path. In short, the first phase of Buddhist historiography was a series of adaptations provoked by the entrance of Buddhism into the Chinese historiographical universe.

The move in the twentieth century away from traditional Buddhist concerns was similarly inspired by international, intercultural dynamics, and followed closely on parallel developments in literati and subsequently academic historiography. Outside of Buddhist circles, the gradual decline of the Qing empire and sense that China had fallen behind the rest of the world in any number of areas—military might, technology, economics, literature, and politics—led to the movement to "doubt antiquity," that is, to question the received tradition, including both the facts and the traditional approaches to investigating the past. This vibrant period of internal reflection by China's leading minds was accompanied by a new and insatiable curiosity about the wider world. In the early decades of the twentieth century, Chinese intellectuals learned foreign languages, studied abroad, devoured and debated new ideas about historiography from Germany, Britain, and the United States, and proposed a plethora of new approaches to Chinese history. The newly founded Chinese universities became the sites where the new history was discussed, developed, and disseminated. Buddhists—laymen, but especially monastics—were in many ways cut off from these trends socially. In the early years, even though a few monks traveled abroad, they did not have the opportunity to learn foreign languages or to study abroad. Early Buddhist seminaries drew inspiration from universities and opened their doors to reform-minded monks, but in the universities there was no place for monks, not to mention nuns, even as students, much less professors. And in the context of a century of revolution and war, Buddhist seminaries, always underfunded and understaffed, never had a chance to compete with the universities. Nonetheless, the changes in the academic world prompted them to adapt their approach to Buddhist history to the new theories, terminologies, and academic fads (recall Taixu, isolated in his monastic cell, studying the latest intellectual trends in newspapers, journals, and translated books he read daily). These trends led to what at present seems to be the disappearance of Buddhist historiography into the larger field of Chinese historiography, which itself is increasingly indistinguishable from academic historiography everywhere else. The reasons for this latest development may be found in the rise of powerful state-run educational systems, globalization, and the success of monastic organizations in adapting to the challenges and opportunities of modernity. In sum, the third phase of Chinese Buddhist historiography was driven by the same process of modernization that affected every sphere of Chinese intellectual life during the period.

The second shift, from conventional biography to genealogies consisting primarily of obtuse dialogue between masters and disciples, is the most difficult to pin to a neat set of causes. Why did the genealogical style of history appear and rise when it did? Perhaps others will one day demonstrate a link to the collapse of the Tang empire and the late-Tang persecution of Buddhism as triggers for a collapse in confidence in the traditional forms of Buddhist historiography, or discover deeper social and cultural trends that led to a search for legitimacy in lineage, or tie the rise of genealogical history to the rise of printing, a burgeoning book market, and changing reading habits. But given the sources we have, such proposals rooted in social and political history will always remain in the realm of loose speculation. The most obvious impetus for the rise of genealogical historiography is the flourishing of sectarian divisions, with each faction attempting to distinguish itself from its rivals. But the genre of lineage history rose together with sectarianism, each spurred on by the other, so that it isn't especially useful to separate the two. We are on more solid ground when we emphasize the appeal of the genealogical genre. Once Buddhist genealogical histories appeared, with their dramatic narratives of disciples who prove their worth in trials of wit and perseverance under charismatic masters, and the puzzles many readers found in these encounters, the genre of genealogical history proved enormously attractive. That is, beyond any external factors, the qualities inherent in the genre of lineage narrative itself no doubt played a major role in its persistent popularity.

This brief romp through an enormous corpus of texts, genres, authors, and approaches over a millennium and a half passes over any number of figures, genres, and innovations. Just as the vast cyclical interpretation of time could be divided up into much smaller units, so too can key shifts in Chinese Buddhist historiography be seen to take place within shorter time frames.

DOCTRINE

One approach to assessing just what is Buddhist about Buddhist historiography is to turn to formal Buddhist doctrines, developed outside of Buddhist historical writings, and then to see how they are employed in historiography. The most sustained attempt to adopt this approach is Song Daofa's recent academic study *Buddhist Historiography* (*Fojiao shiguan yanjiu*), in which he ingeniously proposes seven modes of thought in Chinese Buddhist historiography: immanence, resonance, supernormal powers, karma, decline theory, orthodoxy, and dependent origination. We might add to this list any number of doctrines that crop up frequently in Chinese Buddhist historiography, including the bodhisattva path, buddha nature, the three bodies of a buddha, mind-to-mind transmission, the rhetoric of immediacy, and "doctrinal classification," all much-discussed Buddhist doctrines found in various genres of writing. Some of these doctrines leave a deeper trace on historiography than others; some (in particular the doctrine of karma and the doctrine of the decline of the Dharma) are by their nature fundamentally historical. Rather than beginning with doctrine, I have for the most part worked out from a series of historiographical puzzles: India, genealogy, modernity, and so on. The advantage of this approach is that it reveals ways historical problems dictated the understanding and interpretation of doctrine. It is not the case that doctrinal innovation took place only in formal, doctrinal writing; historians too employed doctrine in creative ways, most apparent in resolving specific historical problems.

Historians turned to the doctrine of the decline of the Dharma not just to evaluate the moral state of the world and warn of its demise but also as a puzzle requiring the philological and chronological skills of the historian to determine his precise position in the grand cycles of time through comparative analysis of a wide range of texts. Historians drew on the doctrine of karma not just to assess the value of the moral life and in particular to pass judgment on history's villains and heroes but also to demonstrate, through their deep familiarity with the historical record, the reality of karma, to prove that it was true. More than this, historians explored the historical record, rife with seeming contradictions and doctrinal conundrums, as a way of thinking through Buddhist thought, through historical narrative probing the limits and potential contradictions of a given set of doctrinal stances.

AGENDA

The Buddhists who wrote history in China were inevitably influenced by the institutions that supported them. This is not especially surprising or pernicious, and is as true for the modern academic as it is for the medieval monk; the important question is which institutions affected them and how. Most of the compilers of

Buddhist history I have discussed were directly or indirectly linked to the court, their works eventually included in one of the officially sanctioned Buddhist canons. In a few cases their works were written directly on imperial command. The court had enormous power over the fate of the Buddhist monastic institutions, as demonstrated in periodic persecutions of Buddhism, at times carried out with ferocious efficiency. Hence it is logical that, in the context of court debates over the relative merits of Buddhism and Daoism, historically minded Buddhists applied their skills to demonstrating that chronologically the Buddha must have lived long before Laozi, making the claim that Laozi founded Buddhism impossible. While we today can easily accept the conclusion that Laozi had nothing to do with the birth of Buddhism, the evidence available to the Buddhist scholars making the claim at the time could just as easily have pointed to a later date for the Buddha—it was their agenda that drove their argument.

More generally, but still with eyes on the court, Buddhists employed the historical record to promote a positive image of Buddhist monks and nuns as moral, loyal, exemplary figures, compiling collections of biographies of eminent monks and exemplary nuns. Buddhists did not compile collections of scurrilous monks or wayward nuns—this was for novelists and playwrights with no commitment to Buddhism. When accounts of seditious or immoral monks were invoked at court, it was usually in the context of arguments by court rivals calling for the persecution of Buddhism. In the same vein of a direct, transparent agenda, Buddhist historians both at and away from the court argued for the superiority of their own lineage over others, to demonstrate the legitimacy of Chan over Tiantai or a particular lineage within Chan over its rivals.

Less cynically, Buddhist historical writings promote Buddhist ideas and values: the power of Buddhist scripture, ritual, meditation, and asceticism; the value of good works like temple construction and vegetarianism; the benefits of the monastic way of life. By examining historical events, Buddhist authors attempted to separate authentic scriptures from apocryphal ones, to promote monastic purity among the sangha, and to identify orthodox, historically reliable lineages, whether or not they themselves were part of them. Uncovering agendas like these does not require expert sleuthing; such motivations are usually obvious and often stated upfront in the introductions to the works themselves. More elusive are the motivations behind often extensive efforts to prove the superiority of one source over another, one name over another, or even one lineage over another when the benefit to the historian and his affiliates is not clear. In many cases, the agenda emerges from a sense of professional pride, an allegiance to the craft of historical research.

CRAFT

For all of my references to the massive corpus of Buddhist historical writings in China, and despite my efforts to read widely and be as comprehensive as I could, in choosing material I have been decidedly old-fashioned in what I consider proper history. I've largely ignored popular narrative, oral accounts, ritual rooted in history, material culture, and, with a few exceptions from the Chan tradition, poorly written history; the historians here are almost without exception members of the elite, writing in a style and format that for the most part mimics that of court historians. The compilers of history I have concentrated on, abbot-appointed, court-appointed, or self-appointed guardians of Buddhist history, were steeped in the classics, ensconced in monastic libraries, and supported by teams of assistants, cooks, and acolytes. Did other types of people—heretics, provincial monks, artisans, women, the illiterate—remember Buddhist history differently? This is a field ripe for more methodologically daring studies of history and memory that would make use of different types of material than I have examined here.

Nonetheless, one advantage to focusing on elite monks and Buddhist literati is their cohesion. This was a group marked by a self-awareness of their tradition. True, some Buddhist historical works have been lost, and there was frequent dissension among Buddhist historians, but it is safe to say that all read the *Records of the Historian* and the *History of the Han* from the court tradition, and the *Collection of Records Concerning the Translation of the Tripitaka* and the *Biographies of Eminent Monks* from the Buddhist tradition. And with this sense of belonging came a shared respect for the standards of historiographical craft. These standards included a voracious appetite for sources—the most admired Buddhist historians read both court history and Buddhist history, scripture and doctrinal treatises, miracle tales, poetry, and vinaya collections. The Buddhist historian, like his court counterpart, was expected to read not just widely but critically, to flag discrepancies in the sources and argue for a version of events that was plausible and chronologically consistent. Finally, the Buddhist historian was supposed to be objective. Of course, no historian is as objective as they think they are. And the close affiliation between author and subject—Buddhists writing about Buddhist history in a context of competition over resources and ideology—made the pull of bias even stronger for Buddhist historians than it is for many others. Nonetheless, we see in many cases Buddhist historians arguing for the superiority of one date or one source over others when their argument advances no particular agenda. And in rare cases, we have even seen Buddhist historians following the dictates of their craft to argue against their own immediate interests. In the modern period, Taixu and especially Yinshun argued that, for the Buddhist historian, allegiance to craft and principle made the writing of history a form of self-cultivation, a way of bettering oneself.

ONE FINAL NOTE

These cold categories of time, doctrine, agenda, and craft might give the impression of clinical, distant scholars, but in fact Buddhist historical writings are filled with emotion. Historians are outraged at the blunders of their predecessors; the words "absurd" (*miu* 謬) and "preposterous" (*guai* 乖) appear frequently in Buddhist historiography. They lament as well the mistakes of the past—the division of the monastic community in India and further sectarian strife in China, the persecution of Buddhism by benighted rulers, the distance, ever increasing, that separated them from the Buddha ("alas!" [*wuhu* 嗚呼] and "we must be vigilant!" [*jingzai* 警哉] are frequent final words to historical commentary). They express as well wonder at the events of the past, at the glory of great monasteries now lost, large translation centers the likes of which were never seen again, and the miracles inspired by holy men long since dead. Reading, editing, and writing history was an opportunity to live in the company of the most eminent monks and nuns and witness their acts of courage, wisdom, and spiritual power. Alongside the vast corpus of writings they left behind, these emotional reactions to the work of the historian and to the past in general perhaps best convey that for Chinese Buddhists, past and present, engagement with Buddhist history is part of what it means to be a Buddhist.

Acknowledgments

I have presented versions of parts of this book in conferences and talks over many years, including for colleagues at the Institute of History & Philology, the University of Bristol, Hong Kong Polytechnic, and Stanford. I presented the chapter on sources for the Center for Buddhist Studies at UCLA; the chapter on karma at McMaster; the chapter on prophecy at a workshop on "Prophecy and Foretelling of Destiny in Buddhism" at Friedrich-Alexander-Universität Erlangen-Nürnberg organized by Mario Poceski, and at a panel on Buddhist historiography at the meeting of the International Association of Buddhist Studies organized by Luke Thompson; and the chapter on modern Buddhist historiography at the Center for Buddhist Studies at Berkeley. In all of these cases, feedback from students and colleagues has been invaluable. The participants at a workshop on Buddhist historiography organized by The Ho Center for Buddhist Studies at Stanford—John Strong, Jacqueline Stone, Stephen Berkwitz, Bryan Cuevas, Stefano Zacchetti, and Paul Harrison—inspired many of the approaches I take here. The graduate students who attended my seminar on Buddhist historiography in 2016 (Allan Ding, Sangyop Lee, Adeana McNicholl, Grace Ramswick, Kedao Tong, Dan Tuzzeo, and Likun Yang) helped me to think beyond China, especially for the introduction. In the early stages of the project, I received financial support (in 2008-9) from the Leverhulme Foundation. Ouyang Nan read through a draft of the manuscript and caught a number of errors. Marcus Bingenheimer read yet another draft, caught another set of errors, and made a number of useful suggestions, all of which I adopted. Elizabeth Morrison read a draft of the manuscript at a later stage, not only correcting many still outstanding errors and stylistic infelicities but also forcing me to rethink my arguments. The three anonymous readers for Columbia University Press caught mistakes and offered many helpful suggestions for improvement. Finally, Leslie Kriesel, Production Editing Manager at Columbia University Press, tightened up my wandering prose on every page, from the first line to the last.

Appendix 1

Chronological List of Major Works

This list is intended as a general reference to the major works cited in the preceding chapters. For more precise information on editions used, see the bibliography. Works are listed in rough chronological order. This is by no means a comprehensive list of Buddhist historical works composed in China; these are just the works that I refer to most often.

500s

Biographies of Famous Monks (*Mingseng zhuan* 名僧傳) by Baochang 寶唱 (b. ca. 466–d. after 517).

Only fragments of this early collection of monastic biographies are extant along with a table of contents.

Collection of Records Concerning the Translation of the Tripiṭaka (*Chu sanzang jiji* 出三藏記集) by Sengyou 僧祐 (445–518).

A bibliography of Buddhist works, listing titles, authors, and circumstances of translation, along with biographies of authors and translators.

The Śākya Genealogy (*Shijia pu* 釋迦譜) also by Sengyou.

An attempt to narrate the history of the Śākya clan from the creation of the world at the beginning of the kalpa up through to Śākyamuni's immediate disciples. Distinct from the seventh-century *Genealogy of the Śākya Clan*, by Daoxuan, listed below.

Biographies of Eminent Monks (*Gaoseng zhuan* 高僧傳) by Huijiao 慧皎 (497–554).

The most influential collection of biographies of monks, divided into ten categories, with an essay by the compiler appended to each category.

"Treatise on Buddhism and Daoism" (*Shi Lao zhi* 釋老志) by Wei Shou 魏收 (507-572).

A treatise contained in Wei Shou's history of the Wei dynasty, *Wei shu* 魏書. Translated by Leon Hurvitz, "Treatise on Buddhism and Taoism."

Record of the Three Jewels Through the Ages (*Lidai sanbao ji* 歷代三寶紀) by Fei Zhangfang 費長房 (completed in 598).

Like the *Collection of Records Concerning the Tripiṭaka*, this work combines bibliography with historical accounts of Buddhist figures and events.

600S

Further Biographies of Eminent Monks (*Xu gaoseng zhuan* 續高僧傳) by Daoxuan 道宣 (596-667).

The second of three major installments in the "Biographies of Eminent Monks" series, for the most part treating monks who lived after the cutoff date for the first *Biographies of Eminent Monks*, though covering as well some earlier monks not included in Huijiao's work.

Genealogy of the Śākya Clan. (*Shijia shi pu* 釋迦氏譜) by Daoxuan 道宣 (596-667).

A history of the Buddha and his ancestors, with discussion of geography as well. Distinct from the sixth-century work *Shijia pu* by Sengyou.

700S

Buddhist Bibliography of the Kaiyuan Era (*Kaiyuan shijiao lu* 開元釋教錄) by Zhisheng 智昇 (completed in 730).

Arguably the most sophisticated and influential of the medieval Buddhist bibliographies.

Record of the Teachers and Disciples of the Laṅkāvatāra Scripture (*Lengqie shizi ji* 楞伽師資記) compiled by Jingjue 淨覺 (683-ca. 750).

A Chan genealogy representing the tradition later known as the "Northern School." Translated into French by Bernard Faure, *Le Bouddhisme Ch'an en mal d'histoire. Genèse d'une tradition religieuse dans la Chine des T'ang*.

Record of the Transmission of the Dharma Treasure (*Chuan fabao ji* 傳法寶記).

A short Chan genealogical history relating the lineage of the Northern School. Translated by John McRae, *The Northern School*, 259.

Record of the Dharma Jewel Through the Generations (*Lidai fabao ji* 歷代法寶記).

A Chan genealogical history compiled in Sichuan. Translated by Wendi L. Adamek, *The Mystique of Transmission. On an Early Chan History and Its Contexts*.

800S

The Biographies of Baolin (*Baolin zhuan* 寶林傳) compiled by Zhiju 智炬 in 801 at the Baolin Monastery.

A collection of biographies of Chan monks, influential in the subsequent "transmission of the lamp" genre.

The North Mountain Record (*Beishan lu* 北山錄) by Shenqing 神清 (d. 814).

A heterogeneous work, not easily classified as historiography, that nonetheless includes original critiques of Buddhist historical writing, most famously Chan works.

900S

Collection of the Hall of the Patriarchs (*Zutang ji* 祖堂集) compiled circa 952.

A large Chan genealogical history comprised of biographies of "patriarchs" with a focus on dialogues between masters and disciples.

Song Biographies of Eminent Monks (*Song gaoseng zhuan* 宋高僧傳) by Zanning (919–1001).

The third major installment in the "Biographies of Eminent Monks" series. A more precise translation of the title is *Biographies of Eminent Monks Compiled During the Song Dynasty*. Unlike the previous two collections in the series, the *Song Biographies* were compiled on imperial command.

A Brief History of the Clergy (*Seng shi lüe* 僧史略) by Zanning (919–1001).

A collection of brief entries on various aspects of the history of Buddhism in China, arranged by theme rather than chronologically. Translated by Albert Welter, *The Topical Compendium of the Buddhist Clergy*.

1000S

The Transmission of the Lamp Compiled in the Jingde Era (*Jingde chuandeng lu* 景德傳燈錄) compiled by Daoyuan 道元 (d.u.) with extensive editing by the court literatus Yang Yi 楊億 et al.

Arranged according to a genealogical tree of masters and disciples, this is the first text in the "transmission of the lamp" genre to receive imperial sanction.

The Expanded Lamp Record Compiled in the Tiansheng Era (*Tiansheng guangdeng lu* 天聖廣燈錄) (completed in 1029).

Record of the Dharma Transmission of the True Lineage (*Chuanfa zhengzong ji* 傳法正宗記) by Qisong (1007–1072).

1100S

Biographies from the Monastic Treasury of the Chan Forest (*Chanlin sengbao zhuan* 禪林僧寶傳) by Huihong 慧洪 (1071–1128).

Records from the Forest [of Chan] (*Linjian lu* 林間錄) by Huihong 慧洪 (1071–1128).

Comprehensive Discussion and Chronology of Buddhism Compiled in the Longxing Era (*Longxing biannian tonglun* 隆興編年通論) by Zuxiu 祖琇 (fl. 1150s–1160s).

A chronological history of Chinese Buddhism, beginning with the entry of Buddhism to China in the Han and proceeding up to the beginning of the Song dynasty, with frequent commentary by the author.

1200S

Comprehensive Orthodox Transmission of the Śākya Clan (*Shimen zhengtong* 釋門正統), first compiled by the layman Wu Keji 吳克己 around 1208 and completed by Zongjian 宗鑑 in 1237.

Informed by Tiantai doctrine, this work follows the structure of the *Records of the Historian*. It was a key source for Zhipan's *Fozu tongji*, listed below.

Compendium of the Five Lamps (*Wudeng huiyuan* 五燈會元) by Puji 普濟 (1179–1253) (completed in 1253).

A large and influential collection of five previous "transmission of the lamp" collections of Chan biographies, organized according to master-disciple lineages.
Comprehensive Account of the Buddhas and the Patriarchs (*Fozu tongji* 佛祖統紀) by Zhipan (fl. 1265-1274).

A large history of Buddhism focused on the Tiantai lineage, in structure based on the *Shiji* (see also the *Comprehensive Orthodox Transmission of the Śākya Clan* above). Partly translated by Thomas Jülch, *Zhipan's Account of the History of Buddhism in China*; and by Jan Yün-hua, *A Chronicle of Buddhism in China 590–960*.

1300S

Complete Accounting of the Buddhas and Patriarchs Through the Ages (*Lidai fozu tongzai* 歷代佛祖通載, by Nianchang 念常 (1282-1341).

1600S

Strict Transmission of the Five Lamps (*Wudeng yantong* 五燈嚴統) by Feiyin Tongrong.
A Chronology of Lineages and Transmission (*Zongtong biannian* 宗統編年) by Jiyin 紀蔭 (fl. 1689).

A chronological history of Buddhism from Śākyamuni to 1689 with a focus on Chan lineages.

1900S

A Brief History of Buddhism (*Fojiao shilüe* 佛教史略) by Taixu 太虛 (completed in 1910).

Taixu, the leading reformist monk of his day, after introducing the life of the Buddha and his teachings, divides his history into the Indian era, the Asian era, and the World era.
Indian Buddhism (*Yindu zhi fojiao* 印度之佛教) by Yinshun 印順 (published in 1942).

A history of Indian Buddhism based on Indic texts translated into Chinese and included in the Chinese canon. Written in Sichuan.

A Discussion of the Determination of the Date of the Buddha's Extinction (*Fomie jinian jueze tan* 佛滅紀年抉擇譚) by Yinshun 印順 (published in 1950).

An argument for the date 390 BCE for the Buddha's nirvana. Written in Hong Kong.

Researching Buddhism with Buddhism (*Yi fofa yanjiu fofa* 以佛法研究佛法) by Yinshun 印順 (completed in 1954).

A collection of essays, including an introduction that discusses the attitude a Buddhist should take when researching Buddhism. Written in Taiwan.

A History of Indian Buddhism (*Yindu fojiao shi* 印度佛教史) by Shengyan (a.k.a. Shengyen) 聖嚴 (published in 1969).

Together with Shengyan's history of Tibetan Buddhism and his history of Japanese and Korean Buddhism, eventually published, in 1980, as *A World History of Buddhism*.

A History of Chan Buddhism in China (*Zhongguo chanzong shi* 中國禪宗史) by Yinshun 印順 (completed in 1970).

A distinctively modern history of Chan, written in Taiwan.

A History of Modern Chinese Buddhism (*Zhongguo fojiao jindai shi* 中國佛教近代史) by Dongchu 東初 (published in 1974).

A study of Chinese Buddhism from the Yuan dynasty through the Republican period, written in Taiwan.

Chinese Buddhism at the End of the Ming (*Meimatsu Chūgoku bukkyō no kenkyū* 明末中国仏教の研究) by Shengyan 聖嚴 (completed in 1975).

Shengyan's PhD dissertation, written in Japanese for Rissho University.

The Origins and Development of Early Mahāyāna (*Chuqi dasheng fojiao zhi qiyuan yu zhankai* 初期大乘之起源與展開) by Yinshun 印順 (published in 1980).

A massive and, for a monastic, thoroughly iconoclastic study of early Mahāyāna. Written in Taiwan.

Appendix 2

Lineage Charts

LINEAGE CHART 1: THE INDIAN PATRIARCHS

1. According to the Fu Fazang Yinyuan Zhuan[1]

Śākyamuni

1. Mahākāśyapa 2. Ānanda 3. Śāṇakavāsa 4. Upagupta 5. Dhṛṭaka 6. Mikkaka 7. Buddhanandi 8. Buddhamitra 9. Pārśva 10. Puṇyayaśas 11. Aśvaghoṣa 12. Kapimala 13. Nāgārjuna 14. Kāṇadeva 15. Rāhulata 16. Samghanandi 17. Samghayaśas 18. Kumārata 19. Jayata 20. Vasubandhu 21. Manorhita 22. Haklena 23. Siṁha. *This ends the transmission of the Dharma.*

2. According to Guanding (differences from above in bold)

Śākyamuni

1. Mahākāśyapa 2. Ānanda 3. **Madhyantika** 4. Śāṇakavāsa 5. Upagupta 6. Dhṛṭaka 7. Mikkaka 8. Buddhanandi 9. Buddhamitra 10. Pārśva 11. Puṇyayaśas 12. Aśvaghoṣa 13. Kapimala 14. Nāgārjuna 15. Kāṇadeva 16. Rāhulata 17. Samghanandi 18. Samghayaśas 19. Kumārata 20. Jayata 21. Vasubandhu 22. Manorhita 23. Haklena 24. Siṁha. *This ends the transmission of the Dharma in India,* but a second branch continued in China from the Fourteenth Patriarch, Nāgārjuna, as follows: Nāgārjuna, *The Dazhidu lun* **(a text),** Huiwen, Huisi, Zhiyi, **Guanding**

3. According to the Transmission of the Lamp Compiled in the Jingde Era
(differences from the Fu fazang *in bold)*

Śākyamuni

1. Mahākāśyapa 2. Ānanda 3. Śāṇakavāsa 4. Upagupta 5. Dhṛṭaka 6. Mikkaka 7. **Vasumitra** 8. Buddhanandi 9. Buddhamitra 10. Pārśva 11. Puṇyayaśas 12. Aśvaghoṣa 13. Kapimala 14. Nāgārjuna 15. Kāṇadeva 16. Rāhulata 17. Saṃghanandi 18. Saṃghayaśas 19. Kumārata 20. Jayata 21. Vasubandhu 22. Manorhita 23. Haklena 24. Siṁha 25. **Vāśasita** 26. **Puṇyamitra** 27. **Prajñātāra** 28. **Bodhidharma**

LINEAGE CHART 2: THE SOUTHERN SCHOOL FROM BODHIDHARMA TO THE FIVE HOUSES (LEAVING OUT MANY SIDE BRANCHES AFTER HUINENG)

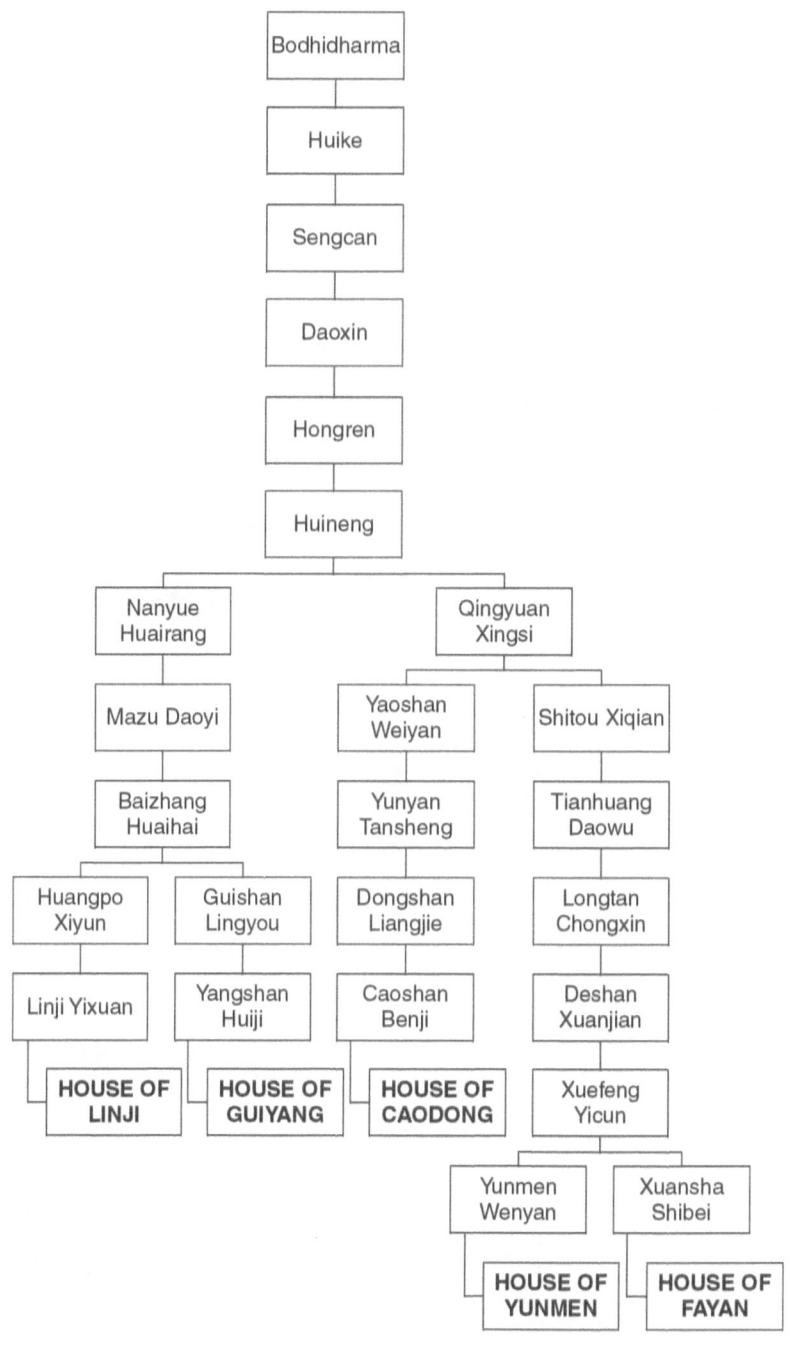

LINEAGE CHART 3: TWO MORE CHAN LINEAGES

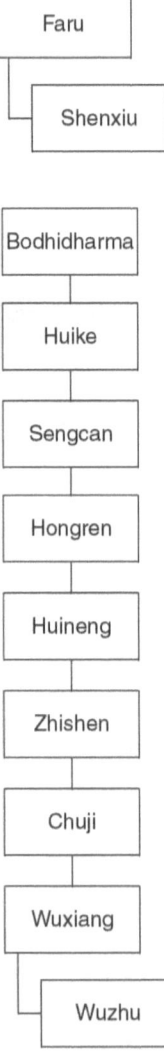

1 According to the *Record of the Transmission of the Dharma Treasure* (with differences from Southern lineage in bold)

2 According to the *Record of the Dharma Jewel Through the Generations* (with differences from Southern lineage in bold)

LINEAGE CHART 4: THE RECORD OF THE TEACHERS AND DISCIPLES OF THE LANKĀVATĀRA SCRIPTURE

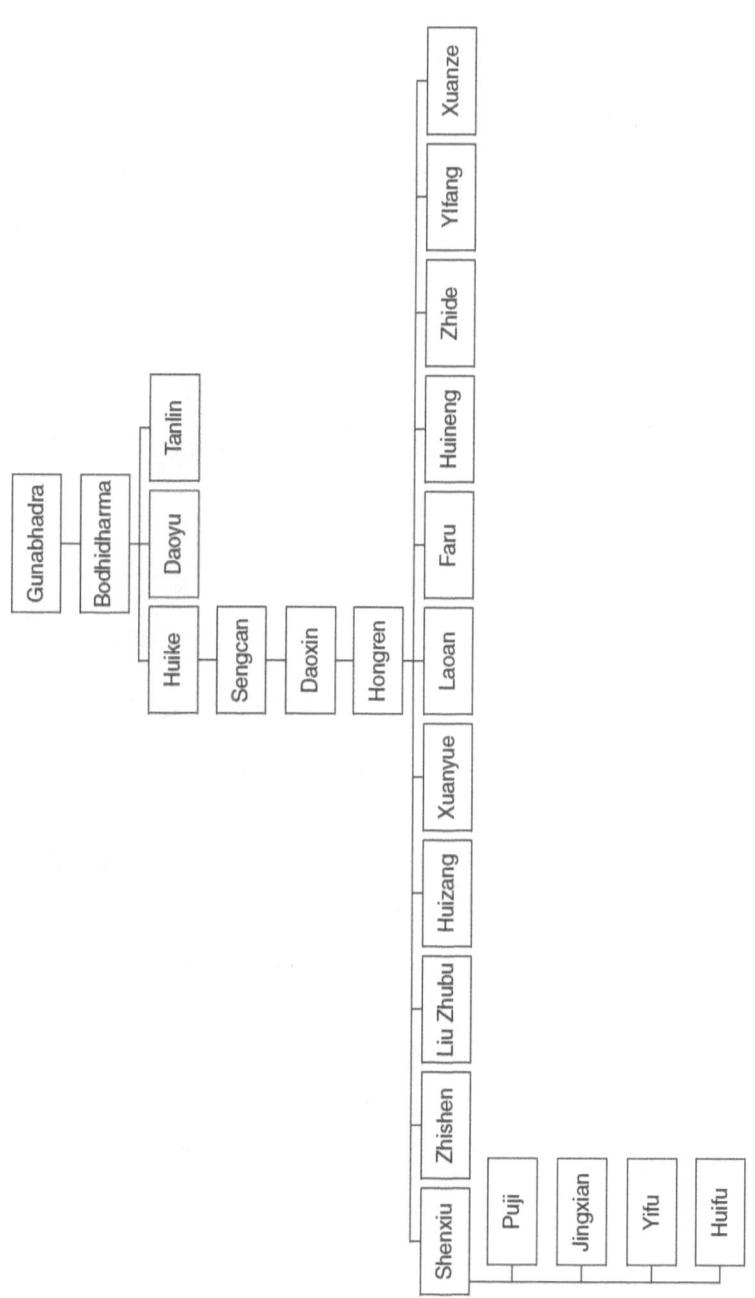

LINEAGE CHART 5: THE TIANHUANG/TIANWANG PROBLEM

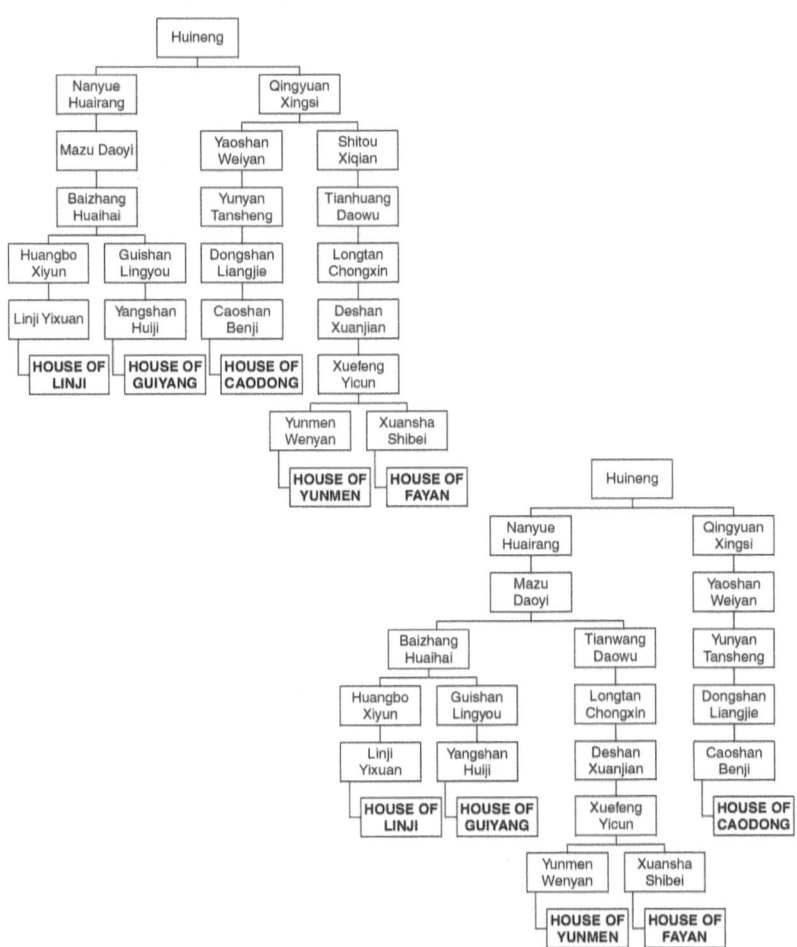

Notes

INTRODUCTION

1. *Yi fofa yanjiu fofa* 以佛法研究佛法 (1972; rpt., Xinzhu: Zhengwen Chubanshe, 2003). The opening essay is translated into German in Marcus Bingenheimer, *Der Mönchsgelehrte Yinshun (*1906) und seine Bedeutung für den Chinesisch-Taiwanischen Buddhismus im 20. Jahrhundert* (Heidelberg: Edition Forum, 2004), 284–301.
2. Qinqin Peng has laid a foundation for this project in her dissertation, "Between Faith and Truth: The Historiography of Buddhism in Modern China (1902–1965)" (Göttingen, 2021).
3. Women were excluded almost entirely from the Buddhist historiographical tradition. None of the works I discuss in this book, including even the *Biographies of Bhikṣuṇīs,* was composed by a woman. The same is true for Chinese historiography more generally; after the notable exception of Ban Zhao 班昭 (45–c. 116 CE), sister of Ban Gu 班固 (32–92 CE) and major contributor to the *History of the Han*, we look in vain for historical works composed by women even into the early modern period.
4. Song Daofa 宋道發 estimates that 186 Buddhist historical works appeared in Chinese before the twentieth century. Of course, defining what constitutes a "Buddhist historical work" is itself fraught. *Fojiao shiguan yanjiu* 佛教史觀研究 (Beijing: Zongjiao Wenhua Chubanshe, 2009), 6.
5. As many references in notes to follow and the bibliography at the end of this book indicate, there is excellent scholarship on Chinese Buddhist historiography in various languages. The pioneering work of Chen Yuan 陳垣, Cao Shibang 曹仕邦, and Helwig Schmidt-Glintzer stands out in particular, as well as more recent work by Song Daofa and Cao Ganghua. Nonetheless, compared to Chinese Buddhist thought, or Chan history, or Chinese institutional history, or Chinese court historiography, the topic of historical writings composed by Chinese Buddhists has been largely overlooked.
6. Even if we accept that conventional historiography is relatively weak in premodern South Asia, the absence of formal historiography does not mean the past didn't matter to South Asians before the modern era. Indian Buddhist texts might be more amenable to a study of how memory is preserved in stories, objects, and ritual, an approach Yosef Hayim Yerushalmi employs in his classic study of Jewish memory and historiography,

216 Introduction

   Zakhor: Jewish History and Jewish Memory, in which he makes explicit comparison between Jewish and Indian memory (Seattle and London: University of Washington Press, 1989).

7. Throughout I follow Keith Knapp in designating the period from 200 to 1000 "medieval." See "Did the Middle Kingdom Have a Middle Period? The Problem of 'Medieval' in China's History," *Education About Asia* 12, no. 3 (2007): 12-17.

8. *Gaoseng zhuan* 高僧傳, T no. 2059, vol. 50. For a chronological list of the major works I draw on, organized by English translation of the title along with a brief description, see appendix 1.

9. Étienne Lamotte, *History of Indian Buddhism. From the Origins to the Śaka Era* (Louvain: Peeters Press, 1988), 198-201. Jan Nattier, *Once Upon a Future Time. Studies in a Buddhist Prophecy of Decline* (Berkeley: Asian Humanities Press, 1991), especially 19-24.

10. *Jingde chuandeng lu* 景德傳燈錄1, T no. 2076, vol. 51, 204d. The *Jingde chuandeng lu* draws here on the *Chang ahan jing* 長阿含經 (Skt. *Dīrghāgama*) 1, T no. 1, vol. 1, 2a.

11. Jan Nattier terms these two types of cycles "Buddhological" (focusing on the appearance and disappearance of buddhas) and "cosmological" (focusing on the origin and destruction of a universe). There is more variety to versions of these cycles than my account above might suggest. See Nattier, *Once Upon a Future Time,* 9-10. For the "cosmological" cycle, see Nattier, *Once Upon a Future Time,* 10-19; Akira Hirakawa, *A History of Indian Buddhism: From Śākyamuni to Nāgārjuna* (Honolulu: University of Hawai'i Press, 1990), 174-75.

12. *Shimen zhengtong* 釋門正統 1, X. no. 1513, vol. 75, 255c-256a.

13. *Shi ji* 史記 (Beijing: Zhonghua Shuju, 1962), 27.1344. Translation from Stephen W. Durrant, *The Cloudy Mirror: Tension and Conflict in the Writings of Sima Qian* (Albany: State University of New York Press, 1995), 127. Feng Youlan comments that "This concept of the interrelationship between man and the physical universe makes of history a 'divine comedy.'" *History of Chinese Philosophy* (Princeton, NJ: Princeton University Press, 1953), vol. 2, 58-71.

14. Mark Edward Lewis, *Writing and Authority in Early China* (Albany: State University of New York Press, 1999), 356. Despite occasional references to these theories in Chinese historical writings, modern scholars have noted that they had remarkably little effect on how Chinese court historians wrote their works or interpreted their facts. See Durrant, *The Cloudy Mirror*, 127 ("neither of the cycles described above is generally applied in *Records of the Historian* to actual events"). And in his study of medieval historiography, Hu Baoguo 胡寶國 writes: "[This] theory did not motivate historians to introduce new ideas; its function remained at a practical political level. Each dynasty was obliged to employ the orthodox concept of the rise and fall of the five virtues to demonstrate the legitimacy of its own rule" (104). Hu Baoguo, *Han Tang jian shixue de fazhan* 漢唐間史學的發展 (Beijing: Shangwu Yinshuguan, 2003), 101-105.

15. The full quotation is "the reading of books found among the Arabs describing historical events, the government of Kings and Arabs generally, is a waste of time." Quoted in Shubert Spero, "Maimonides and the Sense of History," *A Journal of Orthodox Jewish Thought* 24, no. 2 (1989): 129. The comment may reflect a general admiration of Islamic historiography among other Jews at the time. Franz Rosenthal, *A History of Muslim*

Historiography, 2nd ed. (Leiden: Brill, 1968), 140-41. Nonetheless, Maimonides's disdain was not limited to history written by Arabs, leading scholars to question just what aspects of history he objected to and why. See Kenneth Seeskin, "Maimonides' Sense of History," *Jewish History* 18, no. 2/3 (2004): 129-45. For our purposes, quotations like these, together with examples of medieval Muslim scholars who often take an apologetic tone when introducing history, highlight the universal respect for history in China and, seemingly, in Buddhism; I have yet to find an example of a prominent Buddhist thinker declaring open disdain for the study of history.

16. L. S. Perera, "The Pali Chronicle of Ceylon," in *Historians of India, Pakistan and Ceylon*, ed. Cyril Henry Philips (London: Oxford University Press, 1967), 32. The final sentence ("History itself was of little significance therefore except as a means to an end") reflects the view that proper history is devoted to the dispassionate presentation of facts, a desire to reconstruct the past for its own sake rather than to achieve any other purpose. This narrow view of what constitutes history—excluding, for example, all of the vinaya literature, which is profoundly concerned with the past—is prevalent in writings about Indian historiography. Consider R. C. Majumdar's comments in "Ideas of History in Sanskrit Literature": "The works under review do not reach the standard which entitled them to be ranked as 'historical' in the proper sense of the term. They are limited in their objects, eulogistic in character, rhetorical or poetic in style, and aiming more at edification and entertainment than a statement of positive facts." In Philips, ed., *Historians of India, Pakistan and Ceylon*, 20. Again, rhetoric and entertainment, moralizing and utility for the present are essential to many works now considered classics of historiography, from the writings of Sima Qian and Tacitus to Gibbon, Maculay, Prescott, and Braudel. For a more recent assessment of the question of historical consciousness in early Indian writings, including a summary of the history of the discourse, see Romila Thapar, "Historical Traditions in Early India: c. 1000 B.C. to c. AD 600," in *The Oxford History of Historical Writing*, vol. 1, ed. Andrew Feldherr and Grant Hardy (Oxford: Oxford University Press, 2011), 553-76.

17. *The Phoenix and the Ladder. The Rise and Decline of the Christian View of History* (Berkeley: University of California Press, 1964). Patrides was certainly not the only one to recognize the distinction, in the context of comparative historiography, between classical historiography and the teleological view of history of the Jews and after them the Christians. See for instance E. H. Carr, *What Is History* (1961; 2nd ed., London: Macmillan, 1986), 104.

18. Momigliano's warnings against overemphasizing a distinction between the cyclical (Greek) view of time and the progressive (Jewish and Christian) view of time are instructive for the Buddhist case. Momigliano explains that in fact the notions of time were hardly uniform for either group: in particular, the views expressed on cyclical time by Greek philosophers were not shared by Greek historians. He warns, "If one wants to understand something about Greek historians and the real differences between them and Biblical historians, the first precaution is to beware of the cyclical notion of time." Arnald Momigliano, "Time in Ancient Historiography," *History and Theory* 6 (1966): 1-23.

19. Of course any number of other categories for Buddhist historiography could also be valuable. Citing Donald Steel, Keith Jenkins notes that in the 1960s, the five major concepts

identified as constituting history were: time, space, sequence, moral judgment, and social realism. In the 1970s these were refined to: time, evidence, cause and effect, continuity, and change. After suggesting other possibilities, including structure-agency, overtermination, center-periphery, *mentalité*, and paradigm, Jenkins proposes the three categories of epistemology, methodology, and ideology. Keith Jenkins, *Re-Thinking History* (1991; rpt., London: Routledge, 2007). For Buddhist historiography, Song Daofa proposes immanence, resonance, supernormal powers, karma, decline, orthodoxy, and dependent origination, though these themes are more prevalent in Chinese Buddhist historiography than in historiography across the Buddhist world. Song, *Fojiao shiguan yanjiu*.

20. Momigliano singles out the prevalence of prophecy, rather than cyclical versus progressive notions of time, as one of the major differences between Greek and Jewish historiography. As we will see in chapter 4, the distinction in the comparison between Chinese Buddhist and Chinese court history is not so sharp, but is nonetheless significant. "Time in Ancient Historiography," 20.

21. Wilhelm Geiger, trans., *The Mahāvaṃsa or Great Chronicle of Ceylon* (London: Pali Text Society, 1912). On this text, see Heinz Bechert, "The Beginnings of Buddhist Historiography: Mahāvaṃsa and Political Thinking," in *Religion and Legitimation of Power in Sri Lanka*, ed. Bardwell L. Smith (Chambersburg, PA: Anima Books, 1978), 1–12.

22. Delmer M. Brown and Ichirō Ishida, *The Future and the Past: A Translation and Study of the Gukanshō, an Interpretive History of Japan Written in 1219* (Berkeley: University of California Press, 1979).

23. Geiger, *The Mahāvaṃsa*, 154.

24. Geiger, *The Mahāvaṃsa*, 255.

25. Geiger, *The Mahāvaṃsa*, 186.

26. Dan Martin, *Tibetan Histories: A Bibliography of Tibetan-Language Historical Works* (London: Serindia, 1997), 100.

27. Alaka Chattopadhyaya and Lama Chimpa, trans., *History of Buddhism in India* by Tāranātha (Simla: Indian Institute of Advanced Study, 1970), 19, 54.

28. Chattopadhyaya, *History of Buddhism in India*, 188, 238, 240, 344, 345.

29. Chattopadhyaya, *History of Buddhism in India*, 5.

30. Chattopadhyaya, *History of Buddhism in India*, 67.

31. Cao Shibang (Tso Sze-bong) collects examples of medieval Chinese monks reading history in his *Zhongguo shamen waixue de yanjiu: Hanmo zhi Wudai* 中國沙門外學的研究：漢末至五代 (Taipei: Fagu wenhua, 1994), 149–54; 203–11.

32. Edward L. Shaughnessy, "History and Inscriptions, China," in *The Oxford History of Historical Writing*, vol. 1, ed. Andrew Feldherr and Grant Hardy (Oxford: Oxford University Press, 2011), 371–93.

33. I use "court history" here and below (rather than the more problematic "secular history") in contrast to Buddhist history.

34. Etienne Balazs, *Chinese Civilization and Bureaucracy* (New Haven, CT: Yale University Press, 1964), 135. For the qualifications, see Albert E. Dien, "Historiography of the Six Dynasties Period (220–581)," in Feldherr and Hardy, *The Oxford History of Historical Writing*, vol. 1, 510–11.

35. Dien, "Historiography of the Six Dynasties Period," 523.

36. Dien, "Historiography of the Six Dynasties Period," 512.
37. Denis Twitchett, *The Writing of Official History Under the T'ang* (Cambridge: Cambridge University Press, 1992), 10, 13.
38. "History" as a bibliographic category was firmly established in the bibliographical essay of the *Sui History* (*Suishu* 隋書), completed in 636, but the category had begun to take shape in the preceding centuries. Dien, "Historiography of the Six Dynasties Period," 511-12. The classification of Buddhist historical writings in Buddhist bibliographies was complicated by the tendency to separate writings originating in India from those composed in China. That is, in medieval Buddhist bibliographies, most of the works I discuss in this book were lumped together with other Buddhist works composed in China, including doctrinal, apologetic, and ritual texts (see, for instance, *Zhongjing mulu* 眾經目錄 1, *T* no. 2147, vol. 55, 150b, or *Kaiyuan Shijiao lu* 開元釋教錄 13, *T* no. 2154, vol. 55, 624a). Only with the seventeenth-century catalogue of Buddhist works, the *Yuezang zhi jin* 閱藏知津 1, *J* no. B271, vol. 31, 793b did the compiler, Zhixu 智旭 (1599-1655), classify works composed in China into (fifteen) different categories. Most of those I discuss come under his category ten, "accounts and biographies" (*zhuan ji* 傳記), but some of the works I take as "history," he classifies as "chan" or as "collections." Some non-Buddhist bibliographies, such as the bibliographical essays of the official Sui and (Old) Tang histories, did include some Buddhist works like the *Biographies of Eminent Monks* under the category of "history." But others, such as the *New Tang History* and the *Siku quanshu zongmu tiyao* 四庫全書總目提要, consigned all Buddhist historical writing to the catchall category of "Daoist and Buddhist Works."
39. *Hanshu* 62.2735. Translation from Stephen W. Durrant, et al., *The Letter to Ren An and Sima Qian's Legacy* (Seattle: University of Washington Press, 2016), 28-29. I have omitted here the useful notes to the translation. The rest of the book treats the letter this passage comes from in great detail, including the question of its authenticity. The passage is discussed in a historiographical context in the introduction to Xie Baocheng 謝保成 ed., *Zhongguo shixue shi* 中國史學史 (Beijing: Shangwu Yinshuguan, 2006), 19-20; 183-90.
40. *Fozu lidai tong zai* 佛祖歷代通載 3, *T* no. 2036, vol. 49, 498c13-14.
41. *Song gaoseng zhuan* 宋高僧傳 3, *T* no. 2061, vol. 50, 899b18-19.
42. *Zong tong biannian* 宗統編年 20, X. no. 1600, vol. 86, 213a20.
43. Yerushalmi, *Zakhor*; Romia Thapar, "Inscriptions as Historical Writing in Early India: Third Century BC to Sixth Century AD," in Feldherr and Hardy, *The Oxford History of Historical Writing*, vol. 1, 577-600. For Hinduism, see Christian Lee Novetzke, "Memory: Modern Memory Theory, Memory Studies and Hinduism," in *Studying Hinduism: Key Concepts and Methods*, ed. Sushil Mittal and Gene Thursby (New York: Routledge, 2008), 230-50.
44. For a reliable, accessible account of Xuanzang and his legacy, see Benjamin Brose, *Xuanzang: China's Legendary Pilgrim and Translator* (Boston: Shambhala, 2021).
45. That is, the *Biqiuni zhuan* 比丘尼傳, *T* no. 2063, vol. 50; the *Da Song sengshi lüe* 大宋僧史略, *T* no. 2126, vol. 54; and the *Fozu tongji* 佛祖統紀, *T* no. 2035, vol. 49. The historical issue Heng Ching and Haidao debated in the *Biographies of Bhikṣuṇīs* focused on whether the first Chinese nuns underwent the two-year period as probationers (Skt. *śikṣamāṇā*) before receiving full ordination. The focus of discussion for the other two texts was the

extent to which an imperial edict forbidding the ordination of nuns by monks was ever enforced. See Heng Ching (Hengqing), *Xingtan nalü. Hengqing fashi fangtan lu* 杏壇衲履恆清法師訪談錄, based on interviews conducted by Hou Kunhong 侯坤宏 (Taipei: Guoshiguan 國史館, 2007).

46. For this and the subsequent collections of "biographies of eminent monks" scholars give different figures for the total number of biographies. This is because the main biography often contains a short description of the life of a related monk (a "subordinate biography"), but there is disagreement over how long a reference needs to be before it constitutes a subordinate biography.

47. For an overview of the text and scholarship on it, see Kieschnick, "*Gao seng zhuan*," in *Early Medieval Chinese Texts: A Bibliographical Guide*, ed. Cynthia L. Chennault et al. (Berkeley: Institute of East Asian Studies, 2015), 76–80. Kieschnick, "Buddhism, Biographies of Buddhist Monks," in Fedherr and Hardy, *The Oxford History of Historical Writing*, vol. 1, 535–52, discusses Chinese Buddhist biography up to 600, but focuses on Huijiao's *Biographies of Eminent Monks*.

48. The *Chu sanzang jiji* 出三藏記集 (*T* no. 2145, vol. 55) and the *Shi jia pu* 釋迦譜 (*T* no. 2040, vol. 50).

49. The second installment of the biographies of eminent monks, picking up where Huijiao's work left off, was the *Xu gaoseng zhuan* 續高僧傳 by the prominent and prolific monk Daoxuan 道宣 (596–667), *T* no. 2060, vol. 50. It was much larger than Huijiao's work, containing 485 major biographies and 219 subordinate biographies. For an overview, see Kieschnick, "*Xu gaoseng zhuan*," in *Early Medieval Chinese Texts*, 428–31. The third installment was Zanning's *Song gaoseng zhuan*, containing 531 major biographies and 125 subordinate biographies.

50. For an overview of this work, see Albert Welter, *Monks, Rulers, and Literati: The Political Ascendancy of Chan Buddhism* (Oxford: Oxford University Press, 2006), 172–86. I discuss this work and the genealogical genre as a whole in more detail in chapter 5.

51. See Koichi Shinohara, "From Local History to Universal History: The Construction of the Sung T'ien-t'ai Lineage," in *Buddhism in the Sung*, ed. Peter N. Gregory and Daniel A. Getz (Honolulu: University of Hawai'i Press, 1999), 524–76. Helwig Schmidt-Glintzer's *Die Identität der buddhistischen Schulen und die Kompilation buddhistischer Universalgeschichten in China: ein Beitrag zur Geistesgeschichte der Sung-Zeit* (Wiesbaden: Steiner, 1982) is a book-length study of the Buddhist "universal histories" of the Song and Yuan dynasties, outlining the structure of these works and placing them in their political and sectarian context.

52. See for instance *Empty Cloud: The Autobiography of the Chinese Zen Master, Xu-Yun*, trans. Charles Luk (Shaftesbury, Eng.: Element Books, 1988); and Zhenhua, *In Search of the Dharma: Memoirs of a Modern Chinese Buddhist Pilgrim*, trans. Denis Mair (New York: State University of New York Press, 1992).

53. The *Luoyang qielan ji* 洛陽伽藍記, by Yang Xuanzhi 楊衒之 (fl. early sixth century), *T* no. 2092, vol. 51, translated by Wang Yi-t'ung as *A Record of Buddhist Monasteries in Loyang* (Princeton, NJ: Princeton University Press, 1984). Cao Ganghua 曹剛華, *Mingdai fojiao fangzhi yanjiu* 明代佛教方志研究 (Beijing: Zhongguo Renmindaxue Chubanshe, 2011), 1–4; Marcus Bingenheimer, *Island of Guanyin: Mount Putuo and Its Gazetteers* (Oxford: Oxford University Press, 2016), 5–7.

1. INDIA

1. For a concise summary of this book, see Charles Hartman, "Chinese Historiography in the Age of Maturity, 960-1368," in the *Oxford History of Historical Writing, Vol. 2, 400–1400* (Oxford: Oxford University Press, 2012), 46-49.
2. Similarly, with the rise of local history in the form of gazetteers (*difang zhi* 地方志), Buddhist historiography followed suit with works dedicated to important Buddhist mountains and monasteries modeled on their secular counterparts: cities, counties, and provinces. In the most recent manifestation of Buddhist historiography—the scholarly monograph—Buddhists once again followed conventions established by non-Buddhist writers.
3. On the formation of the set of "seventeen histories" in the eleventh and twelfth centuries, see Hartman, "Chinese Historiography in the Age of Maturity, 960-1368."
4. *Han shu* 61 (Beijing: Zhonghua, 1975), 2689-90. For a translation of this passage and discussion, see Richard Mather, "Chinese and Indian Perceptions of Each Other Between the First and Seventh Centuries," *Journal of the American Oriental Society* 112, no. 1 (1992): 1-2. For a broad, reliable survey of Chinese knowledge of India and Indian knowledge of China, see Tansen Sen, *India, China, and the World: A Connected History* (New York: Rowman & Littlefield, 2017).
5. *Hou Han shu* 88 (Beijing: Zhonghua, 1973), 2921; Mather, "Chinese and Indian Perceptions," 2. As the twelfth-century monastic historian Zuxiu 祖琇 (fl. 1150s-60s) observed, "Discussion of Buddhism in historical works began with Fan Ye." *Longxing biannian tonglun* 隆興編年通論 1, *X* no. 1512, vol. 75, 115b.
6. Comparison with historians in other cultures here is instructive, particularly since they demonstrate the common problem of reconciling religious beliefs with the historical record. For a lucid description of chronology in Renaissance scholarship, see Anthony T. Grafton, "Joseph Scaliger and Historical Chronology: The Rise and Fall of a Discipline," *History and Theory* 14 (1975): 157-185.
7. See the brief but perceptive comments of Herbert Franke in "On Chinese Traditions Concerning the Dates of the Buddha," in *The Dating of the Historical Buddha. Die Datierung des Historischen Buddha*, ed. Heinz Bechert (Göttingen: Vandenhoeck & Ruprecht, 1991), vol. 1, 441-442. We approach a similar concern with chronology in court historiography when Sima Qian writes: "My father used to say to me, 'Five hundred years after the Duke of Zhou died Confucius appeared. It has now been five hundred years since the death of Confucius. There must be someone who can set right the transmission of the *Book of Changes*, continue the *Spring and Autumn Annals*, and search into the world of the *Odes* and *Documents*, the rites and music.' Was this not his ambition? Was this not his ambition? How can I, his son, dare to neglect his will?" (Burton Watson, *Ssu-ma Ch'ien: Grand Historian of China* [New York: Columbia University Press, 1958], 50). For discussion of the passage in the *Shiji*, see Stephen W. Durrant, *The Cloudy Mirror: Tension and Conflict in the Writings of Sima Qian* (Albany: State University of New York Press, 1995), 7, and Grant Hardy, *Worlds of Bronze and Bamboo. Sima Qian's Conquest of History* (New York: Columbia University Press, 1999), 116. More generally, in Burton Watson's words, "in Chinese history, unlike that of so many other cultures, there is no

single point in time, such as the creation of the world, the birth of Christ, or the hegira, to which other events are temporally related." *Ssu-ma Ch'ien*, 5. Closer still to the Buddhist link between eschatology and chronology are the Triple Dispensation calendar (*santongli* 三統歷) of the Han scholar-official Liu Xin 劉歆 (d. 23 CE), which included calculations of cosmic end times in the distant future, and subsequent Daoist assertions of the dates of coming cataclysms. See Stephen R. Bokenkamp, "Time After Time: Taoist Apocalyptic History and the Founding of the T'ang Dynasty," *Asia Major. Third Series* 7, no. 1 (1994): 59–88.

8. Heinz Bechert in the introduction to *The Dating of the Historical Buddha* lists nine types of indirect evidence (10). Despite considerable efforts, there is as yet no scholarly consensus on even the century in which the Buddha lived.

9. For the early medieval period, see Erik Zürcher, *The Buddhist Conquest of China* (Leiden: Brill, 2007), 271–274, and, more recently, Yi Liu, "After the Buddha's Nirvāṇa: The *Mofa* Concept of Chinese Buddhism and Its Rise to Prominence," *Studies in Chinese Religions* 4, no. 3 (2018): 277–306. For discussion that includes later material, see Lewis Lancaster, "The Dating of the Buddha in Chinese Buddhism," in Bechert, *The Dating of the Historical Buddha*, 449–457; and especially, Hubert Durt, "La Date du Buddha en Corée et au Japon," in Bechert, *The Dating of the Historical Buddha*, 458–489.

10. While Wei Shou's religious affiliations remain obscure, we can at least surmise that throughout his life he maintained close ties to Buddhists and expressed none of the antipathy for Buddhism that eventually became a standard feature of dynastic histories. References to Wei Shou's participation in Buddhist activities can be found in *Xu gaoseng zhuan* 7.482c and *Guang hongming ji* 廣弘明集 22, *T* no. 2103, vol. 52, 257a. Tsukamoto Zenryū 塚本善隆 demonstrates that Wei Shou was born to a family of devout Buddhists. See his "Gi Shū to Bukkyō" 魏收と佛教 *Tōhō gakuhō* 東方學報 31 (1961): 3–7.

11. *Weishu* 魏書 114 (Beijing: Zhonghua, 1974), 3027. Cf. Leon Hurvitz, "Treatise on Buddhism and Taoism," in *Yun-kang: The Buddhist Cave-Temples of the Fifth Century A.D. in North China*, Seichi Mizuno 水野清一 and Toshio Nagahiro 長廣敏雄 (Kyoto: Jimbunkagaku Kenkyusho, 1956), 40. In fact Wei Shou is quoting from the *Zuozhuan* commentary on the *Spring and Autumn Annals*. See Stephen W. Durrant, Wai-yee Lee, and David Schaberg, *Zuo Tradition: Zuozhuan: Commentary on the "Spring and Autumn Annals"* (Seattle: University of Washington Press, 2016), 149.

12. Or alternately, when Venus (*mingxing* 明星) appeared in the sky. *Taizi ruiying benqi jing* 太子瑞應本起經 1, (到四月八日，夜明星出時。化從右脇生墮地。). *T* no. 185, vol. 3, 473, c1–3. Erik Zürcher makes this point in *The Buddhist Conquest of China* (Leiden: Brill, 2007), 272.

13. These efforts to date events in the life of the Buddha are mirrored in medieval European attempts to precisely date the Last Supper, the trial, and the crucifixion of Jesus. See Ernst Breisach, *Historiography: Ancient, Medieval, and Modern*, 2nd ed. (Chicago: University of Chicago Press, 1994), 131. Breisach does not speculate on the motivation for determining these dates, but I suppose it was for liturgical reasons, or alternatively the product of the decision to adopt a chronological format—both factors we will see at various points in Chinese Buddhist historiography.

14. The Xia is one of three main calendars used during the late Spring and Autumn or early Warring States period, the other two being the Yin and the Zhou calendars. The chief

difference among the three was the first month. Endymion Wilkinson, *Chinese History: A New Manual*, Fifth Edition (Amazon: Endymion Wilkinson, 2018), 58.10.4, "Six Calendars," 780-781.

15. Du Yu (223-285) composed a number of works on the *Chunqiu*, but I have been unable to trace this reference in his extant works.
16. I have been unable to trace the tantalizing references to either the "chronology of Kumārajīva" or the "Stone Pillar Inscription." Neither Catherine Despeux, "La culture lettrée au service d'un plaidoyer pour le bouddhisme. Le 'Traité des deux doctrines' ('Erjiao lun') de Dao'an," in *Bouddhisme et lettrés dans la Chine médiévale*, ed. Catherine Despeux (Paris: Louvain, 2002), 216, nor Hachiya Kunio 蜂屋邦夫, "Hokushū Dōan nikyōron chūshaku" 北周道安「二教論」注釈, *Tōyō bunka* 東洋文化 (Tōkyō: Tōyō Gakkai) 62 (1982): 175-212, glosses these terms.
17. That is, dating back from 569, when Dao'an wrote his work, the "Er jiao lun" 二教論, included in *Guang Hongming ji* 8.142a. For a discussion of Dao'an's work, including a complete translation of the "Er Jiao lun," see Despeux, "Le 'Traité des deux doctrines.'" The passage above is translated on page 216.
18. Fei Zhangfang had been forced to defrock during the persecution of Buddhism in the Northern Zhou. For a study of the historiography of the *Lidai sanbao ji*, see Ruan Zhongren 阮忠仁, "Cong *Lidai sanbao ji* lun Fei Zhangfang de shixue tezhi ji yiyi" 從《歷代三寶記》論費長房的史學特質及意義, *Dongfang zongjiao yanjiu* 東方宗教研究. New Series 1 (1990): 93-129. Tanya Storch examines Fei's work more generally in *The History of Chinese Buddhist Bibliography: Censorship and Transformation of the Tripitaka* (New York: Cambria Press, 2014); see as well the criticism of Storch's characterization of the *Lidai sanbao ji* in Antonello Palumbo's "Review of Storch, Tanya, The History of Chinese Buddhist Bibliography: Censorship and Transformation of the Tripitaka," H-Buddhism, H-Net Reviews, April 2017.
19. On Faxian's passage, see Bechert, "The Date of the Buddha," 233-234.
20. This reference has attracted considerable interest among modern scholars. See Bechert, "The Date of the Buddha," 228-229; Durt, "La Date du Buddha en Corée et au Japon," 486-489. Hubert Durt notes that this oft-repeated date contains an early scribal error (the date should in fact come out to 385 BCE) that was not noticed until the nineteenth century when the Japanese scholar Hirata Atsutane 平田篤胤 (1776-1843) caught it. *Problems of Chronology and Eschatology: Four Lectures on the* Essay on Buddhism *by Tominaga Nakamoto (1715–1746)* (Kyoto: Italian School of East Asian Studies, 1994), 32.
21. At roughly the same time, the great exegete Jizang 吉藏 (549-623) was attempting to solve another chronological problem in Indian Buddhist history. For Jizang it was important for the patriarch Āryadeva to have been a disciple of Nāgārjuna. But according to some sources they were separated by more than 270 years. After listing these sources, Jizang adds three more. Two state matter-of-factly that Āryadeva was a disciple of Nāgārjuna; a third gives a later date that, if accepted, means that Nāgārjuna would only have had to live to around 120 to have been Āryadeva's teacher. Jizang conveniently goes with the three sources that confirm his own theory, though in the grand tradition of Chinese historiography, he at least lists those that contradict it. *Bai lun shu* 百論疏 T no. 1827, vol. 42, 233a. See Stuart Young, *Conceiving the Indian Buddhist Patriarchs in China* (Honolulu: University of Hawai'i Press, 2015), 146, for discussion.

22. *Fozu tongji* 佛祖統紀 1, T no. 2035, vol. 49, 142-144. Writing on the complicated problems involved in determining the dates of another Buddhist figure, Bodhidharma (d.u.), the eleventh-century monk Qisong 契嵩 (1007-1072) cites the puzzle of the Buddha's dates when making the case that historians obsessed with chronology need to maintain perspective in the face of seemingly unsolvable historical riddles: "It is like the stories of the multitude of schools not agreeing on the birthday of the Buddha. How could I say it is not our Buddha?" Translated in Elizabeth Morrison, *The Power of the Patriarchs: Qisong and Lineage in Chinese Buddhism* (Leiden: Brill, 2010), 245. From *Chuanfa zhengzong lun* 傳法正宗論 1, T no. 2080, vol. 51, 776b. As we will see in the last chapter of this book, twentieth-century Buddhist historians continued to grapple with the problem. Hubert Durt's lecture, "Chronology. The Date of the Buddha's Appearance According to Tominaga," details the ingenious analysis of these same sources in the eighteenth century by the scholar Tominaga Nakamoto 富永仲基 (1715-1746). In Durt, *Problems of Chronology and Eschatology*, 23-40.

23. *Da Song sengshi lüe* 大宋僧史略 1, T no. 2126, vol. 54, 235b. Cf. Albert Welter, *The Administration of Buddhism in China: A Study and Translation of Zanning and the Topical Compendium of the Buddhist Clergy* (New York: Cambria Press, 2018), 103-104.

24. Zanning explains that in the Jiangnan region, where Zanning lived much of his life, the ceremonies were held in the fourth month; in the capital at Kaifeng, where he lived for a time after the founding of the Song, they were held on the fourth day of the *twelfth* month.

25. Despite Zanning's plea, the eighth day of the *fourth* month eventually became the standard date for celebrating the Buddha's birth in China, and remains so to this day.

26. Zürcher, *The Buddhist Conquest of China*, 288-320; Livia Kohn, *Laughing at the Tao: Debates Among Buddhists and Taoists in Medieval China* (Princeton, N.J.: Princeton University Press, 1995); and Friederike Assandri, "Inter-religious Debate at the Court of the Early Tang: An Introduction to Daoxuan's *Ji gujin Fo Dao lunheng*," in *From Early Tang Court Debates to China's Peaceful Rise*, ed. Friederike Assandri and Dora Martins (Amsterdam: Amsterdam University Press, 2009), 15-32.

27. In his discussion of the Buddhist response, Zürcher focuses on the latter technique: the fabrication of new scriptures.

28. *Xu gaoseng zhuan* 23.625a.

29. Liu Yi has questioned whether such a debate actually took place in 520, arguing that the assertion that the Buddha died during the reign of King Mu did not appear until some decades later, perhaps as late as the early seventh century. Liu Yi 劉屹, "Mu Wang wushier nian fomieshuo de xingcheng" 穆王五十二年佛說的形成, *Dunhuangxue jikan* 敦煌學輯刊 2 (2018): 166-177.

30. Durt, "La Date du Buddha en Corée et au Japon," 472. In some sources the date is given as the fifty-*third* year of the reign of King Mu (948 BCE).

31. For the Indian antecedents of this belief and the Chinese innovations to it in the fifth and sixth centuries, see Jan Nattier, *Once Upon a Future Time. Studies in a Buddhist Prophecy of Decline* (Berkeley, CA: Asian Humanities Press, 1991).

32. Jamie Hubbard, *Absolute Delusion, Perfect Buddhahood. The Rise and Fall of a Chinese Heresy* (Honolulu: University of Hawai'i Press, 2000), 55-75; Étienne Lamotte, *History of Indian Buddhism. From the Origins to the Śaka Era* (Louvain: Peeters Press, 1988), 192-198.

33. Nattier, *Once Upon a Future Time*, 42–48.
34. Lamotte, *History of Indian Buddhism*, 197–198; *Nanyue Sidachanshi lishi yuanwen* 南嶽思大禪師立誓願文 1, *T* no. 1933, vol. 46, 786. Huisi "dates" the birth and death of the Buddha only according to the sixty-year cycle, and it is on the basis of the same cycle that he predicts the years for the three phases of the decline of the Dharma. He does not indicate which of the "sixtieth" years these dates will refer to. Perhaps he himself did not think the evidence sufficient to determine the date of the Buddha's death.
35. Lamotte, *History of Indian Buddhism*, 198; *Zhongguan lunshu* 中觀論疏 1, *T* no. 1824, vol. 42, 18 b. Wei Shou would not have been using Jizang's timetable, both because Jizang's work appeared after Wei Shou's and because Jizang apparently calculated the death of the Buddha to a different date. In his discussion of the problem in the *Fahua xuanlun* 法華玄論, Jizang's interlocutor asks: "How many years has it been since the Buddha's extinction?" to which Jizang responds, "To this day it has been one thousand, five hundred and ninety-six years" (10, *T* no. 1720, vol. 34, 450b). I have been unable to determine the date of composition of Jizang's text, but he seems to be using a date close to 949 BCE for the Buddha's nirvana. As in the case of Huisi, in his discussion of the dates for the decline of the Dharma, Jizang does not explicitly discuss the date of the Buddha's nirvana.
36. The reference here is to the *Shan jian lü piposha* 善見律毘婆沙 (Skt. *Samantapāsādikā*) 18, *T* no. 1462, vol. 24, 796c.
37. *Lidai sanbao ji* 歷代三寶紀 1, *T* no. 2034, vol. 49, 23a.
38. Franke, "On Chinese Traditions Concerning the Dates of the Buddha"; Lancaster, "The Dating of the Buddha in Chinese Buddhism"; Durt, "La Date du Buddha en Corée et au Japon."
39. Timothy Barrett has suggested intriguingly that the heightened sense of anxiety in the sixth century was brought on in part by a massive volcanic eruption off the east coast of New Guinea that produced a sort of "nuclear winter" throughout the world. See his "Climate Change and Religious Response: The Case of Early Medieval China," *Journal of the Royal Asiatic Society* 17 (2007): 139–156.
40. Even the later date should have put the Buddha's birth before that of Laozi. The motivation for settling on the earlier date may have been a late tradition that Laozi went to India in 716 BCE, as related in a medieval manuscript (Pelliot 4502). See Zürcher, *The Buddhist Conquest of China*, 302.
41. *Zongtong biannian* 1, 75b.
42. Zuxiu, the compiler of the twelfth-century *Longxing biannian tonglun*, a strict chronological history of Buddhism modeled on the *Zizhi tongjian*, prudently begins his work with the entrance of Buddhism to China, perhaps because of the difficulties with determining accurate dates for events and figures in India.
43. A recent example of the importance of chronology in the Chinese historical tradition is the "Xia Shang Zhou Chronology Project" launched in 1996 by no less than the State Council of China 國務院 with the ambitious goal of establishing conclusively the key dates for ancient Chinese history.
44. I quote here from the *Chusanzang jiji* 出三藏記集, which was probably Huijiao's source (19c–20a). Huijiao refers to the prophecy but doesn't quote the Buddha. I have been unable to locate an earlier source for this prophecy in the canon.

45. For the *Da fangdeng daji jing* passage, see 22, *T* no. 397, vol. 13, 159a-b; Lamotte, *History of Indian Buddhism*, 175-176.
46. For the *Mañjuśrīparipṛcchā*, see *Wenshushili wen jing* 文殊師利問經 1, *T* no. 468, vol. 14, 501a; Lamotte, *History of Indian Buddhism*, 534-535.
47. *Gaoseng zhuan* 11.403b.
48. *Nanhai jigui neifa zhuan* 南海寄歸內法傳 1, *T* no. 2125, vol. 54, 205c.
49. Other aspects of Chinese historiography that may have been informed by Buddhism are more difficult to detect. Chen Yinke 陳寅恪 once argued that the format of Pei Songzhi's 裴松之 (372-451) annotated version of the *Sanguozhi* 三國志 was inspired by Buddhist works, but this theory was disputed by Zhou Yiliang 周一良. Chen Yinke, "Zhimindu xueshuo kao" 支愍度學說考, in *Jinming guan conggao chubian* 金明館叢稿初編 (Shanghai: Shanghai Guji, 1980), 163; Zhou Yiliang, "Wei Jin Nanbei chao shixue zhuzuo de ji ge wenti" 魏晉南北朝史學著作的幾個問題, in *Wei Jin Nanbei chao shilun ji* 魏晉南北朝史論集 (Shenyang: Liaoning Jiaoyu Chubanshe, 1998), 49. Zhou Yiliang for his part argued that during the Period of Division, historians in the South emphasized textual analysis in part as a result of inspiration from Buddhist writings. This argument too has been disputed, in this case by Hu Baoguo. See Zhou Yiliang, "Lüe lun Nanchao Beichao shixue zhi yitong" 略論南朝北朝史學之異同, in Zhou, *Wei Jin Nanbei chao shilun ji xubian*, 97-105; Hu Baoguo, *Han Tang jian shixue de fazhan* 漢唐間史學的發展 (Beijing: Shangwu Yinshuguan, 2003), 122. Even in the arguments for Buddhist influence, the influence is said to come from Buddhist exegetical writings, not from Buddhist historiography. A more common assessment of the impact of Buddhism in court historiography for the Period of Division is that of Albert E. Dien: "What is striking about Chinese medieval historiography is how little effect Buddhism had on it, either as subject matter or as influence in its formulation." Albert E. Dien, "Wei Tan and the Historiography of the *Wei-shu*," in *Studies in Early Medieval Chinese Literature and Cultural History: In Honor of Richard B. Mather and Donald Holzman*, ed. Paul W. Kroll and David R. Knechtges (Provo, UT: T'ang Studies Society, 2003), 399-466.
50. The strong, essentialist notion of religious lineage we will see below (and in chapter 5) in the Chan and Tiantai traditions in China does seem different from Indian lineages. In Elizabeth Morrison's words, "The Indian Buddhist tradition offers no shortage of exemplary figures, beginning with the Buddha himself. It does not, however, propose that religious authority lies in the hands of a succession of men who, alone among all Buddhists, are the full spiritual heirs of the Buddha; this powerful notion arose in China." Morrison, *The Power of the Patriarchs*, 2. As Morrison points out, in fact, the strain of Indian Buddhist thought that emphasizes teachings and institutions over individuals runs counter to lineage claims. On genealogy as a form of historical thought in Renaissance Europe, see Anthony Grafton, *What Was History? The Art of History in Early Modern Europe* (Cambridge: Cambridge University Press, 2007), 153-163.
51. Sengyou, perhaps best known for his collection of biographies and prefaces to scriptures, the *Chu sanzang jiji* 出三藏記集, also composed this, the first sustained biography of the Buddha by a Chinese monk. The *Shijia pu* draws on Chinese translations of Indian texts in an attempt to reconstruct a coherent history of Śākyamuni's ancestry and life. For his account of the beginning of human society, Sengyou bases his narrative on the *Āgamas*, combined with the *Dharmaguptakavinaya* (*Sifen lü* 四分律).

52. On the structure of the *Shiji*, see Hardy, *Worlds of Bronze and Bamboo*, 27–60.
53. *Shijia pu* 1.3a. The textual history of the *Shijia pu* is complicated by the transmission of a ten-fascicle version (in the *Qisha* 磧砂 edition of the canon) and a five-fascicle version (in the "Korean edition" of the canon), which was the basis for the version in the Taisho. Chen Jinzhen 陳勁榛 argues that the five-fascicle version represents the text compiled by Sengyou (though the problem is not of great relevance to the discussion here). See his "Sengyou *Shijia pu* yanjiu" 僧祐釋迦譜研究 (MA thesis, Chinese Culture University, 1990).
54. *Shijia pu* 1.8c–9c. For a concise summary of the various numbers of buddhas described in Buddhist sources as a "framework for Buddhist historical thought," see Nattier, *Once Upon a Future Time*, 19–26.
55. *Wei shu* 114.3027; cf. Hurvitz, "Treatise on Buddhism and Taoism," 39.
56. E.g. Daoxuan's *Shijia shi pu* 釋迦氏譜 5, *T* no. 2041, vol. 50, 84b, and books in the "transmission of the lamp" genre, discussed in chapter 5.
57. The same is true in *Shiji*, chapter 13, table 1, "Sandai shi biao" 三代世表, which laid out the order of monarchs from China's most distant past in a period for which dates were scarce. See Michael Loewe, "Tables of the *Shiji* and *Hanshu*: Forms and Contents," in Loewe, *The Men Who Governed Han China: Companion to A Biographical Dictionary of the Qin, Former Han and Xin Periods* (Leiden: Brill, 2004), 215–216.
58. "Sapoduobu shizi ji" 薩婆多部師資記 in *Chu sanzang jiji* 12.89; discussed in Young, *Conceiving the Indian Buddhist Patriarchs in China*, 67–68. For other lists of vinaya, abhidharma, and Dharma masters, see Lamotte, *History of Indian Buddhism*, 203–212. Huijiao refers briefly to six vinaya masters in his essay on the vinaya (*Gaoseng zhuan* 11.403a), which takes him chronologically up to the time of Aśoka.
59. *T* no. 2058, vol. 50. On this text, see Henri Maspero, "Sur la date et l'authenticité du *Fou fa tsang yin yuan tchouan*," in *Mélanges d'Indianisme offerts par ses élèves à M. Sylvain Lévi* (Paris: E. Leroux, 1911), 129–149. Elizabeth Morrison, "Contested Visions of the Buddhist Past and the Curious Fate of an Early Medieval Chinese Buddhist Text" (unpublished manuscript).
60. Specifically, it has been argued that the text was a response to a fifth-century critique of the pedigree of Buddhism in India and an attempt to argue against state persecution of Buddhism in China. See Linda Penkower, "In the Beginning: Guanding 灌頂 (561–632) and the Creation of Early Tiantai," *Journal of the International Association of Buddhist Studies* 23, no. 2 (2000): 250. Young, drawing on Morrison, argues plausibly that the text was "devised to encourage self-reliance" and "emphasized the severance of the Indian patriarchate in order to exhort latter-day Chinese Buddhists to redouble their efforts at upholding the Dharma." Young, *Conceiving the Indian Buddhist Patriarchs in China*, 69–70; 75–76. Morrison, "Contested Visions of the Buddhist Past and the Curious Fate of an Early Medieval Chinese Buddhist Text."
61. For the Tiantai lineage, see Penkower, "In the Beginning." The construction of lineage in the Chan tradition has been carefully examined in a number of works. Representative studies in English include John R. McRae, *The Northern School and the Formation of Early Ch'an Buddhism* (Honolulu: University of Hawai'i Press, 1986); Bernard Faure, *The Will to Orthodoxy: A Critical Genealogy of Northern Chan Buddhism* (Stanford, CA: Stanford University Press, 1997); John Jorgensen, *Inventing Hui-neng, the Sixth Patriarch:*

228   1. India

>   *Hagiography and Biography in Early Ch'an* (Leiden: Brill, 2005); Morrison, *The Power of the Patriarchs*; and Albert Welter, *Monks, Rulers, and Literati: The Political Ascendancy of Chan Buddhism* (Oxford: Oxford University Press, 2006), all of which discuss lineages of Indian patriarchs in Chan historiography.

62. The *Commentary to the Prajñā Scripture of the Humane Kings for the Protection of the State* (*Renwang huguo banruo jing shu* 仁王護國般若經疏) 3 (*T* no. 707, vol. 33, 357c) likely compiled in the mid-seventh to mid-eighth centuries, is a good example of the problems early writers caused for more meticulous historians when they proposed lineages with dates. The text lays out the following lineage: Śākyamuni, Kāśyapa, Ānanda, Madhyantika (60 years postnirvana), Śāṇakavāsa, Upagupta (100 years p.n.), Aśvaghosa (600 years p.n.), Nāgārjuna (700 years p.n.), "Kings" (800 years p.n.). The list leaves gaps in which names are not supplied, and at other points assumes very long life spans. See Young, *Conceiving the Indian Buddhist Patriarchs in China*, 118-120. Tinkering with the dates of the patriarchs went on for some time. Interlineal notes to the *Jingde chuandeng lu*, added some time after the text was completed in 1001, attempt to correct the dates for most. The problem may have been complicated by other accounts that placed Asaṅga (the twelfth patriarch) 350 years after the Buddha's nirvana, and Nāgārjuna (the fourteenth patriarch) at variously 530, 700, or 889 years after the nirvana.
63. On Qisong, see Morrison, *The Power of the Patriarchs*.
64. Morrison, *The Power of the Patriarchs*, 174-175; 212-213.
65. *Chuanfa zhengzong lun* 1.777c.
66. Morrison, *The Power of the Patriarchs*, 177-193.
67. Welter, *Monks, Rulers, and Literati*, 126-128.
68. Zongjian quotes here from Wu Keji 吳克己 (1141-1215), on whose work his own was based. For a biography of Wu Keji, see *Shimen zhengtong* 7.349a.
69. The story of the first transmission with a flower and a smile first appears only in 1101 in the *Jianzhong Jingguo xu deng lu* 建中靖國續燈錄 1, *X* no. 1556, vol. 78, 641b. It is not given in the earlier lamp histories.
70. *Shimen zhengtong* 4.312b.
71. Later, editors of the *Jingde chuandeng lu* attempted to redress this perceived deficiency by introducing interlineal comments into the text, largely from Qisong's *Chuanfa zhengzong ji*.
72. *Shijia pu* 1.10a.
73. Again, the *Shijia pu* provides useful examples of this practice. See, for instance, *Shijia pu* 1.3c.
74. *Fozu tongji* 2.144a. Zhipan was inspired here by the comments of the Tiantai exegete Zhanran 湛然 (711-782) in his *Fahua wenju ji* 法華文句記 2, *T* no. 1719, vol. 34, 178c.
75. *Gaoseng zhuan* 3.343c. Detailed treatments of the varied sources for legends of the Buddha's bowl can be found in Koichi Shinohara, "The Story of the Buddha's Begging Bowl: Imagining a Biography and Sacred Places," in *Pilgrims, Patrons and Place: Localizing Sanctity in Asian Religions*, ed. Phyllis Granoff and Koichi Shinohara (Vancouver: University of British Columbia Press, 2003), 68-107; and Françoise Wang-Toutain, "Le bol du Buddha: propagation du bouddhisme et légitimité politique," *Bulletin de l'École française d'Extrême-Orient* 81 (1994): 59-82.

76. *Daoxuan lüshi gantong lu* 道宣律師感通錄, T no. 2107, vol. 52, 439b. The passage is quoted by Zanning in his own discussion of the problem of reconciling different dates for the Buddha. See *Da Song seng shi lüe* 1.236a; cf. Welter, *The Administration of Buddhism in China*, 107. Daoxuan has his own peculiar source for information about the date of the Buddha's birth. He interviewed a god with a very long life span, who told him he had seen it himself. This sort of revelatory experience and its use as a source is, in Chinese Buddhist historiography, unique to Daoxuan. *Lüxiang gantong zhuan* 律相感通傳 1, T 1898, vol. 45, 879a.
77. *Shijia pu* 1.4b16.
78. *Da Song seng shi lüe* 1.236b. Cf. Welter, *The Administration of Buddhism in China*, 110.
79. For the use of *panjiao* in Chinese Buddhism, see Peter N. Gregory, *Tsung-mi and the Sinification of Buddhism* (Honolulu: University of Hawai'i Press, 2002), 93-172.
80. Young has argued for the importance of the historical component to these *panjiao* schemes. *Conceiving the Indian Buddhist Patriarchs in China*, 117-118.
81. That is, he preached the *Buddhāvataṃsaka-sutra* shortly after his enlightenment, followed later by the Āgamas, the Vaipulya sutras (i.e., the *Vimalakīrti-nirdeśa*, the *Suvarṇaprabhāsōttama*, the *Śrīmālā*, etc.), the *Prajñāpāramitā*, and finally, the *Lotus* and the *Nirvana* sutras. Neal Donner and Daniel B. Stevenson in discussing the interpretation of Tiantai history in the *Fozu tongji* state, "As the most articulated description of the Tiantai sectarian genealogy, the *Fozu tongji* became the chief literary source for later Tiantai historical ideology." *The Great Calming and Contemplation: A Study and Annotated Translation of the First Chapter of Chih-I's* Mo-ho chih kuan (Honolulu: University of Hawai'i Press, 1993), 33.
82. Jizang, for instance, observed that there was no scriptural foundation for ranking the scriptures according to the times they were preached. See Chanju Man, *The History of Doctrinal Classification in Chinese Buddhism: A Study of the* Panjiao *System* (New York: University Press of America, 2006), 175. Zongjian, in his *Shimen zhengtong*, asserts the age of the Buddha for each of the five times: thirty, ten days after enlightenment, for the *Buddhāvataṃsaka*; thirty-two for the lesser vehicle teachings; forty-three for the elementary Mahāyāna sutras; fifty-one for the *Perfection of Wisdom*, and seventy-two for the *Nirvana*. *Shimen zhengtong* 1.258a. Cf. Song Daofa 宋道發, *Fojiao shiguan yanjiu* 佛教史觀研究 (Beijing: Zongjiao Wenhua Chubanshe, 2009), 306-307.

2. SOURCES

1. For instance, Liu Zhiji 劉知幾 (661-721), known for his lengthy reflection on historiography, the *Shitong* 史通, posited three essential qualities that make for a good historian (*san chang* 三長): literary skill (*cai* 才), erudition (*xue* 學), and insight (*shi* 識), where erudition refers largely to knowledge of the sources, and insight into the analysis of these sources. The reference to the "three qualities" appears in Liu Zhiji's biography in *Jiu Tang shu* 舊唐書 102 (Beijing: Zhonghua 1975), 3173; *Xin Tang shu* 新唐書 132 (Beijing: Zhonghua, 1975), 4522. See also Achim Mittag, "What Makes a Good Historian: Zhang Xuecheng's Postulate of 'Moral Integrity' (*shi de* 史德) Revisited," in *Historical Truth, Historical Criticism, and Ideology: Chinese Historiography and Historical Culture from a New Comparative*

Perspective, ed. Helwig Schmidt-Glintzer et al. (Leiden: Brill, 2005), 365. There are instances of source criticism already in the *Shiji* (Xie Baocheng 謝保成, ed., *Zhongguo shixue shi* 中國史學史 [Beijing: Shangwu Yinshuguan, 2006], 187), but attention to source criticism in court historiography begins in earnest in the Six Dynasties period, likely under the influence of classical scholarship. See Hu Baoguo 胡寶國, "Jingshi wenxue yu wenshi zhi xue" 經史文學與文史之學 in Xie, *Zhongguo shixue shi*, 437-449.

2. Expansive knowledge of written sources is just one possible model for the good historian. In premodern Europe, the ideal historian was for many a "man of action" who had personal experience with the events described. George H. Nadel, "Philosophy of History Before Historicism," *History and Theory* 3, no. 3 (1964): 291-315.

3. Grant Hardy, *Worlds of Bronze and Bamboo: Sima Qian's Conquest of History* (New York: Columbia University Press, 1999), 81.

4. Hsing I-tien estimates that in bamboo strips the *Records of the Historian* would weigh approximately 60 kilos (over a hundred in a wooden strip version) and occupy close to 300,000 cubic centimeters, taking up more than 200 times the space of the modern printed version. Hsing I-tien (Xing Yitian) 邢義田, "Handai jiandu de zhongliang, tiji he shiyong—yi Zhongyanyuan Shiyusuo cang Juyan Hanjian wei li" 漢代簡牘的重量、體積和使用--以中研院史語所藏居延漢簡為例, *Gujin lunheng* 古今論衡 17 (2007): 74-75.

5. See E. G. Pulleyblank, "Chinese Historical Criticism: Liu Chih-chi and Ssu-ma Kuang," in *Historians of China and Japan*, ed. W. G. Beasley and E. G. Pulleyblank (London: Oxford University Press, 1961), 135-166.

6. The *Zizhi tongjian kaoyi* 資治通鑑考異. See Xie, *Zhongguo shixue shi*, 818-821. The great twentieth-century scholar Chen Yinke argued that this book had its origins in Buddhist exegetical writings, but this theory has not been widely accepted. See note 49 in chapter 1 above.

7. Several monks wrote brief autobiographies in the Ming dynasty, most notably Hanshan Deqing 憨山德清 (1546-1623) and Ouyi Zhixu 蕅益智旭 (1599-1655), but the genre only became common in the twentieth century with memoirs by a number of leading monks.

8. See Timothy H. Barrett, "Did I-ching Go to India? Problems in Using I-ching as a Source for South Asian Buddhism," *Buddhist Studies Review* 15, no. 2 (1998): 142-156.

9. *Xu gaoseng zhuan* 續高僧傳 16.553b. Daoxuan makes similar observations at a number of points in the same work: 20.589c-90a; 22.615a; 24.642a; and 28.689a.

10. *Gaoseng zhuan* 1.418b. Cf. Arthur F. Wright, "Biography and Hagiography: Hui-chiao's *Lives of Eminent Monks*," in his *Studies in Chinese Buddhism* (New Haven, CT: Yale University Press, 1990). In addition to providing a translation of Huijiao's preface, Wright addresses many of the issues discussed here, though with less detail and limited to Huijiao's work.

11. *Gaoseng zhuan* 1.418b.

12. The rise of epigraphy as a historical source was noted already in the section on steles in the twelfth chapter of Liu Xie's 劉勰 (fl. 500) sixth-century *Wenxin diaolong* 文心雕龍.

13. I refer here to Gregory Schopen's criticisms in "Archaeology and Protestant Presuppositions in the Study of Indian Buddhism," in his *Bones, Stones, and Buddhist Monks: Collected Papers on the Archaeology, Epigraphy, and Texts of Monastic Buddhism in India* (Honolulu: University of Hawai'i Press, 1997), 1-22; and many of his other writings as well.

14. The preface to the *Biqiuni zhuan* 比丘尼傳, written before the *Gaoseng zhuan*, states that the compiler too drew on epigraphy, manuscripts, and oral sources. (*T* no. 2063, vol. 50, 934b). In the preface to the *Further Biographies*, Daoxuan states that he has drawn upon oral accounts, personal observation, manuscripts, and epigraphy (*Xu gaoseng zhuan* 1.425b17-19). In the introduction to his work, Zanning mentions only epigraphy specifically (*Song gaoseng zhuan* 1.709a8-9), but we know from the biographies themselves that he also drew on various sorts of writings, oral accounts, and, in a few cases, personal observation. On the use of epigraphy for biographies of monks, see Koichi Shinohara, "Two Sources of Chinese Buddhist Biographies: Stupa Inscriptions and Miracle Stories," in *Monks and Magicians: Religious Biographies in Asia*, ed. Phyllis Granoff and Koichi Shinohara (Oakville, ON: Mosaic Press, 1988), 119-229.
15. *Shijia pu*.
16. Cao Ganghua 曹剛華, *Songdai fojiao shiji yanjiu* 宋代佛教史籍研究 (Shanghai: Huadong Shifandaxue Chubanshe, 2005), 156-159.
17. *Gaoseng zhuan* 14.419a; *Xu gaoseng zhuan* 1.425a.
18. *Analects* 7.1. Similarly, Sengyou in the preface to his *Śākya Genealogy* writes: "Here I copy and collect many scriptures; I transmit but do not innovate." *Shijia pu* 1.1a. Daoxuan cites the same passage in his *Xu gaoseng zhuan* 22.621a.
19. We know, for instance, that Huijiao copied directly from the bibliographic *Chu sanzang jiji* and the miracle-tale collection *Mingxiang ji* 冥祥記. Scholars have long assumed that he drew directly on the *Mingseng zhuan* as well, but Sangyop Lee has recently demonstrated that there is no evidence that Huijiao used the *Mingseng zhuan* in the compilation of his work. See Lee, "The Invention of the 'Eminent Monk'" Understanding the Biographical Craft of the *Gaoseng zhuan* 高僧傳 Through the *Mingseng zhuan* 名僧傳," *T'oung Pao* 106, no. 1-2 (2020): 87-170.
20. For a brief overview of how perception is analyzed in the context of the overall functioning of the mind in one branch of Buddhist scholastic writing, see Hirakawa Akira, *A History of Indian Buddhism from Śākyamuni to Early Mahāyāna*, trans. and ed. Paul Groner (Honolulu: University of Hawai'i Press, 1990), 156-160.
21. *Shimen zhengtong* 1.256c.
22. *Fozu tongji* 31.306b.
23. *Song gaoseng zhuan* 18.825b-c. I return to this quotation, with more context, below in the section "Historians of the Marvelous."
24. See Burton Watson, *Ssu-ma Ch'ien: Grand Historian of China* (New York: Columbia University Press, 1958), 80. The practice of recording unresolved discrepancies in the historical record was common in Islamic historiography as well. See Chase F. Robinson, *Islamic Historiography* (Cambridge: Cambridge University Press, 2003), 79.
25. This is a distinction of long standing in Chinese historiography, a process of separation that goes back at least as far as the *Zuozhuan*, arguably the first major Chinese historical work. David Schaberg writes: "in China, only a gradual dissociation of anecdotal lore from the ritual, deliberative, and didactic purposes it served in actual social settings could finally produce the phenomenon of a historiography that claimed to record facts without bias." "Platitude and Persona: *Junzi* Comments in *Zuozhuan* and Beyond," in Schmidt-Glintzer, ed., *Historical Truth, Historical Criticism, and Ideology*, 178.

26. Neither "good and fearless," nor "fearless" can be construed as a translation of either Śubhakarasiṃha or śubhakara. Charles Willemen has suggested that "Shanwuwei" is a translation of the Prākrit śubhāgala, and that in Tang times the name was Sanskritized to Śubhākarasiṃha and translated as "lion of purity." See his "Tripiṭaka Shan-wu-wei's Name," T'oung Pao 47, nos. 3–5 (1981): 362–365. Chou Yiliang suggested that Shanwuwei was a nickname taken from one of the monk's translations and is not related to the name Śubhakarasiṃha. See his "Tantrism in China," Harvard Journal of Asiatic Studies 8 (1945): 241–332.

27. Gaoseng zhuan 2.333a. Similar examples of the expression "some say" can easily be found throughout Chinese Buddhist historical writings from later periods as well. A variation of the phrase (huoyan 或言) appears in the Shiji and the Hanshu, both taken as models of proper historiographical practice by virtually every Chinese Buddhist scholar.

28. Gaoseng zhuan, 2.332c. The "three dates" refers presumably to Hongshi 7/11; 8 and 1.

29. Gaoseng zhuan, 2.335c.

30. Song gaoseng zhuan 22.850a.

31. In traditional reckoning, a person is one year (sui) old at birth.

32. Fozu tongji 6.180c18. See also Feng Guodong 馮國棟, Jingde chuandeng lu yanjiu 景德傳燈錄研究 (Beijing: Zhonghua, 2014), 250. In both of these cases the more interesting approach for the historian is to ask why these stories, which chronologically are impossible, were invented and propagated in the first place. What is it about the characters in the stories that made authors want to bring them together despite the obvious chronological obstacles?

33. Consider Finley on the ancient Greeks: "Truth, however, as I have already said, truth in the Rankean sense of 'how things really were,' was neither an important consideration nor a claim one could substantiate. Acceptance and belief were what counted, and the Greeks had all the knowledge of the past they needed without the help of historians." M. I. Finley, The Use and Abuse of History (London: Chatto and Windus, 1975), 29. Or Breisach on the Romans: "Historical truth as pure reconstruction removed from pragmatic aims and resulting from dispassionate study was foreign to all Roman historians." Ernst Breisach, Historiography: Ancient, Medieval, and Modern, 2nd ed. (Chicago: University of Chicago Press, 1994), 58.

34. See, for example, Arthur F. Wright, "Seng-jui Alias Hui-jui: A Biographical Bisection in the Kao-seng chuan," in Liebenthal Festschrift, ed. Kshitis Roy (Santiniketan: Visvabharati, 1957), 272–294; and Jinhua Chen, "One Name, Three Monks: Two Northern Chan Masters Emerge from the Shadow of Their Contemporary, the Tiantai Mater Zhanran 湛然 (711–782)," Journal of the International Association of Buddhist Studies 22, no. 1 (1999): 1–90.

35. Dao'an's teacher, best known as Fotucheng 佛圖澄 (ca. 232–348), was surnamed Zhu 竺.

36. Gaoseng zhuan 5.354. The biography of Dao'an is translated in full with annotations in Arthur E. Link, "Biography of Shih Tao-an," T'oung Pao 46 (1958): 1–48.

37. This is in addition to the other, later monk of the same name discussed in the previous chapter.

38. Gaoseng zhuan 1.324b.

39. T no. 602, vol. 15. The extant version of the Da anban shouyi jing is mixed with commentary that seems to be composed by Chen Hui and Kang Senghui.

40. Preserved in *Chu sanzang jiji* 6.43a.
41. *Yin chi ru jing zhu* 陰持入經註, *T* no. 1694, vol. 33.
42. Antonio Forte, though focusing on An Shigao's descendants, also attempts to recover a historical core from the various legends about this mysterious figure in *The Hostage An Shigao and His Offspring* (Kyoto: Istituto Italiano di Cultura Scuola di Studi sull'Asia Orientale, 1995).
43. *Gaoseng zhuan* 1.326b.
44. *Kaiyuan Shijiao lu* 18.672b. For discussion of Zhisheng's criticism of this text, see Cao Shibang (Sze-bong Tzo) 曹仕邦, *Zhongguo fojiao shixue shi—Dong Jin zhi Wudai* 中國佛教史學史：東晉至五代 (Taipei: Fagu wenhua, 1999), 321-322. Five complete copies of the *Yaoxing sheshen jing* survived at Dunhuang. For discussion of the text itself, see Liu Shufen 劉淑芬, *Zhonggu de fojiao yu shehui* 中古的佛教與社會 (Shanghai: Shanghai Guji Chubanshe, 2008), 215-216.
45. For discussion of these critiques, see chapter 1, "India."
46. For an introduction to Ouyang's historiography, see James T.C. Liu, *Ou-Yang Hsiu: An Eleventh-Century Neo-Confucianist* (Stanford, CA: Stanford University Press, 1967), 100-113.
47. The most trenchant critiques of Ouyang's attitude toward Buddhism in his histories are those of Zhipan (e.g., *Fozu tongji* 38.356c) and Zuxiu, who criticizes Ouyang's work on numerous occasions in his *Longxing biannian tonglun*. On Ouyang's attitude toward Buddhism in the *New History of the Five Dynasties*, see Richard L. Davis, *Historical Records of the Five Dynasties* (New York: Columbia University Press, 2004), liii-liv.
48. *Fozu tongji* 44.405a. Zhipan makes similar criticisms of the same passage later on at *Fozu tongji* 45.414c. For Ouyang Xiu's original passage, accurately reproduced by Zhipan, see *Guitian lu* 歸田錄 1 (Beijing: Zhonghua, 1997), 1. Zhipan's comments are an expansion of those contained in *Shimen zhengtong* 8.353b. Not all monastic historians saw malice in Ouyang Xiu's story. Huihong 慧洪 (1071-1128), who disliked Zanning's work, cited the Ouyang Xiu story as evidence of Zanning's faulty character. *Linjian lu* 林間錄 1, *X* no. 1624, vol. 87, 247b.
49. *Song gaoseng zhuan* 4.725c.
50. *Cheng weishilun zhangzhong shu yao* 成唯識論掌中樞要 A, *T* no. 1831, vol. 43, 608b.
51. *Song gaoseng zhuan* 4.726a.
52. Stanley Weinstein, "A Biographical Study of Tz'u-en," *Monumenta Nipponica* 15 (1959-60): 119-149.
53. *Song gaoseng zhuan* 4.726a.
54. *Song gaoseng zhuan* 4.728a.
55. See *Shiji* 43.1782.
56. The earlier version of this story, incidentally, may well be the inspiration for a famous similar episode in the *Platform Sutra*.
57. *Xu gaoseng zhuan* 23.625a19; *Beishan lu* 北山錄 6, *T* no. 2113, vol. 52, 611a. The story is recorded as well in the *Guang hongming ji* 4.112c. Rather than a malicious fabrication, it is most likely the result of misreading a passage in the *Gaoseng zhuan* that describes a debate that took place between Buddhists and Lu Xiujing at the Tianbao Monastery 天保寺. Tang historians seem to have misread this as the Tianbao *era* (560), a date years

after Lu Xiujing's death. Debate over this earlier account continued into modern times. The twentieth-century scholar of Daoism Chen Guofu rejected the *Gaoseng zhuan* account as "baseless" after noting that an official mentioned as presiding over the debate did not, according to his biography in the *History of the Southern Qi*, take office in the region until five years after Lu Xiujing's death. Chen Guofu 陳國符, *Daozang yuanliu kao* 道藏源流考 (Beijing: Zhonghua, 1963), 41.

58. *Longxing biannian tonglun* 8, 149c.
59. *Gaoseng zhuan* 9.386c–387a.
60. The best discussion of the nature and authorship of these accounts remains Robert Ford Campany, *Strange Writing. Anomaly Accounts in Early Medieval China* (Albany: State University of New York Press, 1996), especially 161–204.
61. *Gaoseng zhuan* 3.339c.
62. On Daoxuan's visions, see Koichi Shinohara, "The Kaṣāya Robe of the Past Buddha Kāśyapa in the Miraculous Instruction Given to the Vinaya Master Daoxuan (596–667)," *Chung-Hwa Buddhist Journal* 13, no. 2 (2000): 299–367; Zhihui Tan, "Daoxuan's Vision of Jetavana: Imagining a Utopian Monastery in Early Tang" (PhD diss., University of Arizona, 2002); and Fujiyoshi Masumi 藤善真澄, *Dōsen den no kenkyū* 道宣傳の研究 (Kyoto: Kyoto Daigaku gakushutsu shuppan kai, 2002), 371–402.
63. *Song gaoseng zhuan* 18.823c–824a.
64. *Taiping guangji* 92.607.
65. *Dazhidu lun* 大智度論 5, T no. 1509, vol. 25, 97c; Étienne Lamotte, *Le traité de la grande vertu du sagesse* (Louvain: Institute Orientaliste Louvain-La-Neuve, 1981), 399.
66. *Shenzu* 神足 (Skt. rddhyabijñā), also known in Chinese as the power to "attain what one wishes" (*ruyitong* 如意通). The term "divine feet" led at times to confusion since "feet" translates "basis." That is, technically the term refers to the basis for a wide range of powers, movement being only one of them.
67. *Shen jing* 神境. Skt. ṛddhiviṣayajñānasākṣātkriyābijñā. See the list of six powers in the *Yujia shi di lun* 瑜伽師地論 36, T no. 1579, vol. 30, 491b.
68. *Gaoseng zhuan* 1.324a. The passage continues with the more pedestrian possibility that the discrepancies in An Shigao's biography may be the result of errors in transmission.
69. *Taiping guangji* 太平廣記 92 (Beijing: Zhonghua Shuju, 1961), 610.
70. *Song gaoseng zhuan* 2.715c–716a and 14.791b. Zanning was apparently referring to a story in the *Kaitian chuanxin ji* 開天傳信記. Although this work is no longer extant, its account of Shanwuwei's meeting with Daoxuan is preserved in the *Taiping guangji* (92.610). The same discrepancy was noted again a few centuries later in the *Shimen zhengtong* 8.362, 8.364b.
71. John Kieschnick, *The Eminent Monk: Buddhist Ideals in Medieval Chinese Hagiography* (Honolulu: University of Hawai'i Press, 1997), 59.
72. *Song gaoseng zhuan* 2.716a.
73. Similarly, while attempting to reconcile accounts that the Indian patriarch Prajñātāra died in India with others that say he came to China, the eleventh-century monk-historian Qisong writes: "Verifying this with accounts and records, [we see that] the twenty-seventh patriarch is not heard to have come [to China] in the Jin but simply entered nirvana in India. If this sage suddenly came and went [from China], he must have come early by means of supranormal powers in order to lay a foundation for Bodhidharma and the Chan lineage. If this is the case, it is a matter of a sage who cannot be fathomed."

3. *Karma* 235

Translated by Elizabeth Morrison in *The Power of the Patriarchs: Qisong and Lineage in Chinese Buddhism* (Leiden: Brill, 2010), 256, from *Chuanfa zhengzong lun* 2.778b.
74. *Song gaoseng zhuan* 18.825b-c.
75. Preserved in *Taiping guangji* 97.649.
76. *Song gaoseng zhuan* 18.827b.
77. This is another episode in the story recounted in the *Song gaoseng zhuan*. Zanning says it took place soon after his sighting of the spirit at the end of the Kaiyuan era (ca. 742). As Zuxiu points out below, An Lushan would have been an adult at that time.
78. See Howard S. Levy, *Biography of An Lu-shan* (Berkeley: University of California Press, 1960).
79. *Longxing biannian tonglun* 16.188a.
80. On Sima Qian's critical approach to omens, see Hardy, *Worlds of Bronze and Bamboo*, 109–111.
81. *Jiu Tang shu* 37.1371. There the appearance of the snake is interpreted as an omen for An Lushan's imminent rebellion.
82. He further notes that Bukong would not have simply murdered a living thing, but would instead have used the incantation compassionately to allow the viper to move on to a better rebirth.
83. *Longxing biannian lu* 16.187b.
84. This book is deeply indebted to the CBETA project, which has produced digitized, easily searchable versions of a vast number of Chinese Buddhist texts, including most of the historical writings I analyze here. Just as remarkably, it has distributed these works widely and free of charge.

3. KARMA

1. From *Laozi* 79, translation from D. C. Lau, *Lao tzu tao te ching* (Middlesex, UK: Penguin, 1985), 141.
2. *Shiji* 61.2124.
3. Cf. William H. Nienhauser Jr., ed., *The Grand Scribe's Records*, vol. 7 (Taipei: SMC, 1994), 1–8.
4. On the *Records of the Historian* as an expression of injustice and pent-up frustration, see Stephen W. Durrant, *The Cloudy Mirror: Tension and Conflict in the Writings of Sima Qian* (Albany: State University of New York Press, 1995).
5. Grant Hardy, *Worlds of Bronze and Bamboo: Sima Qian's Conquest of History* (New York: Columbia University Press, 1999), 63.
6. On the place of the individual in Sima Qian and in early medieval Chinese historiography, see Hu Baoguo 胡寶國, *Han Tang jian shixue de fazhan* 漢唐間史學的發展 (Beijing: Shangwu Yinshuguan, 2003), 102–103; Hardy, *Worlds of Bronze and Bamboo*, 88.
7. *Xu gaoseng zhuan* 26.677c.
8. For a concise, clear introduction to the doctrine of karma, see Rupert Gethin, *The Foundations of Buddhism* (Oxford: Oxford University Press, 1998), 119–125; 215–218. Dan Lusthaus identifies three distinct ways Buddhists discuss karma: as a "mechanical theory of action," as a "moral theory of rewards and punishments aimed at shaping behavior," and as "a soteric project in which karma is the villain." *Buddhist Phenomenology: A*

Philosophical Investigation of Yogācāra Buddhism and the Ch'eng Wei-shih-lun (New York: Routledge, 2002), 168ff. In Chinese Buddhist historical writing, the emphasis is primarily on some combination of the first two categories, specifically, karma as a moral force in historical development.

9. *Xu gaoseng zhuan* 26.677c. Daoxuan addresses this (in response to the question of why an arhat would bother to do good works) in another work. *Sifenlü hanzhu jieben shu xingzong ji* 四分律含注戒本疏行宗記 3, *X* no. 714, vol. 39, p. 879a.

10. For a discussion of karma in the thought of two medieval exegetes and a late-imperial era collection of stories, see Yün-Hua Jan, "The Chinese Understanding and Assimilation of Karma Doctrine," in *Karma and Rebirth: Post Classical Developments,* ed. Ronald W. Neufeldt (Albany: State University of New York Press, 1986), 145–168. For a study of the role of karma in the life of one Chinese monk, see Beverley Foulks, *Living Karma: The Religious Practices of Ouyi Zhixu* (New York: Columbia University Press, 2014), especially chapter 1, "Karma as a Narrative Device in Ouyi's Autobiography."

11. For analysis of attitudes toward the dead in early medieval China, including a discussion of the Daoist interpretation of karma, see Stephen R. Bokenkamp, *Ancestors and Anxiety: Daoism and the Birth of Rebirth in China* (Berkeley: University of California Press, 2007).

12. David Keightley, *Sources of Shang History: The Oracle Bone Inscriptions of Bronze Age China* (Berkeley: University of California Press, 1978), 76–90.

13. Michel Strickmann, *Chinese Magical Medicine* (Stanford, CA: Stanford University Press, 2002), 45–57; Bokenkamp, *Ancestors and Anxiety.*

14. We know little about Li Shizheng other than that he came from Shangdang 上黨, held the posts of scholar of the eastern palace 東宮學士 and supervisor of rites in the palace 門下典儀 in the early Tang, and took as his master the eminent monk Falin 法琳. *Tang hufa shamen Falin biezhuan* 唐護法沙門法琳別傳, 1, *T* no. 2051, vol. 50, 199a; *Da Tang neidian lu* 大唐內典錄 5, *T* no. 2149, vol. 55, 281c.

15. *Guang hongming ji* 14.192b.

16. On Bo Zong (d. 576 BCE), see *Shiji* 39.1680; Yang Xi refers to Yangshe Xi 羊舌肸 (fl. 552 BCE). On Qing Fu (d. 660 BCE), see *Shiji* 33.1532; for Shu Ya (d. 662 BCE), *Shiji* 33.1532.

17. Although discussion of karma is largely focused on the individual in Buddhist scholastic writings, in practice, karma is a family matter in which descendants, in particular children, are expected to create good karma by sponsoring Buddhist endeavors, which they then transfer toward the well-being of their deceased parents. In the end, the gap between ancient Chinese notions of collective family responsibilities for the fate of the family and karma is not as great as it at first seems. Bokenkamp, *Ancestors and Anxiety,* is particularly enlightening on this point.

18. *Guang hongming ji* 14.192a. Similarly, another Buddhist layman, Xi Chao 郗超 (336–377), also drew on historical examples to refute the notion that the family is held responsible for the deeds of an ancestor. *Fengfa yao* 奉法要, in *Hong ming ji* 弘明集 13, *T* no. 2102, vol. 52, 87b; translated in Erik Zürcher, *The Buddhist Conquest of China* (Leiden: Brill, 2007), 168–169, discussed in Strickmann, *Chinese Magical Medicine,* 45–46; and Bokenkamp, *Ancestors and Anxiety,* 170.

19. Wendy Doniger O'Flaherty, ed., *Karma and Rebirth in Classical Indian Traditions* (Berkeley: University of California Press, 1980), ix. Cf. Lusthaus, *Buddhist Phenomenology,* 168.

20. *Jinshu* 晉書 (Beijing: Zhonghua, 1974), 34.1023; cited in *Fozu tongji* 36.338b. Cf. Thomas Jülch, *Zhipan's Account of the History of Buddhism in China. Volume 1,* Fozu tongji, juan 34–38. From the Times of the Buddha to the Nanbeichao Era (Leiden: Brill, 2019), 121. *Longxing biannian tonglun* 9.153b.
21. *Jinshu* 95.2482; cited in *Song gaoseng zhuan* 5.737a. Daoists too took an interest in Bao Jing's case. See Bokenkamp, *Ancestors and Anxiety*, 168-169.
22. This is not the explanation Zhipan gives in his *Fozu tongji*, where he states, "[Yang] Hu's ability to know his past lives is what Buddhists term 'the supernormal ability to know past lives.' [Yang] Hu's study of Buddhism [in previous lives] must have manifested in this incarnation." *Fozu tongji* 36.338b.
23. (Fl. 494). *Gaoseng zhuan* 13.412a.
24. *Song gaoseng zhuan* 14.790b.
25. *Lüxiang gantong zhuan* 1.879c, cited in *Fozu tongji* 36.347a. The two monks do share many characteristics: both composed books on the monastic regulations, historical collections, and Buddhist bibliographic works. Fujiyoshi Masumi devotes an entire chapter to a comparison of them in his lengthy biographical study of Daoxuan, *Dōsen den no kenkyū* 道宣傳の研究 (Kyoto: Kyoto Daigaku gakushutsu shuppan kai, 2002). It has even been suggested that these similarities and the legend that Daoxuan was Sengyou's reincarnation led compilers of the bibliography of the *Sui shu* to wrongly attribute the *Gaoseng zhuan* to Sengyou, apparently assuming that if Daoxuan had compiled a collection of monastic biographies, Sengyou must have done so as well. See Arthur F. Wright, "Biography and Hagiography: Hui-chiao's *Lives of Eminent Monks*," in his *Studies in Chinese Buddhism* (New Haven, CT: Yale University Press, 1990), 98; Yamanouchi Shinkyō 山內普卿, "Kōsōden no kenkyū" 高僧伝の研究, in his *Shina Bukkyōshi no kenkyū* 支那佛教史之研究 (Kyōto: Bukkyōdaigaku Shuppansha, 1921), 4.
26. *Jingde chuandeng lu* 24.407c; *Fozu tongji* 8.190c. More famous still, a previous incarnation of Zhiyi was said to have attended the Buddha's *Lotus* sermon on Vulture Peak. Stuart H. Young, *Conceiving the Indian Buddhist Patriarchs in China* (Honolulu: University of Hawai'i Press, 2015), 128.
27. Zanning should have checked his dates more carefully, as Cai Yong was born a few years before Zhang Heng died. This is equivalent to the clumsy claim discussed above that a spirit of the future An Lushan appeared after An had in fact been born. I have been unable to locate Zanning's source (if he had one) for thinking Cai Yong the reincarnation of Zhang Heng. For Cai Yong's biography, see Chris Conner, "Ts'ai Yung," in *Indiana Companion to Traditional Chinese Literature*, ed. William H. Nienhauser Jr. (Bloomington: Indiana University Press, 1986), 787-788. Bokenkamp begins his book *Ancestors and Anxiety* by citing the story of Cai Yong's relationship with his ancestors as an example of the traditional relationship before the introduction of the concept of rebirth to China with Buddhism. Ironically, some time after Cai's death, Buddhist historians used his case precisely as early Chinese evidence for reincarnation.
28. *Song gaoseng zhuan* 19.830c; *Longxing biannian tonglun* 20.207c.
29. Zhiwei was a seventh-century monk; Xu Ling was a prominent scholar-official. The theory that Zhiwei was a reincarnation of Xu Ling is posited in Zhiwei's biography in *Song gaoseng zhuan* 6.739a. Such examples from Buddhist historiography are easily multiplied.

238   3. Karma

The Tang official Fang Guan 房琯 (697-763) was a monk in a former life, as was Emperor Wen of the Sui, while the violent and unpredictable Emperor Xuan of the Northern Qi was a demon in a former life. *Longxing biannian tong lun* 17.192b; 9.153a; 8.149b.

30. *Song gaoseng zhuan* 18.827a. The *Fozu tongji* conveniently provides a list of a dozen examples of reincarnation in Chinese history, listed chronologically. *Fozu tongji* 52.455b. Huihong's conjecture that Su Dongpo was a prominent monk in a previous existence is the subject of a detailed article by Zhu Gang 朱剛 and Zhao Huijun 趙惠俊 that reveals just how common speculation about previous rebirths was among Song-era literati: "Su Shi qianshen gushi de zhenxiang yu gaixie" 蘇軾前身故事的真相與改寫, *Lingnan Xuebao* 嶺南學報 9 (2018): 123-141. A Ming layman claimed to be the reincarnation of the Song historian-monk Qisong. See Elizabeth Morrison, *The Power of the Patriarchs: Qisong and Lineage in Chinese Buddhism* (Leiden: Brill, 2010), 126.

31. *Gaoseng zhuan* 1.325c-326a.

32. "San bao lun" 三報論 in *Hongming ji* 5.34b.

33. That is, the "knowledge of one's former abodes" (*suzhutong* 宿住通; Skt. *pūrvanivāsānusmṛti*) and the "Heavenly Eye" (*tianyan* 天眼; Skt. *divyacakṣus*). Paul Demiéville, "Sur la memoire des existences anterieures," *Bulletin de l'École Française d'Extrême-Orient* 27 (1927): 283-298.

34. *Chu sanzang jiji* 13.95b. Even when the specifics of events that created relevant karma in past lives are not known, it is not uncommon, either in historiographical works or in other arenas, to claim to detect the effects of karma from a previous life in a more general way. Eric Greene has analyzed medieval meditation texts that explain how one can assess one's karma from previous existences while in meditation. And Justin Ritzinger has interviewed Buddhists in modern-day Taiwan who attribute problems in their everyday lives to karma from past lives. See Eric M. Greene, *Chan Before Chan: Meditation, Repentance, and Visionary Experience in Chinese Buddhism* (Honolulu: University of Hawai'i Press, 2021), chapter 3, "Visions of Karma"; Justin Ritzinger, "Karma, Charisma, and Community: Karmic Storytelling in a Blue-Collar Taiwanese Buddhist Organization," *Journal of Chinese Buddhist Studies* 33 (2020): 203-232.

35. *Guang hongming ji* 14.191a.

36. See Robert Ford Campany, "Return from Death Narratives in Early Medieval China," *Journal of Chinese Religions* 18, no. 1 (1990): 91-125.

37. *Chu san zang ji ji* 15.107c.

38. *Gaoseng zhuan* 134.409b.

39. This is a hell (or "earth prison") in which the residents are forced to climb up the razor-sharp, barbed branches of enormous trees. *Qishi yinben jing* 起世因本經 3, T no. 25, vol. 1, 378c

40. Feng Si must refer to Feng Sixu 馮思勗 (fl. 686). As censor-in-chief, Feng Sixu famously challenged the notorious monk Huaiyi 懷義 (d. 694), favorite of Emperor Wu, for his illegal activities. In response, Huaiyi had Feng Sixu beaten almost to death. *Jiu Tangshu* 183.4741; *Xin Tangshu* 76.3483.

41. The world in which we live.

42. *Song gaoseng zhuan* 5.736a.

43. *Song gaoseng zhuan* 20.840b.

44. *Gaoseng zhuan* 9.388a.

45. Campany, "Return from Death Narratives in Early Medieval China;" and especially Robert Ford Campany, *Strange Writing: Anomaly Accounts in Early Medieval China* (Albany: State University of New York Press, 1996).
46. Xuyun, *Empty Cloud: The Autobiography of the Chinese Zen Master*, trans. Charles Luk (Longmead, UK: Element Books, 1988), 1. As Daniela Campo has shown, in fact it is difficult to determine what parts of the "autobiography" were composed by Xuyun and what by his disciples based on previous written works and oral accounts from Xuyun. *La construction de la sainteté dans la Chine moderne. La vie du maître bouddhiste Xuyun* (Paris: Les Belles Lettres, 2013).
47. *Song gaoseng zhuan* 1.711b.
48. *Song gaoseng zhuan* 15.800a.
49. *Song gaoseng zhuan* 4.728a.
50. In the biography of the fifth Chan patriarch Hongren 弘忍 (602-675?), for instance (*Song gaoseng zhuan* 8.754a), but there are many other examples.
51. In the biography of Zhixuan, *Song gaoseng zhuan* 6.743b.
52. The biography of Shaokang 少康 (d. 805), *Song gaoseng zhuan* 4.728a.
53. Ritzinger, "Karma, Charisma, and Community:."
54. *Suxi* 宿習. Erik Zürcher translates the term as "an ingrained habit," but the implication is normally that these are habits formed in previous lives. For Zürcher's translation and discussion, see Erik Zürcher, "Perspectives in the Study of Chinese Buddhism," *Journal of the Royal Asiatic Society* 2 (1982): 165-166.
55. *Chu sanzang jiji* 5.40b.
56. This is ironic since later in life Daoxuan himself claimed to have been visited by ancient spirits.
57. The quotation is from Confucius. *Analects* 16.9. The translation is from D. C. Lau, *Analects*, 165.
58. The biography of the monk Tandi (d. ca.453) in the *Gaoseng zhuan* recounts how his mother had a dream of a monk who gave her a whisk and a paperweight. When she awoke, the two objects were beside her, and at that moment she conceived. Later, it is revealed that Tandi owned the objects in a previous life. *Gaoseng zhuan* 7.370c.
59. The allusion eludes me. Perhaps Daoxuan is confusing the story of Yang Hu's golden ring, above, with another Tang rebirth story about the poet-official Cui Xian 崔咸 (d. 832), born with a mark beneath his mouth that matched that of a man who vowed to be reborn as Cui Xian's father's child. On Cui Xian's story, see *Jiu Tangshu* 190C, 5060; and Qisong's *Xinjin wenji* 鐔津文集 1, *T* no. 2020, vol. 52, 653b.
60. *Xu gaoseng zhuan* 1.426b.
61. The rivalry between Chao Cuo and Yuan Ang is among the most famous in Chinese history. Chao's accusation that Yuan was taking bribes resulted in Yuan losing all of his official titles. Yuan, for his part, orchestrated Chao's eventual execution. Michael Loewe, *A Biographical Dictionary of the Qin, Former Han and Xin Periods (221 BC–AD 24)* (Leiden: Brill, 2000), 661-663.
62. *Song gaoseng zhuan* 6.744a. In another (apparently later) version of the story, it was not a cyst on his foot but a "face-like sore" on his knee, complete with eyes and a mouth and even capable of speech. Here too, the sore turns out to be Chao Cuo, back from the dead to hound his rival Yuan Ang in his latest incarnation. *Cibei shuichan fa* 慈悲水懺法 1,

63. These three instances of Yuan Ang's forthright criticism are given in Yuan's biography in *Han shu* 49.2267. See also Loewe, *A Biographical Dictionary*, 661-663.
64. Yuan's argument was that the seven kings were angered chiefly by Chao's proposal to reduce their land holdings and that by executing Chao, the emperor could appease the kings and avoid a revolt. See Loewe, *A Biographical Dictionary*, 27-29; 661-63.
65. *Longxing biannian tonglun* 27.244c.
66. *Xu gaoseng zhuan* 16.555b; *Longxing biannian tonglun* 8.149a.
67. *Song gaoseng zhuan* 17.819b.
68. *Song gaoseng zhuan* 17.819b; *Fayuan zhulin* 79.875c.
69. *Fozu tongji* 42.392c. Cf. Jülch, *Zhipan's Account of the History of Buddhism in China, Volume 2*, 316-318.
70. The "three types of catastrophe" (*sanzai* 三災) are calamities that occur at the end of the kalpa in which the world is destroyed.
71. *Fozu tongji* 38.358c; Cao Ganghua 曹剛華, *Songdai fojiao shiji yanjiu* 宋代佛教史籍研究 (Shanghai: Huadong Shifandaxue Chubanshe, 2005), 120.
72. *Song gaoseng zhuan* 3.723a. Though saying only that the time "was not ripe" rather than specifically citing karma, Zhipan too argued that Buddhism had been present in China for a long time before it was actively promoted by the Han court. See *Fozu tongji* 34.327b and Cao, *Songdai fojiao shiji yanjiu*, 123, for discussion.
73. *Song gaoseng zhuan* 6.744c.
74. *Yuanren lun* 原人論 1, T no. 1886, vol. 45, 708c. The translation is from Peter N. Gregory, *Inquiry Into the Origin of Humanity: An Annotated Translation of Tsung-mi's Yüan jen lun with a Modern Commentary* (Honolulu: University of Hawai'i Press, 1995), 123. Huiyuan discussed the same problem in his "San bao lun," 34b.
75. *Da Song seng shi lüe* 2.247a. Cf. Albert Welter, *The Administration of Buddhism in China: A Study and Translation of Zanning and the Topical Compendium of the Buddhist Clergy* (New York: Cambria Press, 2018), 444.
76. The reference to the mind resonates with Huiyuan's treatise on karma, which begins: "There are three types of karmic retribution: immediate retribution, retribution in the [subsequent] life, and retribution in a later life. In immediate retribution, good and bad begin in this body and it is this body that receives the retribution. In retribution in a [subsequent] life, one receives retribution in the next life. In later retribution, one may pass through two lives, three lives, a hundred lives, or a thousand before receiving the retribution. There is no subject [*zhu* 主] of the retribution; it must originate in the mind, and the mind is not governed by any set office [*dingsi* 定司]. [Karmic retribution] responds to the stimulus of events; the stimulus may come faster or slower, and for this reason the retribution may come sooner or later." "San bao lun," *Hong ming ji* 5.34b.
77. On the problem of the mind and body in the functioning of karma, Zongmi writes: "If the eyes, ears, hands, and feet are able to generate karma, then why, while the eyes, ears, hands, and feet of a person who has just died are still intact, do they not see, hear, function and move? If one says that it is the mind that generates [karma], what is meant by the mind? If one says that it is the corporeal mind, then the corporeal mind has material substance and is embedded within the body. How, then, does it suddenly enter the

eyes and ears and discern what is and what is not of externals?... If one were to say that it is just joy, anger, love, and hate that activate the body and mouth and cause them to generate karma, then, since the feelings of joy, anger, and so forth abruptly arise one moment and abruptly perish the next and are of themselves without substance, what can we take as constituting the controlling agent and generating karma?" Gregory, *Inquiry Into the Origin of Humanity*, 124.

78. *Fozu tongji* 38.357c. Cf. Jülch, *Zhipan's Account of the History of Buddhism in China, Volume 2*, 278.
79. *Fozu tongji* 39.360a. Cf. Jülch, *Zhipan's Account of the History of Buddhism in China, Volume 2*, 30–32. For his argument, Zhipan draws on a commentary by Zhiyi, *Guan Wuliangshoufo jing shu* 觀無量壽佛經疏 1, T no. 1750, vol. 37, 190a.
80. *Song gaoseng zhuan* 24.864a. See also Susan Shih-shan Huang's discussion of the story and fifteenth-century illustrations of it in "Illustrating the Efficacy of the *Diamond Sutra* in Vernacular Buddhism," *National Palace Museum Research Quarterly* (*Gugong xueshu jikan* 故宮學術季刊) 35, no. 4 (2018): 54–62.
81. See Chiew Hui Ho, *Diamond Sutra Narratives: Textual Production and Lay Religiosity in Medieval China* (Leiden: Brill, 2019).
82. *Zuishuang* 罪霜, literally the "frost of guilt." The Tang-era text *Kaiyuan zhanjing* 開元占經 explains that a proper judge maintains objectivity in the face of pressure like frost that resists the sun, while the weak judge gives in to manipulation like frost that melts under the sun. *Siku quanshu* 四庫全書 ed., 1–2. Modeling the period after death on court proceedings is not limited to China. Sixteenth-century Spanish wills conceive of heaven as a court and call on saints to act as attorneys for the deceased before God. Carlos M.N. Eire, *From Madrid to Purgatory. The Art and Craft of Dying in Sixteenth-Century Spain* (Cambridge: Cambridge University Press, 1995), 68–73.
83. According to the *Pusa benyuan jing* 菩薩本緣經 3, "The mind is an evil vessel, filled with the poison of enmity." T no. 153, vol. 3, 67.
84. *Song gaoseng zhuan* 24.864a.
85. This refers to the story of the twenty-third Indian patriarch Siṃha, who was beheaded by an evil king. The *Fu fazang* version relates that when the patriarch was beheaded, milk instead of blood poured from his neck. *Fu fazang yinyuan zhuan* 6.321c. The story that the king's arm fell off and that he too died seems to have entered the legend at a later date.
86. *Fozu tongji* 36.342c–343a. Cf. Jülch, *Zhipan's Account of the History of Buddhism in China, Volume 2*, 158–159.
87. Cao, *Songdai fojiao shiji yanjiu*, 118–129.
88. *Longxing biannian tonglun* 25.233b. See also Cao, *Songdai fojiao shiji yanjiu*, 124.
89. *Longxing biannian tonglun* 3.121c.
90. *Fozu tongji* 39.363b. Cf. Jülch, *Zhipan's Account of the History of Buddhism in China, Volume 2*, 62. For Taizong's relationship to Buddhism, including his commissioning of rites for those killed in the establishment of the dynasty, see Stanley Weinstein, *Buddhism Under the T'ang* (Cambridge: Cambridge University Press, 1987), 12.
91. See Hu, *Han Tang jian shixue de fazhan*, 13–19, for Sima Qian's "discovery of the individual." On the importance of individual monks for shaping history in Buddhist historiography, see Cao, *Songdai fojiao shiji yanjiu*, 126–127.
92. *Chu sanzang jiji* 1.1a.

4. PROPHECY

1. In Carr's words, history is "a process of interaction, a dialogue between the historian in the present and the facts of the past." Edward Hallett Carr, *What Is History* (1961; 2nd ed., London: Macmillan, 1986), 29.
2. David Hackett Fischer, *Historians' Fallacies: Toward a Logic of Historical Thought* (New York: Harper & Row, 1970), 257.
3. Hugh Trevor-Roper, on examining the possibilities of predicting future events on the basis of the past, concludes soberly, "We may predict in detail, and conditionally, where we have the means of comparison, and such limited predictions may be scientifically, or at least empirically, tested and so justified and useful; but generally and absolutely there can be no prediction, only a guess; and a guess is, in the strict sense, worthless." "The Past and the Present: History and Sociology," *Past & Present* 42 (1969): 10.
4. Both prophecies are recorded in the *Song shi*. The prophecy of the stone inscription is listed twice, once for the year 979 and once for the year 982 (*Songshi* 宋史 66.1435; 4.67). Zhipan agrees with the dates, but adds the detail that the second stone inscription was written by the famous fifth-century Buddhist thaumaturge Baozhi. *Fozu tongji* 44.407a. Zhipan notes elsewhere that although the first stone inscription might have been manufactured by men, the second was later confirmed by a visit to the emperor by Baozhi himself and so must have been authentic. *Fozu tongji* 43.401c.
5. For a study of this phenomenon in a very different context, see Matthew Neujahr, *Predicting the Past in the Ancient Near East: Mantic Historiography in Ancient Mesopotamia, Judah, and the Mediterranean World* (Providence, RI: Brown Judaic Studies, 2012). Robert E. Lerner's *The Powers of Prophecy: The Cedar of Lebanon Vision from the Mongol Onslaught to the Dawn of the Enlightenment* follows one prophecy repeatedly revised and reinterpreted in Europe from the thirteenth to the seventeenth century, variously seen to predict the coming of the Mongols, the appearance of the Antichrist, the Black Death, and Martin Luther. Included are examples of *ex eventu* predictions (Berkeley: University of California Press, 1983).
6. For a survey, see Richard J. Smith, *Fortune-tellers and Philosophers: Divination in Traditional Chinese Society* (Boulder, CO: Westview Press, 1991). For a hefty collection of excellent essays on individual types of divination (e.g., astrology, hemerology, geomancy, etc.) based on the Dunhuang documents, see Marc Kalinowski, ed., *Divination et société dans la Chine médiévale. Étude des manuscrits de Dunhuang de la Bibliothèque nationale de France et de la British Library* (Paris: Bibliothèque nationale de France, 2003).
7. The *types* of divination most commonly described in formal historical writings are quite limited when compared to the full range of possibilities in other genres of writing, reflected for instance in the materials explored in Smith, *Fortune-tellers and Philosophers*, or Kalinowski, *Divination et société dans la Chine médiévale*. For prognostication in two Chinese Buddhist historical works, see Christoph Anderl and Gang Yang, "Prognostication in Chinese Buddhist Historiographical Texts: The *Gaoseng zhuan* and the *Xu Gaoseng zhuan*," *Acta Orientalis* 73, no. 1 (2019): 1–45.

8. A single passage in *Chang ahan jing* 長阿含經 (Skt. *Dīrghāgama*) 5.34b contains all of these predictions, but many more similar prophecies can be found throughout Buddhist literature. In China, perhaps the most famous predictions the Buddha makes of spiritual progress are those contained in chapters 6, 8, and 9 of the *Lotus Sutra*.
9. *Zengyi ahan jing* 增壹阿含經 (Skt. *Ekōttarikāgama*) 5, *T* no. 125, vol. 2, 567b.
10. Again, there are many references to this prediction. In China at least, the account in the *Fo benxing ji jing* 佛本行集經 (Skt. *Buddhacarita-saṃgrāha*) was well known. 1, *T* no. 190, vol. 3, 655c.
11. *Da Tang Xiyu ji* 大唐西域記 7, *T* no. 2087, vol. 51, 905c; Samuel Beal, *Buddhist Records of the Western World* (London: Kegan Paul, 1906), vol. 2, 46.
12. There are different versions of this division with different interpretations. In his summary, Étienne Lamotte does not list predictions as one of the twelve divisions, but they do appear as such in early texts like the *Saṃyuktāgama* (*Bieyi yi za ahan jing* 別譯雜阿含經 6, *T* no. 100, vol. 2, 415a). Lamotte, *History of Indian Buddhism: From the Origins to the Śaka Era* (Louvain: Peeters Press, 1988), 143-149.
13. *Dazhidu lun* 24.235c; Étienne Lamotte, *Le traité de la grande vertu de sagesse* (Louvain: Institute Orientaliste Louvain-La-Neuve, 1981), 1515-1516.
14. See Li Qingzhang 李清章 and Yan Mengxiang 閻孟祥, "Song Taizong 'shou Fo ji' chuan-shuo kao" 宋太宗受佛記傳說考, in *Hebei daxue xuebao (zhexue shehui kexue ban)* 河北大學學報(哲學社會科學板) 29, no. 1 (2014): 16-18. For the *Fozu tongji* passage, see 43.400b.
15. There are many references to this famous event in Chinese Buddhist histories, for instance in the *Shijia pu* 1.5c. For a more complete survey of sources including Pali and Sanskrit as well as parallels with the biblical story of Simeon, see Lamotte, *History of Indian Buddhism*, 672-675.
16. *Gaoseng Faxian zhuan* 高僧法顯傳 1, *T* no. 2085, vol. 51, 861a. H. A. Giles, *The Travels of Fa-hsien (399–414 AD), or Record of the Buddhistic Kingdoms* (Cambridge: Cambridge University Press, 1923), 37; Jean-Pierre Drège, *Mémoire sur les pays bouddhiques* (Paris: Les Belles Lettres, 2013), 40, 114. For a stele, see "Daosu jiushi ren zaoxiang ji" 道俗九十人造像記 from 543, in Chüan-ying Yen 顏娟英, ed., *Beichao fojiao shike tapian baipin* 北朝佛教石刻拓片百品 (Taipei: Zhongyang Yanjiuyuan Lishi Yuyan Yanjiusuo, 2008), 114-115.
17. Daoheng's future, for instance, is predicted when he is a child by an eremite who sees him on the road. *Gaoseng zhuan* 6.364b. More commonly, such predictions of greatness in infants come from monks. *Xu gaoseng zhuan* 20.590a; *Song gaoseng zhuan* 19.834c; 20.590a.
18. For prohibitions on divination in the monastic regulations, see John Kieschnick, *The Eminent Monk: Buddhist Ideals in Medieval Chinese Hagiography* (Honolulu: University of Hawai'i Press, 1997), 78. Interestingly, one document from Dunhuang shows that monks were not averse to paying a (nonmonastic) professional fortune-teller. Kalinowski, *Divination et société dans la Chine médiévale*, 26.
19. *Gaoseng zhuan* 9.383; see also Arthur Wright, "Fo-t'u-teng, a Biography," *Harvard Journal of Asiatic Studies* 11 (1948): 321-371.
20. Kieschnick, *Eminent Monk*, 76-82. Kalinowski, *Divination et société dans la Chine médiévale*, 26-27. One Dunhuang document testifies to the use of dice in foretelling the future, a practice confirmed by the discovery of dice at Dunhuang. Kalinowski, *Divination et société*, 320. For the dice, see Peng Jinzhang 彭金章 and Wang Jianjun 王建軍, eds., *Dunhuang*

Mogaoku beiqu shiku 敦煌莫高窟北區石窟 (Beijing: Wenwu, 2004), vol. 2, plate 128 (B146: 2.1.3). Also at Dunhuang is the preface to a divination manual that claims the text was brought to China by a monk. Kalinowski, *Divination et société*, 320. Monks continued to tell fortunes in later times and up to the present. In his study of the civil service examinations, Benjamin Elman recounts the story of a monk who, in 1550, predicted examination success for a scholar preparing for his exams. Benjamin Elman, *Civil Examinations and Meritocracy in Late Imperial China* (Cambridge, MA: Harvard University Press, 2013), 173.

21. *Fozu tongji* 44.408a. In a note, Zhipan explains that by predictions of names of kingdoms and of kalpas he is referring to the *Lotus Sutra*, presumably chapter 6. This division shares some features with Cicero's distinction between natural and artificial divination. David Wardle, *Cicero on Divination*, Book 1 (Oxford: Oxford University Press, 2006), especially 48ff.
22. See *Song gaoseng zhuan* 16.808a for one among many examples.
23. *Fozu tongji* 44.408a.
24. *Yijing*, "Xici" 繫辭 11.1; Richard John Lynn, *Classic of Changes: A New Translation of the I Ching as Interpreted by Wang Bi* (New York: Columbia University Press, 1994), 64.
25. *Fozu tongji* 44.408a.
26. As noted above, Wang's attacks are as much on those who manipulate omens as on the omens themselves. See Michael Puett, "Listening to Sages: Divination, Omens, and the Rhetoric of Antiquity in Wang Chong's *Lunheng*," *Oriens Extremus* 45 (2005/06): 271–281.
27. Translated in Tiziana Lippiello, *Auspicious Omens and Miracles in Ancient China. Han, Three Kingdoms and Six Dynasties* (Nettetal: Styler Verlag, 2001), 50. *Hou Han shu* 3.159.
28. Lippiello, *Auspicious Omens and Miracles in Ancient China*, 64. *Sanguo zhi* 三國志 32 (Beijing: Zhonghua, 1982), 888.
29. As we have seen in the sources chapter above, Chinese historians were reluctant to question written records. Nonetheless, there are exceptions. Fan Ye, for instance, at one point suggests that the omens of the reign of Han emperor Guangwu (r. 25–57 CE) were just too numerous to be authentic. Lippiello, *Auspicious Omens and Miracles in Ancient China*, 51; *Hou Han shu* 5.225. Though not a historian, the most famous critic of the standard reporting of omens was Wang Chong. Michael Puett has shown, however, that Wang's criticism did not imply that he rejected the possibility of divine omens; his main concern was with those who misinterpreted natural phenomena as bad omens during times of good governance. Puett, "Listening to Sages." As a court astrologer, Sima Qian no doubt believed in omens and certainly recorded them in his work, but at times questioned the authenticity of some omens as predictive markers, preferring as explanation for historical events more mundane factors like human greed and deceit. Grant Hardy, *Worlds of Bronze and Bamboo: Sima Qian's Conquest of History* (New York: Columbia University Press, 1999), 110. The historian's ambivalence toward omens was expressed most eloquently by Livy: "Since it is a common belief nowadays that the gods give no signs of the future, I am not ignorant that from this neglectful attitude it happens that no prodigies whatever are brought to the attention of the officials of the state or are put down in historical writings. But as I am writing of bygone affairs, somehow or other the disposition of my mind becomes ancient, and an indefinable feeling of awe keeps me from regarding as unworthy of mention in my history those events which the wisest men

of those times deemed important enough to warrant action by the state." Quoted in Franklin Brunell Krauss, *An Interpretation of the Omens, Portents, and Prodigies Recorded by Livy, Tacitus, and Suetonios* (Philadelphia: University of Pennsylvania Press, 1930), 27.

30. Of particular note for the Han are two articles: Hans Bielenstein, "An Interpretation of the Portents in the Ts'ien-Han-shu," *Bulletin of the Museum of Far Eastern Antiquities* 22 (1950): 127-143, in part through statistical analysis, made the case that the reporting of auspicious and inauspicious omens was primarily by officials contemporary to the events rather than later historians or "the common people," as previous scholarship had suggested. Second, Martin Kern in "Religious Anxiety and Political Interest in Western Han Omen Interpretation: The Case of the Han Wudi 漢武帝 Period (141-87 BCE)," *Studies in Chinese History* 10 (December 2000): 1-31, building on Bielenstein's work, explains that the process of reporting and responding to omens was even more complicated in that the same omen could be interpreted as either auspicious or inauspicious by different people or in different times. For a useful survey of auspicious omens from the Han through the Six Dynasties period, and including Buddhist material, see Lippiello, *Auspicious Omens and Miracles in Ancient China*.
31. *Biqiuni zhuan* 2.939c.
32. *Gaoseng zhuan* 2.330a.
33. *Xu gaoseng zhuan* 17.564a.
34. *Xu gaoseng zhuan* 6.468a.
35. *Xu gaoseng zhuan* 6.468b. References to fragrant omens become more common with the *Song gaoseng zhuan*.
36. *Xu gaoseng zhuan* 22.615a. On the rise of vegetarianism in China, see John Kieschnick, "A History of Buddhist Vegetarianism in China," in *Of Tripod and Palate: Food, Politics and Religion in Traditional China*, ed. Roel Sterckx (New York: Palgrave-Macmillan, 2005), 186-212.
37. Kieschnick, *The Eminent Monk*, 31.
38. This idea draws on canonical stories of children gaining vast merit by accidentally making stupa shapes while playing in the sand, a practice praised in the *Lotus Sutra*.
39. *Song gaoseng zhuan* 25.869c.
40. The culture of dreams extended far beyond predictive dreams and beyond Buddhism, my twin focus here. For a nuanced discussion of dreams in medieval China as a whole, see Robert Ford Campany, *The Chinese Dreamscape 300 BCE—800 CE* (Cambridge, MA: Harvard University Press, 2020).
41. Biography of Fashen 法誐 (718-778) in the *Song gaoseng zhuan* 5.736a; swallowing the moon presaged the birth of Kuiji in *Fozu tongji* 29.295a. This example jibes well with contemporary dream manuals from Dunhuang that list a dream of swallowing the moon as a sign of the imminent birth of a noble child. Jean-Pierre Drège and Dimitri Drettas, "Oniromancie," in Kalinowski, *Divination et société*, 375 (citing P3105).
42. The tree appears in a dream of the mother of Yuancheng 願誠 (d. 887) in *Song gaoseng zhuan* 27.883a. For the stupa, see the biography of Zhiyan 智琰 (564-634) in *Xu gaoseng zhuan* 14.531c.
43. *Xu gaoseng zhuan* 17.564a.
44. *Apidamo da piposha lun* 阿毘達磨大毘婆沙論 37, no. 1545, vol. 27, 193c, discussed in Campany, *The Chinese Dreamscape*, 61. There is a similar taxonomy in the *Shanjian lü piposha*

善見律毘婆沙 12.760a, noted briefly in Michel Strickmann, "Dreamwork of Psycho-Sinologists: Doctors, Taoists, Monks," in *Psycho-Sinology: The Universe of Dreams in Chinese Culture*, ed. Carolyn T. Brown (Washington, DC: University Press of America, 1988), 38-39; but Campany argues convincingly that the category Strickmann classifies as prophetic refers instead to thoughts produced in response to karma linked to the past. Campany, *The Chinese Dreamscape*, 59-60.
45. *Fozu tongji* 46.420c. For Huizong's dream, see Patricia Buckley Ebrey, *Emperor Huizong* (Cambridge, MA: Harvard University Press, 2014), 346-348.
46. The first citation refers to *She dasheng lun* 攝大乘論 (Skt. *Mahāyānasaṃgrahaśāstra*) 1, T no. 1593, vol. 31, 118b; *The Summary of the Great Vehicle*, trans. John P. Keenan (Berkeley, CA: Numata Center for Buddhist Translation and Research, 1992), 40-41; the dream kingdom reference is to *Liezi* 3.3a (*SBCK* ed.); Angus Charles Graham, *Lieh-tzu* (London: Murray, 1960), 67.
47. *Song gaoseng zhuan* 21.849b.
48. *Song gaoseng zhuan* 11.775.
49. *Han shu* 56.2498. Translation from Lippiello, *Auspicious Omens and Miracles in Ancient China*, 27. Cf. Michael Loewe, *Dong Zhongshu: A "Confucian" Heritage and the* Chunqiu fanlu (Leiden: Brill, 2011), 88-89.
50. *Shijia pu* 1.5a. The passage he draws on, with some differences (for instance, instead of gems emerging from the trees, Sengyou gives "precious water emerged from underground"), is from *Da fangguang fo huayan jing* 大方廣佛華嚴經 (Skt. *Buddāvataṃsaka-mahāvaipulyasūtra*), 55, T no. 278, vol. 9, 752b.
51. *Shijia pu* 1.5a.
52. Stephen W. Durrant, *The Cloudy Mirror: Tension and Conflict in the Writings of Sima Qian* (Albany: State University of New York Press, 1995), 140; Hardy, *Worlds of Bronze and Bamboo*, 110.
53. *Shijia pu* 1.5c. Sengyou cites the *Ruiying jing* as his source. For discussion of the thirty-two bodily marks of a buddha, see John Strong, *The Buddha: A Short Biography* (Oxford: Oneworld, 2001), 41-43; 157-158.
54. Durrant, *Cloudy Mirror*, 133. For the claim that, in the context of Chinese historiography, Sima Qian showed little interest in strange occurrences, see Hu Baoguo 胡寶國, *Han Tang jian shixue de fazhan* 漢唐間史學的發展 (Beijing: Shangwu Yinshuguan, 2003), 169. Liu Bang had seventy-two black moles on his left thigh, among other unusual features. *Shi ji* 8.342.
55. Robert H. Sharf, *Coming to Terms with Chinese Buddhism: A Reading of the Treasure Store Treatise* (Honolulu: University of Hawai'i Press, 2002), 77-136.
56. *Shijia shi pu* 1.89b.
57. *Fozu tongji* 2.142b. The passages he draws on are from the *Guoqu xianzai yinguo jing* 過去現在因果經 1, T no. 189, vol. 1, 626a, and the *Taizi ruiying benqi jing* 1.474b.
58. *Jingde chuandeng lu* 1.205b, citing the *Puyao jing* as source.
59. *Xu gaoseng zhuan* 26.667c.
60. *Sui shu* 隋書 69 (Beijing: Zhonghua, 1973), 1613; Arthur F. Wright, *The Sui Dynasty* (New York: Knopf, 1978), 19.
61. See Strong, *The Buddha* 38, 57. One could argue that the most famous dream in *Chinese Buddhist history is that of Emperor Ming of the Han, who dreamed of the Buddha and

subsequently ordered that monks and Buddhist scriptures be brought to China. But in this case, the dream, while inspirational, is not in itself prophetic. The dream is discussed in Kenneth Chen, *Buddhism in China: A Historical Survey* (Princeton, NJ: Princeton University Press, 1964), 29-31. See also the discussion of the passage and translation of the received version of the *Scripture in Forty-two Sections* by Robert Sharf in *Religions of China in Practice*, ed. Donald S. Lopez Jr. (Princeton, NJ: Princeton University Press, 1996), 360-377.

62. For this particular version of the story, I draw on the account of the dream in a list of omens given in the Tang work *Fayuan zhulin* 法苑珠林 8, T no. 2122, vol. 53, 341c, which is in turn quoting the *Fo benxing ji jing* 7.683b.
63. *Hanshu* 97A, 3946.
64. For dream prognostication ("oneiromancy") in premodern China in general, see Smith, *Fortune-tellers and Philosophers*, 245-257, and for greater detail, Michel Soymié, "Les songes et leur interprétation en Chine," in *Sources orientale II. Les songes et leur interprétation* (Paris: Le Seuil, 1959), 169-204; Strickmann, "Dreamwork of Psycho-Sinologists: Doctors, Taoists, Monks"; and most thoroughly Campany, *The Chinese Dreamscape*. As we have seen, the presence of dream interpretation manuals in the monastic collection at Dunhuang discloses that monks too looked to their dreams for clues to the future. See Drège and Drettas, "Oniromancie."
65. *Shi ji* 8.342; Lippiello, *Auspicious Omens and Miracles in Ancient China*, 34.
66. Lippiello, *Auspicous Omens and Miracles in Ancient China*, 49-50.
67. *Jiu Tangshu* 10.262-63; 37.1374. *Xin Tangshu* 6.165, 167; 41.1052. *Zizhi tongjian* 資治通鑑 222 (Beijing: Zhonghua, 1956), 7122.
68. *Longxing biannian tonglun* 17.193c. Yet another version of the story, in the *Youyang zazu*, mentions not thirteen but eight treasures. Preserved in the *Taiping guangji* 404.3254-56.
69. *Fozu tongji* 40.376c. Cf. Jülch, *Zhipan's Account of the History of Buddhism in China, Volume 2: Fozu tongji, juan 39–42: From the Sui Dynasty to the Wudai Era* (Leiden: Brill, 2021), 177-178. Zhipan notes this event again at 52.458a.
70. Jiang Wu in his book on seventeenth-century controversies among Chan adherents provides an interesting example of historian monks favoring one Chan lineage over another on the basis of interpreting the historical unfolding of obscure prophecies attributed to Bodhidharma and Huineng 慧能 (638-713). Jiang Wu, *Enlightenment in Dispute: The Reinvention of Chan Buddhism in Seventeenth-Century China* (Oxford: Oxford University Press, 2008), 311-312.
71. Known in the west as Orion and Lucifer.
72. *Wu bu* 五部. A tradition prevalent in Chinese texts holds that the Indian monastic community divided into five schools as a result of a dispute over monastic regulations one hundred years after Śākyamuni's death. Modern scholarship does not accept this tradition. See Lamotte, *History of Indian Buddhism*, 593-595.
73. *Chu sanzang ji ji* 3.19c, 3.20a.
74. *Song gaoseng zhuan* 16.811b.
75. *Gaoseng zhuan* 11.403a. Elsewhere, in a text translated much later, in the Song, the dream is of eighteen men pulling at the white carpet, predicting the division of the regulations into eighteen schools. *Foshuo jigu zhangzhe nü dedu yinyuan jing* 佛說給孤長者女得度因緣經 3, T no. 130, vol. 2, 853a. Other prophetic dreams tell of the decline of the Dharma.

These include the seven dreams of Ānanda, the ten dreams of Prasenajit, and the two dreams of King Kṛkin (*A'nan qimeng jing* 阿難七夢經, *T* no. 494, vol. 14, 146-147, and *Shouhu guojiezhu tuoluoni jing* 守護國界主陀羅尼經 10, *T* no. 997, vol. 19, 572b respectively). See Funayama Toru 船山徹 and Yoshikawa Tadao 吉川忠夫, *Kōsōden* 高僧傳 (Tokyo: Iwanami, 2010), vol. 4, 155.

76. *Chu sanzang jiji* 3, 19c-20a. This story may have been the inspiration for a later account that claimed that Bodhidharma prophesied the division of the Chan school into five houses, with the words "One flower will open with five petals, its fruits naturally forming." *Jingde chuandeng lu* 3.219c.

77. That is, the *Taizi ruiying benqi jing*, 1.475b; *Guoqu xianzai yinguo jing* 2.632a; *Zhong benqi jing* 中本起經 1, *T* no. 196, vol. 4 (I cannot find the reference to the Buddha leaving home at nineteen in the extant version of this text); *Dazhidu lun* 3.80c.

78. See *Foshuo shier you jing* 佛說十二遊經 (Skt. *Dvādaśaviharaṇa-sūtra*) 1, *T* no. 195, vol. 4, 146c; *Zengyi ahan jing* 13.609c; *Zhong ahan jing* 中阿含經 (Skt. *Madhyamāgama*) 56, *T* no. 26, vol. 1, 776b; *Za ahan jing* 雜阿含經 (Skt. *Saṃyuktāgama*) 35, *T* no. 99, vol. 2, 254b; *Chang ahan jing* 4.25b; and *Chu yao jing* 出曜經 (Skt. *Dharmapāda*) 13, *T* no. 212, vol. 4, 680b; "Vasumitra's commentary" probably refers to the *Apidamo dapiposha lun* 阿毘達磨大毘婆沙論 (Skt. *Abhidharmamahāvibhāṣāśāstra*) *T* no. 1545, vol. 27, but I am unable to locate the reference to the Buddha leaving home at twenty-nine.

79. *Fan wang jing* 梵網經 2, *T* no. 1484, vol. 24, 1003c; I cannot locate the *Markless Samādhi* (無相三昧); the *Treasure Store* does not explicitly say that the Buddha was thirty at the age of his enlightenment; here Zhipan draws on Zhanran's analysis (see below) of the account of Rāhula in the *Treasure Store*. *Za baozang jing* 雜寶藏經 (Skt. *Saṃyukta-ratna-piṭaka-sūtra*) *T* no. 203, vol. 4, 496b, translated by Charles Willemen in *The Storehouse of Sundry Valuables* (Berkeley, CA: Numata Center, 1994), 240-45.

80. This is counting the Buddha's age according to the Chinese method (*xusui* 虛歲) by which one is one year old at birth. Hence 80 - 50 = 30; 30 - 6 = 24; 24 + 1 = 25. Zhanran makes this argument in his *Fahua wenju ji* 法華文句記 2, *T* no. 1719, vol. 34, 178c.

81. *Xianyu jing* 賢愚經 10, *T* no. 202, vol. 4, 418c.

82. *Foshuo weiceng you yinyuan jing* 佛說未曾有因緣經 (Skt. *Adbhutadharmparyāya*) 1, *T* no. 754, vol. 17, 575c.

83. *Puyao jing* 普曜經 (Skt. *Lalitavistara*) 8, *T* no. 186, vol. 3, 534b.

84. Zhiyuan died about the time that Zhipan was born. I have been unable to trace this allusion.

85. See *Fahua jing sandabu buzhu* 法華經三大部補注 1, *X* no. 586, vol. 28, 130c.

86. *Fozu tongji* 2.145a.

87. *Da Song seng shi lüe* 1.236b.

88. Jonas Grethlein and Christopher B. Krebs, eds., *Time and Narrative in Ancient Historiography: The 'Plupast' from Herodotus to Appian* (Cambridge: Cambridge University Press, 2012).

89. *Gao seng zhuan* 5.352c.

90. *Gaoseng zhuan* 3.337c.

91. There are two exceptions to this. A narrative can go back in time to explain the circumstances of an additional place or character. For instance, when a biography of the monk Daomi explains that he was dispatched by the emperor to deliver relics to a monastery, the historian pauses to explain that the emperor had been born in that monastery. While

explaining the circumstances of the emperor's birth and the role of a nun in protecting the infant, he pauses to go back in time even further to recount the remarkable childhood of this holy nun (*Xu gaoseng zhuan* 26.667b). It is much more unusual for a historian to use a flashback when describing the actions of the subject of a biography. Here, the exception is when describing an earlier prophecy of the future, a topic I will return to below.

92. On the Huichang persecution, see Stanley Weinstein, *Buddhism Under the T'ang* (Cambridge: Cambridge University Press, 1987), 114-136.

93. In the biography of Musang (Ch. Wuxiang 無相, 680-756) the great monk similarly predicts that when a cypress tree reaches the height of a nearby stupa, the monastery will be destroyed. This comes to pass when the tree reaches the predicted height during the Huichang era and the monastery is destroyed as part of the general persecution. *Song gaoseng zhuan* 1.832c

94. *Song gaoseng zhuan* 19.836a.

95. Keith Thomas notes a similar response to events in sixteenth- and seventeenth-century England: "It was no accident that the periods when prophecies were most prominent in English life were precisely those of rebellion, discontent and violent change—the Reformation and the Civil War, in particular." *Religion and the Decline of Magic* (New York: Scribner, 1971), 425. Or consider Lerner, writing on the medieval period: "For the medieval reader, history and prophecy helped equally to interpret current events because the present was part of a plan that included past and future." *The Powers of Prophecy*, 89. More poignantly still, Campany refers to the case in the 1970s of a large group of schoolchildren who, after surviving a horrific kidnapping, reported dwelling on supposed portents from before the traumatic event. An essential function of the *post eventu* prediction, in Campany's words, is "'to regain a sense of control' by construing the cosmos as ordered and sign-rich after all." *The Chinese Dreamscape*, 123-124.

5. GENEALOGY

1. The genre created by Sima Qian with the *Records of the Historian* is now called the "biography-chronicle" genre (*zhuanjiti* 傳紀體). For the organization of the *Shiji*, see Grant Hardy, *Worlds of Bronze and Bamboo: Sima Qian's Conquest of History* (New York: Columbia University Press, 1999), 27-60.

2. Endymion Wilkinson, *Chinese History: A New Manual*, 5th ed. (Amazon: Endymion Wilkinson, 2018), 48.3; "Zizhi tongjian," 681-682.

3. Wilkinson, *Chinese History: A New Manual*, 7.1.2, "Genealogy," 103.

4. Wilkinson, *Chinese History: A New Manual*, 7.1.2, "Genealogy," 103.

5. To highlight this central metaphor, T. Griffith Foulk prefers to stray from the literal meaning of *deng* as "lamp" and translate the genre as "flame history." T. Griffith Foulk, "Myth, Ritual, and Monastic Practice in Sung Ch'an Buddhism," in *Religion and Society in T'ang and Sung China*, ed. Patricia B. Ebrey and Peter N. Gregory (Honolulu: University of Hawai'i Press, 1993), 200 n. 20.

6. For a concise survey of the lamp histories in the context of an overview of the major genres of Chan literature, see Mario Poceski, *The Records of Mazu and the Making of Classical Chan Literature* (Oxford: Oxford University Press, 2015), chapter 5, "Four Main Genres."

7. Traditional Chinese historiography included speeches and conversations, but never to this extent. In the lamp histories, major events like the circumstances of birth, death, and the founding of monasteries are subordinated to the "encounter dialogue" between masters and disciples.
8. This is not to say that all of the language of these collections is crude. They also contain large amounts of poetry, often including allusions to or quotations of famous literati poems. On poetry in the *Jingde chuandeng lu*, see Feng Guodong 馮國棟, *Jingde chuandeng lu yanjiu* 景德傳燈錄研究 (Beijing: Zhonghua, 2014), 305-360.
9. *Song gaoseng zhuan* 12.779a.
10. *Wudeng huiyuan* 五燈會元 11, *X* no. 1565, vol. 80, 220-221.
11. The scholarship on encounter dialogue and koan is extensive. See for starters John McRae, *Seeing Through Zen: Encounter, Transformation, and Genealogy in Chinese Chan Buddhism* (Berkeley: University of California Press, 2003), 74-100. Steven Heine and Dale S. Wright, eds., *The Koan: Texts and Contexts in Zen Buddhism* (Oxford: Oxford University Press, 2000), includes essays by many of the leading specialists in the field. For an innovative approach to reading one famous encounter, see Robert H. Sharf's "Is Nirvāṇa the Same as Insentience? Chinese Struggles with an Indian Ideal," in *India in the Chinese Imagination*, ed. John Kieschnick and Meir Shahar (Philadelphia: University of Pennsylvania Press, 2014), 141-170.
12. *Jingde chuandeng lu* 1.205b-c.
13. The first clear use of the "five houses" as an organizational principle is in 1039, with the publication of the *Tiansheng guangdeng lu* 天聖廣燈錄, *X* no. 1553, vol. 78. See Morten Schlütter, *How Zen Became Zen: The Dispute Over Enlightenment and the Formation of Chan Buddhism in Song-Dynasty China* (Honolulu: University of Hawai'i Press, 2008), 22.
14. In a parallel development in Islamic historiography, historians constructed genealogical trees linking prominent contemporary families to events in the life of the Prophet. See Franz Rosenthal, *A History of Muslim Historiography*, 2nd ed. (Leiden: Brill 1968), 95-98.
15. For Feiyin's book and the controversy it elicited, see Jiang Wu, *Enlightenment in Dispute: The Reinvention of Chan Buddhism in Seventeenth-Century China* (Oxford: Oxford University Press, 2008).
16. For example, the Chan monk Qisong criticized Tiantai genealogies; the Tiantai monk Zhipan criticized Chan constructions of lineage (discussed in chapter 5); the Chan monk Huihong criticized the nonsectarian Zanning for classifying a monk as a champion of good works (*xingfu* 興福) instead of as a Chan monk (*Linjian lu* 1.587b1).
17. One could argue the opposite: that genealogical history is the product rather than the cause of sectarian dispute. As Albert Welter puts it, "Chan transmission records in the Tang were the product of factional motives. Two factors contributed to factional claims. The first was historical: each generation of Chan students created its own narrative of the past, verifying its own claim regarding lineage transmission, and projecting its own definition of Chan. The second was geographical: different Chan lineages thrived in distinct regions. As Tang authority subsided, regional support for Chan proliferated. From these regional bases of support, Chan factions vied to express the spirit of Chan independence in ways that validated the claims of their own lineage." *Monks,*

Rulers, and Literati: The Political Ascendancy of Chan Buddhism (Oxford: Oxford University Press, 2006), 58.
18. The words "Song dynasty" in the Song gaoseng zhuan are preceded by either "august" (huang 皇) or "mighty" (da 大). Zanning praises the Song as superior to preceding dynasties in both his disquistion on translation and his disquistion on bodily sacrifice.
19. Linda Penkower, "In the Beginning. Guanding 灌頂 (561–632) and the Creation of Early Tiantai," Journal of the International Association of Buddhist Studies 23, no. 2 (2000): 245–296.
20. Mohe zhiguan 摩訶止觀 T no. 1911, vol. 46. Translated with extensive annotation in Paul L. Swanson, T'ien-t'ai Chih-i's Mo-ho chih-kuan (Honolulu: University of Hawai'i Press, 2018), 74–126.
21. See Koichi Shinohara, "From Local History to Universal History: The Construction of the Sung T'ien-t'ai Lineage," in Buddhism in the Sung, ed. Peter N. Gregory and Daniel A. Getz (Honolulu: University of Hawai'i Press, 1999), 524–576.
22. Penkower, "In the Beginning. Guanding 灌頂 (561–632) and the Creation of Early Tiantai," 268–275.
23. Sui Tiantai Zhizhe dashi biezhuan 隋天台智者大師別傳, T no. 2050, vol. 50, 191c; Penkower, "In the Beginning . . . Guanding 灌頂 (561–632) and the Creation of Early Tiantai," 261–263.
24. The Lengqie shizi ji 楞伽師資記 (T no. 2837, vol. 85) has been translated into French by Bernard Faure, Le Bouddhisme Ch'an en mal d'histoire. Genèse d'une tradition religieuse dans la Chine des T'ang (Paris: École française d'extrême-orient, 1989). For discussion of its content, dating, and significance for Chan history, see Faure, The Will to Orthodoxy: A Critical Genealogy of Northern Chan Buddhism (Stanford, CA: Stanford University Press, 1997), chapters 5–7; and John R. McRae, The Northern School and the Formation of Early Ch'an Buddhism (Honolulu: University of Hawai'i Press, 1986), 88–93.
25. Translated in McRae, The Northern School, 255–269.
26. Lengqie shizi ji, 1290c. Yanagida Seizan 柳田聖山, Shoki no Zenshi I: Ryōga shijiki, Denhōbō 初期の禪史 I 楞切師資記、傳法寶記. 禪の語錄 2 (Tokyo: Chikuma shobō, 1971), 321.
27. Faure, describing the passage as "enigmatic," references Yanagida's theory noted below. Le Bouddhisme Ch'an en mal d'histoire, 181–182.
28. Yanagida, Shoki no Zenshi I, 326.
29. Puti damo nanzong ding shifei lun 菩提達摩南宗定是非論, in Shenhui heshang yulu 神會和尚語錄, ed. Yang Zengwen 楊曾文 (Beijing: Zhonghua, 1996), 27.
30. Shenhui heshang yulu, 27. Yet another lineage that I don't cover here is that of the Oxhead School, which departs from the other Chan lineages with the Fourth Patriarch Daoxin, who in this lineage transmits the Dharma not to Hongren but to a monk named Farong 法融. This lineage seems to have died out in China in the eighth century. See John McRae, "The Ox-Head School of Chinese Ch'an Buddhism: From Early Ch'an to the Golden Age," in Studies in Ch'an and Hua-yen, ed. Robert M. Gimello and Peter N. Gregory, Studies in East Asian Buddhism (Honolulu: University of Hawai'i Press, 1983), 169–252.
31. Yanagida Seizan dates the text to 774. See Yanagida Seizan 柳田聖山, Shoki zenshū shisho no kenkyū 初期禪宗史書の研究 (Kyoto: Hōzōkan, 1967), 279. Wendi Adamek gives the more circumspect "probably composed sometime between 774 and 780." Wendi L. Adamek, The Mystique of Transmission: On an Early Chan History and Its Contents (New York:

Columbia University Press, 2007), 6. The authorship is not certain. Adamek represents the consensus when she writes that it was probably composed "at the Bao Tang monastery in Yizhou 益州 by an anonymous disciple or disciples of the above-mentioned Bao Tang founder, Chan Master Wuzhu" (6). Adamek hypothesizes that two nuns at the Baotang Monastery may have composed the text, but the evidence is inconclusive. *The Mystique of Transmission*, 235-237.

32. Adamek, *The Mystique of Transmission*, 330-333.
33. For Zongmi's critique, see Jeffrey L. Broughton, *Zongmi on Chan* (New York: Columbia University Press, 2009), 182-184.
34. Welter, *Monks, Rulers, and Literati*, 110.
35. John Kieschnick, *The Eminent Monk: Buddhist Ideals in Medieval Chinese Hagiography* (Honolulu: University of Hawai'i Press, 1997), 131-135.
36. *Beishan lu* 6.610a; *Song gaoseng zhuan* 13.789c. The source for the story seems to be the *Bai yu jing* 百喻經 3, T no. 209, vol. 4, 551a1.
37. *Beishan lu* 6.611c. See also Elizabeth Morrison, *The Power of the Patriarchs: Qisong and Lineage in Chinese Buddhism* (Leiden: Brill, 2010), 78. This suspicion of the value of lineage is echoed a century later in the writings of the literatus Sun Guangxian 孫光憲 (896-968), who compares Chan lineage charts to the roster of successful candidates in the civil service examination, noting that both are full of imposters. Sun Guangxian, *Beimeng suoyan* 北夢瑣言 (Beijing: Zhonghua Shuju, 2002), 4.88. Discussed in Mark Halperin, "Heroes, Rogues, and Religion in a Tenth-Century Chinese Miscellany," *Journal of the American Oriental Society* 129, no. 3 (2009): 426.
38. Whether or not the *Jingde chuandeng lu* drew directly on the *Hall of the Patriarchs* is not clear; nonetheless, they take roughly the same format.
39. On the compilation of the *Jingde chuandeng lu*, see Welter, *Monks, Rulers, and Literati*, 172-186; and Feng, *Jingde chuandeng lu yanjiu*, 99-147.
40. Welter, *Monks, Rulers, and Literati*, 186-207.
41. On the composition of the *Wudeng huiyuan*, see Huang Junquan 黃俊銓, *Chanzong dianji Wudeng huiyuan yanjiu* 禪宗典籍《五燈會元》研究 (Taipei: Fagu wenhua, 2008).
42. Hasebe Yūkei 長谷部幽蹊, *Min Shin Bukkyō kyōdanshi kenkyū* 明清佛教教團史研究 (Tokyo: Dōhōha, 1993), 282-286, cited in Wu, *Enlightenment in Dispute*, 6.
43. Shinohara, "From Local History to Universal History."
44. This is the focus of Shinohara, "From Local History to Universal History."
45. John C. Maraldo, "Is There Historical Consciousness in Ch'an?" *Japanese Journal of Religious Studies* 12, no. 2/3 (1985): 141-172.
46. The original exchange between Hu and Suzuki took place in an issue of *Philosophy East and West*. Daisetz Teitaro Suzuki, "Zen: A Reply to Hu Shih," *Philosophy East and West* 3, no. 1 (1953): 25-46; Hu Shih, "Ch'an (Zen) Buddhism in China: Its History and Method," *Philosophy East and West* 3, no. 1 (1953): 3-24. For analysis of the debate, see Bernard Faure, *Chan Insights and Oversights: An Epistemological Critique of the Chan Tradition* (Princeton, NJ: Princeton University Press, 1993), 89-94.
47. See John McRae, "Religion as Revolution in Chinese Historiography: Hu Shih (1891-1962) on Shen-hui (684-758)," *Cahiers d'Extrême-Asie* 12 (2001): 59-102. Faure, *Chan Insights and Oversights*, 94-99.

48. See Poceski, *The Records of Mazu and the Making of Classical Chan Literature*, chapters 4 and 5.
49. Maraldo, "Is There Historical Consciouness in Ch'an?," 155, 165.
50. Dale S. Wright, "Historical Understanding: The Ch'an Buddhist Transmission Narratives and Modern Historiography," *History and Theory* 31, no. 1 (1992): 37-46.
51. Wright, "Historical Understanding," 42.
52. Faure deals with similar issues in his chapter on Chan historiography in *Chan Insights and Oversights*, but in the context of a general critique of the limits of objectivism. *Chan Insights and Oversights*, 110-113.
53. Feng Guodong analyzes the ways Song literati read the *Jingde chuandeng lu* in chapter 6 of his *Jingde chuandeng lu yanjiu*.
54. Feng, *Jingde chuandeng lu yanjiu*, 374-383.
55. See, for instance, Zhu Xi 朱熹, *Zhuzi yulei* 朱子語類, 126 (Beijing: Zhonghua, 1986), 3025, discussed below.
56. Yanagida, *Shoki no Zenshi I*, 355; Cf. McRae, *The Northern School*, 259.
57. For the references to the *Further Biographies*, see Yanagida, *Shoki no Zenshi I*, 127, 167; Faure, *Le Bouddhisme Ch'an en mal d'histoire*, 116, 132. For the claim that "the book of Chan teachings in circulation in the world that claims to be the sayings of Chan Master [Hong]ren is a lie," see Yanagida, *Shoki no Zenshi I*, 269; Faure, *Le Bouddhisme Ch'an en mal d'histoire*, 163.
58. Adamek, *The Mystique of Transmission*, 201-202; Erik Zürcher, *The Buddhist Conquest of China* (Leiden: Brill, 2007), 22.
59. *Shuangfengshan Caohouxi Baolin zhuan* 雙峰山曹侯溪寶林傳 1, B no. 81, vol. 14, 12a.
60. *Shuangfengshan Caohouxi Baolin zhuan* 6.112a. "Seventy" must be a mistake (perhaps a scribal error) for "seventeen."
61. *Zu tang ji* 祖堂集 (Zhengzhou: Zhongzhou Guji Chubanshe, 2001), 8, "Longya heshang" 龍牙和尚, 295.
62. *Zu tang ji* 18, "Zhaozhou heshang" 趙州和尚, 587.
63. *Zu tang ji* 20.650.
64. *Zu tang ji* 16, "Huangbo heshang" 黃蘗和尚, 548.
65. In a seminal article on the subject, Bernard Faure suggested that the evidence is so fragmentary that any attempt to reconstruct a historical Bodhidharma is pointless; it is much more fruitful, he argues, to examine how the subsequent legend of Bodhidharma reflects the values of those who invented it, as well as the shared patterns discernible in the creation of several such legendary figures. See "Bodhidharma as Textual and Religious Paradigm," *History of Religions* 25, no. 3 (1986): 187-198. John McRae suggested that even in the earliest accounts of Bodhidharma there are elements that relate to the subsequent history of Chan, but noted that much of the legend of Bodhidharma was invented long after his death. For the critique of Faure, see McRae, "The Hagiography of Bodhidharma: Restructuring the Point of Origin of Chinese Chan Buddhism," in *India in the Chinese Imagination: Myth Religion and Thought*, ed. John Kieschnick and Meir Shahar (Philadelphia: University of Pennsylvania Press, 2014), 125-138; for a lucid account of the growth of Bodhidharma's legend, see McRae, *Seeing Through Zen*, 22-44.
66. For a convenient summary of the growth of the legend of Bodhidharma, see McRae, *Seeing Through Zen*, 24-33. See also McRae, *Northern School*, 15-19. For discussion of two

254　5. Genealogy

important later motifs in Bodhidharma's legend—that he crossed a river on a leaf, often depicted in painting and sculpture, and that he founded Chinese martial arts, see, respectively, Charles Lachman, "Why Did the Patriarch Cross the River? The Rushleaf Bodhidharma Reconsidered," *Asia Major Third Series* 6, part 2 (1993): 237-267; Meir Shahar, *The Shaolin Monastery: History, Religion, and the Chinese Martial Arts* (Honolulu: University of Hawai'i Press, 2008), 12-17; 165-168; 178-180.

67. *Fozu tongji* 14.224a.
68. A high official named Wang You (923-986) was active in the early Song, but there is no reference to him composing a "long calendar" in his official biography.
69. That is, the *Jingde chuandeng lu* had been presented to the emperor and entered into the imperially sponsored Buddhist canon. As we have seen, in the seventeenth century, an order for arrest was put out for Feiyin Tongrong for challenging another imperially sponsored lamp history.
70. *Chuanfa zhengzong ji* 5.742b-744b.
71. Ironically, this is one of the few details in the biography of Bodhidharma that *does* have a historical basis. Qisong apparently read the biography of Xiao Ang in the *Nanshi* 南史 (Beijing: Zhonghua, 1975), 1264, in which there is no mention of his having served as prefect of Guangzhou. But the biography of Xiao Ang in the *Liangshu* 梁書 (Beijing: Zhonghua, 1973), 371, does state that he served briefly as prefect of Guangzhou. There is still a problem of dating, since Xiao left this post to take another a few years before Bodhidharma supposedly arrived. In any event, there is no mention of Bodhidharma in either biography, and the meeting of the two is most likely a later fiction.
72. See *Longxing biannian tonglun* 7.145c. Hu Shi referred to these attempts to correct Bodhidharma's dates as "exchanging one type of false history for another." Hu Shi 胡適, "Ji Zhongyang Tushuguan cang de Song Baoyou ben Wudeng huiyuan" 記中央圖書館藏的宋寶祐本五燈會元, in *Hu Shi quanji* 胡適全集 (Hefei: Anhui Jiaoyu, 2003), 510-511.
73. *Zhu zi yulei*, 126.3007.
74. In fairness to Zhu Xi, it was rare for Buddhist translators to attempt to re-create rhyme in their translations.
75. *Jingde chuandeng lu* 1.206b6-7. For an analysis of these interlineal notes, see Feng, *Jingde chuandeng lu yanjiu*, 294.
76. *Jingde chuandeng lu* 15.320b21; Feng, *Jingde chuandeng lu,* 300ff., for this and other additions and corrections in the interlineal notes.
77. The ensuing controversy, which raged for centuries, is detailed in Wu, *Enlightenment in Dispute,* "Part III: Lineage Matters." See also Jinhua Jia, *The Hongzhou School of Chan Buddhism in Eighth- Through Tenth-Century China* (Albany: State University of New York Press, 2006), 22-26.
78. *Jingde chuandeng lu* 14.309c.
79. *Jingde chuandeng lu* 14.309a; the *Zu tang ji* does the same.
80. *Linjian lu* 248b. The passage is translated in Wu, *Enlightenment in Dispute,* 315-316.
81. *Wudeng huiyuan* 7.141c-142a.
82. *Jingde chuandeng lu* 14.310a. Feng, *Jingde chuandeng lu yanjiu*, 302-302.
83. Wu argues that this analysis of historical evidence owes its fervor to the involvement of literati and the rise of "evidential scholarship" in the period. Both may have contributed to the controversy and the way it was debated, but as we have seen, attention to

source analysis, dates, and names had long been common among monk scholars. Even today, sorting through the sources and determining their validity makes the problem of the two Daowus and their affiliation difficult to resolve. Moreover, the precise motivations of those involved in the debates—some mixture of adherence to historiographical standards and sectarian concerns—are difficult to determine. Chen Yuan 陳垣 speculates on some in *Qing chu seng zheng ji* 清初僧諍記 (Beijing: Zhonghua, 1962).

84. In his historical writings, Qisong, for instance, did not privilege Yunmen, his own lineage. Morrison, *The Power of the Patriarchs*, 158–165.
85. *Song gaoseng zhuan* 1.714a. Yijing, in contrast, constructed the makings of a more elaborate Esoteric lineage of which he was a part. See Stuart H. Young, *Conceiving the Indian Buddhist Patriarchs in China* (Honolulu: University of Hawai'i Press, 2015), 172–173.
86. *Longxing biannian tonglun* 18.198a.

6. MODERNITY

1. On Taixu's confinement, see Don A. Pittman, *Toward a Modern Chinese Buddhism: Taixu's Reforms* (Honolulu: University of Hawai'i Press, 2001), 81–90; and Justin R. Ritzinger, *Anarchy in the Pure Land: Reinventing the Cult of Maitreya in Modern Chinese Buddhism* (Oxford: Oxford University Press, 2017), 59–60.
2. Taixu describes his period of confinement and his daily regimen in his autobiography. *Taixu zizhuan* 太虛自傳, in *Taixu dashi quanshu* 太虛大師全書 (Taipei: Shandaosi Fojing Liutongchu, 1998), vol. 29, 209–219.
3. Scholarship on Chinese intellectual history for this period is excellent. For two lucid surveys of the trends, see Jerome B. Grieder, *Intellectuals and the State in Modern China: A Narrative History* (London: Collier Macmillan, 1981); and Peter Zarrow, *China in War and Revolution 1895–1945* (London: Routledge, 2005).
4. For Liang Qichao's historiography, see Xiaobing Tang, *Global Space and the Nationalist Discourse of Modernity: The Historical Thinking of Liang Qichao* (Stanford, CA: Stanford University Press, 1996). Tang does not, however, discuss Liang's writings on Buddhist history, a relatively minor part of Liang's historical oeuvre. On Buddhism in Liang's historiography, see Qinqin Peng, "Between Faith and Truth: The Historiography of Buddhism in Modern China (1902–1965)" (PhD diss., Georg-August-Universität Göttingen, 2021).
5. For Gu Jiegang's historiography, see Laurence A. Schneider, *Ku Chieh-kang and China's New History: Nationalism and the Quest for Alternative Traditions* (Berkeley: University of California Press, 1971).
6. See Peng, "Between Faith and Truth: The Historiography of Buddhism in Modern China (1902–1965)."
7. In an assessment of Hu Shih's writings on Buddhist history, John McRae laments the lasting influence of some of Hu Shih's approaches and conclusions that McRae shows to be misleading and prejudiced. Nonetheless, some of Hu's work on Buddhism continues to be valuable. See John R. McRae, "Religion as Revolution in Chinese Historiography: Hu Shih (1891–1962) on Shen-hui (684–758)," *Cahiers d'Extrême-Asie* 12 (2001): 59–102.
8. For Taixu's meeting with Hu Shih, see *Taixu zizhuan*, 239. Taixu makes frequent reference to Hu Shih in his writings and wrote at least one letter to him; on Tang Yongtong's connections with Ouyang Jingwu, see Ma Tianxiang 麻天祥, *Tang Yongtong pingzhuan*

湯用彤評傳 (Wuhan: Wuhan Daxue Chubanshe, 2007), 32. This was in the early twenties when Tang was teaching in Nanjing. In contrast to these brief encounters, Hu Shih and Tang were long-standing acquaintances, and Hu read Tang's seminal study of Buddhism in early medieval China in manuscript, commenting on it in his diary. Ma, *Tang Yongtong pingzhuan*, 5-6.

9. On Liang Qichao's changing attitudes toward Buddhism, including his historiography, see Wang Junzhong 王俊中, "Jiuguo zongjiao yi zhexue?—Liang Qichao zaonian de foxueguan ji qi zhuanzhe (1891–1912)" 救國、宗教抑哲學?——梁啟超早年的佛學觀及其轉折 (1891–1912), *Shixue jikan* 史學集刊 31 (1996): 93–116.

10. Joseph R. Levenson, *Liang Ch'i-ch'ao and the Mind of Modern China* (London: Thames and Hudson, 1959), 132. Tellingly, later in life Liang showed increasing sympathy for Buddhism, and it is even said that Buddhist rituals were carried out at his funeral. Levenson, *Liang Ch'i-ch'ao*, 191.

11. For Hu Shih's early life and works, see Jerome B. Grieder, *Hu Shih and the Chinese Renaissance: Liberalism in the Chinese Revolution, 1917–1937* (Cambridge, MA: Harvard University Press, 1970). On the place of Buddhism in Hu's historiography, see McRae, "Religion as Revolution in Chinese Historiography." Unlike Liang Qichao's, Hu Shih's funeral was strictly secular, and he famously banned monks from his mother's funeral.

12. Indeed, he complained that in addition to being erroneously called a Buddhist, he had variously been labeled a Christian and a Muslim, the latter because of his work on the history of Islam in China. See Chen Zhichao 陳智超, *Chen Yuan: shengping, xueshu, jiaoyu yu jiaowang* 陳垣——生平、學術、教育與交往 (Hefei: Anhui Daxue Chubanshe, 2010), 199–200.

13. For Gu Jiegang's interest in non-Han culture, see Schneider, *Ku Chieh-kang and China's New History*, 258–300. For related ideas in Fu Sinian's writings, see Wang Fan-sen, *Fu Ssu-nien: A Life in Chinese History and Politics* (Cambridge: Cambridge University Press, 2000), 98–125.

14. Interestingly, even the academic historians were reluctant to challenge the historicity of the Buddha. In response to Gu's claim that the sage king of antiquity Yu was a myth, beginning as a god and later presented as a man, the prominent philosopher Feng Youlan countered that Yu was instead originally a man around whom legends later grew up, making him into a god, *just like the Buddha*. Schneider, *Ku Chieh-kang and China's New History*, 226.

15. That is, modernity was both a challenge and an opportunity. In his discussion of modernity in the context of Chinese Buddhism, Justin Ritzinger emphasizes that the "pull" of modernity—the opportunities new ideas and institutions provided—was at least as important as the "push," the need to respond to external forces. *Anarchy in the Pure Land*, 4.

16. Wang Fansen, *Fu Ssu-nien*, 62–63.

17. "Lun Shijieshi gang" 論世界史綱, in *Taixu dashi quanshu*, vol. 25, 256–264. Wells had consulted with Fu Ssu-nien for his chapters on China, so ironically Taixu's primary contact with Fu Sinian's historiography was through the Chinese translation of Wells's work. For Wells and Fu, see Wang Fansen, *Fu Ssu-nien*, 57–58.

18. Taixu, *Fojiao shi lüe* 佛教史略, in *Fofa zongxue* 佛法總學, in *Taixu dashi quanshu*, vol. 2, 895.

6. Modernity 257

19. It is revealing to contrast this work with Tang Yongtong's *Brief History of Indian Philosophy* (*Yindu zhexue shi lüe* 印度哲學史略), which, while indeed brief, takes up a respectable 170 pages. Published in 1945, but originating in a class delivered in 1929, Tang's book is based almost entirely on English-language scholarship, supplemented by reference to Chinese primary sources. In the second edition of the book, Tang notes apologetically that his references to Pali and Sanskrit sources come almost entirely (he had had some training in Sanskrit) from English translation rather than from the originals, reflecting the importance Tang gave to primary source criticism (1959; rpt. Beijing: Zhonghua Shuju, 1988). This is in sharp contrast to Taixu who, for all of his interest in the wider world, never drew on foreign-language writing.

20. Taixu composed his work in 1910. Liang Qichao dismisses the legend in his "Fojiao zhi chushuru" 佛教之初輸入 (probably written in the twenties) in *Zhongguo fojiao yanjiushi* 中國佛教研究史 (Shanghai: Sanlian, 1988), 1-24. Liang accepted the possibility that another legend, claiming that Buddhist monks arrived at the court of Qin Shihuang 秦始皇 (r. 221-210 BCE), might be true—a claim scholars now reject. But even in this case, Liang based his argument on examination of evidence rather than simply accepting tradition. Tang Yongtong returned to the problem of the introduction of Buddhism to China with even greater attention to the sources in his *Han Wei Liang Jin Nanbeichao Fojiaoshi* 漢魏兩晉南北朝佛教史, first published in 1938.

21. In order to accord with the Theravāda tradition, Taixu later moved up his assessment of the Buddha's dates. *Fojiao de jiaoshi jiaofa he jin hou de jianshe* 佛教的教史教法和今後的建設, in *Fofa zongxue*, in *Taixu dashi quanshu*, vol. 1, 464-465.

22. See Bernard Faure, "Bodhidharma as Textual and Religious Paradigm," *History of Religions* 25, no. 3 (1986): 187-198; and John McRae, *Seeing Through Zen: Encounter, Transformation, and Genealogy in Chinese Chan Buddhism* (Berkeley: University of California Press, 2003), 22-44.

23. See, for instance, *Zhongguo foxue* 中國佛學, in *Fofa zongxue*, *Taixu dashi quanshu*, vol. 2, 582.

24. Taixu, *Fojiao ge zongpai yuanliu* 佛教各宗派源流, in *Fofa zongxue*, in *Taixu dashi quanshu*, vol. 2, 831-832.

25. Taixu, *Zhongguo foxue*, 574.

26. Taixu, *Zhongguo foxue*, 574.

27. Taixu, *Fojiao ge zongpai yuanliu*, 832-833.

28. Taixu, *Zhongguo foxue*, 565-566.

29. "Putidamo kao" 菩提達摩考, in *Hu Shi juan* 胡適卷, *Ershi shiji foxue jingdian wenku* 二十世紀佛學經典文庫 (Wuhan: Wuhan Daxue Chubanshe, 2008), 408-416.

30. Hu gave the same treatment to the modern monk Xuyun, in a public lecture challenging the details of Xuyun's autobiography on the basis of the historical record. Daniela Campo, *La construction de la sainteté dans la Chine moderne. La vie du maître bouddhiste Xuyun* (Paris: Les Belles Lettres, 2013), 48.

31. "Yu Hu Shizhi shu" 與胡適之書, *Taixu dashi quanshu*, vol. 26, 209.

32. See, for instance, Wright, "Seng-jui Alias Hui-jui: A Biographical Bisection in the *Kao-seng chuan*," in *Liebenthal Festschrift*, ed. Kshitis Roy (Santiniketan: Visvabharati, 1957), 272-294; and Chen Jinhua, "One Name, Three Monks: Two Northern Chan Masters

Emerge from the Shadow of Their Contemporary, the Tiantai Mater Zhanran 湛然 (711-782)," *Journal of the International Association of Buddhist Studies* 22, no. 1 (1999): 1-90.

33. Taixu, *Xin yu rongguan* 新與融貫, in *Fofa zongxue*, in *Taixu dashi quanshu*, vol. 1, 445.

34. Holmes Welch, *The Buddhist Revival in China* (Cambridge, MA: Harvard University Press, 1968), 51-71. Ritzinger is critical of Welch's characterization of Taixu on a number of fronts. See *Anarchy in the Pure Land*, especially 5.

35. See Pittman, *Toward a Modern Chinese Buddhism*; Ritzinger, *Anarchy in the Pure Land*; and Linzy Tsai, "The Rise of the Buddhist University in Taiwan" (PhD thesis, University of Bristol, 2012).

36. For a recent edition with an introduction to Jiang's life and works, see *Zhongguo fojiao shi* 中國佛教史 (Shanghai: Shanghai Guji Chubanshe, 2007). See also Peng, "Between Faith and Truth: The Historiography of Buddhism in Modern China (1902-1965)," 176-178.

37. Two of Jiang's books on meditation, *Yinshizi jingzuofa* 因是子靜坐法 (published in 1914) and *Yinshizi jingzuo fa xubian* 因是子靜坐法續編 (published in 1918), were best-sellers in their day. For a convenient collection of Jiang's works on meditation (reprinted many times since their original publication), see *Jingzuofa jiyao* 靜坐法輯要 (Taipei: Wenjing Chubanshe, 1998).

38. Dongchu 東初, *Zhongguo fojiao jindai shi* 中國佛教近代史 (1974; rpt., Taipei: Dongchu, 1987) vol. 2, 717-720 (available online with Dongchu's complete works at http://dongchu.ddbc.edu.tw/).

39. Zhou Shujia, *Zhou Shujia foxue lunzhu ji* 周叔迦佛學論著集, ed. Su Jinren 蘇晉仁 (Beijing: Zhonghua, 1991), vol. 1, 3-112.

40. Zhou Shujia, *Zhou Shujia foxue lunwen ji*, vol. 1, 113-280.

41. For a detailed chronology of Yinshun's life, see Hou Kunhong 侯坤宏, *Yinshun fashi nianpu* 印順法師年譜 (Taipei: Guoshiguan, 2008). Like Taixu, Yinshun wrote an autobiography, though it is much more reserved in tone. For instance, the passages in which Yinshun describes his marriage were, on his instructions, added only after his death. *Pingfan de yi sheng* 平凡的一生 (Xinzhu: Zhengwen Chubanshe, 2005).

42. Hou, *Yinshun fashi nianpu*, 32.

43. Yinshun describes the passage, his surprise at the accusations, and its consequences for him in his autobiography. *Pingfan de yi sheng*, 79-85. The incident is discussed in Marcus Bingenheimer, *Der Mönchsgelehrte Yinshun (*1906) und seine Bedeutung für den Chinesisch-Taiwanischen Buddhismus im 20. Jahrhundert* (Heidelberg: Edition Forum, 2004), 110-119; and in Ritzinger, *Anarchy in the Pure Land*, 231.

44. Even standard, politically innocuous works like Feng Youlan's 馮友蘭 *History of Chinese Philosophy* (*Zhongguo zhexue shi* 中國哲學史) and Tang Yongtong's *History of Buddhism in the Han, Wei, Jin, and Northern and Southern Dynasties* 兩漢魏晉南北朝佛教史 were banned in Taiwan through the 1970s since they were published in China after the founding of the PRC. Hou, *Yinshun fashi nianpu*, 425.

45. The translation of Tāranātha's *History of Buddhism in India* (*dpal dus kyi 'khor lo'i chos bskor gyi byung khungs nyer mkho*) of 1608 was *Indo bukkyō shi* 印度佛教史 by Teramoto Enga 寺本婉雅, first published in 1928. Hou, *Yinshun fashi nianpu*, 27. The other work was a Chinese translation of the *Cambridge History of India*. Hou, *Yinshun fashi nianpu*, 30.

46. Ritzinger cautions against too easily drawing contrasts with the traditional and characterizing the last century of Buddhism in China with a conventional understanding of modernization (i.e., demythologization, rationalism, and engagement). *Anarchy in the Pure Land,* 4. But in the admittedly limited realm of historiography, the trend toward demythologization and rationalism is in fact prominent.
47. Yinshun, *Zhongguo chanzong shi* 中國禪宗史 (Taipei: Huiri Jiangtang, 1971), 13.
48. Yinshun, *Zhongguo chanzong shi,* 4-5.
49. Yinshun, *Zhongguo chanzong shi,* 5.
50. Yinshun, *Zhongguo gudai minzu shenhua yu wenhua zhi yanjiu* 中國古代民族神話與文化之研究 (Taipei: Zhengwen Chubanshe, 1994).
51. Yinshun, "*Dazhidu lun* zhi zuozhe ji qi fanyi" 大智度論之作者及其翻譯, *Dongfang zongjiao yanjiu* 東方宗教研究 2 (1990): 9-70. For a thorough assessment of the problem that takes into account all of the relevant scholarship, including Yinshun's, see Zhou Bokan (Chou Po-kan) 周伯戡, "*Dazhidu lun* lüe yi chu tan" 《大智度論》略譯初探, *Chung-Hwa Buddhist Journal* 13 (2000):155-165. Stefania Travagnin, "Reception History and Limits of Interpretation: The Belgian Étienne Lamotte, Japanese Buddhologists, the Chinese Monk Yinshun 印順 and the Formation of a Global 'Da zhidu lun 大智度論 Scholarship,'" *Hualin International Journal of Buddhist Studies* 1, no. 1 (2018): 341-369.
52. Marcus Bingenheimer, "Writing the History of Buddhist Thought in the 20th Century—Yinshun (1906-2005) in the Context of Chinese Buddhist Historiography," *Journal of Global Buddhism* 10 (2009): 257.
53. Marcus Bingenheimer emphasizes the extent to which Yinshun's premises and methods mirrored those of traditional Chinese Buddhist historiography. Below, I emphasize instead the ways he was different. See Bingenheimer, "Writing the History of Buddhist Thought in the 20th Century."
54. On the "short chronology," see Heinz Bechert, "The Date of the Buddha—an Open Question of Ancient Indian History," in his *The Dating of the Historical Buddha. Die Datierung des Historischen Buddha* (Göttingen: Vandenhoeck & Ruprecht, 1991), 222-236.
55. Yinshun 印順, *Fomie jinian jueze tan* 佛滅紀年抉擇譚 (Hong Kong: Xingdao Ribao Yinshua Bu, 1950 [listed in the book itself as the "2341st year after the Buddha's nirvana"]), 74.
56. Taixu, "Wo zenyang panshe yiqie fofa" 我怎樣判攝一切佛法, in *Taixu dashi quanshu*, vol. 1, 509-529. See also Yanpei 演培, "Yinshun daoshi dui Yindu fojiao fenqi de quanshu" 印順導師對印度分期的詮述, in *Yinshun daoshi de sixiang yu xuewen* 印順導師的思想與學問, ed. Lan Jifu 藍吉富 (1986; rpt., Taipei: Zhengwen Chubanshe, 2005), 1-28.
57. *Yindu zhi fojiao,* 4; see also Hou Kunhong 侯坤宏, *Zhenshi yu fangbian. Yinshun sixiang yanjiu* 真實與方便‧印順思想研究 (Taipei: Fajie, 2009), 121-125. The preface to *A History of Indian Buddhist Thought* is translated into German and chapter 4 into English in Bingenheimer, *Der Mönchsgelehrte Yinshun,* 220-232; 233-283.
58. David Snellgrove, *Indo-Tibetan Buddhism: Indian Buddhists and Their Tibetan Successors* (Boston: Shambhala, 1987), 79-116; Paul Williams, *Mahāyāna Buddhism: The Doctrinal Foundations* (London: Routledge, 2009), 85-86.
59. In his criticism of Tathāgatagarbha, Yinshun presaged a similar stance later taken by proponents of "critical Buddhism" (*Hihan* Bukkyō 批判仏教) in Japan. See Jamie

260   6. Modernity

Hubbard and Paul L. Swanson, eds., *Pruning the Bodhi Tree: The Storm Over Critical Buddhism* (Honolulu: University of Hawai'i Press, 1997).
60. *Yifofa yanjiu fofa*, 43.
61. *Fojiao shidi kaolun* 佛教史地考論, in *Miaoyun ji* 妙雲集, vol. 22 (1973; rpt., Taipei: Zhengwen Chubanshe, 2000), 286. Cited and discussed in Hou, *Zhenshi yu fangbian*, 274.
62. *Yindu zhi fojiao* 印度之佛教 (1942; rpt. 3rd ed., Taipei: Zhengwen Chubanshe, 1992), 86.
63. One approach has been to simply excise all such material from the biography without comment, as in Michael Carrithers's *The Buddha* (Oxford: Oxford University Press, 1983). Others have argued convincingly that while it is possible to place some elements of the Buddha's biography in chronological order, demonstrating that some legends appeared long after others, it is not possible to separate legendary accounts from a factual core. Edward J. Thomas provides discussion of the problem in chapters entitled "Buddha and Myth" and "Buddha and History" in what is perhaps still the most thorough treatment of the biography of the Buddha: *The Life of Buddha as Legend and History* (1927; 3rd ed., London: Routledge and Kegan Paul, 1975). For a more recent treatment of the Buddha's life that gives due attention to the Buddha's previous lives and in particular to legends that grew up around pilgrimage sites, and also stories related to the Buddha's relics, which in one sense continue his biography up to the present day, see John Strong, *The Buddha: A Short Biography* (Oxford: Oneworld, 2001). Both Thomas and Strong note parallels with scholarship on the life of Jesus, most famously related in Albert Schweitzer's *The Quest of the Historical Jesus* (1906; English translation, rpt., New York: Macmillan, 1978). While one can find a direct connection between Western scholarship on the Buddha and scholarship on Jesus, it is unlikely that Chinese Buddhists like Taixu and Yinshun were at all familiar with the quest for the historical Jesus. Nonetheless, comparison is interesting in that, while the vast scholarship on the biography of Jesus went through phases of rationalization (e.g., the miracle of the conversion of water into wine was a misunderstanding—Jesus must have brought the wine himself) and symbolic interpretation over the course of more than a century, in the Chinese case there was a quick leap from blind acceptance of the tradition to a symbolic interpretation of the meaning of myth in the Buddha's biography all in the space of a few decades.
64. *Taizi ruiying benqi jing*, 472c.
65. *Da ben jing* 大本經 (P. *Mahāpadhānasuttanta*), in *T* no. 1, vol. 1, translated into Chinese in 413.
66. *T* no. 1440, vol. 23, 509b6-7. Quoted in Yinshun, *Chuqi dasheng fojiao zhi qiyuan yu zhankai* 初期大乘之起源與展開 (1981; rpt., Taipei: Zhengwen Chubanshe, 1989), 122.
67. Yinshun, *Chuqi dasheng fojiao*, 153.
68. Yinshun, *Chuqi dasheng fojiao*, 123.
69. *T* no. 1545, vol. 27, 916b24-27; quoted in Yinshun, *Chuqi dasheng fojiao*, 122.
70. Yinshun, *Chuqi dasheng fojiao*, 125.
71. *Fofa gai lun*, 121-136. See also Hou, *Zhenshi yu fangbian*, 258-260.
72. *Chuqi dasheng fojiao*, 480; Hou, *Zhenshi yu fangbian*, 250.
73. Specifically, he argued that Mañjuśrī was the product of a popular amalgamation of Śāriputra and Brāhma; Samantabhadra was an amalgamation of Maudgalyāyana and

Indra. "Wenshu yu Puxian" 文殊與普賢, in *Fojiao shidi kao lun* 佛教史地考論, 233–241; Hou, *Zhenshi yu fangbian*, 248-250.

74. *Chuqi dasheng fojiao,* 483–484 (the text gives "Apolla" for Apollo and "Śrava" for Īśrava); Hou, *Zhenshi yu fangbian,* 251-252. Chün-fang Yü summarizes the theories of Western scholars for the origins of Avalokiteśvara in her *Kuan-yin: The Chinese Transformation of Avalokiteśvara* (New York: Columbia University Press, 2000), 13–14.

75. Yinshun, *Chuqi dasheng fojiao,* 808–809; Hou, *Zhenshi yu fangbian,* 251.

76. Yinshun, *Yi fofa yanjiu fofa* 以佛法研究佛法 (1972; rpt., Xinzhu: Zhengwen Chubanshe, 2003).

77. *Yi fofa yanjiu fofa,* 5. The essay is translated into German in Bingenheimer, *Der Mönchsgelehrte Yinshun,* 284–301.

78. See Williams, *Mahāyāna Buddhism,* 86.

79. On causation in Madhyamaka, see Williams, *Mahāyāna Buddhism,* 73.

80. Yinshun, *Yi fofa yanjiu fofa,* 6.

81. The scheme Yinshun employs here for how one can use Buddhist doctrine to study Buddhist history is based on the traditional "three seals of the Dharma," *san fa yin* 三法印 (Skt. *tri-dṛṣṭi-namitta-mudrā*), namely: all things are impermanent 諸行無常, all things lack inherent existence 諸法無我, and nirvana is perfect quiescence 涅槃寂靜.

82. Yinshun, *Yi fofa yanjiu fofa,* 13

83. For a chronological sketch of Dongchu's life, see Guoche 果徹, "Dongchu laoren nianpu" 東初老人年譜, *Chung-Hwa Buddhist Studies* 2 (1998): 1–48. Dongchu's article on the dates of the Buddha is titled "Guanyu Fotuo shengmie jinian zhi kaozheng" 關於佛陀生滅紀年之考證, first published in 1949 in the journal *Rensheng zazhi* 人生雜誌 and later published as "Fotuo shengmie jinian zhi kaozheng" 佛陀生滅紀年的考證 in Dongchu's monograph *Fojiao wenhua zhi chongxin* 佛教文化之重新, available with his complete works at dongchu.ddbc.edu.tw.

84. Shi Guodong, "Dongchu laoren nian pu."

85. *Zhong Yin fojiao tongshi* 中印佛教通史 (1968; rpt., Dongchu.ddbc.edu.tw), *Zhong Ri fojiao jiaotongshi* 中日佛教交通史 (1970; rpt., Dongchu.ddbc.edu.tw), *Zhongguo fojiao jindai shi* 中國佛教近代史 (1974; rpt., Dongchu.ddbc.edu.tw).

86. The times are also reflected in Dongchu's repeated paeans to then president Chiang Kai-shek ("savior of China, savior of Buddhism," *Zhongguo fojiao jindai shi,* 136), no doubt inspired in part by consideration of Chiang's unrivaled power in Taiwan at the time, though Dongchu's admiration may have been genuine—he wrote a book on Chiang Kai-shek and Buddhism after Chiang's death.

87. Ultimately, Dongchu linked imperialism and even Communism to Christianity, at one point tracing the Cultural Revolution back to the Taiping Rebellion, which he in turn attributed to Christian mischievousness.

88. Shengyan received a PhD from Rissho University in 1975. Yinshun received an honorary PhD in 1973 from Taishō University on the strength of his history of Chan.

89. Another monk-historian active in Taiwan at the end of the twentieth century and worthy of note is Mingfu 明復 (1914-2005). Unlike the other monks discussed in this chapter, Mingfu was born in central China, in Henan, to a prominent family of artists, scholars, and officials. Educated in one of China's elite universities (Fudan), for much of his life

he was in the military, becoming a monk late in life. Founder of the Chinese Buddhist Historical Society 中國佛教史學會, he published mostly articles in Buddhist journals. His work is marked especially by his interest in Buddhist art and literature. His collected works are available in Mingfu, *Mingfu fashi foxue wencong* 明復法師佛學文叢 (Xinzhu: Huamulan Wenhua Chubanshe, 2006).

90. The textual history of Shengyan's autobiography is complicated. He left behind a wealth of autobiographical material, conveniently collected along with his other works at http://ddc.shengyen.org/, including a full-length autobiography, *Guicheng* 歸程. An English-language memoir, made up of translations from his Chinese works supplemented by interviews by Kenneth Wapner and others, appeared in 2008 as *Footprints in the Snow: The Autobiography of a Chinese Buddhist Monk* (New York: Doubleday). This is the work that mentions monastic use of heroin. This English work was then translated into Chinese as *Xuezhong zuji* 雪中足跡 (Taipei: Sancai Wenhua, 2009).

91. Shengyan, *Yindu fojiaoshi* 印度佛教史 (1969; rpt., Taipei: Fagu wenhua, 2006), 172.

92. In addition to *Yindu fojiaoshi*, the other works are *Xizang fojiao shi* 西藏佛教史 and *Ri Han fojiao shilüe* 日韓佛教史略. In 1980, the three works were published together as a *World History of Buddhism* (*Shijie fojiao tongshi* 世界佛教通史 (Taipei: Dongchu).

93. Shengyan, *Yindu fojiao shi*, 36.

94. Shengyan, *Yindu fojiao shi*, 35.

95. Shengyan, *Yindu fojiao shi*, 181–186.

96. Shengyan, *Yindu fojiao shi*, 196.

97. Shengyan, *Yindu fojiao shi*, 239.

98. "Meimatsu Chūgoku bukkyō no kenkyū" 明末中國佛教の研究 (PhD diss., Rissho University, 1975) available at http://ddc.shengyen.org/. The Chinese work is *Mingmo fojiao yanjiu* 明末佛教研究 (Taipei: Dongchu, 1987).

99. David Loy's *A Buddhist History of the West* (Albany: State University of New York Press, 2002) suggests the direction such an approach might take, in his case attempting to apply the lessons of Buddhist thought to the history of the West.

APPENDIX 2. LINEAGE CHARTS

1. Scholars have proposed various reconstructions for the more obscure figures in these lists, a difference that is of little significance since with the exception of a few famous figures (Mahākāśyapa, Ānanda, Upagupta, Aśvaghoṣa, Nāgārjuna, and Vasubandhu) the Indian patriarchs are known only in Chinese sources.

Bibliography

ABBREVIATIONS

B *Da zang jing bu bian* 大藏經補編, ed. Lan Jifu 藍吉富. (Taipei: Huayu Chubanshe, 1986). Reference is to the digitalized version in CBETA 2018 edition.

J *Jiaxing dazang jing* 嘉興大藏經 (Taipei: Xinwenfeng, 1987). Reference is to the digitalized version in CBETA 2018 edition.

T *Taishō Shinshū Daizōkyō* 大正新脩大藏經, ed.Takakusu Junjirō 高楠順次郎 and Watanabe Kaikyoku 渡邊海旭 (Tokyo: Taisho shinshu daizokyo kanko kai, 1924). Reference is to the version, digitalized with some changes, in CBETA 2018 edition.

X *Shinsan Dainihon Zokuzōkyō* 卍新纂大日本續藏經 (Tokyo: Kokusho Kankōkai, 1975-1989). Reference is to the digitalized version in CBETA 2018 edition.

PREMODERN WORKS

(by title; translations of premodern works listed under modern works)

A'nan qi meng jing 阿難七夢經. *T* no. 494, vol. 14.
Apidamo dapiposha lun 阿毘達磨大毘婆沙論 (Skt. *Abhidharma-mahā-vibhāṣā-śāstra*). *T* no. 1545, vol. 27.
Bai lun shu 百論疏. *T* no. 1827, vol. 42.
Bai yu jing 百喻經. *T* no. 209, vol. 4.
Baolin zhuan 寶林傳. See *Shuangfengshan Caohouxi Baolin zhuan* 雙峰山曹侯溪寶林傳
Beimeng suoyan 北夢瑣言. Beijing: Zhonghua Shuju, 2002.
Beishan lu 北山錄. *T* no. 2113, vol. 52.
Bieyi yi za ahan jing 別譯雜阿含經 (Skt. *Saṃyuktāgama*). *T* no. 100, vol. 2.
The Biographies of Baolin. See: *Shuangfengshan Caohouxi Baolin zhuan* 雙峰山曹侯溪寶林傳
Biographies of Eminent Monks. See *Gaoseng zhuan* 高僧傳
Biographies from the Monastic Treasury of the Chan Forest. See: *Chanlin sengbao zhuan* 禪林僧寶傳
Biqiuni zhuan 比丘尼傳. *T* no. 2063, vol. 50.
A Brief History of the Clergy. See *Seng shi lüe* 僧史略
Buddhist Bibliography of the Kaiyuan Era. See: *Kaiyuan Shijiao lu* 開元釋教錄
Chang ahan jing 長阿含經 (Skt. *Dīrghāgama*). *T* no. 1, vol. 1.

Cheng weishilun zhangzhong shu yao 成唯識論掌中樞要. T no. 1831, vol. 43.
A Chronology of Lineages and Transmission. See *Zongtong biannian* 宗統編年
Chuanfa zhengzong lun 傳法正宗論. T no. 2080, vol. 51.
Chu sanzang jiji 出三藏記集. T no. 2145, vol. 55.
Chu yao jing 出曜經 (Skt. *Dharmapāda*). T no. 212, vol. 4.
Cibei shuichan fa 慈悲水懺法. T no. 1910, vol. 45.
Collection of the Hall of the Patriarchs. See *Zutang ji* 祖堂集
Collection of Records Concerning the Translation of the Tripiṭaka. See *Chu sanzang jiji* 出三藏記集
Compendium of the Five Lamps. See *Wudeng huiyuan* 五燈會元
Complete Accounting of the Buddhas and Patriarchs Through the Ages. See *Lidai fozu tongzai* 歷代佛祖通載
Comprehensive Account of the Buddhas and the Patriarchs. See *Fozu tongji* 佛祖統紀
Comprehensive Discussion and Chronology of Buddhism Compiled in the Longxing Era. See *Longxing biannian tonglun* 隆興編年通論
Comprehensive Orthodox Transmission of the Śākya Clan. See *Shimen zhengtong* 釋門正統
Da anban shouyi jing 大安般守意經. T no. 602, vol. 15.
Da ben jing 大本經 (P. *Mahāpadhānasuttanta*). T no. 1, vol. 1.
Da fangdeng daji jing 大方等大集經 (Skt. *Mahāvaipulyamahāsaṃnipātasūtra*). T no. 397, vol. 13.
Da fangguang fo huayan jing 大方廣佛華嚴經 (Skt. *Buddhāvataṃsakamahāvaipulya-sūtra*). T no. 278, vol. 9.
Da Song sengshi lüe 大宋僧史略. T no. 2126, vol. 54.
Da Tang neidian lu 大唐內典錄. T no. 2149, vol. 55.
Da Tang xiyu ji 大唐西域記. T no. 2087, vol. 51.
Daoxuan lüshi gantong lu 道宣律師感通錄. T no. 2107, vol. 52.
Dazhidu lun 大智度論. T no. 1509, vol. 25.
The Expanded Lamp Record Compiled in the Tiansheng Era. See *Tiansheng guangdeng lu* 天聖廣燈錄
Fahua jing sandabu buzhu 法華經三大部補注. X no. 586, vol. 28.
Fahua wenju ji 法華文句記. T no. 1719, vol. 34.
Fahua xuanlun 法華玄論. T no. 1720, vol. 34.
Fan wang jing 梵網經. T no. 1484, vol. 24.
Fayuan zhulin 法苑珠林. T no. 2122.
Fo benxing ji jing 佛本行集經 (Skt. *Buddhacaritasaṃgrāha*). T no. 190, vol. 3.
Foshuo jigu zhangzhe nü dedu yinyuan jing 佛說給孤長者女得度因緣經. T no. 130, vol. 2.
Foshuo shier you jing 佛說十二遊經 (Skt. *Dvādaśaviharaṇasūtra*). T no. 195, vol. 4.
Foshuo weiceng you yinyuan jing 佛說未曾有因緣經 (Skt. *Adbhutadharmparyāya*). T no. 754, vol. 17.
Fozu lidai tong zai 佛祖歷代通載. T no. 2036, vol. 49.
Fozu tongji 佛祖統紀. T no. 2035, vol. 49.
Further Biographies of Eminent Monks. See *Xu gaoseng zhuan* 續高僧傳
Gaoseng Faxian zhuan 高僧法顯傳. T no. 2085, vol. 51.
Gaoseng zhuan 高僧傳. T no. 2059, vol. 50.
Genealogy of the Śākya Clan. See *Shijia shi pu* 釋迦氏譜
Guan Wuliangshoufo jing shu 觀無量壽佛經疏. T no. 1750, vol. 37.
Guang Hongming ji 廣弘明集. T no. 2103, vol. 52.
Guitian lu 歸田錄. Beijing: Zhonghua, 1997.

Guoqu xianzai yinguo jing 過去現在因果經. *T* no. 189, vol. 1.
Han shu 漢書. Beijing: Zhonghua, 1975.
Hong ming ji 弘明集. *T* no. 2102, vol. 52.
Hou Han shu 後漢書. Beijing: Zhonghua, 1973.
Jianzhong Jingguo xu deng lu 建中靖國續燈錄. *X* no. 1556, vol. 78.
Jingde chuandeng lu 景德傳燈錄. *T* no. 2076, vol. 51.
Jin shu 晉書. Beijing: Zhonghua, 1974.
Jiu Tang shu 舊唐書. Beijing: Zhonghua, 1975.
Kaiyuan Shijiao lu 開元釋教錄. *T* no. 2154, vol. 55.
Lengqie shizi ji 楞伽師資記. *T* no. 2837, vol. 85.
Liangshu 梁書. Beijing: Zhonghua, 1973.
Lidai sanbao ji 歷代三寶記. *T* no. 2034, vol. 49.
Liezi 列子 (*Sibu congkan* 四部叢刊 edition).
Lin jian lu 林間錄. *X* no. 1624, vol. 87.
Longxing biannian tonglun 隆興編年通論. *X* no. 1512, vol. 75.
Luoyang qielan ji 洛陽伽藍記. *T* no. 2092, vol. 51.
Lüxiang gantong zhuan 律相感通傳. *T* no. 1898, vol. 45.
Mohe zhiguan 摩訶止觀. *T* no. 1911, vol. 46.
Nanhai jigui neifa zhuan 南海寄歸內法傳. *T* no. 2125, vol. 54.
Nanshi 南史. Beijing: Zhonghua, 1975.
Nanyue Sidachanshi lishi yuanwen 南嶽思大禪師立誓願文. *T* no. 1933, vol. 46.
The North Mountain Record. See *Beishan lu* 北山錄
Pusa benyuan jing 菩薩本緣經. *T* no. 153, vol. 3, 67.
Puti damo nanzong ding shifei lun 菩提達摩南宗定是非論. In *Shenhui heshang yulu* 神會和尚語錄, ed. Yang Zengwen 楊曾文. Beijing: Zhonghua, 1996.
Qishi yinben jing 起世因本經. *T* no. 25, vol. 1.
Puyao jing 普曜經 (Skt. *Lalitavistara*). *T* 186, vol. 3.
Record of the Dharma Jewel Through the Generations. See *Lidai fabao ji* 歷代法寶記
Record of the Dharma Transmission of the True Lineage. See *Chuanfa zhengzong ji* 傳法正宗記
Record of the Teachers and Disciples of the Laṅkāvatāra Scripture. See *Lengqie shizi ji* 楞切師資記
Record of the Three Jewels Through the Ages. See *Lidai sanbao ji* 歷代三寶紀
Record of the Transmission of the Dharma Treasure. See *Chuan fabao ji* 傳法寶記
Records from the Forest [of Chan]. See *Linjian lu* 林間錄
Renwang huguo banruo jing shu 仁王護國般若經疏. *T* no. 707, vol. 33.
The Śākya Genealogy. See: *Shijia pu* 釋迦譜
Sanguo zhi 三國志. Beijing: Zhonghua, 1982.
Sapoduo pinipiposha 薩婆多毗尼毗婆沙 (Skt. **Sarvāstivādavinayavibhāṣa*). *T* no. 1440, vol. 23.
Shan jian lü piposha 善見律毘婆沙 (Skt. *Samantapāsādikā*). *T* no. 1462, vol. 24.
She dasheng lun 攝大乘論 (Skt. *Mahāyānasaṃgrahaśāstra*). *T* no. 1593, vol. 31.
Shi ji 史記. Beijing: Zhonghua Shuju, 1962.
Shi jia pu 釋迦譜. *T* no. 2040, vol. 50.
Shijia shi pu 釋迦氏譜. *T* no. 2041, vol. 50
Shimen zhengtong 釋門正統. *X* no. 1513, vol. 75.
Shouhu guojiezhu tuoluoni jing 守護國界主陀羅尼經. *T* no. 997, vol. 19.

Shuangfengshan Caohouxi Baolin zhuan 雙峰山曹侯溪寶林傳. T no. 81, vol. 14.
Sifenlü hanzhu jiben shu xingzong ji 四分律含注戒本疏行宗記. X no. 714, vol. 39.
Song Biographies of Eminent Monks. See: *Song gaoseng zhuan* 宋高僧傳
Song gaoseng zhuan 宋高僧傳. T no. 2061, vol. 50.
Song shi 宋史. Beijing: Zhonghua, 1977.
Strict Transmission of the Five Lamps. See *Wudeng yantong* 五燈嚴統
Sui shu 隋書. Beijing: Zhonghua, 1973.
Sui Tiantai Zhizhe dashi biezhuan 隋天台智者大師別傳. T no. 2050, vol. 50.
Taiping guangji 太平廣記. Beijing: Zhonghua Shuju, 1961.
Taizi ruiying benqi jing 太子瑞應本起經. T no. 185, vol. 3.
Tang hufa shamen Falin biezhuan 唐護法沙門法琳別傳. T no. 2051, vol. 50.
Tiansheng guangdeng lu 天聖廣燈錄. X no. 1553, vol. 78.
The Transmission of the Lamp Compiled in the Jingde Era. See *Jingde chuandeng lu* 景德傳燈錄
Weishu 魏書. Beijing: Zhonghua, 1974.
Wenshushili wen jing 文殊師利問經. T no. 468, vol. 14.
Wudeng huiyuan 五燈會元. X no. 1565, vol. 80.
Xianyu jing 賢愚經. T no. 202, vol. 4.
Xinjin wenji 鐔津文集. T no. 2020, vol. 52.
Xin Tang shu 新唐書. Beijing: Zhonghua, 1975.
Xu gaoseng zhuan 續高僧傳. T no. 2060, vol. 50.
Yin chi ru jing zhu 陰持入經註. T no. 1694, vol. 33.
Yuanren lun 原人論. T no. 1886, vol. 45.
Yuezang zhi jin 閱藏知津. J no. B271, vol. 31.
Yujia shi di lun 瑜伽師地論. T no. 1579, vol. 30.
Za ahan jin 雜阿含經 (Skt. *Saṃyuktāgama*). T no. 99, vol. 2.
Za baozang jing 雜寶藏經 (Skt. *Saṃyuktaratnapiṭakasūtra*). T no. 203, vol. 4.
Zengyi ahan jing 增壹阿含經 (Skt. *Ekōttarikāgama*). T no. 125, vol. 2.
Zhong ahan jing 中阿含經 (Skt. *Madhyamāgama*). T no. 26, vol. 1.
Zhong benqi jing 中本起經. T no. 196, vol. 4.
Zhongguan lunshu 中觀論疏. T no. 1824, vol. 42.
Zhongjing mulu 眾經目錄. T no. 2147, vol. 55.
Zhuzi yulei 朱子語類. Beijing: Zhonghua, 1986.
Zizhi tongjian 資治通鑑. Beijing: Zhonghua, 1956.
Zong tong biannian 宗統編年. X no. 1600, vol. 86.
Zu tang ji 祖堂集. Zhengzhou: Zhongzhou Guji Chubanshe, 2001.

MODERN WORKS

(Chinese monastics are listed by monastic given name rather than monastic surname: e.g., "Yinshun" rather than "Shi, Yinshun")

Adamek, Wendi L. *The Mystique of Transmission: On an Early Chan History and Its Contexts*. New York: Columbia University Press, 2007.

Anderl, Christoph, and Gang Yang. "Prognostication in Chinese Buddhist Historiographical Texts: the *Gaoseng zhuan* and the *Xu Gaoseng zhuan*." *Acta Orientalis* 73, no. 1 (2020): 1–45.

Assandri, Friederike. "Inter-religious Debate at the Court of the Early Tang: An Introduction to Daoxuan's *Ji gujin Fo Dao lunheng*." In *From Early Tang Court Debates to China's Peaceful Rise*, ed. Friederike Assandri and Dora Martins, 15-32. Amsterdam: Amsterdam University Press, 2009.

Balazs, Etienne. *Chinese Civilization and Bureaucracy*. New Haven, CT: Yale University Press, 1964.

Barrett, Timothy H. "Did I-ching Go to India? Problems in Using I-ching as a Source for South Asian Buddhism." *Buddhist Studies Review* 15, no. 2 (1998): 142-156.

——. "Climate Change and Religious Response: The Case of Early Medieval China." *Journal of the Royal Asiatic Society* 17 (2007): 139-156.

Beal, Samuel. *Buddhist Records of the Western World*. London: Kegan Paul, 1906.

Bechert, Heinz. "The Beginnings of Buddhist Historiography: Mahāvaṃsa and Political Thinking." In *Religion and Legitimation of Power in Sri Lanka*, ed. Bardwell L. Smith, 1-12. Chambersburg, PA: Anima Books, 1978.

——. "The Date of the Buddha—an Open Question of Ancient Indian History." In Bechert, *The Dating of the Historical Buddha*, 222-236.

——, ed. *The Dating of the Historical Buddha. Die Datierung des Historischen Buddha*. Göttingen: Vandenhoeck & Ruprecht, 1991.

Bielenstein, Han. "An Interpretation of the Portents in the Ts'ien-Han-shu." *Bulletin of the Museum of Far Eastern Antiquities* 22 (1950): 127-143.

Bingenheimer, Marcus. *Der Mönchsgelehrte Yinshun (*1906) und seine Bedeutung für den Chinesisch-Taiwanischen Buddhismus im 20. Jahrhundert*. Heidelberg: Edition Forum, 2004.

——. *Island of Guanyin: Mount Putuo and Its Gazetteers*. Oxford: Oxford University Press, 2016.

——. "Writing the History of Buddhist Thought in the 20th Century—Yinshun (1906-2005) in the Context of Chinese Buddhist Historiography." *Journal of Global Buddhism* 10 (2009): 255-290.

Bokenkamp, Stephen R. *Ancestors and Anxiety: Daoism and the Birth of Rebirth in China*. Berkeley: University of California Press, 2007.

——. "Time After Time: Taoist Apocalyptic History and the Founding of the T'ang Dynasty." *Asia Major. Third Series* 7, no. 1 (1994): 59-88.

Breisach, Ernst. *Historiography: Ancient, Medieval, and Modern*. 2nd ed. Chicago: University of Chicago Press, 1994.

Broughton, Jeffrey L. *Zongmi on Chan*. New York: Columbia University Press, 2009.

Brown, Delmer M., and Ichirō Ishida. *The Future and the Past: A Translation and Study of the Gukanshō, an Interpretive History of Japan Written in 1219*. Berkeley: University of California Press, 1979.

Campany, Robert Ford. *The Chinese Dreamscape 300 BCE—800 CE*. Cambridge, MA: Harvard University Press, 2020.

——. "Return from Death Narratives in Early Medieval China." *Journal of Chinese Religions* 18, no. 1 (1990): 91-125.

——. *Strange Writing: Anomaly Accounts in Early Medieval China*. Albany: State University of New York Press, 1996.

Campo, Daniela. *La construction de la sainteté dans la Chine modern. La vie du maître bouddhiste Xuyun*. Paris: Les Belles Lettres, 2013.

Cao, Ganghua 曹剛華. *Mingdai fojiao fangzhi yanjiu* 明代佛教方志研究. Beijing: Zhongguo Renmindaxue Chubanshe, 2011.

———. *Songdai fojiao shiji yanjiu* 宋代佛教史籍研究. Shanghai: Huadong Shifandaxue Chubanshe, 2005.

Cao, Shibang (Sze-bong Tzo) 曹仕邦. *Zhongguo fojiao shixue shi—Dong Jin zhi Wudai* 中國佛教史學史: 東晉至五代. Taipei: Fagu wenhua, 1999.

———. *Zhongguo shamen waixue de yanjiu: Hanmo zhi Wudai* 中國沙門外學的研究: 漢末至五代. Taipei: Fagu wenhua, 1994.

Carr, Edward Hallett. *What Is History*. 1961; 2nd ed. London: Macmillan, 1986.

Carrithers, Michael. *The Buddha*. Oxford: Oxford University Press, 1983.

Chattopadhyaya, Alaka, and Lama Chimpa, trans. *History of Buddhism in India,* by Tāranātha. Simla: Indian Institute of Advanced Study, 1970.

Chen, Guofu 陳國符. *Daozang yuanliu kao* 道藏源流考. Beijing: Zhonghua, 1963.

Chen, Jinhua. "One Name, Three Monks: Two Northern Chan Masters Emerge from the Shadow of Their Contemporary, the Tiantai Mater Zhanran 湛然 (711-782)." *Journal of the International Association of Buddhist Studies* 22, no. 1 (1999): 1-90.

Chen, Jinzhen 陳勁榛. "Sengyou *Shijia pu* yanjiu" 僧祐釋迦譜研究. MA thesis, Chinese Culture University, 1990.

Chen, Kenneth. *Buddhism in China: A Historical Survey*. Princeton, NJ: Princeton University Press, 1964.

Chen, Yinke 陳寅恪. "Zhimindu xueshuo kao" 支愍度學說考. In *Jinming guan conggao chubian* 金明館叢稿初編, 141-167. Shanghai: Shanghai Guji, 1980.

Chen, Yuan 陳垣. *Qing chu seng zheng ji* 清初僧諍記. Beijing: Zhonghua, 1962.

———. *Zhongguo fojiao shiji gailun* 中國佛教史籍概論. Beijing: Zhonghua, 1962.

Chen, Zhichao 陳智超. *Chen Yuan: shengping, xueshu, jiaoyu yu jiaowang* 陳垣—-生平、學術、教育與交往. Hefei: Anhui Daxue Chubanshe, 2010.

Chou, Yiliang (for works in Chinese, see Zhou Yiliang). "Tantrism in China." *Harvard Journal of Asiatic Studies* 8 (1945): 241-332.

Conner, Chris. "Ts'ai Yung." In *Indiana Companion to Traditional Chinese Literature*, ed. William H. Nienhauser Jr., 787-788. Bloomington: Indiana University Press, 1986.

Davis, Richard L. *Historical Records of the Five Dynasties*. New York: Columbia University Press, 2004.

Demiéville, Paul. "Sur la memoire des existences anterieures." *Bulletin de l'École Française d'Extrême-Orient* 27 (1927): 283-298.

Despeux, Catherine. "La culture lettrée au service d'un plaidoyer pour le bouddhisme. Le 'Traité des deux doctrines' ('Erjiao lun') de Dao'an." In *Bouddhisme et lettrés dans la Chine médiévale*, ed. Despeux, 145-227 Paris: Louvain, 2002.

Dien, Albert E. "Historiography of the Six Dynasties Period (220-581)." In *The Oxford History of Historical Writing*, ed. Feldherr and Hardy, vol. 1, 509-34.

———. "Wei Tan and the Historiography of the *Wei-shu*." In *Studies in Early Medieval Chinese Literature and Cultural History: In Honor of Richard B. Mather and Donald Holzman*, ed. Paul W. Kroll and David R. Knechtges, 399-466. Provo. UT: T'ang Studies Society, 2003.

Dongchu 東初. *Zhong Ri fojiao jiaotongshi* 中日佛教交通史 (1970; rpt., Dongchu.ddbc.edu.tw).

———. *Zhong Yin fojiao tongshi* 中印佛教通史 (1968; rpt., Dongchu.ddbc.edu.tw).

———. *Zhongguo fojiao jindai shi* 中國佛教近代史 (1974; rpt., Dongchu.ddbc.edu.tw).

Doniger O'Flaherty, Wendy, ed. *Karma and Rebirth in Classical Indian Traditions*. Berkeley: University of California Press, 1980.

Donner, Neal, and Daniel B. Stevenson. *The Great Calming and Contemplation: A Study and Annotated Translation of the First Chapter of Chih-I's* Mo-ho chih kuan. Honolulu: University of Hawai'i Press, 1993.
Drège, Jean-Pierre. *Mémoire sur les pays bouddhiques*. Paris: Les Belles Lettres, 2013.
—— and Dimitri Drettas. "Oniromancie." In *Divination et société. Étude des manuscrits de Dunhuang de la Bibliothèque nationale de France et de la British Library*, ed. Marc Kalinowski, 369–404 Paris: Bibliothèque nationale de France, 2003.
Durrant, Stephen W. *The Cloudy Mirror: Tension and Conflict in the Writings of Sima Qian*. Albany: State University of New York Press, 1995.
Durrant, Stephen W., Wai-yee Lee, and David Schaberg. *Zuo Tradition. Zuozhuan: Commentary on the "Spring and Autumn Annals."* Seattle: University of Washington Press, 2016.
Durrant, Stephen W., Wai-yee Li, Michael Nylan, and Hans van Ess. *The Letter to Ren An and Sima Qian's Legacy*. Seattle: University of Washington Press, 2016.
Durt, Hubert. "La Date du Buddha en Corée et au Japon." In *The Dating of the Historical Buddha*, ed. Bechert, 458–489.
——. *Problems of Chronology and Eschatology. Four Lectures on the* Essay on Buddhism *by Tominaga Nakamoto (1715–1746)*. Kyoto: Italian School of East Asian Studies, 1994.
Ebrey, Patricia Buckley. *Emperor Huizong*. Cambridge, MA: Harvard University Press, 2014.
Eire, Carlos M.N. *From Madrid to Purgatory: The Art and Craft of Dying in Sixteenth-Century Spain*. Cambridge: Cambridge University Press, 1995.
Elman, Benjamin. *Civil Examinations and Meritocracy in Late Imperial China*. Cambridge, MA: Harvard University Press, 2013.
Faure, Bernard. "Bodhidharma as Textual and Religious Paradigm." *History of Religions* 25, no. 3 (1986): 187–198.
——. *Le Bouddhisme Ch'an en mal d'histoire. Genèse d'une tradition religieuse dans la Chine des T'ang*. Paris: École française d'extrême-orient, 1989.
——. *Chan Insights and Oversights: An Epistemological Critique of the Chan Tradition*. Princeton, NJ: Princeton University Press, 1993.
——. *The Will to Orthodoxy: A Critical Genealogy of Northern Chan Buddhism*. Stanford, CA: Stanford University Press, 1997.
Feldherr, Andrew, and Grant Hardy, eds. *The Oxford History of Historical Writing*, vol. 1. Oxford: Oxford University Press, 2011.
Feng, Guodong 馮國棟. *Jingde chuandeng lu yanjiu* 景德傳燈錄研究. Beijing: Zhonghua, 2014.
Feng, Youlan. *History of Chinese Philosophy*. Princeton, NJ: Princeton University Press, 1953.
Finley, M. I. *The Use and Abuse of History*. London: Chatto and Windus, 1975.
Fischer, David Hackett. *Historians' Fallacies: Toward a Logic of Historical Thought*. New York: Harper & Row, 1970.
Forte, Antonio. *The Hostage An Shigao and His Offspring*. Kyoto: Istituto Italiano di Cultura Scuola di Studi sull'Asia Orientale, 1995.
Foulks, Beverley. *Living Karma: The Religious Practices of Ouyi Zhixu*. New York: Columbia University Press, 2014.
Franke, Herbert. "On Chinese Traditions Concerning the Dates of the Buddha." In *Chan Before Chan. Meditation, Repentance, and Visionary Experience in Chinese Buddhism*, ed. Eric M. Greene. Honolulu: University of Hawai'i Press, 2021.

Fujiyoshi, Masumi 騰善真澄. *Dōsen den no kenkyū* 道宣傳の研究. Kyoto: Kyoto Daigaku gakushutsu shuppan kai, 2002.

Funayama, Toru 船山徹, and Yoshikawa Tadao 吉川忠夫. *Kōsōden* 高僧傳. Tokyo: Iwanami, 2010.

Geiger, Wilhelm, trans. *The Mahāvaṃsa or Great Chronicle of Ceylon*. London: Pali Text Society, 1912.

Gethin, Rupert. *The Foundations of Buddhism*. Oxford: Oxford University Press, 1998.

Giles, H. A. *The Travels of Fa-hsien (399–414 A.D.), or Record of the Buddhist Kingdoms*. Cambridge: Cambridge University Press, 1923.

Grafton, Anthony T. "Joseph Scaliger and Historical Chronology: The Rise and Fall of a Discipline." *History and Theory* 14 (1975): 157-185.

——. *What Was History? The Art of History in Early Modern Europe*. Cambridge: Cambridge University Press, 2007.

Graham, Angus Charles. *Lieh-tzu*. London: Murray, 1960.

Gregory, Peter N. *Inquiry Into the Origin of Humanity: An Annotated Translation of Tsung-mi's Yüan jen lun with a Modern Commentary*. Honolulu: University of Hawai'i Press, 1995.

——. *Tsung-mi and the Sinification of Buddhism*. Honolulu: University of Hawai'i Press, 2002.

Grethlein, Jonas, and Christopher B. Krebs, eds. *Time and Narrative in Ancient Historiography: The 'Plupast' from Herodotus to Appian*. Cambridge: Cambridge University Press, 2012.

Grieder, Jerome B. *Hu Shih and the Chinese Renaissance: Liberalism in the Chinese Revolution, 1917–1937*. Cambridge, MA: Harvard University Press, 1970.

——. *Intellectuals and the State in Modern China: A Narrative History*. London: Collier Macmillan, 1981.

Guoche 果徹. "Dongchu laoren nianpu" 東初老人年譜. *Chung-Hwa Buddhist Studies* 2 (1998): 1-48.

Hachiya, Kunio 蜂屋邦夫. "Hokushū Dōan nikyōron chūshaku" 北周道安「二教論」注釈. *Tōyō bunka* 東洋文化 (Tōkyō: Tōyō Gakkai) 62 (1982): 175-212.

Halperin, Mark. "Heroes, Rogues, and Religion in a Tenth-Century Chinese Miscellany." *Journal of the American Oriental Society* 129, no. 3 (2009): 413-430.

Hardy, Grant. *Worlds of Bronze and Bamboo: Sima Qian's Conquest of History*. New York: Columbia University Press, 1999.

Hartmann, Charles. "Chinese Historiography in the Age of Maturity, 960-1368." In *The Oxford History of Historical Writing, Vol. 2, 400–1400*, 37-57. Oxford: Oxford University Press, 2012.

Hasebe, Yūkei 長谷部幽蹊. *Min Shin Bukkyō kyōdanshi kenkyū* 明清佛教教團史研究. Tokyo: Dōhōha, 1993.

Heine, Steven, and Dale S. Wright, eds. *The Koan: Texts and Contexts in Zen Buddhism*. Oxford: Oxford University Press, 2000.

Heng Ching (Hengqing) 恆清. *Xingtan nalü. Hengqing fashi fangtan lu* 杏壇衲履恆清法師訪談錄, based on interviews conducted by Hou Kunhong 侯坤宏. Taipei: Guoshiguan 國史館, 2007.

Hirakawa, Akira. *A History of Indian Buddhism: From Śākyamuni to Nāgārjuna*. Trans. Paul Groner. Honolulu: University of Hawai'i Press, 1990.

Ho, Chiew Hui. *Diamond Sutra Narratives: Textual Production and Lay Religiosity in Medieval China*. Leiden: Brill, 2009.

Hou, Kunhong 侯坤宏. *Yinshun fashi nianpu* 印順法師年譜. Taipei: Guoshiguan, 2008.

——. *Zhenshi yu fangbian. Yinshun sixiang yanjiu* 真實與方便・印順思想研究. Taipei: Fajie, 2009.

Hu, Baoguo 胡寶國. *Han Tang jian shixue de fazhan* 漢唐間史學的發展. Beijing: Shangwu Yinshuguan, 2003.

—. "Jingshi wenxue yu wenshi zhi xue" 經史文學與文史之學. In Xie, *Zhongguo shixue shi*, 437-449.

Hu, Shi (Hu Shih) 胡適. "Ch'an (Zen) Buddhism in China: Its History and Method." *Philosophy East and West* 3, no. 1 (1953): 3-24.

—. "Ji Zhongyang Tushuguan cang de Song Baoyou ben Wudeng huiyuan" 記中央圖書館藏的宋寶祐本五燈會元. In *Hushi quanji* 胡適全集, 504-520. Hefei: Anhui Jiaoyu, 2003.

—. "Putidamo kao" 菩提達摩考. In *Hu Shi juan* 胡適卷, *Ershi shiji foxue jingdian wenku* 二十世紀佛學經典文庫, 408-416. Wuhan: Wuhan Daxue Chubanshe, 2008.

Huang, Junquan 黃俊銓. *Chanzong dianji* Wudeng huiyuan *yanjiu* 禪宗典籍《五燈會元》研究. Taipei: Fagu wenhua, 2008.

Huang, Susan Shih-shan. "Illustrating the Efficacy of the Diamond Sutra in Vernacular Buddhism." *National Palace Museum Reearch Quarterly* (*Gugong xueshu jikan* 故宮學術季刊) 35, no. 4 (2018): 35-120.

Hubbard, Jamie. *Absolute Delusion, Perfect Buddhahood: The Rise and Fall of a Chinese Heresy*. Honolulu: University of Hawai'i Press, 2000.

Hurvitz, Leon. "Treatise on Buddhism and Taoism." In *Yun-kang. The Buddhist Cave-Temples of the fifth Century A.D. in North China*, ed. Seichi Mizuno 水野清一 and Toshio Nagahiro 長廣敏雄. Kyoto: Jimbunkagaku Kenkyusho, 1956.

Jan, Yün-Hua. "The Chinese Understanding and Assimilation of Karma Doctrine." In *Karma and Rebirth: Post Classical Developments*, ed. Ronald W. Neufeldt, 145-168. Albany: State University of New York, 1986.

—. *A Chronicle of Buddhism in China 590–960—Translations from Monk Chih-p'an's Fo-tsu T'ung-chi*. Calcutta: Visva-Bharati Research Publications, 1966.

Jenkins, Keith. *Re-Thinking History*. London: Routledge, 1991; rpt. 2007.

Jia, Jinhua. *The Hongzhou School of Chan Buddhism in Eighth- Through Tenth-Century China*. Albany: State University of New York Press, 2006.

Jiang, Weiqiao 蔣維喬. *Zhongguo fojiao shi* 中國佛教史. Shanghai: Shanghai Guji Chubanshe, 2007.

Jorgensen, John. *Inventing Hui-neng, the Sixth Patriarch: Hagiography and Biography in Early Ch'an*. Leiden: Brill, 2005.

Jülch, Thomas. *Zhipan's Account of the History of Buddhism in China, Volume 1*, Fozu tongji, juan 34–38. From the Times of the Buddha to the Nanbeichao Era. Leiden: Brill, 2019.

—. *Zhipan's Account of the History of Buddhism in China, Volume 2: Fozu tongji, juan 39–42: From the Sui Dynasty to the Wudai Era*. Leiden: Brill, 2021.

Kalinowski, Marc, ed. *Divination et société dans la Chine médiévale. Étude des manuscrits de Dunhuang de la Bibliothèque nationale de France et de la British Library*. Paris: Bibliothèque nationale de France, 2003.

Keenan, John P., trans. *The Summary of the Great Vehicle*. Berkeley, CA: Numata Center for Buddhist Translation and Research, 1992.

Keightley, David. *Sources of Shang History: The Oracle Bone Inscriptions of Bronze Age China*. Berkeley: University of California Press, 1978.

Kern, Martin. "Religious Anxiety and Political Interest in Western Han Omen Interpretation: The Case of the Han Wudi 漢武帝 Period (141-87 B.C.)." *Studies in Chinese History* 10 (December 2000): 1-31.

Kieschnick, John. "Buddhism, Biographies of Buddhist Monks." In *The Oxford History of Historical Writing*, ed. Feldherr and Hardy, vol. 1, 535-552.

———. *The Eminent Monk: Buddhist Ideals in Medieval Chinese Hagiography*. Honolulu: University of Hawai'i Press, 1997.

———. "Gao seng zhuan." In *Early Medieval Chinese Texts: A Bibliographical Guide*, ed. Cynthia L. Chennault et al., 76-80. Berkeley, CA: Institute of East Asian Studies, 2015.

———. "A History of Buddhist Vegetarianism in China." In *Of Tripod and Palate: Food, Politics and Religion in Traditional China*, ed. Roel Sterckx, 186-212. New York: Palgrave-Macmillan, 2005.

———. "Xu gaoseng zhuan." In *Early Medieval Chinese Texts: A Bibliographical Guide*, ed. Cynthia L. Chennault et al., 428-431. Berkeley, CA: Institute of East Asian Studies, 2015.

Knapp, Keith. "Did the Middle Kingdom Have a Middle Period? The Problem of 'Medieval' in China's History." *Education about Asia* 12, no. 3 (2007): 12-17.

Kohn, Livia. *Laughing at the Tao: Debates Among Buddhists and Taoists in Medieval China*. Princeton, NJ: Princeton University Press, 1995.

Krauss, Franklin Brunell. *An Interpretation of the Omens, Portents, and Prodigies Recorded by Livy, Tacitus, and Suetonios*. Philadelphia: University of Pennsylvania Press, 1930.

Lachman, Charles. "Why Did the Patriarch Cross the River? The Rushleaf Bodhidharma Reconsidered." *Asia Major Third Series* 6, part 2 (1993): 237-267.

Lamotte, Étienne. *History of Indian Buddhism: From the Origins to the Śaka Era*. Louvain: Peeters Press, 1988.

———. *Le traité de la grande vertu du sagesse*. Louvain: Institute Orientaliste Louvain-La-Neuve, 1981.

Lancaster, Lewis. "The Dating of the Buddha in Chinese Buddhism." In *The Dating of the Historical Buddha*, ed. Bechert, 449-457.

Lau, D. C. *Lao tzu tao te ching*. Middlesex: Penguin, 1985.

Lerner, Robert E. *The Powers of Prophecy: The Cedar of Lebanon Vision from the Mongol Onslaught to the Dawn of the Enlightenment*. Berkeley: University of California Press, 1983.

Levenson, Joseph R. *Liang Ch'i-ch'ao and the Mind of Modern China*. London: Thames and Hudson, 1959.

Levy, Howard S. *Biography of An Lu-shan*. Berkeley: University of California Press, 1960.

Lewis, Mark Edward. *Writing and Authority in Early China*. Albany: State University of New York Press, 1999.

Li, Qingzhang 李清章, and Yan Mengxiang 閻孟祥. "Song Taizong 'shou Fo ji' chuanshuo kao" 宋太宗受佛記傳說考. *Hebei daxue xuebao (zhexue shehui kexue ban)* 河北大學學報(哲學社會科學板) 29, no. 1 (2014): 16-18.

Liang, Qichao 梁啟超. "Fojiao zhi chushuru" 佛教之初輸入. In his *Zhongguo fojiao yanjiushi* 中國佛教研究史, 1-24. Shanghai: Sanlian, 1988.

Link, Arthur E. "Biography of Shih Tao-an." *T'oung Pao* 46 (1958): 1-48.

Lippiello, Tiziana. *Auspicious Omens and Miracles in Ancient China: Han, Three Kingdoms and Six Dynasties*. Monumenta Serica Monograph Series 39. Nettetal: Styler Verlag, 2001.

Liu, James T.C. *Ou-Yang Hsiu : An Eleventh-Century Neo-Confucianist*. Stanford, CA: Stanford University Press, 1967.

Liu, Shufen 劉淑芬. *Zhonggu de fojiao yu shehui* 中古的佛教與社會. Shanghai: Shanghai Guji Chubanshe, 2008.

Liu, Yi 劉屹. "After the Buddha's Nirvāṇa: The *Mofa* Concept of Chinese Buddhism and Its Rise to Prominence." *Studies in Chinese Religions* 4, no. 3 (2018): 277-306.

———. "Mu Wang wushier nian fomieshuo de xingcheng" 穆王五十二年佛說的形成. *Dunhuangxue jikan* 敦煌學輯刊 2 (2018): 166–177.

Loewe, Michael. *A Biographical Dictionary of the Qin, Former Han and Xin Periods (221 BC–AD 24)*. Leiden: Brill, 2000.

———. *Dong Zhongshu: A "Confucian" Heritage and the* Chunqiu fanlu. Boston: Brill, 2011.

———. *The Men Who Governed Han China: Companion to A Biographical Dictionary of the Qin, Former Han and Xin Periods*. Leiden: Brill, 2004.

Lusthaus, Dan. *Buddhist Phenomenology: A Philosophical Investigation of Yogācāra Buddhism and the Ch'eng Wei-shih-lun*. New York: Routledge, 2002.

Lynn, Richard John. *Classic of Changes: A New Translation of the* I Ching *as Intepreted by Wang Bi*. New York: Columbia University Press, 1994.

Ma, Tianxiang 麻天祥. *Tang Yongtong pingzhuan* 湯用彤評傳. Wuhan: Wuhan Daxue Chubanshe, 2007.

Majumdar, Ramesh Chandra. "Ideas of History in Sanskrit Literature." In *Historians of India, Pakistan and Ceylon*, ed. Cyril Henry Philips, 13–28. London: Oxford University Press, 1967.

Man, Chanju. *The History of Doctrinal Classification in Chinese Buddhism: A Study of the* Panjiao *System*. New York: University Press of America, 2006.

Martin, Dan. *Tibetan Histories: A Bibliography of Tibetan-Language Historical Works*. London: Serindia, 1997.

Maspero, Henri. "Sur la date et l'authenticité du *Fou fa tsang yin yuan tchouan*." In *Mélanges d'Indianisme offerts par ses éleves à M. Sylvain Lévi*, 129-149. Paris: E. Leroux, 1911).

Mather, Richard. "Chinese and Indian Perceptions of Each Other Between the First and Seventh Centuries." *Journal of the American Oriental Society* 112, no. 1 (1992): 1–8.

McRae, John R. "The Hagiography of Bodhidharma: Restructuring the Point of Origin of Chinese Chan Buddhism." In *India in the Chinese Imagination: Myth Religion and Thought*, ed. John Kieschnick and Meir Shahar, 125–138. Philadelphia: University of Pennsylvania Press, 2014.

———. *The Northern School and the Formation of Early Ch'an Buddhism*. Honolulu: University of Hawai'i Press, 1986.

———. "The Ox-Head School of Chinese Ch'an Buddhism: From Early Ch'an to the Golden Age." In *Studies in Ch'an and Hua-yen*, ed. Robert M. Gimello and Peter N. Gregory, 169–252. Studies in East Asian Buddhism. Honolulu: University of Hawai'i Press, 1983.

———. "Religion as Revolution in Chinese Historiography: Hu Shih (1891-1962) on Shen-hui (684-758)." *Cahiers d'Extrême-Asie* 12 (2001): 59–102.

———. *Seeing Through Zen: Encounter, Transformation, and Genealogy in Chinese Chan Buddhism*. Berkeley: University of California Press, 2003.

Maraldo, John C. "Is There Historical Consciouness in Ch'an?" *Japanese Journal of Religious Studies* 12, no. 2/3 (1985): 141–172.

Mingfu 明復. *Mingfu fashi foxue wencong* 明復法師佛學文叢. Xinzhu: Huamulan Wenhua Chubanshe, 2006.

Mittag, Achim. "What Makes a Good Historian: Zhang Xuecheng's Postulate of 'Moral Integrity' (*shi de* 史德) Revisited." In *Historical Truth, Historical Criticism, and Ideology. Chinese Historiography and Historical Culture from a New Comparative Perspective*, ed. Helwig Schmidt-Glintzer et al., 365–404. Leiden: Brill, 2005.

Momigliano, Arnaldo. "Time in Ancient Historiography." *History and Theory* 6 (1966): 1–23.

Morrison, Elizabeth. "Contested Visions of the Buddhist Past and the Curious Fate of an Early Medieval Chinese Buddhist Text." Unpublished manuscript.
———. *The Power of the Patriarchs: Qisong and Lineage in Chinese Buddhism*. Leiden: Brill, 2010.
Nadel, George H. "Philosophy of History Before Historicism." *History and Theory* 3, no. 3 (1964): 291–315.
Nattier, Jan. *Once Upon a Future Time: Studies in a Buddhist Prophecy of Decline*. Berkeley, CA: Asian Humanities Press, 1991.
Neujahr, Matthew. *Predicting the Past in the Ancient Near East: Mantic Historiography in Ancient Mesopotamia, Judah, and the Mediterranean World*. Providence, RI: Brown Judaic Studies, 2012.
Nienhauser Jr., William H., ed. *The Grand Scribe's Records*, vol. 7. Taipei: SMC, 1994.
Novetzke, Christian Lee. "Memory: Modern Memory Theory, Memory Studies and Hinduism." In *Studying Hinduism. Key Concepts and Methods*, ed. Sushil Mittal and Gene Thursby, 230–250. New York: Routledge, 2008.
Palumbo, Antonello. "Review of Storch, Tanya, The History of Chinese Buddhist Bibliography: Censorship and Transformation of the Tripitaka." H-Buddhism, H-Net Reviews. April 2017.
Patrides, Constantinos Apostolos. *The Phoenix and the Ladder. The Rise and Decline of the Christian View of History*. Berkeley: University of California Press, 1964.
Peng, Jinzhang 彭金章, and Wang Jianjun 王建軍 eds. *Dunhuang Mogaoku beiqu shiku* 敦煌莫高窟北區石窟. Beijing: Wenwu, 2004.
Peng, Qinqin. "Between Faith and Truth." PhD diss., Georg-August-Universität Göttingen, 2021.
Penkower, Linda. "In the Beginning: Guanding 灌頂 (561–632) and the Creation of Early Tiantai." *Journal of the International Association of Buddhist Studies* 23, no. 2 (2000): 245–296.
Perera, Lakshman S. "The Pali Chronicle of Ceylon." In *Historians of India, Pakistan and Ceylon*, ed. Cyril Henry Philips, 29–34. London: Oxford University Press, 1967.
Pittman, Don A. *Toward a Modern Chinese Buddhism: Taixu's Reforms*. Honolulu: University of Hawai'i Press, 2001.
Poceski, Mario. *The Records of Mazu and the Making of Classical Chan Literature*. Oxford: Oxford University Press, 2015.
Puett, Michael. "Listening to Sages: Divination, Omens, and the Rhetoric of Antiquity in Wang Chong's *Lunheng*." *Oriens Extremus* 45 (2005/06): 271–281.
Pulleyblank, E. G. "Chinese Historical Criticism: Liu Chih-chi and Ssu-ma Kuang." In *Historians of China and Japan*, ed. W. G. Beasley and E. G. Pulleyblank, 135–166. London: Oxford University Press, 1961.
Ritzinger, Justin R. *Anarchy in the Pure Land: Reinventing the Cult of Maitreya in Modern Chinese Buddhism*. Oxford: Oxford University Press, 2017.
———. "Karma, Charisma, and Community: Karmic Storytelling in a Blue-Collar Taiwanese Buddhist Organization." *Journal of Chinese Buddhist Studies* 33 (2020): 203–232.
Robinson, Chase F. *Islamic Historiography*. Cambridge: Cambridge University Press, 2003.
Rosenthal, Franz. *A History of Muslim Historiography*. 2nd ed. Leiden: Brill, 1968.
Ruan, Zhongren 阮忠仁. "Cong *Lidai sanbao ji* lun Fei Zhangfang de shixue tezhi ji yiyi" 從《歷代三寶記》論費長房的史學特質及意義. *Dongfang zongjiao yanjiu* 東方宗教研究. New Series 1 (1990): 93–129.

Schlütter, Morten. *How Zen Became Zen: The Dispute Over Enlightenment and the Formation of Chan Buddhism in Song-Dynasty China*. Honolulu: University of Hawai'i Press, 2008.

Schneider, Laurence A. *Ku Chieh-kang and China's New History: Nationalism and the Quest for Alternative Traditions*. Berkeley: University of California Press, 1971.

Schmidt-Glintzer, Helwig. *Die Identität der buddhistischen Schulen und die Kompilation buddhistischer Universalgeschichten in China: ein Beitrag zur Geistesgeschichte der Sung-Zeit*. Wiesbaden: Steiner, 1982.

Schopen, Gregory. "Archaeology and Protestant Presuppositions in the Study of Indian Buddhism." In *Bones, Stones, and Buddhist Monks: Collected Papers on the Archaeology, Epigraphy, and Texts of Monastic Buddhism in India*, ed. Schopen, 1-22. Honolulu: University of Hawai'i Press, 1997.

Schweitzer, Albert. *The Quest of the Historical Jesus*. 1906; English translation, rpt., New York: Macmillan, 1978.

Seeskin, Kenneth. "Maimonides' Sense of History." *Jewish History* 18, no. 2/3 (2004): 129-145.

Sen, Tansen. *India, China, and the World: A Connected History*. New York: Rowman & Littlefield, 2017.

Shahar, Meir. *The Shaolin Monastery: History, Religion, and the Chinese Martial Arts*. Honolulu: University of Hawai'i Press, 2008.

Sharf, Robert H. *Coming to Terms with Chinese Buddhism: A Reading of the Treasure Store Treatise*. Honolulu: University of Hawai'i Press, 2002.

——. "Is Nirvāṇa the Same as Insentience? Chinese Struggles with an Indian Ideal." In *India in the Chinese Imagination*, ed. John Kieschnick and Meir Shahar, 141-170. Philadelphia: University of Pennsylvania Press, 2014.

——, trans. *Scripture in Forty-two Sections*. In *Religions of China in Practice*, ed. Donald S. Lopez Jr., 360-377. Princeton: Princeton University Press, 1996.

Shaughnessy, Edward L. "History and Inscriptions, China." In *The Oxford History of Historical Writing*, vol. 1, 371-393.

Shengyan 聖嚴. *Mingmo fojiao yanjiu* 明末佛教研究. Taipei: Dongchu, 1987.

——. *Shijie fojiao tongshi* 世界佛教通史. Taipei: Dongchu, 1980.

——. *Yindu fojiaoshi* 印度佛教史. 1969; rpt., Taipei: Fagu wenhua, 2006.

—— (Shengyan). *Footprints in the Snow: The Autobiography of a Chinese Buddhist Monk*. New York: Doubleday, 2008.

Shinohara, Koichi. "From Local History to Universal History: The Construction of the Sung T'ien-t'ai Lineage." In *Buddhism in the Sung*, ed. Peter N. Gregory and Daniel A. Getz, 524-576. Honolulu: University of Hawai'i Press, 1999.

——. "The Kaṣāya Robe of the Past Buddha Kāśyapa in the Miraculous Instruction Given to the Vinaya Master Daoxuan (596-667)." *Chung-Hwa Buddhist Journal* 13, no. 2 (2000): 299-367.

——. "The Story of the Buddha's Begging Bowl: Imagining a Biography and Sacred Places." In *Pilgrims, Patrons and Place: Localizing Sanctity in Asian Religions*, ed. Phyllis Granoff and Koichi Shinohara, 68-107. Vancouver: University of British Columbia Press, 2003.

——. "Two Sources of Chinese Buddhist Biographies: Stupa Inscriptions and Miracle Stories." In *Monks and Magicians: Religious Biographies in Asia*, ed. Phyllis Granoff and Koichi Shinohara, 119-229. Oakville, Ont., Mosaic Press, 1988.

Smith, Richard J. *Fortune-tellers and Philosophers: Divination in Traditional Chinese Society*. Boulder, CO: Westview Press, 1991.

Snellgrove, David. *Indo-Tibetan Buddhism: Indian Buddhists and Their Tibetan Successors*. Boston: Shambhala, 1987.

Song, Daofa 宋道發. *Fojiao shiguan yanjiu* 佛教史觀研究. Beijing: Zongjiao Wenhua Chubanshe, 2009.

Soymié, Michel. "Les songes et leur interpretation en Chine." In *Sources orientale II. Les songes et leur interpretation*, 169-204. Paris: Le Seuil, 1959.

Spero, Shubert. "Maimonides and the Sense of History." *A Journal of Orthodox Jewish Thought* 24, no. 2 (Winter 1989): 128-137.

Storch, Tanya. *The History of Chinese Buddhist Bibliography: Censorship and Transformation of the Tripitaka*. New York: Cambria Press, 2014.

Strickmann, Michel. *Chinese Magical Medicine*. Stanford, CA: Stanford University Press, 2002.

——. "Dreamwork of Psycho-Sinologists: Doctors, Taoists, Monks." In *Psycho-Sinology. The Universe of Dreams in Chinese Culture*, ed. Carolyn T. Brown, 25-46. Washington, DC: University Press of America, 1988.

Strong, John. *The Buddha: A Short Biography*. Oxford: Oneworld, 2001.

Suzuki, Daisetz Teitaro. "Zen: A Reply to Hu Shih." *Philosophy East and West* 3, no. 1 (1953): 25-46.

Swanson, Paul L., ed. *Pruning the Bodhi Tree: The Storm Over Critical Buddhism*. Honolulu: University of Hawai'i Press, 1997.

——. *T'ien-t'ai Chih-i's Mo-ho chih-kuan*. Honolulu: University of Hawai'i Press, 2018.

Taixu 太虛. *Fojiao de jiaoshi jiaofa he jin hou de jianshe* 佛教的教史教法和今後的建設. In *Fofa zongxue* 佛法總學, in *Taixu dashi quanshu*, vol. 1, 458-485.

——. *Fojiao ge zongpai yuanliu* 佛教各宗派源流. In *Fofa zongxue* 佛法總學, in *Taixu dashi quanshu*, vol. 2, 761-868.

——. *Fojiao shi lüe* 佛教史略. In *Fofa zongxue* 佛法總學, in *Taixu dashi quanshu*, vol. 2, 894-916.

——. "Lun Shijieshi gang" 論世界史綱. In *Taixu dashi quanshu* vol. 25, 256-264.

——. *Taixu dashi quanshu* 太虛大師全書. Taipei: Shandaosi Fojing Liutongchu, 1998.

——. *Taixu zizhuan* 太虛自傳. In *Taixu dashi quanshu*, vol. 29, 209-219.

——. "Wo zenyang panshe yiqie fofa" 我怎樣判攝一切佛法. In *Taixu dashi quanshu* vol. 1, 513-519.

——. *Xin yu rongguan* 新與融貫. In *Fofa zongxue*, in *Taixu dashi quanshu*, vol. 1, 445.

——. "Yu Hu Shizhi shu" 與胡適之書. In *Taixu dashi quanshu* vol. 26, 209.

——. *Zhongguo foxue* 中國佛學. In *Fofa zongxue* 佛法總學, in *Taixu dashi quanshu*, vol. 2, 531-760.

Tan, Zhihui. "Daoxuan's Vision of Jetavana: Imagining a Utopian Monastery in Early Tang." PhD diss., University of Arizona, 2002.

Tang, Xiaobing. *Global Space and the Nationalist Discourse of Modernity: The Historical Thinking of Liang Qichao*. Stanford, CA: Stanford University Press, 1996.

Tang, Yongtong 湯用彤. *Han Wei Liang Jin Nanbeichao Fojiaoshi* 漢魏兩晉南北朝佛教史. Changsha: Shangwu Yinshuguan, 1938.

——. *Yindu zhexue shi lüe* 印度哲學史略. 1959; rpt., Beijing: Zhonghua Shuju, 1988.

Thapar, Romila. "Historical Traditions in Early India: c. 1000 BC to c. AD 600." In *The Oxford History of Historical Writing*, ed. Feldherr and Hardy, Vol. 1, 553-576.

——. "Inscriptions as Historical Writing in Early India: Third Century BC to Sixth Century AD." In *The Oxford History of Historical Writing*, ed. Feldherr and Hardy, Vol. 1, 577-600.

Thomas, Edward J. *The Life of Buddha as Legend and History*. 1927; 3rd ed., London: Routledge and Kegan Paul, 1975.

Thomas, Keith. *Religion and the Decline of Magic*. New York: Scribner, 1971.
Travagnin, Stefania. "Reception History and Limits of Interpretation: The Belgian Étienne Lamotte, Japanese Buddhologists, the Chinese monk Yinshun 印順 and the Formation of a Global 'Da zhidu lun 大智度論 Scholarship,'" *Hualin International Journal of Buddhist Studies* 1, no. 1 (2018): 341-369.
Trevor-Roper, Hugh. "The Past and the Present: History and Sociology." *Past & Present* 42 (1969): 3-18.
Tsai, Linzy. "The Rise of the Buddhist University in Taiwan." PhD thesis, University of Bristol, 2012.
Tsukamoto, Zenryū 塚本善隆. "Gi Shū to Bukkyō" 魏收と佛教 *Tōhō gakuhō* 東方學報 31 (1961): 1-34.
Twitchett, Denis. *The Writing of Official History Under the T'ang*. Cambridge: Cambridge University Press, 1992.
Wang, Fan-sen. *Fu Ssu-nien: A Life in Chinese History and Politics*. Cambridge: Cambridge University Press, 2000.
Wang, Junzhong 王俊中. "Jiuguo zongjiao yi zhexue?—Liang Qichao zaonian de foxueguan ji qi zhuanzhe (1891-1912), 救國、宗教抑哲學？——梁啟超早年的佛學觀及其轉折 (1891-1912). *Shixue jikan* 史學集刊 31 (1996): 93-116.
Wang, Yi-t'ung. *A Record of Buddhist Monasteries in Lo-yang*. Princeton, NJ: Princeton University Press, 1984.
Wang-Toutain, Françoise. "Le bol du Buddha: propagation du bouddhisme et légitimité politique," *Bulletin de l'École française d'Extrême-Orient* 81 (1994) : 59-82.
Wardle, David. *Cicero on Divination*. Book 1. Oxford: Oxford University Press, 2006.
Watson, Burton. *Ssu-ma Ch'ien: Grand Historian of China*. New York: Columbia University Press, 1958.
Weinstein, Stanley. "A Biographical Study of Tz'u-en." *Monumenta Nipponica* 15 (1959-60): 119-149.
—. *Buddhism Under the T'ang*. Cambridge: Cambridge University Press, 1987.
Welch, Holmes. *The Buddhist Revival in China*. Cambridge, MA: Harvard University Press, 1968.
Welter, Albert. *The Administration of Buddhism in China: A Study and Translation of Zanning and the Topical Compendium of the Buddhist Clergy*. New York: Cambria Press, 2018.
—. *Monks, Rulers, and Literati: The Political Ascendancy of Chan Buddhism*. Oxford: Oxford University Press, 2006.
Wilkinson, Endymion. *Chinese History: A New Manual*. 5th ed. Amazon: Endymion Wilkinson, 2018.
Willemen, Charles. *The Storehouse of Sundry Valuables*. Berkeley, CA: Numata Center, 1994.
—. "Tripiṭaka Shan-wu-wei's Name." *T'oung Pao* 47, no. 3-5 (1981): 362-365.
Williams, Paul. *Mahayana Buddhism: The Doctrinal Foundations*. London: Routledge, 2009.
Wright, Arthur. "Fo-t'u-teng, a Biography." *Harvard Journal of Asiatic Studies* 11 (1948): 321-371.
—. "Seng-jui Alias Hui-jui: A Biographical Bisection in the *Kao-seng chuan*." In *Liebenthal Festschrift*, ed. Kshitis Roy, 272-294. Santiniketan: Visvabharati, 1957.
—. *The Sui Dynasty*. New York: Knopf, 1978.
Wright, Arthur F. "Biography and Hagiography: Hui-chiao's *Lives of Eminent Monks*." In *Studies in Chinese Buddhism*, ed. Wright. New Haven, CT: Yale University Press, 1990.

Wright, Dale S. "Historical Understanding: The Ch'an Buddhist Transmission Narratives and Modern Historiography." *History and Theory* 31, no. 1 (1992): 37-46.

Wu, Jiang. *Enlightenment in Dispute: The Reinvention of Chan Buddhism in Seventeenth-Century China*. Oxford: Oxford University Press, 2008.

Xie, Baocheng 謝保成 ed. *Zhongguo shixue shi* 中國史學史. Beijing: Shangwu Yinshuguan, 2006.

Xing, Yitian (Hsing I-tien) 邢義田. "Handai jiandu de zhongliang, tiji he shiyong—yi Zhongyanyuan Shiyusuo cang Juyan Hanjian wei li" 漢代簡牘的重量、體積和使用—-以中研院史語所藏居延漢簡為例. *Gujin lunheng* 古今論衡 17 (2007): 65-101.

Xuyun. *Empty Cloud: The Autobiography of the Chinese Zen Master*. Trans. Charles Luk. Longmead: Element Books, 1988.

Yamanouchi, Shinkyō 山內晉卿. *Shina Bukkyōshi no kenkyū* 支那佛教史之研究. Kyōto: Bukkyō daigaku Shuppansha,1921.

Yanagida, Seizan 柳田聖山. *Shoki no Zenshi I: Ryōga shijiki, Denhōbō. Zen no goroku* 初期の禪史 I 楞伽師資記、傳法寶記. 禪の語錄, no. 2. Tokyo: Chikuma shobō, 1971.

———. *Shoki zenshū shisho no kenkyū* 初期禪宗史書の研究. Kyoto: Hōzōkan, 1967.

Yanpei 演培. "Yinshun daoshi dui Yindu fojiao fenqi de quanshu" 印順導師對印度分期的詮述. In *Yinshun daoshi de sixiang yu xuewen* 印順導師的思想與學問, ed. Lan Jifu 藍吉富, 1-28. 1986; rpt., Taipei: Zhengwen Chubanshe, 2005.

Yen, Chuan-ying 顏娟英, ed. *Beichao fojiao shike tapian baipin* 北朝佛教石刻拓片百品. Taipei: Zhongyang Yanjiuyuan Lishi Yuyan Yanjiusuo, 2008.

Yerushalmi, Yosef Hayim. *Zakhor. Jewish History and Jewish Memory*. Seattle and London: University of Washington Press, 1989.

Yinshun 印順. *Chuqi dasheng fojiao zhi qiyuan yu zhankai* 初期大乘佛教之起源與展開. 1981; rpt., Taipei: Zhengwen Chubanshe, 1989.

———. "*Dazhidu lun zhi zuozhe ji qi fanyi*" 大智度論之作者及其翻譯. *Dongfang zongjiao yanjiu* 東方宗教研究 2 (1990): 9-70.

———. *Fojiao shidi kaolun* 佛教史地考論. In *Miaoyun ji* 妙雲集, vol. 22. 1973; Taipei: Zhengwen Chubanshe, 2000.

———. *Fomie jinian jueze tan* 佛滅紀年抉擇譚. Hong Kong: Xingdao Ribao Yinshua Bu, 1950.

———. *Pingfan de yi sheng* 平凡的一生. 1971; rpt. with additions, Xinzhu: Zhengwen Chubanshe, 2005.

———. *Yi fofa yanjiu fofa* 以佛法研究佛法. 1954; rpt., Xinzhu: Zhengwen Chubanshe, 2003.

———. *Yindu zhi fojiao* 印度之佛教. 1942; rpt. 3rd ed., Taipei: Zhengwen Chubanshe, 1992.

———. *Zhongguo chanzong shi* 中國禪宗史. Taipei: Huiri Jiangtang, 1971.

———. *Zhongguo gudai minzu shenhua yu wenhua zhi yanjiu* 中國古代民族神話與文化之研究. 1974; rpt., Taipei: Zhengwen Chubanshe, 1994.

Young, Stuart H. *Conceiving the Indian Buddhist Patriarchs in China*. Honolulu: University of Hawai'i Press, 2015.

Yu, Chün-fang. *Kuan-yin: The Chinese Transformation of Avalokiteśvara*. New York: Columbia University Press, 2000.

Zarrow, Peter. *China in War and Revolution 1895–1945*. London: Routledge, 2005.

Zhenhua. *In Search of the Dharma: Memoirs of a Modern Chinese Buddhist Pilgrim*. Trans. Denis Mair. New York: State University of New York Press, 1992.

Zhou Bokan (Chou Po-kan) 周伯戡. "*Dazhidu lun* lüe yi chu tan" 《大智度論》略譯初探. *Chung-Hwa Buddhist Journal* 13 (2000): 155-165.

Zhou, Shujia 周叔迦. *Zhou Shujia foxue lunzhu ji* 周叔迦佛學論著集, ed. Su Jinren 蘇晉仁. Beijing: Zhonghua, 1991.

Zhou, Yiliang 周一良. "Lüe lun Nanchao Beichao shixue zhi yitong" 略論南朝北朝史學之異同. In *Wei Jin Nanbei chao shilun ji xubian* 魏晉南北朝史論續編, 97-105. Beijing: Beijing Daxue, 1991.

——. "Wei Jin Nanbei chao shixue zhuzuo de ji ge wenti" 魏晉南北朝史學著作的幾個問題. In *Wei Jin Nanbei chao shilun* 魏晉南北朝史論, 491-502. Shenyang: Liaoning Jiaoyu Chubanshe, 1998.

Zhu, Gang 朱剛, and Zhao Huijun 趙惠俊. "Su Shi qianshen gushi de zhenxiang yu gaixie" 蘇軾前身故事的真相與改寫. *Lingnan xuebao* 嶺南學報 9 (2018): 123-141.

Zürcher, Erik. *The Buddhist Conquest of China*. Leiden: Brill, 2007.

——. "Perspectives in the Study of Chinese Buddhism." *Journal of the Royal Asiatic Society* 2 (1982): 161-176.

Index

abhidharma, 72, 103
Amoghavajra, 78, 158
analepsis, 8, 129
Ānanda, 137
An Lushan, 75-76, 98, 122
An Shigao, 60-62, 72, 77, 87
apocrypha, 28-29, 32, 44
Asita, 111
Aśoka, 11, 24, 35, 84
autobiography, 19, 50

Bandit Zhi, 80, 82
Ban Gu, 13, 14-15, 23, 81. *See also History of the Han*
Ban Zhao, 215n3
Baochang, 54
Bao Jing, 85
Baolin zhuan. See *Biographies of Baolin*
Baozhi, 57-59, 242n4
Beishan lu, 67
bibliographies, 62-63
Biographies of Baolin, 41, 151-152, 154, 156
Biographies of Bhikṣuṇīs, 17, 231n14
Biographies of Eminent Monks: on An Lushan, 75-76; chronology in, 127-128; on Kang Senghui, 86-87; on karma, 89; political time in, 128; popularity of, 3, 199; sources in, 49, 51-54; structure of, 17, 133. *See also* Huijiao
biography as genre, 133, 135

Bodhidharma: biography of, 53-55; in Chan historiography, 137, 141-144, 150-151; modern historiography on, 168-171; prophecy of, 247n70
Book of Changes, 110, 112
Bo Yi, 79-80
Brief History of the Clergy, 17, 28-30, 106, 99-100, 127-128. *See also* Zanning
Buddha: date of birth, 25-36, 137, 166-167, 185-186, 198; date of enlightenment, 26; date of nirvana, 107, 152, 176-177; life of, 125-126, 180, 189, 229n82, 260n63; omens of birth, 121, 119
buddhas of the past: chronology of, 4-5, 41-42; lineage of, 38-39, 136-137; veneration of, 64; Yinshun on, 180-181
Buddhist Bibliography of the Kaiyuan Era, 63
Bukong, 158

Cai Yong, 86, 98
calendars, 26, 36
Caodong lineage, 157
causation, 9, 104; and karma, 82, 84, 91-97; and prophecy, 109; Yinshun on, 1, 182-184
Chan historiography: accusations of forgery, 63; criticism of Tiantai in, 139; genealogy in, 40-42, 141-142, 145-146; sources in, 53
Chao Cuo, 95-96
chengfu, 82-84

282 Index

Chen Yinke, 165
Chen Yuan, 162-163, 190
children: miraculous powers of, 70; monastic proclivities of, 65, 92-93, 156; previous lives of, 85, 87-88, 95; prophecies about, 111, 114-117, 119-121
Christian historiography, 6, 24
chronology, 8-9, 24-36, 134, 177; and biography, 22; discrepancies in, 60-62, 64, 67-68, 75-76; and genealogy, 40-41, 150, 156; and prophecy, 124-131
Chronology of Lineages and Transmission, 128
Chuandeng yuying ji, 150
Chuan fabao ji. See *Record of the Transmission of the Dharma Treasure*
Chuji, 144
Chu sanzang jiji. See *Collection of Records Concerning the Translation of the Tripiṭaka*
Collection of Gems from the Transmission of the Lamp, 150
Collection of Records Concerning the Translation of the Tripiṭaka, 18, 88-89, 125, 199. See also Sengyou
Collection of the Hall of the Patriarchs, 144, 152
Compendium of the Five Lamps, 134-135, 146, 157
Comprehensive Account of the Buddhas and the Patriarchs: accusations of forgery in, 63; chronology in, 35; on dates of the Buddha, 28; doctrinal classification in, 46; lineage in, 140, 146; on nuns, 17; omens in, 120; prophecy in, 108, 111; sources of, 15, 53; as universal history, 18, 133-134, 166. See also Zhipan
Comprehensive Discussion and Chronology of Buddhism Compiled in the Longxing Era, 67-68, 127-128, 134, 166
Comprehensive Mirror for Aid to Government, 22, 50, 134, 194
Comprehensive Orthodox Transmission of the Śākya Clan, 4-5, 41-42, 55, 63, 140
Confucius, 13-14; approach to sources, 55; compiler of the *Spring and Autumn Annals*, 25; dates of, 31; fate of, 80; on innovation, 54, 58; and karma, 86; as manifestation of a bodhisattva, 30

Congyi, 126
Conversion of the Barbarians, 30-32, 35, 48, 89, 198; decline of, 164, 177
Chronology of Lineages and Transmission, 166
court history: compared to Buddhist historiography, 22, 80-81, 92, 104, 139; definition of, 13, 218n33; India in, 22-23; influence on Buddhist historiography, 12-16, 123, 133-134, 194-195, 226n49; on the marvelous, 69; omens in, 68, 113-114, 118
Cui Xian, 239n59

Daizong, 122
Dao'an (312-385), 59-60, 105, 128-129
Dao'an (fl. 561), 26-28, 35
Daoism, 15, 67-68, 82-84, 88-89, 122, 222n7. See also *Conversion of the Barbarians*
Daojian, 73-75
Daomi, 120
Daoxin, 143
Daoxuan: on Bodhidharma, 153-154; criticism of Huijiao, 53; criticized by Zuxiu, 67-68; on Huike, 150; on karma, 81-82, 94; on the marvelous, 70; meeting with Shanwuwei, 58, 72-73, 77-78; on omens, 120-121; previous lives of, 85, 87, 88, 93; on Sima Qian, 91; sources used by, 44, 51-52. See also *Further Biographies of Eminent Monks*; *Genealogy of the Śākya Clan*
Daoyuan, 146
Dayu, 136
Dazhidu lun, 111, 140, 176
decline theory, 3-5, 129, 197: and dating the Buddha, 25, 32-35, 107, 164, 177, 194; phases of, 33; Yinshun on, 179
Deshao, 86, 88
Devadatta, 66, 111
Dharmakṣema, 102-103
Dharmaruci, 56
divination techniques, 110-111, 112, 117, 131
doctrinal classification, 46, 166, 197, 179
Dongchu, 185-187
Dongshan, 152
Dong Zhongshu, 118

Dotted Record, 28
dreams, 36-37, 85, 92, 115-117, 121
Du Yu, 27
dynastic history. *See* court history

Emperor Daizong of the Tang, 122
Emperor Gao of the Northern Qi, 96
Emperor Huizong of the Song, 64, 116
Emperor Ming of the Han, 97, 127-128, 151, 166, 246n61
Emperor Shizong, 96-97
Emperor Suzong of the Tang, 122
Emperor Taizong of the Song, 111, 139
Emperor Taizong of the Tang, 105
Emperor Taizu of the Song, 64
Emperor Wen of the Sui, 99, 120-121, 238n29
Emperor Wenxuan, 100
Emperor Wu of the Han, 121
Emperor Wu of the Liang, 155
Emperor Wu of the Tang (Wuzong), 95, 130
Emperor Wu of the Zhou, 97, 99
Empress Wu, 89, 144, 151, 238n40
Empress Xiaojing, 121
Emperor Xuan of the Northern Qi, 238n29
Emperor Xuanzong of the Tang, 122
Emperor Yang of the Sui, 100
epigraphy, 50-52, 135, 152, 156-157, 190
esoteric Buddhism, 73, 158, 178-179, 182
ex eventus predictions, 131-132
Expanded Lamp Record Compiled in the Tiangsheng Era, 146

Fang Guan, 238n29
Fan Ye, 23, 113-114, 244n29. *See also Later Han History*
Fan Yu, 13
Faru, 141
fate, 9, 79-84, 88, 91, 103-104
Faxian, 27, 51, 111, 129
Fayan Wenyi, 156-157
Feiyin Tongrong, 138, 147, 157-158
Fei Zhangfang, 27-28, 33-35
First Emperor, 128
five houses of Chan, 138, 156-157, 158
five phases, 6, 24-25

five time periods, 46
Fo mieduhou zhongsheng dianji, 28
forgery, 41, 63, 151, 155
Fotucheng, 69, 105, 112
four marks of existence, 130
Fufazang yinyuan zhuan, 44-45; criticized by Qisong, 63; decline theory in, 39-41; lineage in, 39-41, 140; on Siṃha, 103
Further Biographies of Eminent Monks: birth omens in, 114-115; Bodhidharma in, 153-154; on dates of the Buddha, 31-32; on Huike, 150; in the *Record of the Teachers*, 151; sources of, 51-52, 231n14. *See also* Daoxuan
Fu Sinian, 161-163, 165, 167

Gaodi, 96
Gaoseng zhuan. *See Biographies of Eminent Monks*
genealogy, 18, 133-159; of buddhas, 111; in histories of India, 38-43; reasons for rise of, 196; structuring time with, 8. *See also* lineage
Great Chronicle, 7-8, 10-12, 128-129
Guanding, 40, 140-141
Gu Jiegang, 161, 163-165, 167
Gukanshō, 9
Guṇabhadra, 141-142

Hall of the Patriarchs, 146
Hanfa ben neizhuan, 32
Han Mingdi, 97, 127-128, 151, 166, 246n61
Han shu. *See History of the Han*
Han Wudi, 121
Heng Ching, 16-17
historical consciousness, 147-152
Historiographical Office, 13
History of the Han, 13, 45; dreams in, 121; India in, 23; omens in, 118; reading of, 199. *See also* Ban Gu
History of the Jin, 85
History of the Later Han, 23
History of the Three Kingdoms, 113
Hongren, 141-143
Hongzheng, 101

284   Index

Hou Han shu. See Later Han History
Huahu jing. See Conversion of the Barbarians
Huangbo, 136
Huichang persecution, 130
Huichao, 114
Huihong, 156-157, 250n16
Huijiao: on An Shigao, 60-61, 72; on Dao'an, 59-60, 128-129; on Faxian, 129; on Fotucheng, 69; on the history of the sangha, 36-37; on Kang Senghui, 59-62; on origins, 127-128; on prophecy, 125; on sources, 44, 51-54, 56-57; on Zhiyan, 69-70. See also Biographies of Eminent Monks
Huineng, 138, 143-144, 247n70
Huike, 143, 150
Huilang, 158
Huisi, 32-33, 57-59, 141
Huiwen, 140
Huiyuan, 67-68, 87, 100, 105
Huizong, 64, 116
Hu Shih, 161-162, 167; on Bodhidharma, 169-172, 181; on Chan, 149, 164, 168; debate with Suzuki, 147-148; and Dongchu, 186; sources used by, 190; on Xuyun, 257n30

India in Chinese historiography, 22-48, 124
Indian historiography. See South Asian historiography
Indra, 123
Islamic historiography, 231n24, 250n14

Japanese historiography, 9
jataka tales, 84
Jesus, 93, 260n63
Jewish historiography, 6
Jiang Weiqiao, 172-173
Jiankong, 90-91
jiapu, 134
Jien, 9
Jingde chuandeng lu. See Transmission of the Lamp Compiled in the Jingde Era
Jingjue, 141-142

Jin shu. See History of the Jin
Jīvaka, 91
Jiyin, 35
Jizang, 32-33, 223n21, 229n82
Journey to the West, 16
Juqu Mengxun, 102-103

Kaiyuan Shijiao lu, 63
Kang Senghui, 60-62, 86-87
Kang Youwei, 165
karma, 79-106, 109, 197; and decline theory, 4; in Japanese historiography, 9; in modern historiography, 185, 194; and time, 192; transfer of, 100-101; of Zhiyi, 116
koan, 136
Kuiji, 65-66, 77
Kumārajīva, 27, 56, 58, 114

Lalitavistara, 42
Langran, 93
Laozi. See Conversion of the Barbarians
Later Han History, 13, 113. See also Fan Ye
Lengqie shizi ji. See Record of the Teachers and Disciples of the Laṅkāvatāra Scripture
Liang Qichao, 160-163, 165-167
Liang Wudi, 155
libraries, 15
Lidai fabao ji. See Record of the Dharma Jewel Through the Generations
Lidai sanbao ji. See Record of the Three Jewels Through the Ages
Liezi, 117
lineage. See genealogy
Linji, 135
Linji lineage, 157
Lin Yutang, 174
Li Shizheng, 83-84, 88
Liu Bang, 119, 121
Liu Bei, 113
Liu Songnian, 15
Liu Zhiji, 229n1
Livy, 244n29
local history, 19, 190-191
Luoyang qielan ji, 19

Lu Xiujing, 67-68
Lu Xun, 165

Mahākaśyapa, 42, 137, 156-157, 169
Mahāvaṃsa, 7-8, 10-12, 128-129
Mahāyāna origins, 164, 167, 178, 182, 189
Maimonides, 6
Maitreya, 4-5, 39
Mandate of Heaven, 24
Mañjuśrī, 66
Maraldo, John C., 147-150
memoirs, 19, 50
memory, 16-17, 50
Mingfu, 261n89
Mingseng zhuan, 54
miracle tales, 91; and formal historiography, 69, 135, 199; promotion of scripture in, 101; rebirth in, 88. *See also* zhiguai
Mu Tianzi biezhuan, 28

New Tang History, 123
nirvana date, 25-36, 107, 152, 176-177
North Mountain Record, 67
nuns, 114-115, 120-123, 187, 195, 249n91

objective ideal, 10-12, 67-68, 148-149, 151, 199; of academic historians, 163; in history of Indian Buddhism, 48; when sources disagree, 54-55, 58; of Yinshun, 184
omens, 68-70, 75-76, 86, 109-110, 112-123
oracle bone inscriptions, 13, 82-83, 110
oral sources, 52
Orthodox Lineage, 146
Ouyang Jingwu, 162
Ouyang Xiu, 15, 63-64, 123
Oxhead school, 251n30

panjiao, 46, 166, 197, 179
pilgrimage, 23, 51
plupast, 128-129
printing, 50
prolepsis, 8, 129
prophecy, 107-132; of An Shigao, 60-62; of decline of Buddhism 32-35; in modern historiography, 194; in reconstructing

Indian history, 36-38; Shengyan on, 189; and time, 7-8, 192; of the transmission of the Dharma, 41; Yinshun on, 179
prosography, 17, 193
Putidamo nanzong ding shifei lun, 143
Puyao jing, 42

Qin Shihuang, 128
Qisong, 169; on Bodhidharma, 154; on the Buddha's dates, 224n22; on Indian patriarchs, 40-41, 63, 234n73; reincarnation of, 238n30; on translation errors, 41, 45
Qiyu, 91

Rāhula, 126
reading of historical works, 3
rebirth, 8, 75-76, 79-106
received burden, 82-84
recorded sayings, 135, 148
Record of the Dharma Jewel Through the Generations, 143-144, 151
Records of the Historian: compared to Buddhist histories, 45; on Confucius, 31; on fate, 79-81; influence on Buddhist historiography, 18, 22, 133-134; Laozi in, 30-31; lineage in, 38; omens in, 119; reading of, 150, 199; scale of, 13, 134, 230n4; slander in, 66; structure of, 194, 249n1; used to correct dates, 156. *See also* Sima Qian
Record of the Teachers and Disciples of the Laṅkāvatāra Scripture, 141-143, 151
Record of the Temples of Luoyang, 19
Record of the Three Jewels Through the Ages, 27-28, 33-35. *See also* Fei Zhangfang
Record of the Transmission of the Dharma Treasure, 141-143
relics, 44, 61-62
Rgya-gar Chos'byung, 10-12
Robber Zhi, 80, 82

Sakaino Satoru, 172
Śākya Genealogy, 18, 38-39, 43. *See also* Sengyou

Scripture of the Origins of the Miracles of the Prince, 25
self, 1, 98-100, 178-180, 182, 184
Sengcan, 143
Sengchou, 67
Sengguo, 114-115
Sun Hao, 86
Senghu, 85
Sengshi lüe. *See Brief History of the Clergy*
Sengyou, 18; and Daoxuan, 85, 93; on karma, 93-94, 106; on lineage, 38-39; on omens, 119; on Śākyamuni's cousins, 43; sources used by, 53; on translation errors, 45. *See also Śākya Genealogy*; *Collection of Records Concerning the Translation of the Tripiṭaka*
Shanwuwei, 55, 58, 72-73, 77-78
Shemoteng, 128
Shengyan, 187-191, 193
Shenqing, 67-68, 145, 158
Shenxiu, 141-143
Shiji. *See Records of the Historian*
Shijia pu. *See Śākya Genealogy*
Shimen zhengtong. *See Comprehensive Orthodox Transmission of the Śākya Clan*
Shitou Xiqian, 156-157
Shizong, 96-97
Shu Qi, 79-80
Sima Guang, 22, 50, 134, 194
Sima Qian: and Buddhist historiography, 15, 22; as court historian, 13; on fate, 79-81, 84, 91; on the individual, 105-106; and karma, 81, 104; on omens, 76, 119, 244n29; on time, 5-6; use of sources, 50. *See also Records of the Historian*
Siṃha, 103, 137, 140, 241n85
Song Biographies of Eminent Monks: on karma, 89-93; on Linji, 135; sources in, 51-53, 231n14; on Vajrabodhi, 92-93; on Wanhui, 70-72; on Zhixuan, 95. *See also* Zanning
Song gaoseng zhuan. *See Song Biographies of Eminent Monks*
South Asian historiography, 2, 6-8, 217n16; dates in, 29, 47; karma in, 84; omens in, 110-111, 119

Southern School lineage, 143-144
Spring and Autumn Annals, 13-14, 25-27
standard histories. *See* court history
stele inscriptions, 50-52, 135, 152, 156-157, 190
Strict Transmission of the Five Lamps, 138, 157-158
Śubhakarasiṃha. *See* Shanwuwei
Su Dongpo, 238n30
Sui Wendi, 99, 120-121, 238n29
Sui Yangdi, 100
Sun-kyŏng, 66
supernormal powers, 71-72, 111, 195, 197; knowledge of past lives, 87, 237n22; in modern historiography, 194
Suzong, 122
Suzuki, D. T., 147-148

Taiping guangji, 71
Taixu, 160-161, 163-172, 174, 178, 193
Tandi, 239n58
Taizong (Song), 111, 139
Taizong (Tang), 105
Taizu, 64
Tang Yongtong, 162-163, 165-167
Tanmoliuzhi, 56
Tansheng, 117
Tantric Buddhism, 73, 158, 178-179, 182
Tanwuzui, 31
Tāranātha, 11-12, 175
Tianhuang Daowu, 156-157
Tiansheng guangdeng lu, 146
Tiantai: criticism of Chan, 139; genealogy, 40-42, 140, 146-147; historiography, 18, 53, 63
Tianwang Daowu, 157
Tibetan historiography, 2, 11-12
time, 3-5, 192-196; analepsis, 129; in court history, 24-25; cyclical, 5-6, 107, 121; liturgical, 8, 29-30; plupast, 128-129; political, 128; prolepsis, 129; and prophecy, 7-8, 192
translation: forgery of 39, 94, 156; history of, 17, 127-128, 133, 200; mistakes in, 30, 41-42, 45-47, 63
Transmission of the Dharma Jewel, 150-151

Transmission of the Lamp Compiled in the Jingde Era: authorship of, 15; Bodhidharma in, 153-154; on buddhas of the past, 42; changes to, 156-157; criticized, 57-58, 155-156, 228n62, 228n71; decline theory in, 4; extracts from, 150; genealogy in, 18; omens in, 120; origins in, 128; rise to prominence of, 145-146; scale of, 134; structure of, 136-138
travel accounts, 23
"Treatise on Buddhism and Daoism," 14, 25-26. *See also* Wei Shou
Treatise on Establishing What is True and What False in the Southern School of Bodhidharma, 143

universal histories, 18. *See also Comprehensive Discussion and Chronology of Buddhism Compiled in the Longxing Era; Comprehensive Account of the Buddhas and the Patriarchs; Chronology of Lineages and Transmission*

Vajrabodhi, 158
vegetarianism, 115
von Ranke, Leopold, 165

Wang Chong, 112, 244n29
Wang Shao, 121
Wang Sui, 150
Wanhui, 70-71
Wei Gao, 86
Wei History, 14. *See also* Wei Shou
Wei Shou, 14, 25-26, 33-34, 38-39. *See also* "Treatise on Buddhism and Daoism"
Wells, H. G., 165-166
women, 16-17, 24, 33-34, 215n3. *See also* nuns
Wenxuan, 100
Wright, Dale S., 149-150
Wudeng huiyuan. See Compendium of the Five Lamps
Wudeng yantong. See Strict Transmission of the Five Lamps
Wuxiang, 144
Wu Zetian, 89, 144, 151, 238n40
Wuzhu, 144

Wu Zixu, 80
Wuzong, 95, 130

Xiangzheng ji, 28
Xiaojing, 121
Xi Zuochi, 59-60
Xuandi, 238n29
Xuanzang, 16, 116: and Daoxuan, 94; meeting with Kuiji, 65-66, 77; on prophecy, 111; sources used by, 51; teacher of Sun-kyŏng, 93
Xuanzong, 122
Xu Fuguan, 186
Xu gaoseng zhuan. See Further Biographies of Eminent Monks
Xu Ling, 86
Xuyun, 92

Yama, 88-89, 101-102
Yan Fu, 165
Yang Hu, 85
Yang Yi, 146
Yan Hui, 80
Yijing (book), 112
Yijing (monk), 37
Yinshun, 1, 19, 172-186
Yogācāra, 183-184, 190
Yuan Ang, 95-96, 98
Yumen lineage, 157
Yunmen Wenyan, 156-157

Zanning, 139; on An Lushan, 98; on Cai Yong, 98; court links, 15; criticized by Huihong, 156; criticized by Ouyang Xiu, 64; criticized by Zuxiu, 75-76; on Daojian, 73-75; on dates of the Buddha, 28-30, 35, 45-46; on dreams, 117; on the Huichang persecution, 130; on karma, 97, 101-102; on Kuiji, 65; on lineage, 158; on omens, 115; on origins, 127-128; praise of imperial family, 139; on prophecy, 124-125; on rebirth, 86; on "recorded sayings," 144-145; on the self, 99-100; on Shanwuwei, 72-73; use of sources, 51-53, 55-57; on Wanhui, 71-72; on Zhixuan, 98. *See also Song Biographies of Eminent Monks*

Zhang Heng, 86, 98
Zhang Qian, 129
Zhanran, 126
Zhao Dun, 66
zhengshi. See court history
Zhenru, 122-123
zhiguai, 69, 74. See also miracle stories
Zhipan: on the Biographies of Baolin, 154; on life of the Buddha, 28, 43, 45; on the Conversion of the Barbarians, 32; on divination, 112-113; on doctrinal classification, 46; on dreams, 116; on karma, 97, 100, 102-103; on Ouyang Xiu, 64; on prophecy, 108, 123-127, 132; on Tang Taizong, 105; use of sources by, 15, 53, 57. See also Comprehensive Record of the Buddhas and the Patriarchs
Zhishen, 62-63, 144
Zhiwei, 86
Zhixuan, 95-96, 98
Zhiyan, 69-70
Zhiyi, 86, 114, 116, 140-141, 146
Zhiyuan, 126
Zhou Shujia, 173
Zhoushu yiji, 32, 44
Zhou Wudi, 97, 99
Zhuge Liang, 86
Zhu Xi, 155-156
Zizhi tongjian. See Comprehensive Mirror for Aid to Government
Zongjian, 41. See also Comprehensive Orthodox Transmission of the Śākya Clan
Zongmi, 98, 100, 144
Zuozhuan, 28, 231n25
Zutang ji. See Collection of the Hall of the Patriarchs
Zuxiu: on Bodhidharma, 155; on karma, 96; on lineage, 158; on Lu Xiujing, 67-68; on meeting between Shanwuwei and Daoxuan, 77-78; on origins, 127; on the persecution of Buddhism, 104-105; on prophecy, 123; on Zanning, 75-76

GPSR Authorized Representative: Easy Access System Europe, Mustamäe tee 50, 10621 Tallinn, Estonia, gpsr.requests@easproject.com

www.ingramcontent.com/pod-product-compliance
Lightning Source LLC
Chambersburg PA
CBHW022039290426
44109CB00014B/912